D1292811

Patterns in Network Architecture

Patterns in Network Architecture

A Return to Fundamentals

JOHN DAY

Upper Saddle River, NJ • Boston • Indianapolis • San Francisco
New York • Toronto • Montreal • London • Munich • Paris • Madrid
Cape Town • Sydney • Tokyo • Singapore • Mexico City

The publisher offers excellent discounts on this book when ordered in quantity for bulk purchases or special sales, which may include electronic versions and/or custom covers and content particular to your business, training goals, marketing focus, and branding interests. For more information, please contact:

U.S. Corporate and Government Sales
(800) 382-3419
corpsales@pearsontechgroup.com

For sales outside the United States please contact:

International Sales
international@pearsoned.com

Visit us on the Web: informit.com/ph

Library of Congress Cataloging-in-Publication Data:

Day, John D., 1947-

Patterns in network architecture : a return to fundamentals / John Day.

p. cm.

ISBN 0-13-225242-2 (hbk. : alk. paper) 1. Computer network architectures. 2. Computer networks—Design. 3. Computer networks—Philosophy. 4. Internet—History. I. Title.

TK5105.52.D39 2007

004.6—dc22

2007040174

ISBN-13: 978-0-132-25242-3
ISBN-10: 0-132-25242-2
Text printed in the United States on recycled paper at RR Donnelley in Crawfordsville, Indiana.
First printing December 2007

This Book Is Safari Enabled

The Safari® Enabled icon on the cover of your favorite technology book means the book is available through Safari Bookshelf. When you buy this book, you get free access to the online edition for 45 days.

Safari Bookshelf is an electronic reference library that lets you easily search thousands of technical books, find code samples, download chapters, and access technical information whenever and wherever you need it.

To gain 45-day Safari Enabled access to this book

- Go to http://www.awprofessional.com/safarienabled
- Complete the brief registration form.
- Enter the coupon code 4PA7-DKVC-8HJ5-XZCP-CMGH.

If you have difficulty registering on Safari Bookshelf or accessing the online edition, please e-mail customer-service@safaribooksonline.com.

Editor-in-Chief
Karen Gettman

Acquisitions Editor
Chuck Toporek

Managing Editor
Gina Kanouse

Senior Project Editor
Kristy Hart

Copy Editor
Keith Cline

Indexer
Erika Millen

Editorial Assistant
Romny French

Cover Designer
Chuti Prasertsith

Composition
Gloria Schurick

Proofreader
San Dee Phillips

To Heinz von Forester,
who taught me how to think
and
To Dite, Kathleen, and Kinmundy,
who gave me a foundation for life

Contents

Preface

There is something fascinating about science. One gets such wholesale returns on conjecture out of such a trifling investment of fact.

—Mark Twain, *Life on the Mississippi*

The Seven Unanswered Questions

This didn't start out to be a book.

It started out simply as an attempt to distill what we know about networks after 35 years of beating on the problem. What principles, rules of thumb, guidelines, and so on could be distilled from what we had seen independent of politics, and religion, and even the constraints of technology. What could be said with as little qualification as possible? Were there a few constraints that could be introduced that would allow us to do a great deal more? What did we really know that didn't change? What some might call science.

Over the years, I saw ideas go by that had not been pursued, directions taken that didn't seem quite right; sometimes little things, sometimes not so little (but always affected by politics, market interests, group think, and sometimes just the imperfect state of our understanding). But the ideas were points that had the potential to be those subtle inflections on which much bigger things hinged. Usually they were sloughed off with a fatalistic "Awww! Simplifying here would only increase complexity elsewhere." But would it?

As I pursued this seemingly quixotic quest, patterns began to assemble themselves that I had not seen before. Patterns that lead to a major collapse in complexity. The structure of networks turns out to be much simpler than we imagined. There are far fewer protocols. And capabilities such as multihoming, mobility, and scaling turn out to be a consequence of the resulting structure, not complexities to be added. No cumbersome mechanisms are required. The increased orthogonality and regularity of the structure makes the solutions to other problems easier and straightforward. On the surface, what emerged appears not that different from what we had been doing. And upon first reflection, some are likely to think, "Sure, we all knew that." But deeper, it is very different and requires a cognitive shift that isn't always easy to make. And this shift is made more difficult because not all the concepts key to making the transition are common knowledge.

In addition to just codifying principles and rules of thumb, a few key unsolved problems that were at the crux of a better understanding, problems that needed the kind of unfettered thought impossible in the heat of product development or standards deliberation.

I have often said, only half jokingly, that "the biggest problem with the ARPANET was we got too much right to begin with." Meaning that for a project for which there had been no prior experience, for which there was considerable doubt it would even work, there was some brilliant work and some brilliant insights to the point that it was "good enough," and there was no overwhelming need to address the problems it did uncover (which really just says we weren't pushing hard enough on the edges). One of the most striking phenomena in the early ARPANET was the number of times that when presented with what appeared to be a dichotomy, an "oil and water" problem, they found an elegant simple synthesis that wasn't either extreme but in which the extremes were "merely" degenerate cases (and that at the same time told us something we hadn't previously understood).[1]

As one would expect with any first attempt, some were mistakes, some things were unforeseen, some shortcuts were taken, some areas went unexplored, and so forth. But even so, the network worked much better than anyone had any reason to expect. Almost immediately, the ARPANET went from a subject of research to a necessary and useful resource.[2]

During its development, a constant guiding metaphor was operating systems. We always looked to operating systems to provide insight to the solution of problems and for what should be built. (Many involved in that early work have attributed the success of the ARPANET in great part to the fact that it was built by people with operating system, not communications, backgrounds and have lamented that it is no longer the case.) By 1974, with the network essentially operational, there was great excitement about what could be done with the Net.[3] (It was really a small version of the excitement we saw in the early 1990s

---

[1] I say "they" because I was just a "junior" grad student at the time, and while I was there, I can take no credit for these insights but could only hope that I learned from watching them emerge.

[2] This book isn't yet another history of the Net (although there is a lot of that here). I have found that one cannot give an honest explanation of why things are the way they are based solely on technical arguments.

[3] Contrary to recent characterizations that we saw the use of the Net as "conversational," nothing could be further from the truth. We saw it as a heterogeneous resource-sharing facility, and that was the impetus for experiments and production distributed systems such as Englebart's NLS, National Software Works, CCA's Datacomputer, the NARIS land-use management system that utilized a distributed database spread of over the United States invisible to its users, processing ERTS satellite images across multiple systems, heavy use of Rutherford High Energy Lab and the UCLA 360/91 by U.S. particle physicists, and so on, all prior to 1976.

when everyone else discovered the Net.) However, there were some outstanding problems that we knew about; some expediencies we had taken (as one must always do in any real project) that needed to be fixed. They were as follows:

- **Replacing NCP.** Probably foremost in our minds coming out of the ARPANET was the realization that the Host-Host Protocol would not scale to a large network, where *large* was a few thousand hosts. The separate control channel shared by all hosts was a bottleneck. The protocol was overly complex and tied a little too closely to the nature of the IMP subnet. What sort of protocol should replace it?

- **Cleaning up the structure.** Given that operating systems loomed large in the early thinking and Dijkstra's THE paper (1968) was only few years old, it was natural that layering was used to organize the functionality. However, it is difficult to say that the initial implementation of the ARPANET was layered very cleanly. There was still a lot of beads-on-a-string in the design.[4] The interactions of the Host-Host Protocol and the IMP subnet were less than clean. But by 1974, the idea of physical, data link, network, and transport layers—probably best reflected in the implementation of CYCLADES with its clean separation of CIGALE and TS—was becoming well accepted. Beyond that, there was less certainty. And later, we would find that the lower four layers weren't quite "right" either but were a bit more complicated. But we couldn't say we had a good understanding of what layers were.[5] *What was the right architecture for heterogeneous resource-sharing networks?*

- **The upper layers.** We had just scratched the surface of what applications could be developed. We had three basic applications, once again using operating systems as our guide. We simply replicated the services of an operating system in a network. One we nailed (Telnet); one needed more work (FTP); and one we blew (RJE). Not a bad record. There was a general sense that there was more "structure" in the upper layers we had not yet been able to tease out. Even though some thought that Telnet and FTP were all you needed,[6] some people had all sorts of ideas for other applications. We needed a better understanding of what applications would be

---

[4] This is not an uncommon state of affairs in science that the first step in the transition from one paradigm to another still has a foot in both. "Beads-on-a-string" refers to the phone company model of networking, as exemplified by X.25, ISDN, ATM, and MPLS, that existed prior to 1970 and still exists today.

[5] Actually we still don't, as textbook authors like to point out (and if the ongoing architecture discussions are any indication).

[6] Mail was two commands in FTP.

useful, how the upper layers were structured, and how they worked with the rest of the system. And as it would turn out, this is a place where our operating system model failed us. These first three applications are all examples of a special case. Oddly enough, this might have been a critical juncture in the development of the Net...or lack thereof. *What did the upper layers look like?*

- **Application names and directory.** Early in the development, the model of operating systems told us that we should have application names and network addresses. As with operating systems, application names would be location independent, whereas addresses would be location dependent. In fact, I remember my mild disappointment when it was announced that well-known sockets would be used as a stopgap measure, rather than defining application names and a directory. It was understandable. Coming up with a naming scheme and building a directory would have taken considerable time. We had only three applications and only one instance of each of them in each host. Application names and a directory weren't really *needed* immediately. Eventually, we would have to go back and do it right before there were too many applications. *What did naming and addressing look like in networks?*

- **Multihoming.** In 1972, Tinker Air Force Base joined the Net and took us at our word that the Net was supposed to be robust. They wanted redundant network connections. Upon hearing this news, I distinctly remember thinking, "Ah, great idea!" and a second later, thinking, "O, *#@*, that isn't going to work!" By making host addresses IMP port numbers (i.e., naming the interface not the node), the routing algorithm couldn't tell that these two addresses went to the same place: our first really fundamental mistake.[7] *But* the solution was immediately obvious! Using the operating system model, it was clear that we needed a logical address space over the physical address space. We needed separate address spaces for nodes and for interfaces. The only trouble was it wasn't clear what these address spaces should look like. It was well understood from operating systems that naming and addressing was a hard problem fraught with pitfalls. Get it right and many things are easy; get it wrong and things are hard, inefficient, and maybe impossible. And we knew the difference between getting it right and getting it wrong could be subtle. *We needed to proceed carefully. What was the nature of this "logical" addressing?*

---

[7]   Well, not really. It would be a mistake if supporting redundant connections had been intended, but it hadn't. It was hard enough just building a network that moved data. But this is an indication of how quickly the Net began to be considered "production."

- **Location-dependent addresses.** And furthermore, it wasn't at all clear what *location dependent* meant for network addresses. It was a simple problem in operating systems. Location dependence of memory addresses was easy and well understood. It was also well understood for cities built on grids. But data networks were seldom regular grids. What location dependent meant in a general mesh network without being route dependent was far from clear. It couldn't be tied to the graph of the network because that changed too often. It needed to be some sort of abstraction of the graph that indicated where without indicating how to get there. *But how to abstract an arbitrary graph was less than obvious. What does location dependent mean in a network?*

- **Adopting connectionless.** The ARPANET was primarily a connection-oriented network. The ARPANET IMP subnet had more in common with X.25 than with IP. This was a reasonable conservative choice for a first attempt, when we had no idea how it would actually work or how a network was supposed to be built and a somewhat built-in assumption that the network had to be as reliable as possible. Experience with reassembly, flow control, and such showed that a tightly controlled deterministic network had major problems. The insight that less control (less reliable) would be more effective came as an intriguing surprise, but an insight that made a lot of sense. The experience of CYCLADES with the use of connectionless datagrams in a network that essentially created reliable communications with unreliable mechanisms was elegant, simple, and convincing.[8] However, a better understanding was needed of how the connectionless model behaved. Because it had been used only at low bandwidth in relatively small networks, a better understanding was needed of how it would work as it was scaled up. After all, it is seldom the case that the pure form of anything works well in the real world. The simplicity and elegance of the new paradigm of connectionless looked promising. It also provided concepts for a replacement for the Host-Host Protocol. We also needed a deeper understanding of the difference between the connection model and the connectionless model. Even with our excitement for connectionless, we had to admit that there did appear to be times when connections made sense. However, I must admit it took some of us a long time to admit that (me included). *What were the properties of the connectionless model and its relation to connections and how would it scale in a production system? Was there a single model that would encompass both as degenerate cases?*

---

8 The connection-oriented packet-switching model is a straightforward, even obvious, approach to the problem, whereas the connectionless model is an inspired shift in thinking.

These were the major issues facing networking as we transitioned from the ARPANET to the Internet. What happened next? Let's consider how the Internet rose to the challenge of these problems.

Converging on TCP

There were basically four contenders for replacing NCP:

(1) **XNS - Sequence Packet,** which was similar to the (2) **CYCLADES TS** protocol. A packet-sequenced, dynamic window transport protocol with multiple PDU types, establishment, release, ack, and flow control. Both XNS SeqPkt and CYCLADES separated the transport and network functions, analogous to TCP and IP.

(3) **Delta-t,** developed at Lawrence Livermore Lab, was a radically new idea in protocols with a more robust timer-based synchronization mechanism that essentially eliminated connection establishment and used separate PDU types for ack and flow control. Delta-t also separated the transport and network functions. And, of course...

(4) **TCP,** a byte-sequenced, dynamic window transport protocol with a single PDU format and control bits to distinguish various state changes. It also allowed the two simplex channels to be released separately. In its initial version, TCP did not separate the transport and network functions.

A few unique features of TCP stirred some discussion:

- The single PDU format was supposed to streamline processing rather than the additional code to parse several different PDU types. It was expected that this would save both per-packet processing and code space. Given the low speeds of processors, this was a very real concern. At the time, this looked like a move toward simplicity, but with more understanding of protocols it turns out it isn't.[9] In addition, treating the control bits as control bits in the implementation creates more code complexity. The recommendation for current implementations is to treat them as if they were an opcode. In fact, looking at traffic statistics in the Net today, it is clear that syns, fins, and acks are treated as different PDU types (i.e., the number of 40-byte packets).

- The single PDU format also had the advantage of piggybacking acks. Calculations at the time showed that piggybacking reduced overhead by 35%

---

[9] It is hard to believe, but in 1974, there had been very few data protocols designed, and they all looked very different. More so than they do today.

to 40%. This savings occurred because at the time the vast majority of traffic on the Net was character-at-a-time echoing of Telnet traffic by BBN Tenexes (the then-dominant system on the Net). However, because there aren't many Tenexes on the Net today, the savings today is negligible, well under 10%.[10]

- For a 1974 environment where one size fit all, TCP had marginal advantages in some areas, for others it posed significant burden; for example, bandwidth constraints were still common, making the header size problematic for some environments. Today its advantages have disappeared. Its inability to adapt easily to a wider range of operations are an obstruction to meeting the requirements of a modern network. Delta-t or TS would probably have been a better choice. They were not only well-suited for the environment at the time (delta-t was used for years within the DoE), but both could also have been easily adapted to modern demands without significantly changing their structure.

As shown in Chapter 3, "Patterns in Protocol," the general structure of this class of protocols naturally cleaves into a pipelined data transfer part, loosely coupled with a more general-purpose computational half that requires synchronization for the bookkeeping-associated error and flow control. The single PDU format complicates taking advantage of this structure and complicates making the protocol adaptable to the requirements of different applications, leading to an unnecessary proliferation of protocols. The single PDU format makes less sense. TCP was very much optimized for the characteristics of the mid-1970s.

Why was TCP chosen? There are many reasons. At the time, with the exception of the delta-t synchronization mechanism, the differences among the four protocols were not that great. And overwhelming arguments could not be made for any of these protocols; that is, none was the overwhelming choice. None of the arguments mentioned above was understood then. And, it was expected whatever the choice, it would be used for a few years in this research network and replaced. After all, NCP was a first attempt in building a network. TCP was our first attempt in this new direction. No one expected that we would get it right the first time. At least, one more attempt would probably be needed to "get it right." However, probably the foremost factor in the choice was that the Internet was a DoD project and TCP was paid for by the DoD. This reflects nothing more than the usual realities of interagency rivalries in large bureaucracies and that the majority of reviewers were DARPA contractors.

---

[10] Do the math. Twenty-character input and 40 characters on output were accepted averages for terminal traffic at the time.

Splitting out IP (nothing new for addressing). Splitting IP from TCP seemed a necessity. The transport protocol and IP do very different functions (as will become clear in Chapter 6, "Diving Layers"). The only unfortunate aspect in the creation of IP was that nothing was done about the multihoming problem. IP continued to name the interface. But this was understandable. IP was split out in 1975, soon after the problem was recognized. Although we understood what the multihoming problem was and theoretically what its solution was, there was still much about addressing that was unclear. More theoretical and practical work was necessary. However, it did put us in the uncomfortable position of an *Internet* address naming a *subnetwork* point of attachment.

NCP is phased out. Finally, after eight years of development, TCP was deployed in 1982. The Internet did its first (and nearly last) Flag Day switch from NCP to TCP. In the same time frame (late 1970s, early 1980s), the (in)famous BBN 1822 Host–IMP hardware interface was being phased out in favor of a standard interface. For hosts connecting to a packet switch, the choice was, in most cases, IP over X.25; for others, it was the new-fangled Ethernet. NCP had served well for more than a decade, much longer than anyone expected.

Saltzer on addressing. In 1982, Jerry Saltzer at MIT published one of the most cited papers on naming and addressing in computer networks. Saltzer (1982) outlined how a network must have application names, which map to node addresses, which map to point of attachment addresses, which map to routes. These are all of the necessary elements of a complete addressing architecture.[11] The only missing piece then is figuring out what location-dependent means in a graph. While everyone cites this paper and agrees that it is the right answer, there have been no proposals to implement it. But in all fairness, Saltzer doesn't provide much help with how his abstractions might be applied to the existing Internet or what *location dependent* means in a graph.

Host table gets unwieldy—DNS but no application names or directory. From the beginning of the ARPANET, the *Network Information Center* (NIC) had maintained a text file of the current list of hosts and their corresponding IMP addresses. Every few weeks, the latest version of the file was downloaded. Then weeks became every week, became every other day, and by 1980 or so it was becoming hard to manage manually as a simple text file. This was bound to happen with the Internet continuing to grow. So now was a good time to take the first step to resolving some of the addressing problems, by putting a scheme of application names and a directory in place. But there were still only three applications in the Net, and each host had only one of each. There was still no

---

[11] There is only one refinement we will need (and will turn out to be crucial, see Chapter 5) that did not exist or was very rare when Saltzer wrote, so it is not surprising that he did not consider it.

real need for all the trouble of a directory. And everyone was quite comfortable with the way it had been done for the past 15 years.[12] So, DNS was created essentially as a hierarchy of distributed databases to resolve synonyms for IP addresses, replacing the old host table. This approach was partly due to the strong attachment to the idea of naming hosts that was begun with the ARPANET (even though a careful analysis of naming in networks shows that naming hosts is not relevant to the addressing necessary for communications). As long as there were well-known sockets and only one occurrence of an application in each host, DNS was all the "directory" that was needed: a means to maintain a user-friendly form of the IP address. Even though there had been discussions of a directory since the early 1970s, an opportunity to show some vision was lost. Already the attitude of introducing no more change than necessary to address the current problem had set in. Was this prudent engineering, shortsightedness, protecting the status quo, or a bit of all three?

Congestion collapse. In 1986, the Internet encountered its most severe crisis. The network was suffering from congestion collapse. The classic congestion curve of increasing throughput followed by a nosedive became a daily occurrence. Long delays caused by congestion led to timeouts, which caused retransmissions that made the problem worse. Although the connectionless model had become the *cause célèbre* early in the 1970s, the ARPANET was fundamentally a connection-oriented network (unless Type 3 messages were explicitly used). Even after the move to IP, many host attachments to packet switches and routers were made with BBN 1822 or X.25, both of which flow controlled the host. As more and more hosts were attached by connectionless LANs with no flow control, and as 1822 and X.25 were phased out, there was less and less flow control in the network. The only flow control that existed was in TCP. But TCP flow control was intended to prevent the sending *application* from overrunning the destination *application,* not with preventing congestion somewhere in the network. Congestion collapse was inevitable. No one had ever experimented with the properties of connectionless networks as they scaled up.[13] Now it had to done on-the-fly.

This was a major crisis. Something had to be done and done quickly. The Internet was basically unusable. But the crisis was much deeper than simply keeping an operational network up and running. Control theory going back to Weiner said that feedback should be located with the resource being controlled.

---

[12] No wonder there were people who thought it was *supposed* to be done this way. Fifteen years ago in computing is nearly ten generations—ancient history!

[13] There had been calls for experimental networks, and some small ones had been built, but not large enough to investigate these problems. They were too expensive. No one was willing to fund simulations of large networks. Not to mention that there were detractors who questioned whether such simulations would be meaningful.

But congestion could happen at any switch in the network. To include congestion control would essentially mean going to a connection model, not a connectionless model. First, it was known that connection-oriented designs did not work that well and had bad survivability properties. Second, for the past 15 years, the networking community had been fighting off the phone company giants in debates over connectionless and connections (see Chapter 3). We couldn't admit defeat, and we didn't think we were wrong.[14] Many believed there was a middle ground, a synthesis, but so far no one had been able to find it. All proposals seemed to fall into one extreme or the other. In any case, there certainly wasn't time for new theoretical insights. Something had to be done quickly.

Van Jacobson proposed a congestion-avoidance scheme to be inserted into TCP. It consisted of the now well-known slow-start, doubling the congestion window with every round-trip until congestion is detected (and then exponential backoff). Essentially, congestion avoidance creates congestion and then backs off. This solution maintained the connectionless model and provided a quick fix to the congestion problem, while researchers tried to understand how to do congestion control and maintain the seminal properties of a connectionless network. Furthermore at this point, it was much easier to change the TCP implementations than to redesign all the switches. Perhaps as important, this juncture also signals a qualitative shift in networking from flow control being discrete counting of buffers to continuous control theory mechanisms. However, after the crisis was past, there was such relief that no one went back to try to understand what a full solution might look like. And with an all-too-human trait, rationales appeared to justify why this was the "right" solution. There were without doubt several reasons: the "it works don't change it" attitude;[15] the strong adherence to the end-to-end principle; pressure from the outside to adopt connection-oriented solutions; and so on. But congestion collapse had been put behind us so that today there is a consensus that congestion control *belongs* in TCP. But wasn't it a stopgap? Could the conditions that led to congestion collapse occur again? What would it take? Perhaps, a killer app that generated large amounts of traffic, but didn't use TCP? What if the bulk of traffic on the Net were not using TCP? Like with, say, video?

SNMP. The ARPANET had always had good network management,[16] but it was a function internal to BBN that was running the Net. In the early 1980s, as

---

14 And they weren't.

15 At the time, few of the networking people involved had a strong background in control theory, very few were comfortable with the issues, and so there was greater reticence to start changing something so large that was working.

16 The stories are legend: BBN calling Pacific Bell to tell them their T1 line from Santa Barbara to Menlo Park was having trouble and Pacific Bell not believing that they weren't calling from either Santa Barbara or Menlo Park, but from Boston.

more corporate networks were created, network management had become a topic of concern. By the mid-1980s, experience with the IEEE 802.1 management protocol had shown that the elemental "Turing machine" approach,[17] although simple and straightforward, was inadequate. It was also clear by this time that the key to network management was less the protocol and more the object models of the systems to be managed. The Internet community pursued two approaches: a simple Turing machine-like, polling[18] protocol, SNMP without object-oriented characteristics; and a more sophisticated extensible object-oriented, event-driven protocol, HEMS. It is probably significant that unlike the ARPANET, which came up with innovative solutions to problems, the Internet of the late 1980s took a step away from innovation by adopting SNMP. There was strong emphasis at the time on the apparent simplicity, supposedly leading to smaller code size and shunning concepts that were seen as too esoteric.[19] As it turned out, SNMP implementations are larger than either HEMS or CMIP.[20] Its rudimentary structure and lack of object-oriented support, along with a red herring that we will look at in Chapter 4, "Stalking the Upper-Layer Architecture," has proven to be a major obstacle to the development management in the Internet.

The Web. In the early 1990s, the Web began to take off. The Web had been around for a while, but was basically just another version of Gopher. Until NCSA at the University of Illinois extended it with a browser. One of the major efforts of the supercomputer center was investigating how to present data more effectively. As part of that, one of their programmers hit upon the idea of putting a GUI on the Web that made any object on the page "clickable." The Web took off and put new requirements on the Net.

The Web becomes the first major new application on the network in 20 years, and as one would expect it created a number of new problems. First of all, this is the first application that did not come from the operating system metaphor. For the Web, the protocol and the application are not one and the same. There may be more than one application using the Web protocol and more than one instance of the same application at the same time on the same host. With no application naming structure in place, the Web had to develop its

---

[17] Everything is done with Set and Get on attributes.

[18] The use of polling in SNMP has always been perplexing. In the ARPANET, polling was seen as a brute-force approach that didn't scale and represented mainframe think. It was an anathema. It would never have been considered, and anyone proposing polling in those days would have been laughed out of the room.

[19] Push-down automata, object-oriented, and so on. There was a strong anti-intellectual attitude then (and still is to some extent) that real programmers "don't need no book learning." They innately know how to design and write code.

[20] The OSI management protocol, which was event-driven and was object-oriented.

own naming scheme, the now ubiquitous URL. However, once again, this did not lead to consideration of the deeper structure of what this was saying about the requirements for naming. Instead, there was considerable interest in extending the existing scheme with the work on Universal Resource Names.

With network management, we again see the focus on the short term and how to fix a specific problem, but little focus on what this is telling us about the general problem.

IPng. In the early 1990s, the Internet was growing by leaps and bounds. At the rate things were going, there was going to be a shortage of IP addresses, although of greater concern was the growing router table size. The IAB embarked on a program to determine a course of action. After a thorough process considering the pros and cons of a new protocol effort or adopting an existing protocol, they recommended a two-pronged approach of conservation and replacing IP with the OSI version called CLNP. Conservation consisted of IANA tightening the number of addresses handed out, the use of private addresses, instituting CIDR to facilitate aggregation of routes, and forcing most requests for addresses through the major providers to reinforce the move to CIDR.

The years of isolation between the Internet and OSI had done their job. The proposal to adopt an OSI protocol precipitated a huge uproar, which led to the IAB reversing itself, and the IPng process was begun to select a new protocol. The requirements for an acceptable IPng were drafted, which among other things required that the address continue to name the interface, not the node (even though it had been known since 1972 that a network address, let alone an *internetwork* address, should not name a *subnet* point of attachment). Basically, the only problem the resulting IPv6 solves is lengthening the address. In particular, it did nothing to arrest the growth of router tables and nothing to solve 20-year-old deficiencies in the addressing architecture.[21] And what it does do, it makes it worse. Furthermore, the transition plan to IPv6 called for network address translation (NAT). As it turned out, owners of networks liked NATs for other reasons. Once one had a NAT and private address space, there was little reason to adopt IPv6. Had the IPv6 group chosen to fix the addressing problem and come to grips with the fact that IPv4 was not an *Internet* protocol, they could have fixed the problem and avoided the use of NATs.

Why did the IETF not fix a problem that had been known for 20 years? Several reasons:

---

[21] It pains me to watch the IETF resorting to spin for IPv6 to cover up its inadequacies. It used to know how to call a lemon, a lemon.

1. CLNP did fix it, and there was a strong attitude that if OSI did it, the Internet wouldn't.[22]

2. Very few people in the IETF (maybe a dozen or so out of about 1,000) understood the problem.[23] What should be named in a network architecture was not taught in universities. In fact, even today one will be hard pressed to find a networking textbook that covers this topic.

3. There was a belief that any multihoming would be to different providers,[24] which would either have no peering point or they would be so distant that it would unnecessarily complicate the routing, if not be impossible. There were also excuses about addresses being provider-based, but this is an artifact of naming the interface and misses the point of Saltzer's paper that point of attachment addresses are "physical addresses" but node addresses are "logical addresses."

Internet traffic is self-similar. In 1994, a paper was published by a group at Bellcore showing that measurements of Internet traffic on various Ethernets exhibited self-similarity. Some found this a revelation—that this was the first inkling that traffic was not Poisson—when, in fact, this fact had been known since the mid-1970s.[25] This observation created huge interest, and a lot of researchers jumped on the bandwagon. There was more than a little infatuation with the idea that the Internet was described by the hot new idea of fractals, chaos, the butterfly effect, etc. Although not reported in that paper, there were immediately deep suspicions that it wasn't Internet traffic *per se* or Ethernet traffic that was self-similar, but that the self-similarity was an artifact of TCP congestion control. This was later verified. TCP traffic is more strongly self-similar than UDP traffic, and Web traffic is somewhat less self-similar than TCP traffic. The lower self-similarity of Web traffic is most likely a consequence of the "elephants and mice" phenomenon. But interestingly enough, the result that TCP congestion control was causing chaotic behavior did not precipitate a review of how congestion control was done. The general view of the community seemed to be that this was simply a fact of life. This is in part due to the ideas being currently in vogue and the argument being made by some that large systems all exhibit self-similar behavior, so there is nothing to do.

---

[22] Of course, there were very logical rationales for not changing it that sounded good if one didn't look too closely, but it doesn't change the underlying reaction.

[23] This argument plays out on an IETF list every few months. Some still arguing that they should be able to take their *address* wherever they go. Nothing has been learned in the past 15 years.

[24] Which is only sometimes the case in the real world.

[25] The problem was that bursty traffic required a new approach to modeling. No one had come up with one (and still haven't).

That brings us to roughly the early 1990s, to the time frame when I started this exercise, just as the IPng was heating up.[26] The seven unanswered questions we started with were still unanswered and in the back of my mind (as they always had been). It was not my intention to try to solve them. It is a daunting list. But with each pattern that emerged was measured against whether they contributed to solving them. I was looking for a clear understanding of where we were. However, three issues had to be looked at. Two of the issues experience had shown could wreck an architecture if not confronted and solved. We have already touched on them: finding a meaningful synthesis of connection and connectionless, and working out naming and addressing (and in particular what location dependent means). The religious war over connections and connectionless had been at the root of too many disasters. A true synthesis was desperately needed. And, of course, just looking at the seven unanswered questions, you can see that a number of issues all revolve around a clear understanding of naming and addressing. The third arose from my experience with hundreds of protocol designs more than 20 years, seeing the same things over and over. I wanted to separate mechanism and policy as we had in operating systems—just to see what would happen.[27]

Keep in mind that this wasn't my job, my thesis, or my research grant. This was just something I did in my spare time. The initial foray was very productive. Separating mechanism and policy revealed patterns I hadn't seen before and renewed interest in patterns I had seen 15 years earlier (but at the time did not seem to go anywhere). By 1994, the outlines of the model presented here were clear. There weren't seven layers or five layers, but a single layer of two protocols along with optional information that recursed. The limitations of technology and our focus on differences had hidden the patterns from us. This collapse in complexity immediately solves a long list of problems.

Although there were some key problems to solve, it was never a case of finding just anything that solved them. They were threads to pull on in untangling the knot confronting us. Merely finding something that would work was not enough. The solution had to fit into a larger "theory." If it didn't, either the solution or the theory needed to change. I quickly learned (and was often

---

26 I remember being at IETF meetings where IPng was under heavy discussion and having just had the fundamental insight, but having not as yet completely worked it through.

27 Along the way, I picked up a fourth coming out of my frustration with the fact that although we revel in the idea that network traffic is bursty, we then do everything we can to get rid of the burstiness and what I saw as a missing piece: We have a body of literature on ack and flow-control strategies but not on multiplexing (except as a physical layer phenomenon). Although I have made significant progress on this topic, it isn't covered in this book because it just isn't an "architecture" problem.

reminded) that it was more important to go where the problem told me, rather than to do what I thought was best. (Some readers will think I have completely lost it; others who have had the experience will know precisely what I mean.)

In the mid-1990s, however, no one believed there was any reason to look at "new architectures." And in any case, I wasn't done yet, so I just kept mulling over the patterns. Sometimes I put the work down for a year or more. Then some new insight would reveal itself and I would dive into it for a while. Sometimes I would see the pattern the problem was showing me, but it was so at odds with conventional directions that I wouldn't fully embrace it. But there would be continuing hints that doing what the problem was saying would be better. Finally, my resistance would collapse and further simplifications and insights resulted.[28]

What emerged was a much simpler model of networking. A complexity collapse. We knew the outlines of what addressing had to be fairly early. Jerry Saltzer gave us the basics in 1982. But a slight extension to Saltzer to accommodate a case that didn't yet exist yielded a result that dovetailed neatly with the emerging structure of protocols (i.e., it repeated). The results were reinforcing each other. This was getting interesting. This would happen more and more. Someone would remark about something that was hard to do, and it turned out to be straightforward in this model. When capabilities that were not specifically designed in turn out to be supported, it is usually an indication you are on the right track.

The problem of location dependence was much harder. It had always been clear that addresses had to be location dependent, but route independent. It took years of reading and thinking. But slowly I came to the conclusion that for addresses to be location dependent in a meaningful way, they had to be defined in terms of an abstraction of the graph of the network. Looking for mathematical tools for abstracting graphs led to topology and the conclusion that an address space has a topological structure. Throughout the 1990s, I talked to people about this, and by the late 1990s, I had a way to go and an example.

Later, an off-handed teaching question about a detail of protocol design led to revisiting fundamentals that we all knew, and this turned out to shed new light on the structure and further simplification.

So, does this book solve all of our problems? Hardly. But it does lay out the fundamental structure on which a general theory of networking can be built. It does give us a place to stand outside the current box we find ourselves in and see what we have been missing. It turns out that it wasn't so much that what was missing was huge, but it was *key* to a simple solution. I have tried to strike a balance between readability and formality. But one of my goals here has been to try

---

[28] This was the case with the structure of error- and flow-control protocols.

to find the minimal set of concepts necessary to represent the problem. This model is very close to being that. This is a fundamental model. Much of what we have done over the past 30 years is still quite applicable. But this model gives us a much better basis for reasoning about networks independent of any particular network or technology. My hope is that this will spark insights and ideas by others, and I look forward to them.

As noted earlier, several concepts that are key to understanding this model are not generally known. We will rely heavily on what Seymour Papert[29] calls the only concepts that make computer science worth learning: problem decomposition, abstraction, and recursion. Abstraction has fallen into to disuse for the past couple of decades, but we will put it to good use here. Furthermore, the architecture we are led to requires a considerable cognitive shift. Therefore, this book is organized to take the reader from what we know to a new way of looking at things. To bridge the gap, so to speak. Even so, this will not be easy for the reader; there is some hard thinking ahead.

We first start with a return to fundamentals, to remind us of the minimum assumptions required for communication and for the tools for working with abstractions. In Chapters 2 and 3, we look at the familiar world of protocols and separating mechanism and policy. Here, new patterns emerge that indicate there are probably only three kinds of protocols, and then later we find that one of them is more a "common header" than a protocol. We are also able to make considerable progress in resolving the conflict between connections and connectionless.[30]

In Chapter 4, we review our experience with "upper layers" and learn some things that we did right and some things to avoid. As strange as it might sound, we find some key concepts here that will be useful in constructing our fundamental model, while at the same time concluding that there is no "upper-layer architecture." Then in Chapter 5, "Naming and Addressing," we take a hard look at that ever-difficult and subtle topic, naming and addressing. We give special emphasis to Saltzer's 1982 paper expanding on it slightly, noting how the current infatuation with the "loc/id split" problem is a dead end. By the time we reach Chapter 6, we have a pretty reasonable picture of the problem and the elements will we need and can consider the problem of assembling them into a system. Here we embark on a simple exercise that any of us could have done at any time over the past 30 years only to find it yields the structure we have been looking for. (A revolting department!) This chapter is key to everything.

---

29 I wish I could cite a reference for this. Seymour assures me he said it, but he can't remember where, and I can't find it!

30 We don't address the problem of connectionless scaling because this isn't strictly an architectural problem, although the structure presented here facilitates a solution.

In Chapter 7, "The Network IPC Model," we do the unpleasant task of assembling all the pieces we have uncovered in the previous six chapters into the elements of the new model and consider its operation. This entails emulating Johnson's harmless drudge as we define all the concepts required. Messy work, but it has to be done. We consider how new nodes join a network and how communication is initiated. Chapter 8, "Making Address Topological," returns us to naming and addressing to consider the problem of what *location dependent* means and how to make useful sense of the concept. In Chapter 9, Multihoming, Multicast, and Mobility," we look at how multihoming, mobility, and multicast/anycast are represented in this model and some new results that are a consequence of this model. In Chapter 10, "Backing Out of a Blind Alley," we take stock, consider the process that led to seven fundamental issues going unsolved for more than a quarter century, and look to the future.

Acknowledgments

This Preface can't end without expressing my immense appreciation to the long list of people who have contributed their time and effort to this book and to my thinking, all of the people whose ear I have bent over the years working through these ideas. The list in its entirety is far too long, but let me hit the high points: Sue Hares, Lyman Chapin, Margaret Loper, Charles Wade, Glenn Kowack, Geneva Belford, Fred Goldstein, George Schimmel, William Zimmer, Sue Rudd, Chris Williams, Fernando Gont, Sharon Day, and a special thanks to Lynn DeNoia for asking the important questions. The reviewers and friends who had to endure so much: Jonathan Smith, Michael O'Dell, Pekka Nikkander, Ibrahim Matta, Tony Jeffree, and Joel Halpern. Catherine Nolan, Mark Taub, Keith Cline, and Chuck Toporek at Prentice Hall for tackling a different kind of book.

And of course, my wife, Meg, whose love and support sustained me throughout this project (although, I think she was never quite sure it would ever end).

—John Day, Lake Massapoag, 2007

About the Author

John Day has been involved in research and development of computer networks since 1970, when they were 12th node on the "Net." Mr. Day has developed and designed protocols for everything from the data link layer to the application layer.

Also making fundamental contributions to research on distributed databases, he developed one of two fundamental algorithms in the updating of multiple copies. He also did work on the early development of supercomputers and was a member of a development team on three operating systems. Mr. Day was an early advocate of the use of *Formal Description Techniques* (FDTs) for protocols and shepherded the development of the three international standard FDTs: Estelle, LOTOS, and extending SDL. Mr. Day managed the development of the OSI reference model, naming and addressing, and a major contributor to the upper-layer architecture; he also chaired the US ANSI committee for OSI Architecture and was a member of the Internet Research Task Force's Name Space Research Group. He has been a major contributor to the development of network management architecture, working in the area since 1984 defining the fundamental architecture currently prevalent and designing high-performance implementations; and in the mid-1980s, he was involved in fielding a network management system, 10 years ahead of comparable systems. Recently, Mr. Day has turned his attention to the fundamentals of network architectures and their implications (as discussed in this book).

Mr. Day is also a recognized scholar in the history of cartography, on Neolithic Korea, and on Jesuits in 17th-century China. Most recently, Mr. Day has also contributed to exhibits at the Smithsonian and a forthcoming chapter in *Matteo Ricci Cartographia*.

Chapter 1

Foundations for Network Architecture

Architecture is doing the algebra, before doing the arithmetic.

A good (network) architect suffers from the topologist's vision defect. He can't tell a coffee cup from a doughnut.

Architecture is maximizing the invariances and minimizing the discontinuities.

Introduction

A field cannot consider itself a science until it can progress beyond natural history; moving from describing what is, to positing principles or theories that make predictions and impose constraints.[1] And it shouldn't be just any theory; we need a theory that has the fewest assumptions and the greatest breadth: a theory with the fewest concepts, the fewest special cases, that includes the extremes as degenerate cases of a more encompassing model. Computer science, in general, and networking, in particular, has been slow to make this transition. Several times during the past 30 years, I toyed with such ideas, but never with a very satisfactory result. A few years ago, however, I started making a few notes: once again, attempting to cull principles from our experience in networking to get a clearer picture of what we know and what we don't. I was doing this for its own purposes before tackling another problem. Quite unexpectedly, patterns that had not previously been apparent (at least not to me) began to assemble

---

[1] The distinction between natural history and science was drawn by the ecologist Robert MacArthur in his seminal work *Geographical Ecology* (1972).

1

themselves. Charles Kettering [2] believed that within every problem lies its solution; we only have to learn to listen to the problem—in a sense, learn to "follow the grain" of the problem. This time, as these patterns emerged, it seemed logical to see where they would lead (but not without a few of those embarrassing moments when I went astray, reverting back to our old ideas, only to have the "problem" set me straight).

This book does not claim to be proposing a "new paradigm" or "a whole new way of looking at networking" (as is common), nor does this theory accommodate everything that has been done before. (It would be incredibly fortuitous if every protocol ever designed obeyed principles as yet unrecognized. However, these principles do shed light on why things were done as they were.) Nor do I claim that this theory answers all of our questions, but it does answer many of them. It does make things simpler, and with that simplicity, one now has a powerful framework from which to tackle many open questions. In some cases, the solutions were staring us in the face: We had the tools, but we just weren't looking at them the right way.

Why had we (including myself!) not seen them before? There are many reasons, but probably the most significant were the following:

- **Early imprinting.** The domain of the problem space of networking in the early 1970s was microscopic in comparison with the domain of the problem space today. Some patterns were simply not yet visible or were masked by the constraints of those early systems. Quite naturally, those early assumptions continued to condition our thinking.

- **Early success.** Our initial efforts were really pretty good. Some very bright people made some significant insights early that were either correct or very close, which meant there wasn't that much to fix. (Our biggest problem was that we got too much right to start with!)

- **Moore's law.** The two-edged sword of Moore's law not only dropped the cost and increased the capability of equipment at an unprecedented rate, but it also allowed us to avoid fundamental problems by simply "throwing hardware" at them.

- **Socioeconomic forces.** These forces (probably the most significant factor in this list) constrained solutions because before the fledgling research had done more than scratch the surface, it was thrown into a fierce competitive

---

[2] The prolific inventor and engineer (1876–1958) who along with Alfred P. Sloan made General Motors the largest corporation in the world.

battle over who would dominate the merging computer and telecommunications market, where technical solutions were used to determine who made money. Starting very early, this battle distorted our understanding, creating a "bunker mentality" of warring camps that inhibited the pursuit of deeper understanding and real progress. We still live with this legacy today.

What this book does claim is that a small number of principles can, when applied to our current ideas of network architecture, lead to a much simpler, more unified theory of networking. This theory can be exploited to great advantage in the design, development, manufacturing, deployment, and management of networks. It should also contribute to a new rigor in our research. And thus, results can be more easily compared and evaluated, making it easier to understand their implications (that is, which results are more general and which are more specific). What is remarkable is that we were not that far off. With a few adjustments here and there, recognizing that some things were more similar than different, things fell into place, and a much simpler structure emerged. There was, in some sense, a complexity implosion.

Were we close enough to use existing protocols? Unfortunately, not in all cases. Some of our existing designs have just too many warts and lack the hooks necessary for things to work sufficiently smoothly to achieve the benefit of these results. However, most of the techniques we have perfected can be used to transition in a straightforward manner to an architecture based on these principles. Many in our field have often waxed eloquently about how special and how different from other scientific fields computer science is. It *is* different but not in a way that should leave us complacent. The most important difference between computer science and other scientific fields is that:

We build what we measure.

Hence, we are never quite sure whether the behavior we observe, the bounds we encounter, the principles we teach, are truly principles from which we can build a body of theory, or merely artifacts of our creations. Far from being something that should allow us to relish our "special" position, this is a difference that should, to use the vernacular, "scare the bloody hell out of us!"

Recognizing that the optimal decisions for a good implementation will change with technology, but believing that there are general principles for networking, I have worked with the assumption that principles will be independent of implementation; but I have tempered that with the recognition that rampant generality is seldom beneficial and the "right" answer also leads to a good implementation.

In what follows, I try to present the architecture in brief. The primary intent is to describe the elements of the theory and identify the train of reasoning that leads to the conclusions (without boring the reader with the fits and starts that actually occurred, and thus avoiding further embarrassment). Very few concepts here are truly new, but some of these concepts may be used in different or novel forms from those for which they were originally proposed. In some cases, I contrast the implications of this architecture with traditional views, but for the most part this is left as an exercise for the reader. Thinking about this architecture is a bit like working with a non-Euclidean geometry. The objects being manipulated are familiar, but the axiom set we are working from is somewhat different. So, the reader must always be aware (and we will stress) that the concepts and results must be interpreted not in the conventional axiom set but in this alternative. The result is a much simpler network architecture that will have higher performance, lower manpower needs, and most important of all, it scales.

Before delving into the pragmatics of networking, however, we need to remind ourselves of where we came from.

Beginning at the Beginning

In 1921, a young philosopher returning to Cambridge from service in the German army during WWI published a short 75-page book with an Introduction by Bertrand Russell that had an immediate and revolutionary effect on philosophy and mathematics. It basically made obsolete much of the past 2,000 years of philosophy, pointing out that many of the problems considered by philosophy were pseudo-problems and as such were either nonsensical or could have no solution. The book made it clear that words meant only what we want them to mean (opening the door for modern propaganda), that the entire world could be described by a finite list of precise logical statements. The book gave rise to the Vienna Circle, logical positivism, and symbolic logic and would have a major impact on the field of computer science when it arose roughly 25 years later. The philosopher was Ludwig Wittgenstein, the book was *Tractatus Logico-Philosophicus,* and it began like this:

1.   The world is all that is the case.

1.1   The world is the totality of facts, not things.

1.11 The world is determined by being the facts, and their being all the facts.

In such a rigid logical structure through six fundamental statements with a varying number of substatements, the book develops a link between logical propositions and reality:

2. What is the case—a fact—is the existence of states of affairs.

3. A logical picture of facts is a thought.

4. A thought is a proposition with a sense.

5. A proposition is a truth-function of elementary propositions.

6. The general form of a truth function is $(\rho, \xi\ N(\xi))$. This is the general form of a proposition.

And so on, concluding with perhaps the most revolutionary and devastating statement ever made in philosophy, mathematics, or science:

7. That of which we cannot speak we must pass over in silence.

In one straightforward sentence, the *Tractatus* destroyed any hopes of putting what was then called moral philosophy (ethics, morals, and religion) on any kind of formal base. Because the terms could not be precisely defined and the value judgments were always cultural or relative, nothing could be said. Proper civilized behavior could not be argued from first principles, as many from Plato to Kant had tried to do. The *Tractatus* was immediately embraced by mathematics and science as holding out a Holy Grail that all of science and mathematics could be described by a precise logical system as complete as Euclid's *Geometry*, Newton's *Principia*, or Maxwell's *Treatise*. Attempts were made to create logical models of various branches of science, and when computers came along, the *Tractatus* was used as not only the basis for logic and programming languages, but also as the basis for artificial intelligence and database systems. The database field coined the phrase *conceptual schema* to describe the collection of logical statements that would define a domain, an enterprise. Later, artificial intelligence called the same concept a *knowledge base* and developed expert systems. Both of these are implementations of what Wittgenstein meant when he wrote 1.1. In both, "the world is all that is the case," and the world is represented by a collection of logical propositions.

The same approach was applied to distributed systems. For two parties to communicate, they must have a shared conceptual schema; they must have a common language or protocol and some common understanding about what strings in the language stand for. Without this, communication is impossible, whether between machines or between people. The important things to a protocol are the things it understands. This approach provided a very nice model for communications, even in the more mundane error-control protocols. The shared conceptual schema of protocol state machines was the information exchanged about flow control, acknowledgments, addresses, and so on. The user's data was outside their shared conceptual schema and was ignored (or passed to another protocol machine). Data is this incomprehensible stuff that shows up every so often and is ignored and passed on.

But beyond this, the usefulness of this approach finds its limits, although we will have use for it when we come to applications. Like any good engineer (and He *had* studied earlier as an aeronautical engineer), Wittgenstein, had taken the easy way out and provided an existence proof but did not tell us how to construct these logical worlds (or to know when we had all the necessary facts). Although there is much to be gained by understanding the *Tractatus*, we are primarily interested in what it teaches us about reducing problems to their bare bones to see what is *really* going on (but also to take a lesson from the penultimate statement of the *Tractatus*):

> **6.54** My propositions serve as elucidations in the following way: anyone who understands me eventually recognizes them as nonsensical, when he has used them—as steps—to climb up beyond them. (He must, so to speak, throw away the ladder after he has climbed up it.)

At several points in what follows, we will find it necessary to throw away the ladder. Concepts and constructs that have helped us to get where we are will be discarded so that we may get beyond them. It is not so much that these concepts are wrong (after all, we might never have reached our new insights without them) but more that they have done their job and now it is time to move beyond them. At these points, the reader may have to work a little harder to reinterpret familiar concepts from a new perspective. I try to warn the reader when this is necessary.

Let us start by first considering two meta-level topics that will be important to us as we proceed:

1. The abstract method by which we will proceed (the "nature of the algebra," if you will)

2. The role of formal methods in network architectures

But we will always want to keep in mind some sage advice:

In the practical arts, the theoretical leaves and blossoms must not be allowed to grow too high, but must be kept close to experience, their proper soil.

—*Clausewitz*

If we have a correct theory but merely prate about it, pigeonhole it and do not put it into practice, then that theory, however good, is of no significance. Knowledge begins with practice, and theoretical knowledge is acquired through practice and must return to practice.

—Mao Zhe Dong

I have referred to these quotes as a philosophical triangulation. When two important voices of the right and the left say the same thing, it is probably right. In the course of this journey, we will have reason to delve into what might seem like some fairly esoteric topics for the practical task of engineering networks. The insights here have been gained from practice. These forays into theory will allow us to do the algebra, simplify the arithmetic, and thereby simplify the practice. The first of these uses of theory is applying levels of abstraction to the problem.

Levels of Abstraction

Levels of abstraction represent an important tool for managing the complexity of a system or architecture. There is a common misconception that top-down design starts at the user interface and goes down to the hardware. This is not the case. This confuses the levels of abstraction in the design process with the layers of the system being designed.

Top-down design starts at a high level of abstraction, which is refined through successive levels, each level less abstract than the one above, to the implementation. Even though the implementation may itself create objects, which hide complexity and therefore are considered more abstract (and possibly layered), from the design perspective the entire implementation is all at the same level of abstraction.

This is important because it allows the designer to ensure that the use of "first-order effectors" across all *layers* of the system being designed is consistent, before moving the design to a lower level of abstraction and lesser-order effects. Two orthogonal forms of abstraction have been found useful in architectures: levels of design and specification, and the layering of the architecture. Because there will be much more to say about layering in Chapter 6, "Divining Layers,"our discussion here is brief.

The concept of layering evolved in the late 1960s and early 1970s in the design of operating systems and software in general. Layering is an expansion of the "black box" concept developed by Norbert Weiner. A user of a black box can only observe what the box does (that is, the service it provides), not how it does it; the mechanisms that implement its external behavior are hidden. In fact, there may be many mechanisms to generate the same external behavior. In software, layering was used to build up layers of abstraction so that the specifics of the hardware (processor and peripherals) could be masked from the applications and to allow more efficient resource management by the operating system and provide a portable, more user-friendly environment for programming.[3]

For operating systems, layering tends to represent a collection of black boxes that take a class of different mechanisms (for example, device drivers) at one level of abstraction and present an interface with a higher level of abstraction (for example, device independent) to the layer above. Each layer added a level of functionality that created a greater abstraction with the hardware as the bottom layer and the user as the top layer. Similarly in networks, layering provided abstraction from the specifics of a network hardware technology.[4] For example, the network layer creates an abstract service that is independent of the underlying media. This was seen as very similar to what operating systems did to make all terminals and storage devices look the same to programs.

Although the use of layers has evolved in operating systems from Dijkstra's THE, and even as innovative developments in operating systems continue, the layering of microkernel, kernel, user is fairly well accepted. Why are layers in networks still controversial? To a large extent, it is due to the effects of the war alluded to earlier. By the time the industry settled on designs based on Multics/UNIX or DEC's VMS and a few others for specialized environments, there had probably been 20 to 30 major operating systems (probably more) of radically different architectures developed and thoroughly tested over a period of about 10 years. In contrast, for networks, we settled on the current approach after considering just three or four networks over three or four years. We simply did not explore the problem space as much. It is a much greater effort to create a new kind of network than a new kind of operating system. Further, the effect of the "war" tended to push thinking into one camp or another.

Recently in networking, there has been a flight from layers by some, although it is unclear to what (a response to the perception that the traditional layered approach was interfering with solving the problems). But we must be careful. As

---

[3] The concepts for creating portable operating systems and other software applications derive from the same source: The system is layered with a canonical interface at one of the middle layers and the hardware specific layers below that.

[4] The seven-layer OSI model was the creation of Charles Bachman based on his experience at Honeywell with database systems and with Multics.

noted earlier, communications requires a set of objects with a shared conceptual schema. Given that we may want to hide some of the complexity of that shared schema, so that we can build other objects with different shared schemas that use it, would seem to indicate that these collections of objects with the common shared schemas have a structure something like a "layer." The concept of layer seems inherent in the problem. The question is what constitutes the "right" schema for these "layers."

For design and specification of network architecture, four levels of abstraction have proved useful: the model, the service, the protocol and interface, and the implementation. We start with a model or architecture, and each lower level of specification refines the abstraction of the level above to add more detail. This step-wise refinement is a method of exposition and specification, not necessarily one of design. While the design process makes use of these levels of abstraction, the process must move up and down successively approximating the final solution. However, this approach does allow components of lower levels of abstraction to be modified with no effect on higher-level components and little or no effect on components at the same level of abstraction. A good architecture will both specify constraints and allow sufficient flexibility for a wide range of implementations.

The aphorisms at the beginning of this chapter attempt to characterize what constitutes a good architecture.[5] The more formal definition I have used is close to the common dictionary definition of *architecture*:

A set of rules and constraints that characterize a particular style of construction

Like the weather, it is not possible to have no architecture (although some have tried hard not to); at worst, one has the Karnack or accidental architecture—that is, given the system, what is the architecture?[6] One must distinguish, for example, between Victorian architecture and a Victorian building built to that architecture: type versus instance. Most activity in the field of architecture consists of creating buildings to an existing architecture (that is, creating instances of a class). In this case, we are developing a new architecture. Not a radically new architecture, but one definitely based on our experience and using many components of previous architectures. However, it is our belief that this

---

[5] This word is much abused in our field. I have seen papers where "architecture" was used as synonymous with hardware.

[6] For those too young to remember, this is an allusion to a recurring skit on U.S. television by Johnny Carson on *The Tonight Show*, where The Great Karnak divines the answer to questions before they are posed to him.

new architecture avoids many of the ornate and cumbersome constructions required in the past and will generate much simpler, more powerful constructs and few special cases. Many capabilities that have required explicit functionality will be found to be degenerate cases in this model. Many capabilities that were difficult to accommodate are included easily. And most important, it is a model that inherently scales. At the same time, however, we are also trying to identify architectural principles that are invariant with respect to media and implementation. (And where we do make choices, I make them as explicit as possible.)

Model

The definition of the *model* of a layer, service, protocol, or distributed application is one of the more important aspects in the process of design and specification. The model, in essence, defines the shared conceptual schema of the communication. It defines the objects in the universe of discourse, their attributes, the operations that can be performed on them, how they relate to each other, the communication of information among them, and so on.

Models exist for all protocols, but they are most important for distributed application protocols. Because the models for the lower-layer protocols are concerned with ensuring the integrity and resource management of the communication, they are essentially similar, self-contained, and require little or no interaction with the entities outside the protocol itself. Here the model is primarily of use as an explanatory tool to facilitate the description of the protocol's behavior. Application protocols differ qualitatively from the lower-layer protocols. Application protocols are concerned with modifying state on objects *external* to the protocol itself, while data transfer protocols modify state *internal* to the protocol. For example, a file transfer protocol modifies the state of the operating system's file system (external), where TCP modifies its state vector internal to the protocol. Unfortunately, there are a wide variety of file systems with widely varying properties. Although the corresponding systems may have different models, the application layer protocol must establish a common model for the communicating systems. In effect, the model describes the semantics of the distributed application. In recent years, this degree of rigor has been replaced by the implementation.

There will be much more to say about this when we discuss upper-layer architecture. Keep in mind that specifications are required for four levels of abstraction: the *model*, which we are primarily concerned here; the *service* and the *protocol*, as described in the following sections; and the *implementation*, which at least in source code is still an abstraction. Most of what is discussed in this book is at the model or architecture level. Our focus will be on the models for protocols and layers and how they all fit together to create a working system. We try to identify the properties that allow them to fit together well and, in some cases, directions that lead to a less-than-good fit. We also consider specific protocols and architectures to illustrate various points.

Service

Using techniques to hide mechanism has always been important to the design and implementation of complex systems. Hiding mechanisms has been used throughout computer science: the concept of procedure in most programming languages, layers of an operating system, the object-oriented model, and so on. All of these techniques use the concept of hiding mechanisms behind an abstract view to manage complexity. This has the effect that the interactions with the object are simplified and allow the mechanisms by which the object provides its function to be modified without affecting the user. This greatly enhances its utility.

In communications, we embodied this idea of hiding mechanisms in the construct of layering. The concept of layer was essentially the concept of a process or object recast in what was thought to be a less-rich environment with only a few types of "objects" and very limited forms of interactions among them. The layer boundaries hid the mechanisms of a layer from the layer above and below. The crucial difference from operating systems was that a layer was a "distributed black box" whose internal mechanisms were coordinated by the exchange of information, forming a loosely coupled shared state.

The concept of service is one of the more important concepts in the development of communication architectures. The definition of *service* as used here is an abstraction of the interface between layers that is system independent.

Service is a level of abstraction higher than protocol and interface and a level of abstraction lower than the architecture or model. It is from this abstraction that the importance of the concept is derived. On one hand, the concept of service allows one to hide the mechanisms of a protocol from its user, thereby simplifying the user's interactions with the protocol. At the same time, it allows the behavior of one protocol to be decoupled from another, thereby allowing the protocol some flexibility in responding to its users by not tying its behavior

Words Mean What We Want Them To

The *International Telecommunication Union* (ITU) and others with a telephony background use the concept of service and interface as a boundary between systems or boxes. Therefore, when most ITU documents use the terms *service* or *interface,* they are really talking about properties of a protocol; for instance, X.25 is an interface specification between a *Data Terminal Equipment* (DTE) and a *Data Communication Equipment* (DCE). This is how some were deluded into believing that they could automatically generate a protocol from an abstract service definition, such as X.407. It is, in fact, easy to generate a protocol from a protocol specification. However, it is only possible to generate a protocol from a service specification for a very small tightly constrained class of protocols and impossible for the vast majority.

too tightly to its interactions with its users. Providing this decoupling at critical junctures is crucial to the successful design of complex systems such as these.

Although closely related, a service is *not* an interface. Interfaces are local to a particular system. An interface must be concerned with several elements—such as maximum buffer size, procedure entry/exit or system call conventions, buffer management, and interface flow control—that must be integrated with the local operating environment. It is important to leave as much flexibility as possible in these local matters to ensure that efficient and cost-effective implementations can be built for a variety of operating environments. For purposes of architecture, therefore, the concept of service is used to describe the aspects of an interface that all interfaces must have regardless of how the local issues are solved. Every protocol will be associated with a service definition, but some interfaces may not exist in an actual implementation. In other words, a given implementation may choose to not explicitly implement certain interfaces, in cases where those interfaces would not be used. The choice of a representational method will carry with it certain implications. These, of course, must be explicitly understood so that interfaces using radically different models can be created. Issues such as whether calls block must be addressed.

In general, a service is defined to be independent of the protocol. Any number of protocols can satisfy a particular service; and so, with a well-designed service, it should be possible to change protocols without changing the service. This is especially true with the lower layers. A service defines a set of requirements and constraints on the operation of both the service user and the service provider (that is, the protocol state machine). This is less often the case with applications, where interfaces are necessarily required to reflect the specific nature of the application (although, a greater degree of decoupling of interactions between the layer boundary and elements inside the layer makes many of these considerations moot).

A *service definition* consists of two parts:

1. A set of service primitives, which specify the operations to be performed on the service and a set of parameters that are used as arguments to the operations

2. A set of rules that determine the legal sequences in which the service primitives can be invoked

With a nod to Frege (1892) two service definitions will be considered equivalent when the two service definitions have the same service primitives, parameters, and partial state machines. And two service definitions will be considered as similar if the two service definitions have the same primitives and partial state machines. Most often when we speak informally of two services being the same, it is this latter relation that we have in mind. This form of similarity implies that although different parameters may be passed, the behavior is the same.[7]

A service definition is defined for a layer; it is specified as a partial state machine for the interaction of the user of the layer and the protocol machine (PM) in the layer of a single system. A protocol may have to adapt its behavior to the constraints of the service definition. This can happen when the service is defined as independent of the protocol (and to some degree it should be) or when a new protocol is being developed to an existing service definition. A service definition never states explicitly that a service primitive submitted to one PM causes another service primitive to appear at the peer PM. Any such association is made by the protocol. A service definition specifies requirements on the service user and the service provider (that is, the protocol). There are two primary reasons for this discipline:

- It allows the protocol designer some flexibility in choosing the correspondences of actions on one side to actions on the other.

- It also enforces the view that the behavior of the service is defined completely in terms of the events it has seen, not in terms of behavior presumed to have happened elsewhere.

With any interface design, there is always the question of how much to hide and how much to expose. As usual, some think that everything should be exposed, whereas others believe nothing should. Experience has shown that although it may be interesting to expose as much as possible, this leads to systems with high maintenance costs and poor scaling properties. It is important to present the user with an abstraction that captures the important elements. Remember, we want to find the right abstraction that allows the user to specify what is required without actually giving access to the mechanisms. Creating a good service model requires a good understanding of the system. If there is not a good service model, the system is not well understood. It does require some

---

[7] The genesis of the concept of "service" came during the OSI effort and was motivated not by a desire for formalism, but by the desire of manufacturers to protect their turf and avoid standards defining internal interfaces or APIs. As often happens in the dynamics of the standards process (not unlike the hostage syndrome) as the work progressed, the resistance to defining such APIs waned, but the abstraction was found useful and remained.

hard work to achieve that understanding, but that is supposed to be what we do. Exposing everything is taking the easy way out.

One could argue that the expose-everything approach is only applicable in data communications, where the network has a single physical medium and hence a single interface. In a network, layers have limited scope with different media and, with the expose-everything model, different interfaces. A user application will not have access to every interface of every segment that its data traverses, nor will the user application even know what kind of interface traversed. To modify the parameters for these intervening segments, the information must be communicated to where it is used. Because it is impossible to know all the interfaces that might be encountered, one will need some abstract model of the parameters that can be used as a common representation of the parameters. And, so, we are back to the don't-expose-everything model. The fact that the expose-everything model has gotten any consideration in networking at all is difficult to fathom. It is really only applicable to data communications.

Protocol and Interface

The protocol and interface level of specification is probably the most important. This is the last point before jumping off into specific implementation design decisions. A *protocol* specification defines the rules and behavior required by any entity participating in the transfer of data. The protocol specification defines the sequences of message exchanges among the participants. There will be much more to say about protocols later, but here I merely want to establish them as a level abstraction between the service and model on the one hand and the implementation on the other. A protocol specifies the minimal state machine that any implementation must conform to. Traditionally, the protocol specification does not specify implementation considerations such as buffering strategies, interactions with the local operating environment, and so forth. Protocol specifications should be taken as requirements documents, not design specifications.

The protocol specification should not diverge too far from the "normal" implementation strategy. Experience shows that this can lead implementers too far astray. Even though implementations may take on any form to meet the requirements of the environment in which they may exist, the specification should not make it difficult to discover the "normal" implementation strategy. Conformance testing should be restricted to only those behaviors that are externally visible, and thus give the implementers as much freedom as possible to construct efficient implementations. This is a good place to reiterate the oft-quoted rule that an implementation should be conservative in what it generates and liberal in what it accepts. In particular, the point of testing is not to ensure that any implementation can detect any infraction by another implementation but to ensure that the probability is as low as possible of a misbehaving implementation being fielded that will cause catastrophic failures in other systems.

Standard (or common) *application programming interfaces* (APIs) may be defined for specific languages and operating systems at important junctures in an architecture to facilitate the development of portable software. For the same reasons that some implementations will not implement explicit interfaces, APIs are not necessary at all layers. For example, in the lower layers, the transport service has been one such important juncture. In general, this service should be similar to the *interprocess communication* (IPC) service of the operating system. (The only difference being in the syntax of the names used to access a peer.) In some cases, it may be necessary for the local system to emulate the model of local interface functions to conform to the API. If the API's model of these functions differs significantly from those of the local system, there may be significant performance or resource penalties on the system.

Implementation

This is the lowest level of abstraction, where the rubber meets the road. As indicated previously, an implementer is free to construct an implementation in any form as long as the external behavior is consistent with the specification. The implementation must address all the issues not covered by the protocol specification, such as local buffering strategies, interactions with the operating system, and so on. And an implementation must be carefully written to ensure that any data received does not cause aberrant behavior.

Specifying Protocols

Specifying the protocol and specifying the interface are critical steps. Experience has shown that simple prose is very insufficient and relying on just the implementation can over specify and lead to monoculture problems. Good specification is needed to communicate the protocol to others, provide a basis for analysis, and so forth.

Informal Specifications

It is equally important that there are informal and formal specifications for protocols. Good specifications for protocols are crucial not only to communicating the protocols to other designers and implementers, but also as part of the design process. It is equally important to keep in mind the nature of specification. An informal specification of a protocol is not a journal article about the protocol.

An article and a specification serve two very different but related purposes. An article is primarily intended to give the reader an understanding of the overall behavior of the protocol, so the reader has an idea of "where things are going" and a general idea of what happens when things go wrong. An article is intended to be read from beginning to end.

Although a specification may be read from beginning to end (it is seldom an enjoyable affair, nor should it be), the primary purpose of a specification is as a reference document—most often used to look up what happens in a particular situation. Therefore, it should be organized such that it is easy to find the answer to such questions. It is this property that makes a specification difficult to read from beginning to end but easy to use for the engineer building an implementation or attempting to answer specific questions. The article (or an abridged version) may be included in the specification as a narrative overview, as introductory material. Although there are many variations on this outline, with some items being omitted and others included, the benefit of the outline is to remind the writer of what must be written, often an invaluable service.

Formal Description Techniques

Beginning in the mid-1970s, the first attempts were made to apply *Formal Description Techniques* (FDTs) to programs. These attempts were interesting, but the generality of most real-life programs led to formal descriptions that were often much more complex than the programs they described. At about the same time, experience with the early prose protocol specifications showed that even the ones thought to be very good were woefully ambiguous when used by people outside the initial developers. So whereas FDTs for general-purpose programming were mainly concerned with proving correctness, the use of FDTs in networking was also concerned with being able to unambiguously communicate the specification to other implementers. In the late 1970s, several researchers realized that applying FDTs to protocols could be much more successful because of the constraints on their behavior. Considerable activity in this area meant that by 1978 it was possible to publish an annotated bibliography of 60 papers on the topic (Day and Sunshine, 1978)[8]. A thorough evaluation of nearly 25 different FDTs by applying them to the Abracadabra Protocol (alternating bit protocol) to understand their properties, lead to the development of three standard languages for the formal description of protocols: one for each of the two major paradigms of formal description, *Extended Finite Stale Machine Language*

---

[8] This may be the first network-produced paper. I had been living and working for two years as the University of Illinois at Houston (TX) telecommuting over the Net; the database for the bibliography was on a PDP-11/45 in Urbana, Illinois; and the paper was edited on Multics at MIT and then shipped to Carl Sunshine in California, who did the final editing and printing and then surface mailed it to the conference in Liége, Belgium.

(Estelle), using an extended state machine model, and *Language Temporal Ordering Specification* (LOTOS), using a temporal logic model; and one for the ITU, *Specification and Definition Language* (SDL), also using an extended state model. Others have been defined since but are variants of either of these two models or one of the others. By the early 1980s, there were compilers and automatic verification tools for all three languages.

If certain guidelines are followed, FDTs are beneficial in the design and development of a protocol. They have proven useful in uncovering numerous bugs, races, hazards, and deadlocks during the design process. Unfortunately, the use of FDTs is greater in the design of hardware than in software. They have been applied to software applications where correct or fail-safe operation is crucial. The use of a good FDT should greatly shorten the design and development cycle. However, certain rules of thumb should be applied:

- The FDT should be no more complex than the programming language used for implementation. Otherwise, there is a greater probability of an error in the formal description than in the implementation (a sort of "complexity artifact" effect).

- The FDT should be useful as a design tool. If the model of the FDT does not fit the mode of design, it will get in the way of the design process. This means its use will be avoided, and the probability increases that the translation of the design to a formal description will contain errors.

- An FDT is just another form of programming. To be understandable, it must be documented just as code must be. In other words, a formal description does not preclude the need for an informal specification or inline comments.

- There should be analytical tools that can analyze the formal description to ensure against protocol deadlock, data loss, races, hazards, and other pathological behaviors.

- The formal description should not require more specificity than necessary. A formal description is not an implementation and should not impose constraints on implementations.

- It should be easy to move from the informal to the formal specifications when referencing the specification.

There are basically three forms of such techniques or languages:

- **Mathematical or language-based.** The mathematical techniques have been intended for specifying general algorithms, rather than tailored to defining the much smaller subset of algorithms represented by protocols. They are generally based on a predicate calculus approach. This generally makes them much more complex and difficult to use.

- **Finite state machine.** The finite state machine methods usually consist of a small number of extensions to an existing programming language that facilitate the representation of the state machine and the rules associated with it.

- **Temporal logic.** Temporal logic approaches describe the protocol in terms of statements on the relative ordering of events and their actions.

The mathematical approaches have generally been more complex than the programs they described and, thus, fail our first criteria. In general, there has been more success with FDTs that were designed with distributed system problems in mind. First, because protocols are more constrained than a general algorithm, much more can be done. I had great hopes for the temporal logic approach because it was not only precise, but also more nearly minimal. It said the least about the implementation. They implied the least about the nature of the implementation, thus prejudicing the implementer as little as possible to an implementation design. However, it is difficult to find anyone who can design in a temporal logic language. In most cases, the design is done in a finite state machine model and then translated to temporal logic statements.

Over the years, researchers and graduate students return to these topics, applying them to new areas of networking with some new interesting results being proved. However, no major new approaches to the formal description method have come to light. Formal descriptions in Estelle and LOTOS were written as part of the development of all or most of the OSI protocols. Timing of the development of the FDTs necessitated that some of the formal specifications were written after the protocols were defined, but there were cases where the formal specification was done in parallel with development. In both cases, the formal descriptions discovered bugs and ambiguities that were then corrected.

Formal descriptions of the *Internet Protocols* (IPs) have not been part of the *Internet Engineering Task Force* (IETF) process. Although in the early 1980s, an Estelle description of *Transport Control Protocol* (TCP) was done, and various academics have done formal specifications of IETF standards, the IETF has not embraced the use of FDTs and continues to specify protocols much as they were in 1975. This is consistent with IETF skepticism of advanced methods. The approach to producing specifications remains pretty much unchanged since the early 1970s, relying primarily on the implementation as the specification.

This tendency to use the implementation as the specification has the drawback of not cleanly separating what is part of the protocol and must be conformed to and what is system and implementation dependent. In particular, some implementations may take particular shortcuts that are deemed reasonable for their environment but which then constrain the behavior of the protocol. In a world with few system types, this problem is less severe, but it can easily lead to considerable differences in the conception of the protocol that will not be answered by an informal specification.

This also has the disadvantage of playing on a prime engineering virtue: laziness. There is a natural tendency to just port the code rather than write new code from scratch thereby making the implicit assumption that the existing implementation is as good as it can get; seldom a good assumption. There have been more than a few recent examples of this.

There is always the question of what should take precedence if a discrepancy exists between the implementation, the formal description, and the prose description. One's first impression is that the formal description should, of course, take precedence because it was presumed to be the most rigorous. But upon reflection, one comes to a much different answer: By their nature, all written specifications are merely approximations of the intent of the designers. The real specification can only be presumed to reside in the designers' heads. When a discrepancy is found, we cannot presume any of the specifications take precedence; instead, we must return to the intent of the designers and infer what the specifications should say. This should serve as our approach in evaluating FDTs.

Where to from Here

Now that we have the preliminaries out of the way, we are ready to start the hard work of this book. First, in Chapter 2, "Protocol Elements," we analyze the common data transfer protocols in the abstract, using the experience of the past 30 years as data to work through the implications of separating mechanism and policy. Then, in Chapter 3, "Patterns in Protocols," we consider the patterns revealed by applying what we did in Chapter 2 and then take steps toward resolving the conflict between connection and connectionless networking. But before moving to consider architectures of protocols, we must first collect more data based on our experience. Therefore in Chapter 4, "Stalking the Upper-Layer Architecture," we look at application protocols and the pursuit of the "upper-layer architecture." Our purpose here is not so much to be encyclopedic but to consider protocols with unique structures that deepen our understanding. Somewhat surprisingly, we discover that there is no upper-layer architecture, but there is a model for constructing distributed applications. In Chapter 5, "Naming and Addressing," we review our experience with that most subtle and difficult aspect of networking: naming and addressing.

All of this then gives us the tools we need to consider how to assemble a network architecture in Chapter 6, "Divining Layers." But here we find that we have no definition of a layer. We have conventions and habits, but nothing we can stand on. This leads to an exercise that will appear too elementary to many readers but yields results that are exceptionally elegant and form the foundation of a powerful network architecture. Although this architecture requires only a small number of changes to the existing architecture, these changes could never have been achieved by starting with the current architecture and modifying it piecemeal. The result is a definition that is both the same and different. In one sense, the structure we arrive at changes nothing. The old model is largely still there. In another way, however, it radically alters everything. We come to the conclusion that there aren't seven layers or five or even four, but *one layer that recurses* (a layer that encompasses all three phases [not just two] of communication, enrollment, allocation, and data transfer simply and elegantly). We move from the realm of the fixed to the relative: that a layer is a distributed application that provides interprocess communication for a given range of bandwidth and quality of service. The greater the range of bandwidth in a network between the applications and the backbone, the more layers; the less range, the fewer the layers. However, no one system implements any more layers than a host or router today, and in some cases, fewer. Furthermore, the fundamental nature of the resulting model is such that it scales indefinitely over any range of bandwidth, distance, or user population.

In Chapter 7, "The Network IPC Model," we consolidate our gains by laying out the basic architecture or reference model based on the patterns uncovered in the previous chapters. This lays the foundation for exploring the properties of the architecture—not the least of which are the major implications it has for security and bringing in aspects previously believed to require ad hoc procedures.

Chapter 8, "Making Addresses Topological," introduces topological addresses and examines an approach to making addresses location dependent without being route dependent (and still reflecting the structure of the network). A general approach to topological addresses is developed and then applied it to the ubiquitous hierarchy of subnets with shortcuts we see in the wild. For now, this is considered only in the context of traditional routing algorithms, although we are well aware that this opens the door for new investigations. This chapter also considers how networks of layers might be created, and we see how *network address translations* (NATs) either do not exist or are an integral part of the model depending on your point of view.

Chapter 9, "Multihoming, Multicast, and Mobility," considers how the capabilities are inherent to the structure of the recursive architecture and topological addresses, requiring no additional protocols or mechanisms, and Chapter 10, "Backing Out of a Blind Alley," looks back at where we've been and how we got there, wraps up a few loose ends, and reviews the implications of the book.

The development of this model does not assume any particular set of protocols or any particular media. It is based on a very few fundamental assumptions. Consequently, it would appear that this represents the fundamental structure of networking. Does this mean that we have answered all the questions? Hardly. All we have done is created an opportunity for new advances in network science and engineering. And perhaps, we have also pointed the way to teaching networking as a university-level subject based on principles and theory, rather than as simply a vocational course describing what is deployed today.

Chapter 2

Protocol Elements

A good engineer is a lazy degenerate. He prefers degenerate cases to special cases and will sit around (thinking) until he finds a simple solution, rather than immediately launch into a brute force approach.

In other words, the role of an architect is to use the tools he has to make things simple. (Anyone can make things more complicated!)

Introduction

We are now ready to begin our exploration of network architecture. The philosophy is mostly behind us, and we can now get down to the part everyone wants to talk about. But remember, we are doing the "algebra" first. We're trying to keep as close to first principles and independent of implementation dependencies as we can—not because implementations are bad, but because they represent trade-offs for specific situations and are data for first principles. First and foremost, we are interested in those properties that are independent of the trade-offs, and next we are interested in understanding the nature of the trade-offs and when certain choices should and should not be made. We want to postpone this binding as long as we can to see what patterns appear. The longer we can do that, the more likely the patterns we see are fundamental and not specific to a given problem domain.

Protocol Architecture

This chapter covers the theory and architecture of protocols. We consider the general structure of protocols and lay the foundations for the use of the separation of mechanism and policy to reveal invariant patterns in protocols. We briefly consider the range of functions that are generally included in a protocol, although we do not consider which functions go with which kinds of protocols. We make our first stab at that in Chapter 3, "Patterns in Protocols."

Elements of a Protocol

All data communications is a side effect.

The theory of *finite state machines* (FSMs) has traditionally been used to describe and analyze protocols. This "black box" model is not the only descriptive method, and certainly not the only implementation approach, but it does provide a reasonable theoretical framework that can be made as formal as we need. It enforces the concept that the FSM (or *protocol machine*, PM) itself is not an amorphous object but is created from smaller modular elements (this will become more important when we consider application layer protocols and upper-layer architecture) and that a small number of concepts can be used over and over again to construct a network architecture. We will use this model to combine modular elements of protocols and PMs into larger structures.

The traditional definition of an generally goes as follows:

An is defined by

An input alphabet   a set $A = \{A_1, \ldots, A_m\}$

A set of states $S = \{S_1, \ldots, S_n\}$

An output alphabet   a set $O = \{O_1, \ldots, O_p\}$

Two functions: $F_1(A, S) \rightarrow (S)$ and

$F_2(A, S) \rightarrow O$

The function F_1 maps an element of the input alphabet and the current state to the next state; the function F_2 maps the same inputs to an element of the output alphabet.

Often, a state machine is represented by a graph (Figure 2-1), where the nodes represent the states and the arcs represent the function F_1, the mapping or transition from one state to the next; and the arcs are labeled with input/output of the function F_2, or by a state table with the rows (columns) representing the current state and the column (rows) are the next state. The cells are then filled by the inputs/outputs. There are many interesting properties of FSMs, and you can

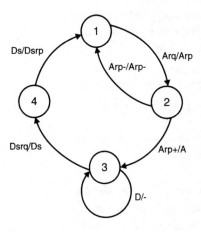

Figure 2-1 A typical FSM diagram.

find more information about those in textbooks. For purposes of this book, it is assumed you are reasonably familiar with these concepts.

As noted earlier, the FSM model has been used as a formal specification method. For practical uses, it is modified slightly; and where we need it, it will be this modified form that we will use. The FSM is not practical in its pure form for describing more than fairly simple mechanisms. For more complex algorithms that involve even simple counting, ordering, and so on, an FSM would require a state space roughly the magnitude of the product of the magnitudes of each of the parameters! For example, a pure state machine model might have three major states, "start," "doing it," and "done." If it also involves a single 8-bit counter, then there are $3 * 2^8$ or 768 states. If there are two 8-bit counters, then there are on the order of $3 * 2^8 * 2^8 = 3 * 2^{16}$ states or roughly 190,000 states! This makes a state analysis difficult, if not impossible, and makes it clear why this is referred to as "the state explosion problem."

Word from the Author

I can hear it now: "I know all of this! This is CS 101!" And you probably do. But remember, "We build what we measure." We need to pull back to the fundamentals. Strip away all of our implicit assumptions so that we can see in stark relief what is going on. So we know explicitly when we make assumptions and why. We are trying to include sufficient formality to ensure important properties have been exposed without making the explanation too painful. So, please bear with me, and remember it could have been a lot more formal (that is, painful).

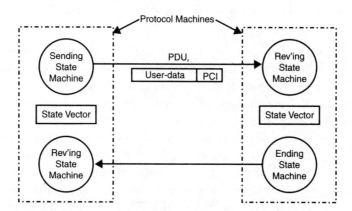

Figure 2-2 A typical protocol machine.

To make the model more tractable, the FSM technique is combined with programming or formal language techniques. An FSM is modified to consist of an input and an output alphabet, a set of procedures, and a state vector that includes the "major" states and any variables associated with the state, such as sequence numbers, counters, and so forth. The procedures are minimized to the greatest degree possible and modify elements of the state vector. The state vector consists of any information whose value must be maintained between inputs (This approach was first formalized by Danthine [1977], although it is a natural approach to take and may have been independently arrived at by others).

This modified state machine takes as input an element from the input alphabet and the current major state, and it invokes a procedure. The procedure executes an algorithm that uses an element of the input alphabet, the major state, and the state vector as inputs, modifies only the state vector, and emits one or more elements of the output alphabet. The state vector represents that information that must be maintained between executions of the procedures. The major states represent the point in the overall algorithm that the FSM has reached (for example, "beginning," "waiting for something," "middle," "end").

The inherent structure of protocols allows this hybrid approach to be quite successful where the FSM or program-proving techniques alone can be problematic. By combining, both state machines and the algorithms are sufficiently constrained for purposes of verification and proving both approaches remain tractable. This construct can be considered to fairly closely mimic most protocol implementation strategies, which is part of its power and usefulness. With this structure, we now set out to model protocols and communication.

Protocol

For two systems to communicate, they must have a shared conceptual schema. In other words, they must already have some common understanding about their world and the things in it that they want to talk about. If one correspondent says, "Do X," the correspondents must first know what "Do" and "X" mean, as well as what it means to "do X."

For those who want to jump ahead and propose "self-describing protocols," there is no such thing. This merely moves the shared common schema up a level, and then the definition of the description language must be part of the shared conceptual schema. No matter how minimal, there must be some shared schema. These are often concepts relating to ordering messages, determining the acceptability of a message, detecting errors, performing some operation, and so on. These concepts held in common are embodied in FSMs. The set of rules and procedures that each system participating in the communication is required to follow to maintain the coordination of their shared schema is called a *protocol*. The FSMs that implement the protocol will be referred to as protocol state machines or just *protocol machines* (PMs). (We will use *PM* only for those FSMs that describe protocols and reserve *FSM* for those that may or may not be PMs.)

Often, the operations that are performed require that each FSM maintain information on the state of the other. Clearly, this information is seldom accurate. And as discussed later, the amount of this shared state and the degree of consistency of the information are crucial considerations. The protocol defines the procedures and interactions necessary to initialize and maintain the shared state among the sending and receiving systems. Protocols in computer communications are used for two broad classes of problems: coordination over a distance and action at a distance.

In practical terms, the protocol specification becomes the specification of the communicating FSMs (Figure 2-2). Theoretically, this is not a requirement. Specifications techniques do exist—namely, the temporal logic techniques noted previously—that can specifying a protocol without reference to constructs similar to an implementation, such as a PM. But as noted, very few can actually design with these techniques. Therefore, the FSM approach is followed throughout this book to model protocols. This is not intended to in any way constrain implementation strategies but only to serve as a model. However, keep in mind that nonstate machine implementation strategies exist.

A PM models a single instance of communication, a single flow. It is often the case that the supporting service and the user of a PM are also PMs. Therefore, we must refer to the ranking of PMs (and other objects) so the (N)-PM is the focus of our attention; the (N+1)-PM above which uses the (N)-PM; and the (N-1)-PM below which is used by the (N)-PM. All PMs of a particular protocol in a given system may be referred to as a *protocol machine type* (PMT). In general, a system will have more than one PMT for each protocol of a particular rank. (We will figure out what a layer is in Chapter 6, "Divining Layers.")

A protocol may be either symmetric, also called peer where the communicating PMs have the same behavior that is, the same state machine; or, asymmetric where the communicating PMs will have distinctly different behaviors that is, different state machines.

In the latter case, it may be useful to distinguish subtypes of PMs, which are usually given names such as user/server, client/server, master/slave, and so on. Many application protocols are asymmetric, whereas data transfer protocols tend to be symmetric (or should be, as anyone who has tried to build an *interprocess communication* [IPC] facility on top of a synchronous *Remote Procure Call* [RPC] system can testify). Recognizing that some applications are inherently asymmetric and that protocols often find use in ways not foreseen by their authors, it may be worthwhile to expend the extra effort to consider whether a protocol normally seen to be asymmetric might not have a symmetrical model, because a symmetrical protocol will, in general, be more flexible and easier to use. We will see an example of this with Telnet in Chapter 4, "Stalking the Upper-Layer Architecture."

A circuit is just one long packet.

Associations, Connections, Flows, and Bindings

Because communicating systems do not share state (that is, memory), one PM must be able to notify the other of important changes in state. This is accomplished by exchanging finite quanta of information. These quanta carry information that is used to update a PM's view of its correspondent's state. This continual exchange of information quanta between the PMs creates a weak "field" or binding between the PMs. These bindings are characterized by the amount of shared state and by the "strength" of the binding. The strength of the binding is a measure of how tightly coupled the PMs are (that is, the degree to which one PM's perception of the state of its correspondent can be allowed to deviate from reality). It has been useful to recognize a form of binding within systems, and three degrees of bindings between systems: a minimal binding requiring no exchange of updates; a weak binding with some dependence but not affected if some updates are lost; and a strong binding, which requires updates to be received to avoid pathological behavior.

In some specifications, this binding is referred to with terms that connote a "connection" or "flow." Although the terms can be very useful, the use of these terms can vary widely. Therefore, this book adopts the following terminology for the forms of this relation:

- An *association* represents the minimal shared state and minimal coupling, often associated with connectionless communication.

- A *flow* has more shared state but not tightly coupled (no feedback), as found in some network protocols.

- A *connection* has a more tightly coupled shared state (with feedback), as with so-called end-to-end transport protocols.

- A *binding* has the most tightly coupled shared state, generally characterized by shared memory.

A connection and a flow are specializations of an association. Whereas a connection or flow has all the properties of

State Machines Versus Threads

There is some question as to whether an FSM or thread approach to implementation is better. They are, in some sense, duals. An FSM implementation consists of a "harness" that executes the proper action by indexing into the state table, given the input and current state. A thread represents a specific path through a state machine for some sequence of events. In essence, there must be a thread for each path. Each state transition is a point where the thread blocks, waiting for the next action. From a coding perspective, this means that for an FSM, one will write one "harness" for all paths, whereas for the thread approach one will write a "harness" for each path. The difference in code size, although probably slightly larger for the threaded approach, should not be significant in most cases.

The major difference, if there is one, is that if one writes the threads without doing a state table, the programmer must ensure that all cases are covered, whereas the state table serves as a reminder to specify the action for every entry in the table. It might not seem like much, but it is a task that we humans seem to be particular bad at! So, even though from a coding perspective the two approaches are pretty close to equivalent, the FSM discipline may avoid a few bugs.

an association, the reverse is not true. Later, as we develop further properties of protocols, we discuss more about the differences among these three concepts.

Interfaces

A protocol does not exist on its own. Something else must drive it—provide it with its *raison d'être*. In general, this is another FSM and often another PM in the same system that requires the services that this protocol provides. (Traditionally, this driving FSM has been drawn as "above" the PM, and in this discussion it's often referred to that way.) The PM and the FSM above must also exchange information to coordinate their behavior. However, it is prudent and important for the driving FSM to view the PM as a "black box," thus hiding the complexity of the PM's operation from the FSM above and hopefully simplifying the FSM. This "black box" boundary is traditionally called an *interface*. (Interface is used in two very distinct ways: In computer science, as described here and in telecommunications as a protocol between types of systems, generally where one system is owned by the network.) Because exchanges of information across an interface are in the same system, the mechanism for the exchange achieves a much tighter coupling than even a connection. In implementation terms, this is often referred to as a *system call* or as implemented by other mechanisms to effect isolation. This exchange between FSMs in the same system is often referred to as an *application programming interface* (API).

> **Learning to Count**
>
> Although the use of these terms in the field vary widely, they seem to more or less correspond to the use here. However, these definitions differ from their use in the OSI reference model. In OSI, the definitions of connection and association are essentially reversed. The (N)-connection is really an (N+1)-connection. According to the OSI reference model, the shared state between two (N)-entities (PMs) is an (N–1)-connection! Someone couldn't count.

Therefore, for the PMs in different systems to coordinate their behavior, the input alphabet of a PM, in fact, must consist of two subsets:

1. The exchange of information to coordinate the FSM above and the PM,

2. The exchange of information to coordinate among the PMs

Architecturally, these two exchanges are very similar, even though the mechanisms are quite different. For this discussion, the first is referred to as an interface, the second as a protocol. Because protocol exchanges are between PMs in different systems, a much looser coupling results. Interfaces may be implemented as local system or procedure calls, whereas protocol exchanges require self-contained quanta of information to be transferred between the PMs. A practical protocol specification will specify the interaction with an upper interface—that is, the user of the protocol, the interaction between the PMs, and the interaction with the lower interface (or the supporting communication service).

An implementation of the protocol must exist in all the communicating systems that participate in the data transfer. This implementation is modeled as a PM. The PM (Figure 2-3) has four kinds of interactions:

- The (N)-interface with the user, which may be another protocol machine, an (N+1)-PM, or an application

- The exchange of messages or *protocol data units* (PDUs) with the peer (N)-PM(s) to maintain the shared state

- The (N−1)-interface with some (N−1)-PM that provides a certain level of quality of service

- The local interface, for various operating system services, such as timers

(For simplicity, rather than referring to the user, the (N+1)-PM, or the application in every case, (N+1)-PM will be used to stand for all three.)

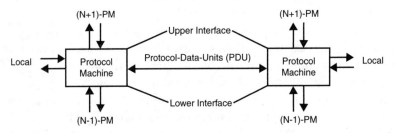

Figure 2-3 The relation of an (N)-PM to other PMs.

An interface represents a separate state machine shared between an (N)-PM and (N+1)-PM or an (N)-PM and (N−1)-PM always in the same system. Of course, when an interface is defined, the specification cannot be entirely complete. The specification can characterize what an (N+1)-PM must do but clearly cannot specify everything it does. For a protocol specification, the interface specification represents a partial state machine that must be meshed with the state machine of the (N−1)-PM or the (N+1)-PM, depending on whether it is the lower or upper interface. It is important to note that for any application to interact with a protocol (that is, for the application to communicate with another application), it must incorporate the state machine necessary to interact with the protocol's interface. When the partial state machine for the interface is joined with its upper or lower partner, it creates a strong binding between the two PMs.

This is an idealized logical model. These interfaces, and even the PM, may not be identifiable in a given implementation in a system. However, the model provides a formal framework for describing the architecture for creating the appropriate protocol specifications and is fairly easy to map into any implementation approach.

Data Units

As noted earlier, to communicate from one place to another, finite quanta of information must be exchanged. Over the years, these "finite quanta" have been given a variety of names, such as frame, cell, packet, segment, message, and so on, depending on the inclination of the author and the kind of protocol. All of these are different terms for the same concept. To avoid confusion, we will adopt the neutral term *protocol data unit* (PDU).

The structure of a PDU (Figure 2-4) has evolved to consist of three major elements: a header, and less frequently a trailer, to carry the information necessary to coordinate the PMs, and the user data. This is an important distinction: "Information" is what is understood by the PM, and "data" is what is not understood (and usually passed to the PM or application above). To remind us of this, we refer to the part that is understood by the (N)-PM (the header and trailer) as *protocol control information* (PCI), and the user's data as *user-data* because the (N)-PM does not understand it. This distinction is clearly relative. What is information (PCI) to the (N+1)-PM is merely part of the data to the (N)-PM. Similarly, the (N)-PCI is merely more user-data to the (N−1)-PM and so on. This distinction is crucial to much of what follows. It is important that one always be clear about what is information and what is data at any given point.

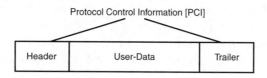

Figure 2-4 A PDU is sometimes called a message, a segment, a frame, a packet, or many other terms. They are all the same, just in different places.

PDUs are sometimes likened to processor instructions: Based on the parameters of the instruction (PCI) and the state of the processor (PM), the execution of PDUs performs operations on the state of the processor (PM). Unlike instructions, which carry an address to reference the data on which they operate, PDUs must carry the data themselves

Various types of PDUs are used to transfer PCI among peer PMs. These PDUs may or may not contain user-data. There is no architectural limit to the size of these PDUs. There might, however, be engineering considerations that impose size limitations on the PDUs in specific environments. For example, for a protocol operating in an error-prone environment, a smaller PDU size may increase the probability that a PDU is received error free, or that the overhead for retransmission is minimized. Or in a network of real-time sensors, the systems may have very limited buffer space, so smaller PDUs may be necessary.

Headers

Most PCI is contained in the header. Most fields in data transfer protocols are fixed length to simplify processing. Fixed-length fields generally precede any variable-length fields. A length field that gives the total length of the PDU is strongly recommended. The header of any protocol should have a protocol identifier to identify the type of protocol and a protocol version to identify the version of the protocol, as well as a field that indicates the function of the PDU. The PCI will also include a field that encodes the action associated with the PDU (for example, set, get, connect). Like instructions, this field may be either horizontally or vertically encoded; that is, it may consist of either a string of control bits, each indicating functions of the processor to be invoked, or an opcode, which stands for the specific combination of functions. In general, horizontal encoding requires more space than vertical encoding because there are generally many combinations of bits that are not legal. Horizontal encoding is generally faster in hardware, whereas vertical is faster in software. TCP uses horizontal encoding. This was an experiment that has not stood the test of time. If the implementation treats the control bits as control bits, it leads to less-efficient implementation. Papers (Clark et al., 1989) have recommended treating them as an opcode, and this seems to be what most implementations do. Consequently, opcodes are generally recommended over control bits.

Trailers

The PDUs of some protocols have a trailer. The most common use is to carry the *cyclic redundancy code* (CRC). The advantage of the CRC in the trailer is that the CRC can be computed as each byte arrives without waiting for the whole

PDU to be received. Generally, the use of a trailer is found in protocols operating near the physical media. When a PDU is in memory, the advantages of a trailer are less useful. Consequently, the use of trailers in protocols higher up is infrequent.

The general guidelines for the use of a trailer might be characterized as follows; but it is important to stress that it isn't so much the absolute characterization of the conditions as their relation to each other:

- The information in a trailer is such that it cannot be known at the time the header is created; that is, it is a function of the header and the user-data.

- The processing time for the PDU is much less than the time required for the PDU to be sent or received, and the delay thus incurred would be a significant fraction of the delay quota for the traffic.

The Nature of the Service Boundary

Earlier service was used as the abstraction of the interface, hence, the term *service data unit* (SDU) is used to refer to the unit of data provided to the PM by the (N+1)-PM across the service boundary as a service data unit (SDU) (reserving the term *interface* for the implementation-specific case, such as a UNIX interface or a Windows interface). To a PM, an SDU consists entirely of user-data but will have a size that is convenient to the (N+1)-PM. The service primitive invoked to pass the SDU to the PM will also pass other parameters to the PM for handling the SDU. Generally, one of these is a local "port-id" that identifies this end of the flow or connection this SDU is to be sent on. The port-id is local to the system (that is, only known within the system and only unambiguous within it) and shared by the (N+1)- and (N)-PMs to refer to related communications. The PM may have to segment the SDU into several PDUs or may aggregate several SDUs into a single PDU so that the PDU is a size convenient to the requirements of the (N)-protocol. (This nomenclature follows the OSI Reference Model, not because I favor the OSI model, which I don't, but because it is an existing nomenclature that tries to define common terms. I can find no good reason to invent new terms other than for the sake of generating new terms. For those who still have a visceral reaction to anything OSI, all I can say is, OSI is long dead, get over it.)

It's a Side Effect

Thus, we see that information is what the PM understands and data is what it doesn't. When a PM receives a PDU, it happily goes along processing each of the elements of PCI, updating its state and generating new PDUs until it reaches this stuff it doesn't understand; then, it shrugs and throws this incomprehensible junk (user-data) over the wall (to the (N+1)-PM) and happily goes back to processing the stuff it understands. The transfer of data is a side effect!

Stream Versus Record

One of the enduring debates in protocol design is, given that the (N+1)-PM delivered an (N)-SDU of a particular size to the (N)-PM and that under some conditions it may have been fragmented or concatenated *en route,* what does the (N)-PM deliver to the remote (N+1)-PM? What was sent or what was received?

Although it may often be the case that an SDU would be a single (N+1)-PDU, it might be more than one. Seldom would it only be part of a PDU. In any case, the (N)-SDU was a unit that the (N+1)-PM found to be significant for its processing. The early debate was between record and stream modes, derived from early operating system practices. The older mainframe systems tended to operate on fixed-length records, whereas more modern systems such as Sigma 7, Tenex, Multics, and its derivative UNIX communicated in terms of undifferentiated byte streams. Record mode was always considered as something that simply had to be lived with. There was general agreement that record mode was too inflexible and cumbersome.

Stream mode was considered a much more flexible, elegant approach that provided greater layer independence. A stream might deliver any combination from whole SDUs to pieces of an SDU to multiple SDUs or even part of two SDUs. Stream mode requires that the (N+1)-layer be able to recognize the beginning and end of its SDU/PDUs and be able to assemble them for processing. The (N+1)-protocol must have a delimiting mechanism and cannot rely on the layer below to tell it where the beginning and end of the PDU are.

Over time, a third approach evolved, which was a generalization of record mode. In this mode, SDUs were not fixed length. The rule in this approach was that the *identity* of SDUs was maintained between the sending and receiving users. No name was ever given this mode, so let's call it the *idempotent mode,* referring to its property of maintaining the identity of the SDU invariant. Because SDUs may be of any length, this differs significantly from traditional fixed-length record mode. This mode requires that the (N)-layer deliver SDUs in the form it received them. If the (N)-protocol needs to fragment an SDU, it is (N)-protocol's responsibility to put things back the way it found them before delivering the SDU to the (N+1)-PM. (There is something compelling about a "do anything you want but clean up your mess when you're done" approach!) This form is more consistent with good programming practice. Similarly, if the (N)-protocol combines several SDUs into a single PDU for its own reasons, it must deliver them as separate SDUs to the remote user. Consequently, the (N + 1)-PM does not have to understand (or be modified for) every potential (N)-PM fragmenting or concatenation condition, nor make assumptions about what the (N)-PM will do. Maintaining the identity of SDUs maintains symmetry in an architecture. And symmetry is always good.[1] But, it does require the assumption that the layer below is well behaved. The essential difference between the two is that the idempotent mode is a *user's* point of view, whereas stream mode is more the *implementer's* point of view.

It makes no difference in the receiving system, the amount of work is the same: Either the receiving PM or the receiving user, the (N+1)-PM, must do the reassembly. In other words, the work is either done at the bottom of the (N+1)-layer (stream) or the top of the (N)-layer (idempotent). There are no strong logical or architectural arguments for one or the other. Although if it is done by the (N+1)-PM, it may have to be implemented several times (if there are many (N+1)-PMTs i.e, applications). Then, good software engineering practice supports the (N)-PM performing the function.

That said, it will be easier for protocols with sequence space granularity of octets to do stream mode (for instance, TCP), and more work to keep track of where the SDU boundaries are.[2] For protocols that do sequencing to the granularity of PDUs, the amount of work is the same if there is no concatenation. If the protocol concatenates, however, it must be able to find the boundaries between SDUs. In which case, stream mode will be less work for the (N)-protocol. Overall, the work as seen by the system is the same.[3]

But it does not have to be an either/or choice. It is possible to provide both. For the solution, we take a lesson from how Telnet modeled half and full duplex as degenerate cases of a single mechanism, and from the glib comment that "all data communications is a side effect" (mentioned previously). We just note that a stream is simply a very long SDU! If the protocol has the ability to indicate the boundaries of SDUs and negotiates whether it may deliver partial SDUs (in order) to the (N+1)-layer, the (N+1)-layer can have either interface discipline. Stream mode negotiates partial delivery and at a minimum indicates the end of an SDU only on the last PDU sent. Idempotent mode negotiates no partial deliv-

---

[1]   Yes, similar arguments can be made for stream. However, the argument that "I should get things back in the same form I gave them to you" is reasonable. Stream may impose additional overhead on the (N+1)-protocol that from its point of view is unnecessary (It knows what it is doing; why should it be penalized because the supporting protocol doesn't.)

[2]   There are rumors of applications using the TCP Urgent pointer as a means to delimit SDUs.

[3]   Having been a strong proponent of stream-mode from the beginning of the Net, I have spent considerable thought coming to this conclusion. Fixed record was clearly not a good idea; and although stream mode is elegant, it does ignore our responsibility to the "user" to clean up our mess.

ery and indicates the end of SDUs at the appropriate times. Flags in the protocol might be defined as shown here:

Supporting Both Stream and Idempotent

Delivery of Incomplete SDU Allowed	More Data	Description
0	0	Self-contained PDU, equivalent to Don't Fragment
0	1	Idempotent
1	0	Stream (with huge buffers!)
1	1	Stream

Constructing Protocol

A PM must interpret four inputs:

1. Interactions with the upper interface

2. PDUs from its corresponding PM(s)

3. Interactions with the local system

4. Interactions with the lower interface

Good Solutions Are Never Obsolete

This illustrates why it is important to study good designs. Here we have used the Telnet half-duplex solution (see Chapter 4) to solve what appears to be an either/or choice. Many students would complain about being taught the Telnet solution: "Why are we wasting time on this. Half-duplex terminals are a thing of the past. I will never need this!" Perhaps not, but as you have just seen, the *form* of problem recurs, and so the same solution in a somewhat different guise can be applied.

All of these can be considered to be equivalent to procedure or system calls of the following form:[4]

<procedure name>(<param 1>,<param i>*)

The PDUs can be seen as procedure calls in that the PDU type is the name of the procedure and the elements of the PDU (that is, PCI and user-data) are the parameters:

<PDU type>(<PCI element><PCI element>*, user-data)

Associated with each of these are actions to be taken depending on the state of the PM (that is, the body of the procedure). The action taken by each procedure is to interpret the parameters and update the state vector associated with the PM and possibly cause other PDUs to be sent or interactions with the local system or the upper- and lower-interfaces to occur. Coordinating all of this is a control function or state machine that enforces the proper sequencing of these actions according to the state of the PM.

---

4 It pains me to have to do this, but the use of the * in the procedure or system calls is referred to as a *Kleene star* and means "zero or more" ocurrences. There was a time in computer science when such explanations were unnecessary.

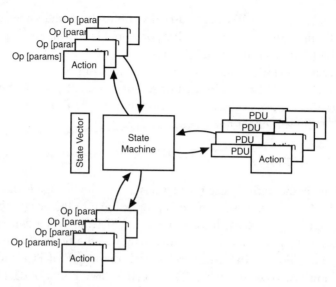

Figure 2-5 A more detailed model of a PM.

The local interactions access local resources, such as memory (buffer) or timer requests. Processing the PDUs invokes the mechanisms of the protocol. In some protocols, a distinct set of PDUs is associated with a particular mechanism, forming a module. Such a module is formed from a subset of PDUs and their procedures with its own state machine. Strictly speaking, any such module as this is a protocol. These service primitives and PDUs invoke the mechanisms of the protocol. For data transfer protocols, the types of interface procedures are all the same: synchronize/finish and send/receive with appropriate parameter values.

The primary task of a PM is to maintain shared state. There are three loci of shared state in any PM: the upper- and lower-interface loci, or *bindings*, between an (N)-PM and an (N+1)-PM and between an (N)-PM and an (N–1)-PM; and the protocol locus, often called a *connection* or *flow*, between apposite (N)-PMs. The shared state is maintained by the exchange of PCI. The shared state between PMs in adjacent layers is maintained by the parameters exchanged in procedure or system calls between layered PMs in the same system,[5] whereas the shared state between apposite PMs in different systems is maintained by the exchange of protocol PCI. The primary difference between the two kinds of shared state is that for a connection or flow, PCI may be lost. For an interface binding, it can be assumed that the exchange of PCI is reliable, and often, shared access to memory can be assumed.

---

[5] We are still building a logical model here. Actual implementations may or may not explicitly implement an interface. As long as the rules of the protocol are obeyed, no interface is necessary.

State changes in a PM are caused by inputs from the upper interface (for example, an application or (N+1)-PM, or from PDUs from the apposite PMs, or from the local layer apparatus [for instance, timeouts]). Whether inputs from the layer below cause changes in state is a matter of policy. In other words, if an (N–1)-flow should be de-allocated or fail unexpectedly, it is a matter of policy whether this causes a subsequent state change in the (N)-flows multiplexed on the (N–1)-flow. It might not.

The Size of PDUs

Determining the optimal size for PDUs is a traditional engineering trade-off. In general, PDU processing overhead is proportional to PCI length, but independent of PDU length. Regardless, processing efficiency is maximized by making the PDU as long as possible. Similarly, bandwidth efficiency is maximized, the greater the amount of user-data relative to the length of PCI. However, other factors mitigate toward smaller PDUs, such as the amount of data significant to the application may be small, buffering constraints in systems, fairness (that is, interleaving PDUs), the error characteristics of the media, and so on. Fragmentation (or segmenting) and concatenation may be used to match PDU sizes or improve efficiency between layers or between different subnets based on different media.

There is an optimal range for PDU size in each protocol, including applications, that will depend on where the protocol occurs in the architecture. For upper-layer protocols, this will be most strongly affected by the requirements of the application. Boundaries will tend to be created at points that have logical significance for the application. These sizes will give way to the requirements of the lower layers, while being moderated in the middle layers by system constraints (for example, the operating system and constraints on multiplexing). For lower-layer protocols, the size will be more determined by the characteristics of the subnetwork or the media. As noted previously, the PDU sizes for error-prone environments such as wireless will be smaller, thereby decreasing the opportunity for errors.

One would expect larger PDU sizes in less-error-prone media. For backbone networks where traffic density is the highest, one would expect media with very high bandwidths, very low error rates, and larger PDU sizes to take advantage of concatenation to increase efficiency. As bandwidth and traffic density increases, one wants to process fewer bigger PDUs less often rather than more smaller PDUs more often. Smaller PDUs will occur at lower bandwidths to minimize the time window for errors and increase the opportunity for interleaving other PDUs (that is, fairness). Smaller PDU sizes are more likely at the periphery, and size increases as one moves down in the layers and in toward the backbone. (Or as traffic density increases, for example toward the backbone, one wants to switch more stuff less often, not less stuff more often!) The ratio of PDU size to bandwidth and the ratio of PCI to PDU size should be relatively constant or decrease as one moves down in the architecture.

One of the factors in determining PDU size is to keep the ratio of the PCI size to the PDU size small. This ratio is an engineering choice, but as a rule of thumb, generally, 5% to 10% is considered acceptable. Address fields are the greatest contributor to PCI size. Upper-layer protocols with wider scope will have longer addresses, and lower-layer protocols with less scope will have shorter addresses. Thus, we can expect some inefficiency in the upper layers as applications generate potentially shorter PDUs (but of a size useful to the application) with longer addresses; but increased efficiency at the lower layers as PDUs get longer, concatenation occurs, and addresses get shorter. Concatenation is not supported by the current Internet protocols early on because of the slower processor speeds and later because of the delay incurred waiting for PDUs to concatenate. Given that these networks start to congest at 35% to 40% utilization, and consequently, ISPs try to operate well below that threshold, this isn't surprising. At higher utilizations, one should be able to concatenate with only marginal impact on delay.

Mechanism and Policy

In operating systems, the concept of separating mechanism and policy has a long tradition. Only recently has this been used in network protocols, although there are exceptions (for example, Hadzic et al., 1999; Snoeren and Raghavan, 2004; Arpaci-Dusseau, 2003; RFC 4340, 2006; and others). However, this work has concentrated on the engineering aspects and tended to ignore what this tells us about the structure of networks and protocols. Here we develop a model for the separation of mechanism and policy, and then in the next chapter look at its implications. A protocol is composed of a set of functions that achieve the basic requirements of that protocol, whether that is error control, reading a file, flow control, two-phase commit, or so on. The choice of functions is made based on the operating region in which the protocol is intended to exist and the desired level of service that is to result from its operation. Each function is divided into a mechanism and a policy (see Figure 2-6).

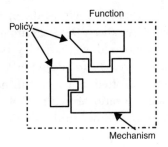

Figure 2-6 A mechanism may have one or more policies.

Mechanisms are static and are not changed after a protocol is specified. The order of interpreting the fields of the (N)-PCI is determined by the PM (that is, defined by the protocol specification). In general, policy types occur in pairs: a sending policy and a receiving policy. For example, for the function detecting data corruption, a specific CRC polynomial is the policy. The sending policy computes the polynomial, and the mechanism inserts it into the PDU. The receiving policy computes the polynomial on an incoming PDU, and the mechanism compares the result with the field in the PCI.[6] There are exceptions. For example, a policy to choose an initial sequence number would only occur in the sending PM. Hence, initialization policies or policies associated with timeouts may not occur in complementary pairs. The number of distinct types of policy associated with each mechanism depends on the mechanism but is generally only one. The number of policies of a specific type is theoretically unlimited, although in practice only a few are used. In general, there is typically a sending policy and a complementary receiving policy for the respective sending and receiving PMs. The coordination of the mechanisms in the sending and receiving PMs is accomplished by the exchange of specific fields of information in the (N)-PCI (see Figure 2-7). A single PDU may carry fields for multiple mechanisms in the (N)-PCI. A major consideration in the design of protocols is determining which fields are assigned to which PDU types.

---

[6] One might be tempted to call these inverses but they really aren't. More complements of each other.

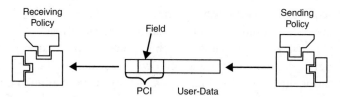

Figure 2-7 Fields in PCI coordinate the complementary mechanisms in the sending and receiving PMs.

For any one mechanism, a variety of policies may be applied to it. For example, consider the basic sliding-window flow-control mechanism used in many protocols. The sliding window is part of the protocol specification. When specified, this mechanism is not modified. However, there are a variety of policies for flow control: from simply extending new credit on receipt of a PDU, to periodically sending new credit, to high/low watermarks, and so on. Different policies might be used for different connections at the same time. Similarly, acknowledgment is a mechanism, but *when* an ack is sent is policy.

In the upper layers, OSI found that it was necessary to negotiate a "context." The presentation context selected the abstract and concrete syntax of the application, whereas the application context was to "identify the shared conceptual schema between the applications." The concept of the presentation context was fairly well understood, but the application context never was. (see Chapter 4, for a more complete discussion of this.) Not recognizing that both cases were simply mechanisms for negotiating policy also meant that OSI failed to recognize that this was a general property of all protocols, not just of the upper two layers. Protocols should include a mechanism for specifying or negotiating policy for all mechanisms during synchronization or establishment.[7]

Policies chosen at the time communication is initiated can be modified during data transfer, if care is taken. Some policy changes may require that they be synchronized with the data stream to prevent pathological behavior. For example, changing the CRC polynomial for detecting corrupt data would require such synchronization so that receiver knew when to stop using the previous policy and use the new one. It can be shown that this sort of strong synchronization is

---

[7] Many early protocols contained elaborate mechanisms for negotiating policy during connection establishment. However, it was soon learned that this was more effort than simply refusing the connection attempt with some indication of why and letting the initiator attempt to try again with a different request.

essentially equivalent to establishing a new flow. Hence, including this capability in the protocol would generally be deemed as simply adding unnecessary complexity. However, some changes, such as changing the frequency of extending flow-control credit or of sending acknowledgments, would not require such synchronization and would not incur the same overhead. Although quite useful, it is less obvious that policy negotiation should be allowed during the data transfer phase. In general, changing policy during the data transfer phase requires synchronization that is essentially equivalent to establishing a new flow or connection.

Any ability to change policy on an existing connection or flow will have to be carefully handled to avoid aberrant behavior. The process, which determines which policies should be used or when they are changed, is outside the protocol. This may be requested by the layer above (or by the user), which knows its use of the protocol is changing. More likely, it will be effected by "layer management" to ensure that the parameters agreed with the layer above are maintained or in response to changes observed in the characteristics of the layer below and to ensure that the resource-allocation strategy of the layer is maintained.

By separating policy and mechanism,[8] the operating range of a protocol can be increased, and its ability to optimally serve a particular subset of an operating region can be greatly enhanced. The choice of policy depends on the traffic characteristics of the (N–1)-association and the *quality of service* (QoS) required by the user. The task of the (N)-PM is to translate these QoS characteristics as requested by the (N+1)-PM into a particular choice of mechanisms and policies based on the service from the (N–1)-PM. As a rule of thumb, one would expect protocols nearer the media to have policies dominated by the characteristics of the media and consequently fewer policies would apply. For protocols further from the media, there would be a wider variety of policies that might apply. (However, other considerations may limit the number of policies that might occur.)

There has been much talk of policy in the network literature, but generally limited to application protocols, such as routing, and recently there has been limited experimentation with applying this elsewhere. If one inspects the myriad proposals for "new protocols" that have appeared over the years, one will find that no new mechanisms have been proposed for nearly 25 years.[9] These "new" protocols are primarily rearrangements of headers and old mechanisms with

---

[8] This use of mechanism and policy can be traced to a paper on the operating system for C.mmp (Levin et al., 1975).

[9] A reasonable but not definitive indication that there aren't any more (or at least not very many more) to discover. (Either that or it indicates that research over the past 25 years has not been very innovative!)

different policies. Given a well-designed protocol that separated mechanism and policy, one would need many fewer protocols. It would be much easier to understand the properties of various policies and their interactions. There have been proposals for protocols with optional mechanisms and policies that are specified at execution time. In general, these protocols have considerable overhead either in bandwidth, processing, or both. This concept, along with a pragmatic approach to selecting policy, should achieve a useful middle ground. The mechanisms of a protocol are fixed at the time of specification, whereas selecting policies is postponed until synchronization or establishment. Mechanisms are fixed, although an appropriate policy could, in effect, make it null.

As an example of the power of this concept both to simply and easily achieve what might be considered a major change to a protocol and to give us deeper insights into the nature of protocols, consider the following: It had always been thought that another transport protocol would be required for voice. With voice, the PDUs must be ordered, but short gaps in the data stream can be tolerated. So, it was thought that a new protocol would be required that allowed for small gaps (instead of the protocol just retransmitting everything). However, a new protocol is not required; all that is necessary is to modify the acknowledgment policy...and lie. There is no requirement to tell the truth! If the gap is short, send an ack anyway, even though not all the data has been received. There is no requirement in any existing transport protocols to tell the truth!

This also tells us something very important about the semantics of ack: Ack does not mean, as commonly thought, "I got it"; instead, it means, "I am not going to ask for a retransmission" or perhaps more to the point, "I'm fine with what I have received." This might seem like playing with words, but it makes a major difference in how we conceive the use of acknowledgments. Consequently, in this book what might be referred to in other protocols as the acknowledgment mechanism is often referred to as *retransmission control*.

QoS Versus NoS

Quality of service (QoS) is a term that has been applied to the set of characteristics, such as bandwidth, delay, error rate, jitter, and so forth, that the user desires the communication to have. Proposals for QoS parameters (and sometimes rather extensive proposals) have been made many times over the past two or three decades, but few protocols have paid more than lip service to doing anything about it (to some extent with good reason). If you look carefully at these parameters and ask, "When a QoS parameter is changed, which policies of the protocol change and how?" you often finds that the answer is "none."

There are two reasons for this. Any change in policy that could affect that parameter is a resource management issue, often a change in the buffering strategy: a topic generally not addressed by protocol specifications and normally considered the exclusive domain of the implementation. There is nothing that a protocol can do to affect the parameter.

Consider delay. Clearly, a protocol can minimize making delay worse, but it can do nothing to improve it. Parameters of this latter type are called *nature of service* (NoS). The distinction between QoS and NoS is essentially recognition of the old adage that "you can't make a silk purse from a sow's ear," but perhaps we can make the sow's ear a bit more acceptable. These are parameters largely determined by "nature." We may be able to avoid making them worse, but there is little or nothing that can be done to make them better.

QoS represents a set of characteristics that the (N+1)-PM desires from the (N)-PM for a particular instance of communication (the silk purse). NoS represents the set of characteristics that an (N–1)-PM is actually providing and is likely to be able to provide in the future (the sow's ear). The (N)-PM uses the difference between the QoS and NoS to select the protocol, mechanisms, or policies to match the desire with the reality. However, limits apply to what a particular protocol can do to improve a particular NoS to match the particular QoS that is requested. The nearer the (N)-PM operates to the physical media, the more constraining the NoS may be; that is, the technology dependencies limit the amount of improvement that can practically be accomplished by a single protocol. In some cases, some forms of error control may be more efficient or more effective if they are postponed to protocols operating further from the physical media. This and the fact that multiplexing at different layers allows for better strategies for aggregating PDUs are some of the reasons that there is more than one layer on top of the physical media. On the other hand, additional layers limit the achievable bandwidth and delay characteristics, thus mitigating against too many layers. This is one of many trade-offs that are continually being balanced in the design of network architectures. We return to this topic later when we discuss particular QoS strategies.

A Short Catalog of Data Transfer Mechanisms

Over the years, a number of mechanisms have been found to occur in many protocols. This section briefly reviews a few of the more common protocol mechanisms so that we have something concrete to refer to in our subsequent discussions.

Delimiting

A *delimiter* is a mechanism used to indicate the beginning and end of a PDU. There are two basic methods for delimiting PDUs: external and internal delimiting. In external delimiting, a special bit pattern, usually called a *flag sequence,* is defined to denote the start and end of the PDU. The problem with this approach is that either data transparency is forfeited, because the flag sequence cannot occur as a bit pattern in the PDU, or some "escape" mechanism is used to insert extra bits into the PDU to avoid the flag sequence, which are then removed by the receiver before any other PDU processing is done. Another common form of external delimiting is to use the lower layer to delimit the PDU. This may take the form of a length field in the (N–1)-PCI or in the physical layer in the bit encoding used (for instance, the use of Manchester encoding to delimit MAC frames in Ethernet). In internal delimiting, the PDU contains a length field as an element of PCI from which the number of bits or octets to the end of the PDU can be calculated. A degenerate form of internal delimiting is that the supporting service provides only complete PDUs with a length field passed as a parameter as part of the interface. External delimiting is generally found in data link protocols, such as HDLC or the IEEE local-area network protocols. Network and transport protocols have generally used internal delimiting.

Initial State Synchronization

Before data transfer can begin, the shared state of the PMs must be initialized. The *initial state synchronization* mechanism achieves this initialization. Four basic forms are generally found:

1. The creation of local bindings with the (N+1)-PM and (N–1)-PM; no PDUs are exchanged (used by protocols that require minimal shared state).

2. The former plus the exchange of request and response PDUs, the so-called *two-way handshake* used for protocols that do not have feedback mechanisms.

3. A more robust form consisting of the former, a request, a response, and an ack by the initiator when the response arrives, the so-called *three-way handshake* used by protocols with feedback.

4. A simple timer-based mechanism based on bounding maximum PDU lifetime, maximum time sender will try to resend a PDU, and maximum time receiver will wait before ack'ing (Watson, 1981).

The first is used for connectionless communication, in protocols such as *User Datagram Protocol* (UDP). The second is used for protocols with tightly coupled mechanisms; that is, all state updates are feed-forward, or the probability of an error during synchronization is unlikely, or where it is impossible to cause aberrant protocol behavior, and/or where the probability of an error in the supporting communication service is unlikely. The third is used for protocols with loosely coupled mechanisms or where the probability of an error during synchronization is likely to cause aberrant protocol behavior, and/or where the probability of an error in the supporting communication service is likely.

Belnes (1974) showed that to reliably deliver a single packet, a five-way exchange was required. Note that this is equivalent to synchronization with a three-way handshake, followed by the release request/response. With the advent of client/server, a subsequent paper refined this result to prove what semantics were possible with five or fewer messages (Spector, 1982). We look at this further in Chapter 3.

Protocols such as HDLC, X.25, TP Class 2, and most application protocols use the two-way handshake. Protocols such as TCP, TP4, and XNS Sequenced Packet use the three-way handshake. (Note that the choices made in these protocol designs reflect the views of their designers, which may or may not be consistent with the conditions of the actual operating environment.) The timer-based approach can be used in place of either the two-way or three-way handshake by simply bounding maximum packet lifetime, maximum round trip time, and maximum number of retries. In addition, state synchronization can be combined in application protocols with cryptographic authentication mechanisms that utilize a four-way handshake (Aura and Nikander, 1997).

Policy Selection

As previously noted, the functions of a protocol are composed of a mechanism and a policy. The mechanism is that part of the function that is a fixed part of the protocol. The *policy-selection* mechanism allows selection of policy during allocation and under certain conditions to change policies during the data transfer. Several protocols have this kind of mechanism, such as HDLC and IEEE 802.3. Many protocols have a list of parameters associated with the establishment procedures. Often these are not strongly tied to the mechanisms in as direct a manner as intended here. And often, these have more to do with the operating environment of the protocol or its management. HDLC has an extensive mechanism for selecting various options, but again only some of these are related to mechanism/policy (for instance, choosing different CRCs, width of flow-control windows).

Addressing

Protocols operating in multiaccess environments must contain some means to identify the source and destination of the PDUs. This is done by including *addressing* fields in the PCI. The addresses must be large enough to name all elements that can be communicated without relaying at the layer above.

Flow or Connection Identifier

Protocols that support multiple instances of communication (that is, associations, flows, or connections between the same two stations) also require a *connection-* or *flow-id*. Traditionally, this has been accomplished using the local "port-ids" or file handles as a pair to disambiguate one flow from another. Protocols use flow or connection identifiers to distinguish multiple flows between source/destination address pairs. Such an identifier must be unambiguous within the scope of the (N)-protocol. Generally this is done concatenating local port-ids of the source and destination, as noted earlier. If these port-ids are unambiguous within the system (not just within the protocol), then flows of multiple protocols of the same rank can be multiplexed without a problem. However, if they are not, additional identifiers will be necessary to distinguish the (N)-PM to which the (N)-PDUs belong. Note that the protocol-id field can only be used for this purpose if there is only one occurrence of each protocol in a system.

Relaying

Most networks are not fully connected meshes. Consequently, some protocols may improve the connectivity provided by the supporting service by *relaying* a PDU from one PM to the next. This mechanism is accomplished by including a PCI element that contains the address of the destination. In most cases, the PCI will also contain the address of the source. When a PDU arrives, the relaying mechanism inspects the address and determines whether it is addressed to one of its (N+1)-PMs. If it is, it is delivered to the appropriate (N+1)-PM. If it is not, the PM consults information it maintains and determines the (N–1)-PM that can get the PDU closer to its destination, a mechanism called *forwarding*. Generating this forwarding information is a task of flow management utilizing routing algorithms. The astute reader will have noticed that there is no discussion of addressing in this chapter of basic concepts. Oddly enough (I was surprised, too.) while important, addressing is not basic. The interpretation of an address and consequently the theory of addressing is a policy of the relaying mechanism.

Multiplexing

Multiplexing is the mapping of the flows of (N)-PMs onto flows of (N–1)-PMs. Networks are not fully connected meshes, and so when PDUs are relayed, PDUs from different flows and from different sources will be sent on the same outgoing flow. A system may have a number of (N)-PMs passing PDUs associated with flows to fewer (N–1)-PMs. These flows are passed to an (N)-PM, which must combine them into a single flow at a lower rank.

Ordering

Most but not all protocols assume simple *ordering*—that is, PDUs will arrive in the same order they were sent. However, some supporting communication services do not guarantee this property. This mechanism is provided by including a sequence number as an element of PCI that is incremented in units of octets (length of the user data in the PDU) or in units of PDUs so that the PDUs may be ordered at the receiver. A large number of protocols include this mechanism (TCP, X.25, TP4, HDLC, and so on). Application protocols generally assume order is provided by the supporting service and do not explicitly include this mechanism. As previously noted, some applications require ordering but do not require all PDUs to be received if not too many are lost. Other forms of order are required by other applications.

Fragmentation/Reassembly

The practical constraints of networking often require that SDUs and user-data be *fragmented* into smaller PDUs for transmission and then *reassembled* at the other end. This is generally accomplished through a variety of means by including PCI elements: a single bit that indicates whether this is the last fragment, the use of the sequence number, or by a distinct enumeration of the fragments. Techniques may also involve the length field of the PDU used for delimiting and detecting data corruption.

Combining/Separation

Conversely, the protocol may achieve some efficiency by *combining* SDUs into a single PDU. Once again, a variety of techniques have been used, ranging from fixed-length SDUs to a chain of length fields (and so on).

The efficiency of fragmentation and combining is directly affected by the scope within which the resulting PDUs must be recognizable. For a fragmented PDU to be concatenated with any other PDU, it must be identified within the scope of the layer. However, for a PDU to be concatenated only with PDUs from the same system requires identifiers of less scope (and hence shorter PCI).

Data Corruption

During transmission, the contents of a PDU can be corrupted. There are two fundamental mechanisms for dealing with this problem:

- **The use of a checksum or CRC[10] to detect the corruption.** The code is computed on the received PDU. If it fails, the PDU is discarded and other mechanisms ensure its retransmission.

- **The use of forward error correcting code.** Forward error correcting code can detect and correct some number of errors, in which case the PDU may not have to be discarded.

The codes used must be chosen based on the nature of the error environment. For example, the traditional view has been that protocols closer to an electrical media (for instance, data link protocols such as HDLC or the various LAN protocols) are more subject to burst errors and thus require codes that can detect bursts of errors (for example, CRCs). However, optical media have different error characteristics and thus require a different kind of error code. And protocols more removed from the media (for instance, IP, TCP, X.25, or TP4) are more likely to encounter single-bit errors (memory faults) and therefore use error codes that detect single-bit errors. In addition, the error characteristics may interact adversely with other aspects of the protocol design, such as the delimiters.[11] In general, a careful error analysis of both the protocol and the proposed operating environment must be done to determine the appropriate data-corruption detection strategy. In particular, you must consider the effect of PDU size on the strength of the polynomial. A particular polynomial will only achieve the advertised undetected bit error rate up to some maximum PDU length. Beyond that maximum, the undetected bit error rate goes up.

---

[10] The oddest things turn up during review! In this case what CRC stands for. It turns out that by the early 1970s there was some ambiguity as to whether CRC stood for *cyclic redundancy check* or *cyclic redundancy code*. Both are used in the literature almost interchangeably. Clearly, the polynomial was referred to as a code. Perhaps, *check* was the action of computing the code. Or was it a confusion with *checksum?* Usage seems to have made CRC stand for any and all uses, regardless of what kind of polynomial they are. We won't worry about the details here, but it would be interesting if someone could figure out how and what (if any) difference was intended and where and when it arose.

[11] A rather famous case: HDLC uses external delimiters and thus to achieve data transparency must stuff bits in the data stream to avoid the delimiter from occurring in the PDU. Because the inserted bits cannot be part of the CRC calculation, the undetected bit error rate goes up (significantly) as the number of 1s in the PDU increases (Fiorine, et al, 1995).

Lost and Duplicate Detection

Because relaying occurs in various supporting services and the normal response to congestion or corrupt PDUs is to discard the PDUs, entire PDUs may be lost. Because these PDUs must be retransmitted, this may lead to duplicate PDUs being generated. The sequence number PCI element used for ordering is also used for *lost and duplicate detection*. The receiving PM keeps track of the sequence numbers, as PDUs arrive. If a PDU arrives out of order, the PM knows there is a gap and may after some time assume the missing PDUs are lost and request a retransmission, either explicitly or implicitly; see the Retransmission Control section below. If a PDU arrives for a sequence number that has already been received, it is a duplicate and is discarded.

Flow Control

A *flow-control* mechanism is used to avoid the sender sending data faster than the destination can receive it. Two basic forms of flow control are used:

- **A credit scheme,** where the destination tells the receiver how many messages it can send before receiving more credit. This scheme is sometimes linked to the acknowledgment mechanism such that the flow-control policy extends more credit whenever an ack is received.

- **A pacing scheme,** where the destination indicates to the sender the rate at which data can be sent.

Both schemes may use units of either octets or PDUs.

Retransmission Control or Acknowledgment

As noted earlier, simplistically the *acknowledgment* mechanism is used by the destination to tell the receiver that the PDUs have been successfully received. The most prevalent scheme includes the sequence number as an element of PCI that indicates that all PDUs with sequence numbers less than this have been received. If the sender does not receive an ack for a sequence number after a given period of time, it automatically retransmits all PDUs up to the last PDU sent. When an ack is received, the sender may delete PDUs from its list of potential retransmissions with a lower sequence number. For environments with a large bandwidth-delay product, a more complex mechanism of selective ack or *negative acknowledgment* (nack) is used to notify the sender of specific errors and thus limit the number of PDUs retransmitted and to shorten the time taken to recover from the error (that is, not wait for the retransmission timeout). However, retransmission may incur unacceptable delay.

As we have seen, a number of mechanisms make use of the sequence number-ing of the PDUs. The lost and duplicate, flow-control, and retransmission-con-trol mechanisms have been linked by a concept called the *sliding-window mechanism*. The sender and receiver keep a sliding window based on the sequence numbers of the PDUs they send and receive. The left edge of the win-dow represents the last PDU ack'ed or ack-received. The width of the window is the amount of credit that the flow-control mechanism has extended. Thus, the width of the sender's window represents the number of PDUs or octets that can be sent. The width of the receiver's window is the number of PDUs or octets the receiver expects to receive before credit expires. Any PDU outside the window is discarded. Any PDU with a sequence number less than the left edge is a dupli-cate, and the PDU is discarded. The right edge is the largest sequence number the sender can send (before more credit is extended) or the receiver is expected to receive.

The retransmission mechanism modifies only the left window edge; the flow-control mechanism modifies only the right window edge. Any linkage between the two is done through policy. The lost and duplicate detection mechanism refers to the left and right edges of the receive window and to any sequence numbers of PDUs that have arrived in the window to detect duplicates or gaps. Duplicates are discarded, and gaps may be filled by withholding acks and forc-ing the sender to retransmit (generating a selective ack/nack) or perhaps be ignored (as in our case of lying).

Compression

The *compression* mechanism is used to improve the transmission efficiency by applying data compression to the user-data. The policy for this mechanism selects the compression algorithm to be used. "Header compression" or apply-ing compression to the (N)-PCI is found in certain environments. Header com-pression requires some assumptions about the (N–1)-protocol and the (N)-protocol to ensure that the (N)-layer recognizes what it should do. It should be noted that (N–1)-user-data includes the (N)-PCI.

Authentication

The *authentication* mechanism is used to allow the destination to authenticate the identity of the source. The policy associated with this mechanism determines the particular authentication algorithm used. Cryptographic techniques are gen-erally employed to provider greater confidence in the exchange. There are sev-eral different authentication mechanisms of varying capabilities, and various policies may be used with them to further adjust their properties.

Access Control

This *access-control* mechanism is used to prevent unauthorized use of a resource. For communication, this generally involves whether the requestor is allowed access to the resource being requested. Again, cryptographic methods are generally employed to securely communicate the permission (access) associated with the requestor. In general, access-control is performed only after authentication. Access-control mechanisms use different policies to guarantee a given level of security and control.

Integrity

The *integrity* mechanism provides communication with protection against the insertion or deletion of PDUs in an unauthorized manner. This mechanism provides greater integrity than the generally weaker measures described previously, such as data-corruption detection or lost and duplicate detection. Cryptographic methods are generally used to ensure this greater degree of integrity. Generally, the policies for integrity will be the cryptographic algorithms and the associated key size used.

Confidentiality

The *confidentiality* mechanism attempts to ensure that the contents of user-data carried in PDUs or whole PDUs of a communication are not divulged to unauthorized processes or persons. Cryptographic mechanisms are generally used to implement this mechanism. Generally, the policies for confidentiality will be the cryptographic algorithms and the associated key size used.

Nonrepudiation

The *nonrepudiation* mechanism attempts to ensure that no process that has participated in an interaction can deny having participated in the interaction. Cryptographic methods are generally used to implement this mechanism.

Activity

An *activity* mechanism is used on connections that have long periods of no traffic. This mechanism, often referred to as a *keepalive*, enables the correspondents to determine that their apposite is still there and in a consistent state. The policy associated with this mechanism determines the frequency or conditions for invoking the mechanism. There are significant arguments that mechanisms such as these are not required (or perhaps more precisely, are only required by application protocols). Of course, timer-based protocols do not require these mechanisms.

Phases of Operation

The concept of phases of operation in protocols has been around for decades. I have taken the term *enrollment* from discussions of application management in the early 1980s. *Establishment* and *data transfer* are in common usage. All forms of communication progress through three phases:

1. Enrollment

2. Establishment or synchronization

3. Data transfer

Procedures associated with all three phases must be performed by the senders and the receivers for communication to occur, regardless of whether any PDUs are exchanged.

Each phase consists of one or more operations and their inverses—that is, the operation of the phases is nested. Thus, for communication to occur, first enrollment must occur, then allocation, and finally data transfer. It is not necessary for every protocol to perform all phases. Network management, ad hoc procedures, or some other protocol may perform enrollment or allocation on behalf of a given protocol.

The Enrollment Phase

The *enrollment phase* creates, maintains, distributes, and deletes the information within a layer that is necessary to create instances of communication. This phase makes an object and its capabilities known to the network, any addressing information is entered into the appropriate directories (and routing tables), certain parameters are set that characterize the communication this protocol can participate in, access-control rules are established, ranges of policy are fixed, and so on. The enrollment phase is used to create the necessary information for classes or types of communication. However, in some cases (for instance, multicast and some security services), enrollment specifies information for a particular instance (that is, flow). The enrollment phase has always been there but often ignored because it was part of the messy initial configuration and setup (which was often manual). Frankly, it just wasn't fun and had more in common with having to clean up your room than good engineering! In general, enrollment is performed by ad hoc means (often manual) or application protocols. A given enrollment protocol or procedure will generally be used for more than one data transfer or application protocol. The enrollment phase creates an information base of parameters and policies that will be used to instantiate particular PMs. When the PMs are created in the establishment phase, they will inherit the set of attributes associated with their protocol that were recorded during the enrollment phase. These attributes may be modified by the allocation phase parameters and subsequent operation of the PM during the data transfer phase. In practice, this phase is often characterized by two subphases: registration and activation.

The *registration* operation makes the information necessary to create an instance available within the network (that is, distributed to directories in the network). The information is available only to systems within the scope of this protocol and its layer. *Deregistration* deletes the registration of the protocol from the network. In general, deregistration should be withheld until all existing instances have exited the allocation phase. There are no active instances of the protocol; that is, there are no active flows.

In general, it is useful to separately control the registration and the actual availability of the protocol to participate in communication. *Activation/deactivation* is the traditional operation of taking a facility "offline" without deleting the system's knowledge that the facility exists. If a protocol has been registered but not activated, instances (PMs) cannot be created that can enter the allocation phase. Deactivation, in general, does not affect currently existing instances in the allocation or data transfer phases but does prevent new ones from being created.

De-enrollment is synonymous with deregistration. Completion of deregistration completes de-enrollment. De-enrollment may not have any affect on PMs in the allocation or data transfer phases unless the PMs must refer back to the original enrollment information, in which case they will abort.

To date, most architectures have relied on ad hoc procedures for enrollment. The registration and activation operations and their inverses may be performed by network management, as in setting up permanent virtual circuits or with a connectionless protocol. In some cases, the enrollment phase is performed when someone calls up someone else and says, "Initiate such and such so that we can communicate" or a standard that defines "well-known" sockets on which a listen is to be posted for communication with a particular application to take place. *Dynamic Host Configuration Protocol* (DHCP, RFC 1541), the assignment of MAC addresses, well-known sockets, key management, and such are all examples of aspects of enrollment. HDLC has included mechanisms for enrollment in the *Exchange Identification* (XID) frames used to select options to be made available, although this combines aspects of enrollment and allocation. With the advent and use of directory protocols and address-assignment protocols, the enrollment phase is becoming much less ad hoc and much more a regular automated phase.

The Establishment or Synchronization Phase

The *synchronization phase* creates, maintains, and deletes the shared state necessary to support the functions of the data transfer phase.

The primary purpose of this phase is to create the initial shared state in the communicating PMs to support the functions of the protocol. The synchronization phase ensures that the PMs initially have consistent state information. (Although *consistent* does not necessarily imply the same state information.) The behavior associated with this phase can range from simply creating bindings between the (N+1)-PM and the (N)-PM (connectionless) to an explicit exchange of initial state information to synchronize state between two PMs (so-called connections) depending on the amount of shared state required to support the functions of the data transfer phase. It is during this phase that the specific QoS requirements for data transfer acceptable to the user are made (or modified) if they were not fixed during the enrollment phase. At the completion of the synchronization operation, the communication transitions to a state such that it may transfer data. The desynchronization operation is invoked when the (N+1)-PM has completed the data transfer phase and wants to terminate the shared state created during the synchronization phase.

There are two broad classes of protocols, termed *in-band* and *out-of-band*. In-band protocols are defined such that the synchronization and data transfer phases are specified as a single protocol, whereas in an out-of-band protocol the synchronization and data transfer phases are distinct protocols.

The mechanisms used for the synchronization phase depend on the mechanisms in the protocol. The stronger the coupling of the shared state, the more reliable the synchronization phase mechanisms must be. In general, protocols with feedback mechanisms require more robust synchronization procedures than those without.

The Data Transfer Phase

The *data transfer phase* is entered when the actual transfer of data is effected according to the requested QoS among the addresses specified during either of the previous two phases. For application protocols, the data transfer phase may be further subdivided into specialized subphases.

Conclusions

We have gotten off to an easy start: developing the traditional model of finite state machines, applying them to protocols, and considering the structure of protocols. We used this to construct an abstract model of our understanding and take a quick survey of the mechanisms that make up protocols. We have introduced the concept of separating mechanism and policy and showed that it can further clarify our understanding. We wrapped up, noting that communication goes through three distinct phases: Our first recognition that these protocols fit into a larger environment.

Clearly, we could, if we so desired, construct a much more complete and formal definition of the interfaces, protocols, and their mechanisms to create a useful construction kit for investigating how to assemble architectures. But truthfully, it is too soon to embark on that exercise. All in all, this chapter represents our current understanding of the basics of protocols, interfaces, and so on. As we continue to look at what we know and consider the implications it has for architecture, we may find it necessary to revise our understanding, to throw away one or more ladders. Not because our ideas were wrong necessarily, only incomplete. To give a hint of where we may find ourselves, that our current view is more an *in vitro* picture, rather than an *in vivo* view of these elements in a complete network architecture.

The going gets progressively tougher from here. In the next chapter, we consider our first hard problem: resolving the dichotomy of connection and connectionless. When you give up trying to think about it and listens to the problem, the result is a bit surprising. We will also use the separation of mechanism and policy to extract invariants in the structure of protocols and discover some patterns.

Chapter 3

Patterns in Protocols

The trick with reductio ad absurdum is knowing when to stop.

Introduction

In this chapter, we begin to get to the crux of the matter: finding patterns in the architecture of networks. And not just any patterns, but patterns that go beyond natural history and make predictions and provide new insights. The task is made more difficult by the nature of computer science; that is, we build what we measure. Unlike physics, chemistry, or other sciences, the patterns that form the basis of our field are seldom fixed by nature, or they are so general as to provide little guidance. For us, it is more difficult to determine which patterns are fundamental and not an artifact of what we build.

Even in what we think of as the traditional sciences, finding the problem at the core of a set of problems is not always obvious. (Although it always seems so in retrospect.) For example, one of the major problems in the late 16th century was predicting where cannonballs would fall. Rather than proposing an elaborate and expensive project to exhaustively explore their behavior with a highly instrumented collection of cannons of various makes, caliber, and amounts of powder and from this try to determine the equations that would predict the path of the cannonballs, Galileo had the insight that the answer lay not with firing cannons but with some hard thinking about a simple abstraction that was at the core of the problem. The key for Galileo was to break with Aristotle and imagine something no one had ever seen or had any reason to believe could exist: frictionless motion. Then formulate what we know as the first law of motion, "A body at rest or in motion will tend to stay at rest or in motion...." (Fermi and Bernardini, 1961; a little gem of a book). Imagine how absurd and idealistic such a construct must have appeared to his colleagues. Everyone knew that an object put in motion slowed to a stop unless a force was

57

acting on it. One saw it every day. What was this dream world that Galileo inhabited? Push an object and it goes on forever? Absurd! [1]

Galileo could then confirm his insight by rolling inexpensive balls down an inclined plane or simply dropping them from high places. Had Galileo gone directly for the problem at hand, he would never have found the answer. It was far too complex. To start from nothing to find equations of motion that accommodate factors of air resistance, wind drift, shape of the projectile (not perfect spheres), and so on would have been all but impossible. Galileo had the insight to find the model at the core of problem. (One wonders if Galileo had the same problems getting funding for experiments that were not of immediate practical application that one would have today. Luckily, an inclined plane and a few balls don't cost much now or didn't then.) We must also look for the model at the core of our problem to find the concepts that will pull it all together. And like Galileo, we may find that some hard thinking is more productive and less expensive.

It would seem that because we have much more leeway in our choices and very little help from nature to determine which ones are right, that it will be difficult to justify choosing one over another. To some extent this is true, but we are not totally adrift. The experience of the 16th- and 17th-century scientists allowed, by the early 18th century, for science to arrive at some guidance we can fall back on: the *Regulae Philosphandi* from Newton's *Principia* of 1726 (as paraphrased by Gerald Holton, 1988):

1. Nature is essentially simple; therefore, we should not introduce more hypotheses than are sufficient and necessary for the explanation of observed facts. This is a hypothesis, or rule, of simplicity and *verae causae*.

2. Hence, as far as possible, similar effects must be assigned to the same cause. This is a principle of uniformity of nature.

3. Properties common to all those bodies within reach of our experiments are assumed (even if only tentatively) as pertaining to all bodies in general. This is a reformulation of the first two hypotheses and is needed for forming universals.

4. Propositions in science obtained by wide induction are to be regarded as exactly or approximately true until phenomena or experiments show that they may be corrected or are liable to exceptions. This principle states that propositions induced on the basis of experiment should not be confuted merely by proposing contrary hypotheses.

---

[1] While Galileo also uncovered other principles, this is probably the most counterintuitive.

Not only are these good for nature, but also for finding fundamental structures. As the reader is well aware, the path to finding such solutions is seldom a nice, straightforward progression. Along the way, there are always twists and turns, blind alleys, backtracking, and some intuitive leaps that we will only see later, the straightforward path that led to them followed by throwing away of one or more ladders. I will do what I can to protect you from the worst of these, while at the same time giving you a sense of how I came to these conclusions. All the while, we will try to listen to what the problem is telling us. We will assume that what others have done was for good reason and offers clues to patterns that may have remained obscured. But be aware that there is some hard thinking ahead. You will be asked to set aside preconceived notions to see where a new path leads, and some things you thought were fact were artifacts of our old ways. It is not so much that the old ways of thinking were wrong. They were necessary to a large extent for us to make progress. We had to see how the problem behaved to have a better understanding of the principles underlying it. In fact, it is unlikely that we could have gotten to a better understanding without them. Any scientific theory is always a working hypothesis: an indication of our current understanding; something to be improved on.

Before we can begin that process, however, we must address the great religious war of networking. A war that has raged for the past 30 years or more and at this point has been and remains probably the greatest barrier to progress in the field. The war revolves around two topics that are not only technical but also historical, political, and worst of all economical. (*Worst*, because ideas that change business models and that can make money are the most threatening, outside actual religion.) The conflict is between the two major architecture paradigms, beads-on-a-string and layers, and the conflict between connection and connectionless. The war continues unabated to this day. And although it may appear that because the Internet has been such a success that the connectionless layered approach has won the day, this is far from apparent. Virtually every proposal for new directions or new technology falls into one camp or the other. And it seems that beads-on-a-string proposals are once again on the rise. Proponents lobby hard for their favorites and demean proposals of

A Word of Warning

This topic has been the most hotly contested in the short 30+ year history of networking. No one has come to blows over it (as far as I know), but it has been awfully close at times. Strong emotions and shouting matches have not been uncommon. Conspiracy theories abound, and some of them are even true. So the reader should be aware of the intensity these issues tend to generate and the powers that are brought to bear. I will try to be even-handed and will conclude I have succeeded if I am criticized for being unfair by both sides. But not everyone can be right.

And full disclosure: As long as we are on a topic of such sensitivity, I should make you aware of my own history with these topics. I was involved in the early ARPANET an avid proponent of the connectionless approach found in CYCLADES and the Internet. I was one of those responsible for ensuring that the Europeans held up their bargain to include connectionless in the OSI reference model. It is not uncommon for supporters of the *post, telephone, and telegraph* (PTT) position (that is, bellheads) to change the subject of discussion when I walked in a room. On the other hand, some members of the *Internet Engineering Task Force* (IETF) probably assume I am a connection-oriented bigot (probably because I have been a long-time critic of the disappearance of the vision and intellectual risk taking that made the early Net a success).

the other camp. Some loudly champion views that they see as inherently good for the Net because they reflect some Utopian myth without showing how they solve real problems or yield real benefits. None of the proposals generate that sense of a "right" solution and, hence, none get any traction. Unless we can find a resolution to this crisis, especially one that provides a synthesis of connection and connectionless, networking will continue its imitation of the Faber Marching Band (in the movie *Animal House*).

One of the things that most impressed me about the early work of the ARPANET *Network Working Group* (NWG) was its ability when confronted with two extreme positions to find a solution that was a true synthesis. Not the typical standards committee approach of simply jamming both views together and calling them options, but a solution that went to depth and found a common model that encompassed the extremes as degenerate cases. Time after time, the NWG found these solutions. Not only were they an elegant synthesis, but also simple and easy to implement. OSI was too politicized to do it, and the IETF seems to have lost the spirit to do it.

It appears that there are times when both connections and connectionless make sense. After all, the architectures that support connectionless have connections, too. We need to understand when one or the other is preferred. I have believed there had to be something we weren't seeing: a model in which connections and connectionless were both degenerate cases. I have spent many hours over many years struggling with the problem looking for a model that maintained the best of both worlds. Perhaps we can find one here.

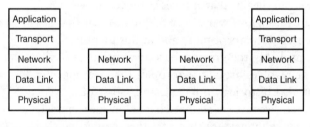

Figure 3-1 Typical network architecture of the early 1970s.

The Two Major Architecture Paradigms

The Layered Model

By one of those quirks of history, the first major computer networks (ARPANET, CYCLADES, and NPLnet) were built primarily, not by communications experts, but by computer experts, in particular operating systems experts. In 1970, software engineering was barely two decades old, and design principles were only beginning to coalesce. Operating systems were the most complex programs of the day; and if computers were to use networks, it would have to be through the operating system. Therefore, it is not surprising that Dijkstra's paper (1968) on the elegant and simple layered design of the THE operating system and Multics (Organick, 1972), the basis of UNIX, would influence early attempts to find a structure for the new networks. This combined with the justification of the ARPANET as a resource-sharing network served to impart a strong influence of operating systems. The first applications were modeled on providing the major functions of an operating system in a network.

This exercise of finding abstractions to cover the variety of heterogeneous systems also led to a deeper understanding of operating systems. (In my own case, trying to replicate semaphores in a network lead to a solution to reliably updating multiple copies of a database [Alsberg, Day; 1976].) The primary purpose of Dijkstra's layers was the same as any "black box" approach: to provide an abstraction of the functions below and isolate the users of functions from the specifics of how the function worked and from specifics of the hardware. Higher layers provided higher abstractions. This also allowed the functions within a layer to be modified without affecting the layers on either side. In addition, the tight constraints on resources led Dijkstra to believe that there was no reason for functions to be repeated. A function done in one layer did not have to be repeated in a higher layer. The Dijkstra model had gained currency not only in operating systems but in many other application areas, too. It seemed especially well suited for the distributed resource-sharing network, where not only were computers sending information to each other, but the switches to move traffic between source and destination hosts were also computers, albeit minicomputers, but still general-purpose computers nonetheless. Hence, an architecture of at least five layers was fairly commonly accepted by 1974 (see Figure 3-1):

1. A physical layer consisting of the wires connecting the computers

2. A link layer that provided error and flow control on the lines connecting the computers

3. A relaying layer that forwarded the traffic to the correct destination

4. A transport layer responsible for end-to-end error and flow control

5. An applications layer to do the actual work

At least five layers; because as we will see in the next chapter, the ARPANET had adopted a quite reasonable approach of building one application on the services of another; no one at this point believed they understood what this structure was, but it was assumed there was more structure. It was unclear how many layers there should be above transport.

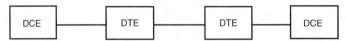

Figure 3-2 A typical beads-on-a-string architecture of the early 1970s (same as Figure 2-1).

The Beads-on-a-String Model

The early research computer networks were not the first networks. The telephone companies had been building networks for nearly a century, and these were large international networks. Clearly, they had developed their own network architecture suited to their needs. However, the properties of the architecture reflected not only the circuit-switched technology of the telephone networks but also their economic and political environment. From their founding in the 19th century until after the middle of the 20th century, the telephony networks were electrical (physical circuits). Even in the last half of the 20th century as switches used digital communication for control, this control was alongside the telephony network. Interfaces were always between devices. Although this architecture has never been given an official name, I have always called it the "beads-on-a-string" model after the figures common in their specifications: different kinds of boxes strung together by wires.

The beads-on-a-string model reflects the unique environment occupied by the telephone companies (see Figure 3-2). It has been primarily promulgated by the CCITT/ITU and the telephone companies and manufacturers closely associated with them. First, until recently, all telephone switching was circuit switched, and hence there was only one layer, the physical layer. Strictly speaking, these networks consisted of two physically distinct networks: one that carried the traffic and a separate one for controlling the switching. More recently, these are referred to as the data plane and control plane. (Another indication of the Internet's slide into telephony's beads-on-a-string model.) The communication generated by these two planes is sometimes multiplexed onto a common lower layer rather than physically distinct networks. This split between the voice and switch control was well established. There was no reason for a layered model. This also leads to a very connection-oriented view of the world. Second, until recently telephone companies were monopolies that either manufactured their own equipment or bought equipment built to their specifications from a very small number of manufacturers. Hence, where standards were required, they were to define interfaces between boxes, between a provider and someone else (that is, another telephone company or, if absolutely necessary, a customer). In the preferred solution, all equipment used by the customer is owned by the telephone company. This was the situation prior to deregulation. Therefore, a major purpose of the model is to define who owns what (that is, define markets). In this environment, it is not surprising that a beads-on-a-string model evolved. And herein lies one of the first differences between the layered and beads-on-a-string model: the definition of interface. In the layered model, an interface is between two layers internal to a system, within a box. In the beads-on-a-string model, an interface is between two boxes.

One can imagine the combination of confusion and indignation with which the telephone companies faced the idea of computer networks at the beginning of the 1970s. On the one hand, this was their turf. What were these computer companies doing infringing on their turf, *their* market? On the other hand, these research networks were being built in a way that could not possibly work, but did, and worked better than their own attempts at computer networks. In Europe, the telephone companies, known as PTTs, were part of the government. They made the rules and implemented them. In the early 1970s, it was a definite possibility that they would attempt to require that only PTT computers could be attached to PTT networks. Everyone saw that communication between computers was going to be a big business, although it is unlikely that the PTTs had any idea how big. (As late as the late 1980s, phone company types were still saying that data traffic would never exceed voice traffic.) The PTTs saw an opportunity for value-added networks, but they did not like the idea of competition or of companies creating their own networks.

The situation in the United States was very different. AT&T was a monopoly, but it was a private corporation. It thought it understood competition and saw this as a chance to enter the computer business. But the European PTTs knew they did not like the layered model because as we will soon see, it relegated them to a commodity market. The layered model had two problems for PTTs. Because most of the new (they called them value-added) services were embodied in applications and applications are always in hosts, which are not part of the network, there is no distinction between hosts owned by one organization and hosts owned by another. Any

Why Do We Care?

"This is all interesting history that may have been important in your day, but it is hardly relevant to networking today!"

Oh if that it were the case. First, it is always good to know how we got where we are and why we are there. There is a tendency in our field to believe that everything we currently use is a paragon of engineering, rather than a snapshot of our understanding at the time. We build great myths of spin about how what we have done is the only way to do it to the point that our universities now teach the flaws to students (and professors and textbook authors) who don't know better. To a large extent, even with deregulation, little has changed.

To be sure, the technology is different, the nomenclature has changed, the arguments are more subtle; but under it all, it is still the same tension. Who gets to sell what? Who controls the account? How does this affect

continues

continued

my bottom line? The same economic and political factors are still driving the technology. And the providers are still trying to find a way to turn the layered model to their advantage, whether they call it value-added service, AIN, IPSphere, or IMS. It is still the same game. Any time one hears of wonderful services for applications "in the network," it is one more ruse to draw a line between what they can sell and no one else can. Today, one hears router vendors making statements that sound uncannily like the PTTs of 1980s. Product offerings are never about elegant paragons of engineering but offensive and defensive moves in the game of competition. If you don't see how a particular product does that for a vendor, you aren't thinking hard enough.

new services were open to competition. The second problem was connectionless, which we cover in the next section.

The PTTs much preferred an approach that allowed them to use their monopoly. They dug in and would not concede an inch to the computer industry without a fight. This "bunker mentality" became and remains a characteristic of both sides. Each side was deathly afraid that the slightest concession to the other side would lead to a collapse of their position. For the layered advocates, it was the immense political power of the PTTs; and for the PTTs, it was the immense market and technological pressure of the computer industry that drove their fear. But also, the lack of any technical middle ground contributed to the tension. For both sides, there did not seem to be any ground to give that did not lead to the collapse of one's position.

To illustrate this mindset and how architecture was used for competitive ends, consider the simple example in Figure 3-3 from the period. In both the ARPANET and the PTT packet networks, many users gained access by dialing a terminal into a computer that had a minimal user interface that enabled the user to then connect to other computers on the network. In the ARPANET, there were two kinds of these: one that was a stand-alone host (usually if not always a PDP-11) connected to an *Interface Message Processor* (IMP), or a version of the IMP with a very small program to handle the user interface called a *Terminal Interface Processor* (TIP). (But the TIP software looked like a host to the IMP software.) As Figure 3-3 shows, the configuration of boxes was the same in both networks.

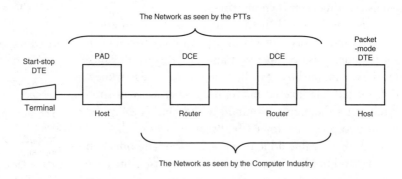

Figure 3-3 Two views of the same thing.

The PTTs called the equivalent of a TIP a *Packet Assembler Disassembler* (PAD). The PAD was not a small host or a switch but an *interface* between start-stop mode DTEs[2] (that is, simple terminals) and packet-mode DTEs (hosts). Why go to all this trouble? Why not just call it a small host? Because that would mean that someone other than a PTT could sell it. PTTs own the interfaces. The PTTs did not want competition in the network access business. Was it really that big a business? At a conference in the late 1970s at the unveiling of their network, the head of one such network when asked what he would think of PAD products being offered by other companies, replied in a moment of frankness, "Not very much!"

However, by defining an asymmetrical architecture, the PTTs essentially created a point product that had nowhere to go, an evolutionary dead end. This distinction between trying to cast what are clearly application functions as "in the network" and having some special status persists to this day. Its manifestation has become more and more interesting as phone companies have become populated with young engineers brought up on the Internet and as the Internet has become more and more dominated by carriers and router vendors trying to escape a business model becoming more and more a commodity. The PTTs were more than willing to consider layers within their interfaces. For example, X.25, the interface between packet-mode DTEs and DCEs defines three layers. The PTTs have consistently attempted to use the beads-on-a-string model to legislate what was "in the network." This approach is found in ISDN, ATM, MPLS, AIN, WAP, and so on.[3] It doesn't take long for even manufacturers of Internet equipment to find that selling on performance and cost is hard work and to begin to advocate more functionality "in the network." (Not long ago, a representative of a major router manufacturer very active in the IETF waxed eloquent about how future networks would have all of this wonderful functionality in them, sounding just like a telephone company advocate of 15 years earlier. Of course, the poor guy had no idea he was parroting views that were an anathema to the whole premise of the Internet.)

The fundamental nature of the beads-on-a-string model provides no tools for controlling complexity or for scaling. The desire to distinguish provider and consumer imparts an inherent asymmetry to the architectures that adds complexity and limits extensibility. We have already discussed some of the general advantages of layering, but there is an additional property that can be quite useful: scoping, which has been defined as the set of nodes addressable without

---

[2] Data Terminating Equipment, not owned by the provider. DCE, Data Communicating Equipment, owned by the provider.

[3] It is striking how similar the first WAP standards of today are to the videotex standards of the early 1980s; e.g., France's Minitel, a similarity that as far as I know went uncommented on.

relaying at a higher layer. In general, the scope of layers increases with high layers. For example, addresses for a data link layer must only be unambiguous within the scope of the layer, not for all data link layers. This provides another tool for controlling complexity and localizing effects, as anyone who has had to contend with a large bridged LAN can attest. Although the layer model avoids these problems, it also has problems. Layering can control complexity up to a point, but it does not address scaling. There has been a tendency to require layers where they are not necessary (causing inefficiencies). Attempts to improve the efficiency of layers by having fewer of them has the effect of reducing the layered model to the beads-on-a-string model or at the very least creating an architecture of "beads with stripes" as we see in today's Internet. But more on this later, now we must turn our attention to the other half of the problem.

The Connectionless/Connection Debate

Background

The preceding section introduced the two major paradigms of networking and began to contrast them. However, that is only half the story. Completely intertwined with the tension between the beads-on-a-string model and the layered model is the connection versus connectionless debate. Given its circuit-switched roots, beads-on-a-string is quite naturally associated with the connection approach, whereas with the popularity of the Internet, layered networks are generally associated with connectionless technologies. However, just to muddy the waters, there are connectionless architectures that try to avoid layers, and layered connection-oriented network architectures, too. In this section, we look at this aspect of the problem in more detail and see how it might be resolved.

Paul Baran, in a RAND Report, proposed a radical new approach to telecommunications (Baran, 1964). Baran's concept addressed the shortcomings of traditional voice networks in terms of survivability and economy. Baran's idea was twofold: Data would be broken up into fairly short "packets," each of which would be routed through the network; if a node failed, the packets were automatically rerouted around the failure, and errors were corrected hop-by-hop. Baran's ideas were the basis for the first packet-switched network, the ARPANET, a precursor to the connection-oriented X.25 networks of the 1970s. However, Louis Pouzin developing the CYCLADES network at IRIA (now INRIA) in France, took the idea one step further. Pouzin reasoned that because the hosts would never trust the network anyway and would check for errors regardless, the network did not have to be perfectly reliable and, therefore, could be less expensive and more economical. Pouzin called this a datagram or connectionless network. Soon afterward, the ARPANET added a connectionless mode. The datagram network quickly became a *cause célèbre* of the research world, and connectionless became the religion of the Internet. CYCLADES was a research project that despite being an unqualified success and placing France at the leading edge in networking was turned off in the 1970s, primarily because it treaded on the turf of the French PTT. Had it been left to develop, France might have been a leader in the Internet, rather than a straggler. Clearly, some of the most insightful intellectual work was coming out of France. Consequently, the datagram concept had not been very thoroughly explored when CYCLADES ended. It is not clear that when it was adopted for the Internet there was an awareness that deeper investigation was still waiting to be done. In any case, the ensuing connection/connectionless debate created the bunker mentality that ensured it would not get done.

This proved to be a very contentious innovation. The computer science community embraced the elegance and simplicity of the concept (and its compatibility with computers),[4] while the telephone companies found it an anathema. The ensuing connectionless/connection war has been a Thirty Years War almost as bad as the first one. The war has been complete with fanatics on both sides and not many moderates. The PTTs have been the most ardent supporters of the catholic connection world to the point of being unable to conceive (at least, as many of them contended in many meetings) the existence of communication without a connection. The protestants of the Internet community, representing the other extreme, concluded that everything should be connectionless, while conveniently ignoring the role of connections in their own success. As with any religious issue, the only reasonable approach is to be an agnostic.

The first battle in the war was over X.25. The connectionless troops were late in discovering this push by the telephone companies into data networking and were largely unprepared for the tactics of the Comité Consultatif International Téléphonique et Télégraphique (CCITT) standards process.[5] Strictly

Was Packet Switching Revolutionary?

Interestingly, it depended on your background. If you had a telecom background, where everything was in terms of continuous signals or bits, it definitely was. If your background was computers, where everything is in finite buffers, it was obvious. What could be more simple, you want to send messages, pick up a buffer, and send it.

---

[4] The success of the early ARPANET had as much to do with the level of funding as the success of the technology.

[5] With decades of experience, the ITU participants had developed political maneuvering to a level of sophistication that the largely academic connectionless troops were unprepared for.

Not One, But Two 800-Pound Gorillas

Although not directly related to the problem we must address here, it should be noted that the new network paradigm not only threw a wrench in the PTTs view of the world, but in IBM's as well. Not because it was layered, but because it was a *peer* architecture. IBM's *System Network Architecture* (SNA) was a hierarchical architecture. A peer architecture can always be subset to be hierarchical, but a hierarchical architecture can not be extended to be peer. This new idea in communications had (inadvertently) invalidated the business models of two of the largest economic forces on the planet. This is no way to make friends! The two 800-pound gorillas were really...mad!

It is no wonder there was so much contention in the standards debates. IBM needed to delay as much as possible without appearing to. But for the PTTs, this was a direct threat; they needed to squelch this. But Moore's law was working against both of them. The falling equipment prices favored the new model. Although it was a real possibility that had IBM designed SNA as a peer architecture and subset it for the 1970s market, given its market position, none of this might ever have happened.

speaking, X.25 defined the interface to the network and not the internal working of the network. The initial PTT response to a datagram service in X.25, called Fast Select, was a single packet that opened, transferred data, and closed a connection in a single packet (a connectionless connection and a characteristic of this genre of proposals down to ATM and MPLS). Although a datagram facility was finally included in X.25, it was seldom, if ever, used.

The primary focus of the X.25 debate became whether hop-by-hop error control (X.25) could be as reliable as end-to-end error control or whether a transport protocol such as TCP was always required. The PTTs contended that their networks were perfectly reliable and never lost data, and end-to-end transport was therefore unnecessary. This was an absurd claim that the PTTs never came close to achieving. But the real point was this: Would any IT director who wanted to keep his job simply assume the network would never lose anything? Of course not. So, if the hosts were doing end-to-end error checking anyway, the network could do less error checking.

This brings us to the second problem PTTs had with the layered model. The transport layer effectively confines network providers to a commodity business by essentially establishing a minimal required service from the network (Figure 3-4). Commodity businesses do not have high margins. Much of the purpose of the PTT approach was to keep the computer manufacturers out of the network and the PTTs in a highly profitable business. End-to-end transport protocols and the layered model had the effect of either confining PTTs to a commodity business or creating high-margin, value-added opportunities open to competition—neither of which was appealing to the PTTs. As you will see as we work through this timeline, the debate over whether there should be a transport protocol further reinforces the bunker mentality in the two camps, entrenching a boundary that leaves the last vestige of beads-on-a-string in place and effectively arresting the development of network architecture for the next 30 years.

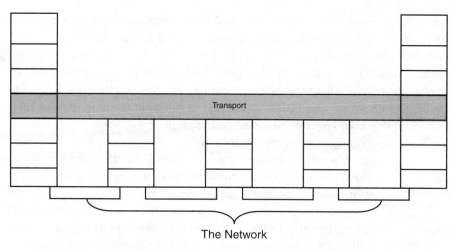

The Network

Figure 3-4 The transport layer effectively seals off the network from high-margin applications.

The second and much more contentious battleground for most of this debate was the OSI work. The connectionless proponents began with the upper hand, but the European delegations quickly capitulated to PTT influence,[6] leaving mostly the United States to champion connectionless. The insinuation of the PTT's strong presence was aided by a parochial stance by European computer companies to not adopt anything done in the United States and, thereby, not give the United States an advantage in the market. (Even though at this point, no major commercial vendor was considering product that supported Internet protocols.) The Europeans had a good transport protocol (developed for CYCLADES). This protocol among others, including TCP, had been the subject of an open process conducted by *International Federation for Information Processing* (IFIP) WG6.1 and was selected as a proposed international end-to-end transport protocol (Cerf et al., 1978) in January 1978.

---

[6] Actually, it was a combination of the PTTs and IBM. IBM chaired and was a heavy influence in all the European ISO delegations. There was an IBM chair in the United States, too, but the U.S. delegation had AT&T and DEC, among others, to balance IBM. The U.S. IBM members for the most part constrained themselves to the administrative issues and stayed away from the technical issues. European computer companies needed détente with the PTTs because they had to coexist with them and as balance against U.S. and Japanese companies. The desire of the European computer companies and PTTs to not simply adopt or improve on what the United States already had, along with others in the United States pushing competing agendas, played right into IBM's strategy. The ultimate example of this came in the battle over a transaction-processing protocol. Let's just say that the Europeans might have done better had they read Uncle Remus.

OSI began a few months later, and the IFIP recommendation was carried into ISO by the IFIP representative and adopted as the basis for Class 4 of the OSI Transport Protocol. But the Europeans insisted on X.25 as the connection-oriented network protocol.[7] After a bitter battle, the United States was able to insert connectionless in the architecture but had to accept constraints that made any interworking of connection mode and connectionless mode impossible. Connectionless could operate over connection mode or vice versa, but there was no means to interwork them as peers. As it turned out, this was less a problem. However, it was enough for the United States to move ahead to develop connectionless routing and data transfer protocols. As the 1980s wore on, X.25 was being relegated to a role as a subnetwork access protocol similar to its use in the Internet in the early 1980s, with connectionless operating over it as a subnetwork independent protocol. The European bunker mentality to not leverage the existing U.S. advances caused them to forfeit any opportunity they might have had to assume a leadership role. The European faith in the ability of centralist initiatives to override consumer demand lost them the war (sound familiar?). The connection/connectionless debate between the United States and Europe and the factions within the United States to dominate the direction of OSI (DEC, IBM, COS, NIST, MAP, and so on) created so much internal strife within OSI that it essentially self-destructed. It lost any cohesive market focus.[8] This left the Internet, a research network, as a production network without having ever been made into a product.

The Internet community (the U.S. and the international academic community) maintained a fairly pure parochial connectionless stance, while the ITU, European computer companies, and PTTs similarly maintained a fairly pure parochial connection

The Battle over Connectionless

As with any consensus organization (standards or legislative), a topic is never really resolved. Issues can always be raised again. Connectionless is a case in point. The United States voted No on the first ballot to move the OSI reference model (RM) to a standard in 1980 in Berlin. The vote was conditional on including connectionless. There was much angst among clueless American commentators who didn't understand that a Yes vote with comment under ISO rules meant that none of your comments had to be accepted; you had voted Yes, after all. Voting No conditionally was the only way to get your comments addressed. (National bodies with active participation in a standard always voted No on condition; that major comments were accepted for just this reason.)

That No vote was resolved with an agreement to develop a connectionless addendum to the OSI RM. There then ensued three years of meeting two or three times a year for a week at a time to hammer out a document that added connectionless to the RM. Every word was contested and argued

continues

---

[7] It is hard to believe in retrospect that as late as 1990, Europeans were still expecting X.25 to be the future of networking. How X.25 could have supported the bandwidths and applications is hard to imagine.

[8] By 1978, France, Germany, and the United Kingdom had all produced high-level government reports focusing on networking as a major future technology, and considerable funding followed soon after. However, all attempts to build a "European ARPANET," although technically successful, were never able to survive PTT pressures. In the end, the difference was not technological but that the United States was willing to provide far greater subsidies (through the DoD) for the Internet (and AT&T and IBM never saw it as compitition), while Europe more or less allowed the market to decide. The greater subsidies by the DoD and NSF allowed the Internet to achieve critical mass, while the competitive marketplace was still developing. However, these political and economic susidies were not accompanied by a commensurate transition from research demo to product. Leaving the result lacking critical structure.

stance. The European standards stance had a majority connection-oriented bias rooted in the influence of the PTTs and a pragmatic stance by some in the computer industry that the PTTs were part of the reality. The U.S. standards group was primarily connectionless with a connection-oriented tendency by the IBM participants. (It must also be recognized that in the 1970s and 1980s the split between connection and connectionless was to a large extent, but not entirely, generational. This is no longer the case.) Thus, the protectionist attitudes toward the status quo in Europe ultimately undermined Europe's strategy for economic parity (sound familiar?). The connectionless forces were woefully outnumbered. The "solution" was less than satisfactory and, in fact, never really resolved. The Europeans attempted to legislate connectionless either out of existence or constrain it to such a degree to make it useless. (There are arbitrary statements in the OSI RM limiting the use of connectionless.) The solution in OSI can only be likened to a cease-fire along a demilitarized zone rather than a real solution. By the same token, this was the forum where the concepts were given the greatest scrutiny. But, the scrutiny led to only heated debate and an uneasy truce, not to any deeper understanding.

Connectionless was seen (by both sides) as having no shared state and requiring no establishment phase and was, therefore, fundamentally simpler, cheaper, more flexible, and elegant. Connections were seen by the connectionless crowd as too much unnecessary overhead and too much state to store for simple store-and-forward networks and by the connection-oriented crowd as the only way to provide any reasonable service.[9] The connection proponents forced the connectionless proponents to recognize that there was some shared state in connectionless that had to be created before communication could begin. But that (thought the connectionless types) was really minor stuff that could be ignored; connectionless was really different from having a connection! Although the connectionless advocates convinced the connection advocates (also known as bellheads) that connectionless did have advantages in routing and recovery from failures, everyone *knew* that any real network had to

continued

over by the Europeans. Every word and phrase was inspected to ensure that it did not give an advantage to one side or the other. Finally in 1983, in Ottawa, the document was ready to be progressed to a standards vote. The chair of the Architecture Working Group found me eating lunch in the food court of the Rideau Center and said he wasn't sure the votes were there for it to pass. As Head of Delegation for the WG, this was my problem. We had an agreement, but that was three years ago. (Because the Chair was a connectionless advocate, he was sympathetic to our cause, but there was only so much he could do.) We had negotiated everything there was to negotiate. Finally, it came down to no connectionless addendum, no further U.S. participation.

It was passed and became an approved standard two years later. However, the issue was never really resolved and continued to be contested in every meeting.

---

[9] On the other hand, the PTTs insisted that no end-to-end reliability was required because their networks were perfectly reliable, even though everyone knew better. Here they insisted on the use of TP0 (at the transport layer because there won't be any errors), whereas in the application layer where no one will notice. There was Reliable Transfer Session Element (RTSE) (X.228), a transport protocol, pretending to be an application protocol. This was even found in Wireless Access Protocol (WAP) 1.0!

have connections. How else could you charge for usage? In particular, both groups saw the interface provided at the layer boundary as being very different for the two. Below the transport layer, existing network architectures kept the two very distinct, if they even considered both.

Fairly early in this debate, the moderates thought they saw a resolution by viewing connectionless and connections as simply two extremes on a continuum of a single property: the amount of shared state necessary among the protocol machines. Connectionless is not, as some have contended, no shared state; instead, it is a minimal shared state. However, the two models seemed so radically different that it seemed impossible to find a unified model that was a true synthesis that didn't just push the two techniques together. There seemed to be no way to make them interwork seamlessly. It seemed that there wasn't much of a continuum but more of a dichotomy: There was either very little state (as in IP) or a lot (as in X.25, TCP, and so forth) and few, if any, examples in between. What weren't we seeing?

Finding for a Synthesis: The Easy Part

In all architectures, these were represented as very different services; that is, they presented very different interfaces to the user, by very different mechanisms. Clearly any resolution would have to solve two problems:

1. A unified approach of the service. (The external "black box" view must be the same.)

2. A unified approach to the function, a single mechanism that encompasses both extremes.

The primary characteristic that any unified model would have to have would be that the behavior seen by the user would be the same whether using connectionless or connections (a common interface). As always, a good interface can cover up a multitude of sins, regardless of how successful we are at the second part of the problem. For connectionless communications to be possible, the sender must have some reason to believe that there will be an instance of the protocol associated with the destination address that will understand the message when it is received and some binding to a user of the protocol at the destination so that data can be delivered to someone. Hence, there are procedures that must be performed for this to be the case. This does not entail the exchange of protocol. Both connectionless and connections require some sort of setup. Both require that first, the addresses on which they are willing to communicate be made known. This is done in the enrollment phase. Then, when the user is ready to send or receive data, resources need to be allocated to support the communication, and bindings must be made between an application and a lower-layer protocol machine. The only way to get a common interface would be for both to present the same behavior to the user.

Depending on the traffic characteristics, the operation of the layer can be made more effective and efficient if the layer maintains more shared state information to better control the rate of transmission and to recover from errors. The more of this shared state information maintained, the more connection oriented the communication. To some extent, it becomes a trade-off between putting information in the header of each message (and consuming more bandwidth, but less memory) and associating more state information with the protocol (and consuming more memory but less bandwidth). In any case, managing this shared state occurs entirely among the cooperating protocol state machines and is not visible to the user. Connectionless and connections are functions within the layer. The user of the service has no need to know which mechanisms are used by the protocol machines, only the resulting characteristics seen by the user. The internal behavior of the layer should not be visible outside the black box.

Given that some setup is required, even if PDUs are not generated, implies that a common interface behavior would resemble behavior of the connection interface (that is, create, send/receive, and delete). However, it does not have the sense of creating a "connection," so the common terms *connect* and *establish* seems wrong. A more neutral concept that truly leaves the decision of the mechanism internal to the layer is needed. Let's go back to the roots of networking to look for analogs in operating systems to find an appropriate abstraction of the operation we are performing. The user is requesting the service below to "allocate" communication resources, just as one requests an operating system to allocate resources (and bandwidth is just the first derivative of memory). *Allocate*, however, does not imply whether there is a *connection*.

What's in a Word?
Words make a difference. They affect how we think about something. The terms chosen to describe a concept are a crucial part of any model. The right concepts with terms that give the wrong connotation can make a problem much more difficult. The right terms can make it much easier. Adopting the mindset of the terms may allow you to see things you might not otherwise see.

Thinking in terms of allocate makes clear what probably should have been clear all the time: The layer should decide whether it uses a connection, not the user of the layer. The user should not be choosing how resources should be provided, but what characteristics the resources should have.[10] The user should be requesting communication resources with certain characteristics: bandwidth,

---

10   This is at odds with the current fad that the user should be able to control the mechanisms in the network. This is not unlike old arguments for assembly language because more control was needed than the compiler allowed. It is even less true here.

delay, error rate, and so on. It is the layer's task to determine how it should satisfy the request, given the characteristics from its supporting service and all other requests. How it is done is of no concern to the user. Working from the concept of allocate, it becomes apparent that the choice is a trade-off between static and dynamic allocation of resources; we are throwing away a ladder:

> *The more deterministic (less variance), the more connection-like*
> *and static the resource allocation;*
> *The less deterministic (greater variance), the more connectionless and*
> *dynamic the resource allocation.*

This fits our experience. As traffic becomes denser (that is, nearly constant), connections are more effective. When traffic is more stochastic, connectionless makes more sense. As one moves down in the layers and/or in from the periphery toward the backbone, one would expect traffic to shift from being less dense to more dense and, therefore, from being more connectionless in nature to more connection-like. To insist that either connectionless or connections is best in all circumstances is foolish.

Generally, connections are associated with greater reliability, but reliability is a separate consideration. The reliability of a communication is only one aspect of the characteristics associated with connections. Simply requiring more than best effort is not necessarily a reason to choose a connection. The choice to be made within the (N)-layer depends on the difference between what is requested by the (N+1)-layer and what is provided by the (N–1)-layer. It is quite possible to have a very reliable (N–1)-layer, and so the (N)-layer might use a connectionless mechanism when high reliability is requested by the (N+1)-layer. Or the (N+1)-layer might have requested ordering, and the (N–1)-layer was highly reliable but did not provide ordering. So, the (N)-layer would need a weak form of connection to satisfy the allocation requested. Reliability is not always the deciding factor, but traffic density is.

Connectionless and connection oriented are a characterization of functions chosen depending on the traffic characteristics and the QoS desired. They are not themselves traffic characteristics or QoS or anything that the user needs to be aware of. They are mechanisms that may be used to provide specific traffic characteristics. Every communication must be enrolled and must request an allocation of resources and only then may it send and receive data.

Now we need to address the second part of the problem: finding a model that unifies the function of connectionless and connection. This is a much harder problem. Solving the first one was relatively easy. We essentially created a rug to sweep the mess under. Now we have to deal with the mess! However, we'll need to put this off until after we have worked out more of the structure of protocols.

The Types of Mechanisms

A protocol mechanism is a function of specific elements of PCI (fields) and the state variables of the PM that yields changes to the state variables and one or more PDUs. These elements of PCI are conveyed to the peer PM(s) by one or more PDUs to maintain the consistency of the shared state for that mechanism. As we have seen, some mechanisms may use the same elements. (For example, sequence numbers are used both for ordering and lost and duplicate detection.) But is there more to say about the types of mechanisms in protocols?

To investigate the structure of protocols and the effect of separating mechanism and policy, I did a gedanken experiment in the early 1990s. In the 1970s, we had developed a standard outline based on the finite state machine (FSM) model for informal prose specifications of protocols. For each PDU type, the conditions for generating it and the action upon receipt are described. Carefully following the outline proved to be quite effective. For the experiment, the outline was extended to accommodate adding a new mechanism to a protocol (see Appendix A, "Outline for Gedanken Experiment on Separating Mechanism and Policy"). Then, in strict accordance with the outline, the mechanisms of a typical transport protocol were specified. Some of the results of this experiment were discussed in Chapter 2, "Protocol Elements." Looking at the result, one finds that the fields of the PCI associated with the mechanisms naturally cleave into two groups:

- Tightly bound fields, those that must be associated with the user-data (for instance, the Transfer PDU)

- Loosely bound fields, those for which it is not necessary that the fields be associated with the user-data

For example, tightly bound fields are those associated with sequence numbers for ordering, or the CRC for detecting data corruption that must be part of the PCI of the Transfer PDU. Loosely bound fields are associated with synchronization, flow control, or acknowledgments may be, but do not have to be, associated with the Transfer PDU. A protocol may have one PDU type, with all PCI carried in every PDU (as with TCP), or more than one (as with XNS, TP4, SCTP, or X.25).

Therefore, we can define the following:

- A tightly coupled mechanism is one that is a function of only tightly bound fields.

- A loosely bound mechanism is a function of at least one loosely bound field.

How Many PDUs in a Protocol?

One of the major (and much argued about) decisions to be made in the design of a protocol is the number and format of the PDUs. We know that there must be at least one PDU to carry the user's data, which we will call the Transfer PDU,[11] but how many others should there be? Beyond the considerations discussed in the preceding section, there would seem to be no architectural requirements that would require multiple types of PDUs. There are engineering constraints that would argue in specific environments for or against one or more PDU types to minimize the bandwidth overhead or processing.

An oft-quoted design principle recommends that control and data be separated. The natural bifurcation noted previously would seem to reinforce this design principle. Because a PDU is equivalent to a procedure call or an operator on an object, associating more and more functionality with a single PDU (and the Transfer PDU is generally the target because it is the only one that has to be there) is "overloading the operator." TCP is a good example of this approach. Minimizing the functionality of the Transfer PDU also minimizes overhead when some functionality is not used.[12] However, there is nothing in the structure of protocols that would seem to require this to be the case.

For data transfer protocols, the minimum number of PDU types is one, and the maximum number would seem to be on the $O(m+1)$ PDU types—that is, one Transfer PDU plus m PDU types, one for each loosely bound mechanism—although undoubtedly, some standards committee could define a protocol that exceeds all of these bounds). For most asymmetric protocols, the maximum may be on the $O(2m)$, because most functions will consist of a Request and a Response PDU. In symmetric protocols, the "request" often either does not have an explicit response or is its own response. Hence, there are $O(m)$ PDU types.

Good design principles favor not overloading operators. It would follow then that there should be a PDU type per loosely coupled mechanism. Separate PDU types simplify and facilitate asynchronous and parallel processing of the protocol. (This was not a consideration with TCP, which in 1974 assumed that serial processing was the only possibility.) Multiple PDU types also provide greater flexibility in the use of the protocol. Loosely coupled mechanisms can be added to a protocol so that they are backward compatible. (For a protocol with one

---

11 The names of PDUs are generally verbs indicating the action associated with them, such as Connect, Ack, Set, Get, etc. Keeping with this convention, we will use Transfer PDU, completely aware that in many protocols it is called the Data PDU.

12 Overloading the Transfer PDU but making the elements optional may minimize the impact on bandwidth but increases both the amount of PCI and the processing overhead when they are.

A Closer Consideration of the Number of PDUs in a Protocol

There were two major arguments for a single PDU format in TCP: 1) ease of processing and 2) piggybacking acks. Piggybacking acks reduce the bandwidth overhead over the life of the connection. This is a classic engineering trade-off, whether to incur a little more overhead in some packets for less overhead overall (global efficiency of the connection) or have more smaller packets (local efficiency, but) with perhaps more overhead over all. In any protocol, each packet type will have several common PCI elements, X, that must be present (addresses/socket-ids, opcode, and so on). With multiple packet types, for our purposes, let's assume a Transfer PDU, T, and an Ack PDU, A, and then a protocol with different types of PDUs will have to generate XT and XA PDUs, in contrast with a protocol with one packet type, which will generate XAT, potentially a savings of X bytes.

In the 1970s, measurement of network traffic found that piggybacking acks would reduce overhead by 30% to 40%. To under- stand why, consider that the vast majority of Net traffic in the 1970s was Telnet connections between terminals to remote hosts with the minority traffic being FTP for file and mail transfers. The most prevalent system on the Net was the BBN Tenex. Tenex insisted on character-at-a-time echoing over the Net. This generated many very small packets: The Telnet user would send a one-character packet with a one-character echo from the server, both which had to be ack'ed. The length of an input string averaged about 20 characters (each one ack'ed) with an average of a 40-character output string, which would be in one message with one ack.

A quick back-of-the-envelope calculation will show that if T is 1 byte (character at a time), and X is bigger, at least 8 bytes (2 socket-ids, an opcode, and probably a couple of other things), and A is 4. This alone accounts for a 35% savings in the character echoing and the "efficient" response in one message. File transfers and such and Telnet connections that used local echo would not see this gain as much because there was more data in the packets and fewer acks were required. This traffic would bring the overall improvement down to the 20% to 30% range that was observed. There was considerable overhead per character sent and piggybacking acks provided a significant savings. Because each PDU required two address fields, simply concatenating a Transfer and Ack PDU (that is, XTXA) still incurred considerable overhead.

However, today's network traffic is not dominated by Tenex Telnet sessions. Even if we assume Request/Response pairs averaging 20 and 40 bytes, this reduces the advantage to roughly 10%. If Request/Response pairs are 100 bytes, the advantage is reduced to roughly 1%. So the advantage of piggybacking acks quickly becomes negligible. Given that Internet traffic data shows significant modes at 40 bytes (syns and acks with no data), 576 bytes (default maximum unfragmented size) and 1500 (Ethernet frames) would seem to imply that piggybacking is not as advantageous today as it was in 1974.

There is also little advantage to a single header format. The opcode of the multiple PDUs is replaced by control bits. Each control bit must be inspected in every PDU even if the state of the PM would indicate that some bits should not be set. This creates more processing overhead rather than less. The solution as proposed in several papers on code optimization of TCP is to treat the control bits as an opcode! If one looks at the implementation optimizations proposed for TCP in these papers (Clark et al., 1989), one finds that they fall into two categories:

1. They are equally applicable to any protocol, or

2. They make the single-format PDU protocol (for instance, TCP) more closely emulate a protocol with multiple PDU format (for example, TP4).

But even this leaves considerable discretion to the protocol designer. For example, are acknowledgment and negative acknowledgment separate mechanisms or the same mechanism that differ only in a single bit? Are data-based flow control and rate-based flow control different mechanisms or the same mechanism only differing in the units used for credit? Probably not worth worrying about. What PDU types will be generated most often by the traffic seen in the network?

PDU type, adding a mechanism will generally require changing the one PDU format.) Similarly, a mechanism can be made optional by simply using a policy that never causes the PDUs to be generated. (For a protocol with a single PDU type, the PCI elements must be sent whether they are used, or a more complex encoding is required to indicate whether the elements are present.) With multiple PDU types no overhead is necessary to indicate a PDU absence. From this it would seem that more rather than fewer PDU types would generally be preferred.

Does this and the discussion in the sidebar mean that protocols should always have more than one PDU type? Not necessarily. This is not a case of right or wrong, true or false. The choices made are based on the requirements of the operating environment. As we have seen, TCP was designed for an environment with a very large proportion of very small PDUs. Clearly, the choice was correct; it saved 30% to 40% in bandwidth. In an environment that does not have a lot of small PDUs, and especially one with a large range of traffic characteristics, optimization for small PDU size loses its weight while the need for greater flexibility gains weight, indicating that under different conditions a different solution might be more appropriate.

Contrary to the often knee-jerk response to these decisions, the choice of a mechanism is not right or wrong but a case of appropriate boundary conditions. It is important to remember the conditions under which these sorts of choices are appropriate. Although it might seem unlikely that network requirements will ever return to the conditions of remote character echoing, history does have a way or repeating itself, although usually in a somewhat different form.[13]

The Types of Protocols

If we consider the list of mechanisms in Chapter 2, several patterns begin to emerge. First, there are mechanisms that might appear in any protocol, such as delimiting, allocation, policy negotiation, data-corruption detection, and so on. The other pattern that seems to emerge is the similarity in transport protocols and data link protocols. They both are primarily concerned with end-to-end error and flow control. It is just that the "ends" are in different places; they have different scopes. Similarly, network and MAC protocols are similar in that they primarily deal with relaying and multiplexing. But also, in the relaying and

---

[13] Which is what makes the topologist's vision defect so useful. These vision-impaired architects are able to recognize when this new doughnut looks like that old coffee cup!

multiplexing protocols, policy is always imposed by the sender; and in the error- and flow-control protocols policy is always imposed by the receiver: They are *feedback* mechanisms.

The distinction of loosely coupled and tightly coupled shared state is more definitive, not tied to qualitative ideas of more versus less or loose versus tight or hard versus soft shared state or the effects of lost state, but to an observable property: the presence of feedback. The tightly coupled protocols have feedback mechanisms; the protocols with more loosely coupled shared state have no feedback mechanisms. The operation of protocols with no feedback is less effected by inconsistent state than protocols with feedback. Thus, the distinction between flow and connection that has been found useful in finding a middle ground in the connection/connectionless controversy characterizes the presence or absence of feedback in a protocol. Connections include feedback mechanisms; associations and flows do not. Similarly, the more robust three-way handshake allocation mechanism is required for protocols with feedback (a two-way handshake for protocols with no feedback).

The astute reader will also have noticed one other pattern: These two types of protocols tend to alternate in architectures. The MAC layer does relaying and multiplexing, the data link layer does "end-to-end" error control; the network layer relays, the transport layer does end-to-end error control; mail protocols relay, hmm no end-to-end error control and sometimes mail is lost. We will consider this in greater detail in Chapter 6, "Divining Layers," but for now we can make two observations:

1. Relaying always creates the opportunity for PDUs to be lost. Therefore, to guarantee reliability, there must always be an error-control protocol on top of a relaying protocol.

2. This would seem to indicate that there are really only three fundamental types of protocols:

   - **Two data transfer protocols:** Relaying and multiplexing protocols and error- and flow-control protocols with different policies

   - **Application protocols**

To avoid repeating cumbersome phrases, error- and flow-control protocols will be often referred to as error-control protocols, and relaying and multiplexing protocols as relaying protocols. Keep in mind, however, that the other aspect is always there.

Policies will be chosen to optimize the performance based on their position in the architecture. Protocols nearer the application will have policies suited to the requirements of the application. Because there are many applications over these protocols, we can expect them to use a wider variety of policies. Protocols nearer to the media will be dominated by the characteristics of the media. Since these protocols have less scope and are specific to a specific media, we can expect them to use a smaller range of policies. Protocols in between will be primarily concerned with resource-allocation issues. Combining this with our observations about connection and connectionless, we can expect more connection-oriented protocols as we move toward the core and more connectionless protocols toward the edge.

The functions of multiplexing, routing, and relaying provide numerous opportunities for errors to occur. Analysis and experience has shown that relaying (that is, hop-by-hop protocols) can never be absolutely error free and that an error-control protocol operating with the same scope as the relaying layer is required to ensure error-free operation between a source and a destination. This was the great X.25 versus transport protocol debate of the mid-1970s and early 1980s.

This alternating of protocols is seen in traditional best-effort networks: The data link protocol provides "end-to-end" error control for relaying by physical or MAC protocols. The transport protocol provides "end-to-end" error control for relaying by the network protocols; one often resorts to "end-to-end" methods to ensure that relaying mail has been successful and so forth. This separation is seldom completely clean in existing protocols. In fact, we even see protocols designed with multiple roles in the same protocol.

Although there is nothing inherently wrong with two adjoining error-control protocols or two adjoining relaying protocols, there are strong arguments against such configurations. Two adjoining error-control protocols is fairly pointless because the scope of the two layers must be the same. (There has been no relaying that would increase the scope.) Unless the first protocol is relatively weak, there should be no errors missed by the first one that will not be detected or corrected by the second. This is essentially doing the same work twice. If there are such errors, the second protocol should be used in place of the first. In a legacy network, however, it might not be possible to do anything about the existence or absence of the first protocol, in which case the second protocol may be necessary to achieve the desired QoS. This is probably the only instance in which one should find two adjoining error-control protocols. Therefore, we should conclude that the two kinds of protocols should alternate in the architecture, and if they don't, it is probably an accident of history.

The fundamental nature of relaying protocols is to be always treading on the edge of congestion, and PDUs are lost when congestion cannot be avoided. Two adjoining relaying protocols would tend to compound the errors, thereby decreasing the NoS of the second relaying protocol and thus impacting the QoS, and the performance, that an eventual error-control protocol could achieve. In addition, two adjoining relaying protocols will usually (but not always) imply that the (N+1)-protocol has wider scope than the (N)-protocol.

It is generally prudent (more efficient, less costly, and so on) to recover from any errors in a layer with less scope, rather than propagating the errors to an (N+1)-protocol with a wider scope and then attempting to recover the errors. If the probability of the relaying protocol introducing errors is low, an intervening error-control protocol may be omitted. For example, Ethernet LANs and related technologies are generally deemed sufficiently reliable that no "end-to-end" error control is necessary. For a wireless environment, however, the opposite could be the case. By the same token, the error-control protocol does not have to be perfect but only provide enough reliability to make end-to-end error control cost-effective. For example, the data link layer might tolerate an error rate somewhat less than the loss rate due to congestion at the layer above. However, these sorts of decisions should be based on measurements of the live network rather than on the hype of marketing or the conviction of the designers.

An application protocol can operate over any data transfer protocol. An application protocol can have direct communication only with systems within the scope of the next-lower layer. However, an application protocol operating over a relaying protocol will be less reliable than one operating over an error-control protocol with the same scope (for example, mail).

Relaying and error-control protocols have been embedded into applications. The examples are legions of people arguing that the overhead of a transport protocol is just too great for their application. But then, they are inexorably drawn through successive revisions, fixing problems found with the actual operation of their application until they have replicated all the functionality of a transport protocol but none of its efficiency because their application was not designed for it from the beginning. We have already alluded to the relaying protocol that is part of a mail protocol such as *Simple Mail Transfer Protocol* (SMTP). This application could easily be partitioned into a relaying protocol that did not

Why We Can't Design the Perfect Transport Protocol

There has been much discussion and many proposals for new and "better" transport protocols over the years to replace TCP—none with very much success. There was always some major category of traffic that the proposal did not handle well. On the other hand, we have been fairly successful with new data link protocols.

The separation of mechanism and policy makes the reason for this clear. Transport protocols are intended to support the requirements of their applications. There are roughly six or eight mechanisms in a transport protocol. By not separating mechanism and policy, we have (unintentionally) been saying that we expect to find a single point in an eight-dimensional space that satisfies all the requirements. When put this way, this is clearly absurd! There are no panaceas, but there is a lot of commonality! If we separate mechanism from policy, the problem can be solved.

Why was there more success with data link protocols? Data link protocols are tailored to address the requirements of a particular physical medium. Hence, their performance range is narrower. Thus, a single set of policies will satisfy the problem.

differ much from those found below it and the actual mail application. The traditional checkpoint-recovery mechanism found in many file transfer protocols is an error-control protocol. Less obvious is the traditional *Online Transaction Processing* (OLTP) protocols, which involve a two-phase commit. OLTP can also be implemented as a form of data transfer protocol with different policies.

The effect of separating mechanism and policy is to separate the invariances (the mechanisms) in the structure of the protocols from the variances (the policies). From this we see that there seems to be fundamentally two kinds of data transfer protocols: a relaying protocol and an error-control protocol. The major differences in the examples of the two sets are the differences in syntax and the requirement for fields of different lengths. At low bandwidth, large sequence numbers add too much overhead to the PCI and are unnecessary. At very high bandwidth, even longer sequence numbers might be required.

This seems to be a rather minor difference. Can we make it an invariant, too? A self-describing syntax (that is, tag-length-value) would incur too much overhead for protocols operating in performance-sensitive environments. In any case, such flexibility is not required at execution time in data transfer protocols. One could have the "same protocol" (that is, procedures) but a small number (three or four) of different PCI formats. These PCI formats would be very similar, only the lengths of the PCI elements would be somewhat different; and for data transfer protocols, the only fields that might vary are those related to addresses, sequencing, and flow control. It should be possible to define the protocols such that they are invariant with respect to syntax. (Addresses are just used for table lookups, and sequence numbers only differ in the modulus of the arithmetic.) Greater commonality in protocol behavior could have a beneficial effect on network engineering.

So, there actually are only two data transfer protocols described in terms of a single abstract syntax with a few concrete syntaxes. The only question is the degree to which various media-specific characteristics and other "bells and whistles" are necessary or whether they are part of some other functions?

The Architecture of Data Transfer PMs

A PM consists of actions associated with inputs, either from PDUs, from local timeouts and system calls for buffer management, or from the upper or lower interfaces whose sequencing is controlled by a state machine. The distinction in the types of mechanisms and protocols allows us to say more about the architectural structure of the protocol machines for data transfer protocols. Actions are divided between mechanism and policy. Further, the patterns, which we have seen in the mechanisms, are not just a nice taxonomy but have implications for implementation. Clearly, some mechanisms must be done before others. For example, the CRC must be done before anything else in the PDU is looked at, lost and duplicate detection must be done before retransmission control, and so on. For now, let's ignore the normal engineering constraints and the constraints of serial processors and consider the amount of asynchrony inherent in a data transfer protocol. Let's follow the pattern we have seen of loosely coupled and tightly coupled mechanisms.

If we separate loosely bound mechanisms to the right and tightly bound mechanisms to the left (see Figure 3-5), a much more interesting thing happens. The left side consists of the processing of the Transfer PDU and consists only of fragmentation/reassembly, ordering, and queuing. The right side handles allocation, flow control, and acknowledgments. CRC checking and delimiting is done in common to all PDUs. The left side has little or no policy associated with it, other than whether simple ordering is on or off. The connection-id (or port-ids) select the state vector. All operations are simple operations based on the sequence number and SDU delimiters and the queuing of the PDUs. The right side is all policy. The right side maintains the state vector and executes the policies for retransmission control (that is, acking and flow control). The right side requires general-purpose calculations; the left side requires much less general computation, just straightforward queuing and ordering algorithms. Others have noted a similar dichotomy but ascribed it to merely an artifact of certain implementation-specific considerations. Here we see that it underlies a much more fundamental structural property of protocols.

But what is striking is that the two sides are not at all tightly coupled! In fact, they are virtually independent. The only effect the right side has on the left is to start and stop queues and infrequently discard one or more PDUs from a queue, and it probably isn't too particular which ones. Furthermore, we have made no assumptions about the protocol other than to assume the mechanisms it should contain. The design implied by this diagram supports either an in-band or out-of-band design simply by mapping the left and right side to the same or different output queues. It also allows retransmission (acks) and flow control to be completely asynchronous from the data transfer. Protocol processing has generally been seen as serial in nature (for instance, TCP); an implementation along these lines exhibits a high degree of parallelism. This approach could be pipelined and would seem to indicate significant improvements in protocol performance. This is not the place to consider this in detail, but it should be mentioned that security mechanisms fit nicely into this architecture, too.

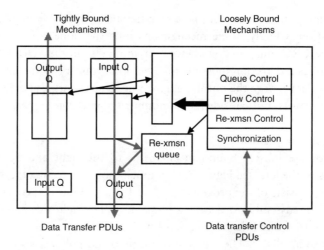

Figure 3-5   Error- and flow-control protocols naturally cleave into a data transfer part with only tightly bound mechanisms and a control part with only loosely bound mechanisms.

Clearly, the optimal protocol design to take advantage of this would have separate PDUs for the loosely coupled mechanisms, which would be processed by the right side and a Transfer PDU that was processed by the left side. This would maximize the parallelism in the processing and the parallelism in the interactions with the remote PM. (This is not a hard requirement. This approach could be used with a protocol that did not have separate PDUs, but more complex hardware would be required to duplicate headers and route them. One would be making the mistake that OSI made of allowing desire to go against the grain of the problem, its nature. Nature generally gets its retribution.)

As we have seen in the past, there has been a school of thought that tried to minimize the number of PDU types. This was based on assumptions unique to software and hardware constraints and traffic characteristics of the mid-1970s. A single PDU type simplified processing and allowed acks to be piggybacked with the return traffic. These conditions are no longer relevant. This additional overhead just to carry a 16- or 32-bit sequence number was rightfully considered excessive. From the principles we have developed here, we can see that there is no multiplexing in an error-control protocol, so such overhead is virtually nonexistent, and the other conditions that held then no longer exist. If the loosely coupled mechanisms are implemented with separate PDUs, they become degenerate cases. If the policies for them are null, these PDUs are simply never sent. There needs be no explicit action to not accommodate them.

This also begs the question as to whether this is one protocol or two. Protocols with only tightly bound mechanisms need only a two-way handshake. Such a protocol would have the left side of Figure 3-5 and only state initialization on the right. Protocols with loosely bound mechanisms would use a three-way handshake and have more functionality on the right side of Figure 3-5 for the bookkeeping to maintain shared state. Even more intriguing is the fact that if one looks at the format of the Transfer PDU with just tightly bound mechanisms, one finds that it bears a strong resemblance to UDP-like protocols. The only difference being whether the "message-id" field is interpreted as a sequence number. This raises the possibility of a single protocol structure accommodating the entire range from pure connectionless to full connection by merely changing policy.

Finding a Synthesis: The Hard Part

Earlier in this chapter, we considered the problem of finding a synthesis of the *connection/connectionless* (co/cl) schism that has plagued networking from its beginnings. We identified that there were two parts of the problem: a common interface model and a common functional model.

We need both to accommodate co/cl as degenerate cases. For the service/interface model, we abstracted the problem into a resource-allocation model and required the user to specify the parameters of the communication being requested so that the choice is inside the black box. The first part was relatively easy to solve. (Sweeping a problem under the rug always is.) Now we must look at the more difficult problem: finding a common model for the function of connection and connectionless.

Generally, the difference between co/cl has been characterized by the amount of shared state and degree of consistency (that is, how tightly coupled the state is required to be for correct operation). In this view, co/cl are extremes along a continuum from less state loosely coupled to more state tightly coupled. If this is the case, there should be other operating points along the continuum.

Analysis of this problem begins quite early with Belnes's analysis (1976) of the requirements to deliver a single message reliably. He concludes that a five-way exchange will reliably deliver a single message even if either host resets. The four-way exchange will suffice as long as neither host fails. This gives some idea of the amount of shared state required for reliable delivery. Watson (1981) developed a timer-based approach to a transport protocol based on the rather ingenious perspective that all connections exist and have existed for all time. We maintain state information about them in a cache only when they are active. The exchange of PDUs merely serves to refresh the cache, and when activity ceases for some time, we no longer keep the cached information on the exchange. This yields a very robust and simple approach to a transport protocol. But all of these techniques are concerned with creating the reliable delivery of data over an unreliable network. Watson is able to prove that the timers in delta-t are both necessary and sufficient. Watson's delta-t protocol warrants far more attention than it has received.

Lamport et al. (1982) analysis of the Byzantine Generals problem somewhat confuses the issue with an unfortunate analogy that proves an interesting puzzle. For networking, the result of this analysis is that within a single protocol operating over an unreliable media, it is impossible to determine whether the last message arrived at its destination. This is not the same thing as saying that the generals can't know whether an ack was received, or perhaps more precisely it does if the generals fail to construct a proper communication architecture.

This is a beads-on-a-string view of the problem predicated on overloading the semantics of the acknowledgment so that it acts both to acknowledge the conversation of the generals and to acknowledge the delivery of messages. In a properly layered architecture with explicit establishment and release at both the application and transport layers, the generals can know the state their conversation terminated, although it is not possible to know whether their reliable communication channel terminated correctly. Here, the general's last message is not the last message sent. In other words, we can't know whether the transport connection terminated correctly, but we can know whether the application layer protocol terminated correctly. After that is done, we don't care whether the transport connection terminates correctly. Note that with a protocol like Watson's delta-t with no explicit establishment and release this won't be the case. However, if the connection/release discipline is followed by the application layers, the generals can know whether they reached agreement and whether the application connection terminated correctly. They still won't know whether the last message (a disconnect ack of some sort) arrived.

Spector (1982) considers the same problem as Belnes from a somewhat different perspective. Rather than consider whether an exchange is reliable and under what conditions it is not, Spector considers the problem from the other end, so to speak: Given a particular exchange, what can we say about whether an operation took place? Spector considers the perspective of request/response PDUs for client/server applications (just becoming popular then) and considers the semantics of the reliability of a remote operation performed in the presence of lost messages (but not duplicates):

- "Maybe," a single PDU with no response

- "At least once," a simple request response (that is, two-way handshake)

- "Only once," a three-way handshake, which has two subtypes depending on failure cases

Clark (1988) characterizes the shared state problem in more qualitative terms of soft versus hard state and whether failures are subject to "fate-sharing." Clark contrasts replicating state with fate-sharing. The abstraction he is contrasting is the hop-by-hop nature of X.25 with the end-to-end error control of TCP, TP4, or delta-t. Today, we would compare the TCP/IP approach with ATM or MPLS. The X.25 protocols are definitely more complex, but the reason is somewhat counterintuitive. Although Clark's point is fundamentally correct, this comparison is significantly different from the case Spector was considering or the case below that applies Clark's soft state concept to signaling protocols. But to see it, let's first consider later attempts to formalize the soft state concept.

While intuitively appealing, the soft state idea has resisted formalism until recent attempts: (Raman and McCanne, 1999; Ping et al., 2003; and others). But here again, the gradations of shared state are found in application protocols (for example, signaling and peer-to-peer (sic) protocols, not so much in data transfer protocols). Ping et al. describe five cases of decreasing "softness" between pure soft state and hard state. A careful look at them in comparison with what we have already looked at is helpful but that the results here assume that the only operation being performed is "replacement," not any operation that depends on the previous state (that is, increment or decrement):

1. The first case is *pure soft-state* (ss), which is described as a sender sending a trigger PDU to a receiver. The sender sets a timer and refreshes the state whenever the timer expires by sending the current value of the state information in a new trigger PDU. The receiver records the content of the trigger PDU when it arrives and sets its own timer, which is reset whenever a new message arrives. If the receiver's timer expires, it deletes the state.

This characterization is a weak form of Spector's maybe case with Watson's view of connections. (We are assuming that "trigger" and "request" are roughly equivalent, although recognizing not entirely equivalent.) The receiver may not receive any of the sender's PDUs. Also, Ping distinguishes a

Getting the Proper Perspective

We have made the point that it is always important to view things from the point of view of the "organism," not the observer (a lesson I learned from Heinz von Forester, a pioneer in cybernetics). He often illustrated the point with a story to show the fallacy in B. F. Skinner's theory of conditioned response.

Heinz would begin his story with that twinkle in his eye in his Viennese accent: "We are going to teach an urn!" At this point, the student is thinking, an urn? A vase? What does he think he is doing? "We put an equal number of red and white balls in the urn," Heinz would continue. "We are going to teach the urn to only give us red balls. To teach the urn, we reach in and pull out a ball. If it is a white ball, we *punish* the urn and throw it away. If it is a red ball, we *reward* the urn and put it back. Eventually, the urn learns to only give us red balls!"

Clearly, the reward/punishment is in the eye of the observer, not the organism, the urn. These false distinctions turn up often. It is important to keep a clear perspective about to whom distinctions are important. This is often the source of significant simplifications.

"false removal" of state when the receiver's timer expires before a new trigger PDU arrives. This constitutes looking at the system from the point of view of an omniscient observer (see the sidebar), rather than strictly from the point of view of the participants. How does the observer know the intent of the sender? Perhaps, the trigger is late because recent events at the sender caused the sender to change state from "stop sending" to "more to send." Essentially the sender had intended to let the state expire and then did otherwise. (Anthropomorphizing state machines is dangerous.) How does the sender even know that the state is being discarded? Does it care? Whether state is kept or discarded by the receiver has no effect on the sender. From the sender's or receiver's point of view, there is no such thing as "false removal." This is dangerous reasoning. The action of protocol machines cannot be based on what is surmised to have happened elsewhere, but only on the inputs it sees. No assumptions can or should be made about what generated those inputs.

2. The second case is soft state with explicit removal (ss+er), which is described as the first case with an explicit ER PDU sent by the receiver when its timer expires, and the state is deleted telling the sender that the state has been removed. This gives us a weak form of "at least once." If the ER is received, the sender will know that at least one of its trigger PDU was received, but it does not know which one, and there is no indication in the problem state that it matters to the sender. Note that the ER PDU is only useful from the point of view of the observer, not the sender. The sender need not take any action whatsoever. If the sender did not intend the state to be deleted, the next trigger timeout will rectify the situation with no explicit action by the sender in response to the ER. If it did intend the state to be deleted, and it was, there is nothing the sender needs to do.[14] This is a case of not recognizing a degenerate case and, worse, turning it into a special case. The semantics of the ER is as an "indeterminate ack" or that "at least one trigger PDU arrived." There is no indication in the problem specification that this affects the state of the sender. From Watson's point of view, the ER as explicit removal is redundant because a connection/flow is never terminated; the receiver just ceases maintaining cache space for it. Once again, we see distinctions that are in the eye of the observer, not the organism.

---

[14] It is easy to see that any timeout value for the ER is going to arrive at a time less than the normal update period. Because the ER is not an ack, it must be sent after more than one trigger is missed, and therefore we can conclude that missing more than one trigger is not critical to the system. If it is, the sender should have had a higher update rate to begin with.

3. The third case is soft state with reliable trigger (and explicit removal) (ss+rt), which is defined by the receiver sending an ack to each trigger. The sender starts a retransmission timer when the trigger PDU is sent. (We assume this is the only reliability mechanism, that there are no lower layer functions providing reliability.) If it expires with no ack being received, it retransmits the same trigger PDU. State removal is explicit, as in the second case. This corresponds to either a strong form of the "at least once" case or a weak form of Spector's "only once," depending on whether one takes a glass half-full or half-empty view. If an ER PDU is received and there is an ack outstanding, the sender will not know whether its last trigger PDU was received. Ping et al. are unclear, but it does appear that if an ack is not received by the time the trigger timer expires, a new trigger PDU is sent regardless. (This follows from our assumption that replacement is the only operation.) This would imply that the old ack is no longer relevant and the sender is now waiting for the ack from the new trigger PDU. This could persist so that the sender never receives an ack or an ER. Similarly, if the ER is lost, the sender will not know that the state has been deleted, but then it doesn't affect the sender at all.

4. The fourth case is soft state with reliable trigger/removal (ss+rtr), which is defined as using "reliable messages to handle not only state setup/update but also state removal" (italics in original). Ignoring the fact that Ping et al. do not make clear how the explicit removal is made reliable without running afoul of the Byzantine generals problem, this is the same as the previous case—because, as we have seen, the only information the ER adds to the semantics is the knowledge that at least one trigger was received, and there is no indication that the sender needs this information.

5. The fifth case is hard state (hs), which is defined as using reliable PDUs to set up, update, and remove state, but it is not stated how they are made reliable. Ping et al. state that "neither refresh messages nor soft-state time-out removal mechanisms are employed," and go on to say that a significant problem with hard state is the removal of orphaned state and reliance on an external signal to remove it.

   The authors do not make it clear, but generally hard state has been applied to protocols such as TCP or delta-t. It is unclear here whether we are considering this class of protocols as some impractical straw man with no timers. The problem of orphaned state arises directly from the requirement that both the sender and receiver know that they have terminated normally. It is the Byzantine generals problem that ensures that this cannot be the case. In the case constructed by Ping et al., that both sender and receiver know that a common point in the conversation was reached was not a requirement.

So to some extent, we are comparing apples and oranges. This class of hard state protocols does (where it matters) use timers and uses them to eliminate orphaned state. In the case of delta-t, however, orphaned state cannot occur by definition. The primary characteristic of hard state protocols is that the operations of some mechanisms are such that if the state of the sender and receiver are inconsistent, the protocol will deadlock. Hard state protocols have the mechanisms to avoid these conditions, increasing their complexity. It is the degree of consistency and amount of shared state necessary to avoid these conditions that makes them hard state protocols.

As we can see over the years, the emphasis of this issue has shifted from the shared state of data transfer protocols[15] to the shared state for client/server applications to signaling protocols and more generally to what are essentially distributed databases, largely following the popular topics of the time. To some extent, this also parallels our increasing understanding of where the crux of the problem lies. As we have seen, the results from Ping et al. reduce to variations on Spector's cases as seen through Watson. These results are consistent with our findings here. For a data transfer protocol, there are basically three cases: a pure connectionless protocol (maybe), a protocol with only tightly coupled mechanisms providing feed forward requires only a two-way handshake for synchronization, and a protocol with loosely coupled mechanisms providing feedback (at least once) and requiring a three-way handshake for synchronization (only once). Three points don't make much of a continuum.

In addition to the lack of points on a continuum, the shared state approach also doesn't address the hop-by-hop versus end-to-end aspect of the issue. In the traditional connection solutions, resource management is done on a hop-by-hop basis. Connectionless has always been associated with a "best-effort" service with a greater degree of "quality" provided end to end by a higher-layer protocol. However, as connectionless networks have grown and their use broadened, this has presented problems. As the range of applications has grown (mainly over past decade or so), the perceived need for levels of services other than "best effort" have also grown. While overprovisioning has generally been seen as a solution for this collection of issues, it is realized that this is not a long-term solution, nor is it always available. The conundrum for those of us who prefer the flexibility and resiliency of the connectionless model has been that any

---

[15] I say data transfer protocols here because with X.25 we are comparing error control at the data link layer and resource allocation and flow control at X.25 Layer 3, with resource allocation of IP at Layer 3, and TCP error and flow control at Layer 4.

attempt to address these issues has led directly to a connection-like solution. One or the other, no synthesis. However, this has not led to the conclusion that the connection model was right after all. The connection-oriented solutions have suffered from the classic problems of static resource allocation, tended to not perform much better if not worse than the connectionless ones, and have encountered complexity and scaling problems. And yes, in all honesty, we must admit there has been a bit of ego involved in not wanting to admit connectionless might not be the answer.

But even among the calmer minds, there has been a sense that there is something we have missed. The intensity of the networking Thirty Years War has tended to push us to one extreme or the other. If one were in the debates at any time over the past 30 years, one could see that the fear of not knowing where a compromise would lead kept compromises from being explored and reinforced the combatants into their trenches. From looking at the proposals, that certainly seems to be what has transpired. All of this and only the three points on our continuum is perhaps an indication that the "degree of shared state" is a red herring, or at least not an approach that will yield the synthesis we were looking for. But perhaps the preceding observation will give us an opening.

What is most interesting is to return to Clark's characterization that the problem with hard state is that "because of the distributed nature of the replication, algorithms to ensure robust replication are themselves difficult to build, and few networks with distributed state information provide any sort of protection against failure." X.25 provides error control on links with a variation of HDLC, LAPB. HDLC, as we saw, does "end-to-end" error control; the ends are just closer together. The replication is primarily associated with resource allocation and flow control. Given what we have just seen with Ping et al. analysis of signaling protocols, one begins to realize that it is not possible to compare just the data transfer protocols. The different approaches to data transfer protocols tend to include functions that the other assumes are elsewhere or vice versa. This is an apples and oranges comparison.[16] One must include the signaling or "control plane" aspects in the analysis, too. We need to look at the whole problem.

When we do this, something quite remarkable begins to emerge: The connection-oriented approach is actually trying to minimize the amount of shared state. Its fragility derives (as Clark alludes to) from its inability to respond to failure. If a link or node along a virtual circuit breaks, the nodes participating in the virtual circuit don't have sufficient information to take action. They don't have *enough* state information. *It is brittle because when it breaks, no one knows what to do.* The connectionless approach avoids this in a somewhat

---

[16] I have to admit I dislike this terminology because it is so heavily associated with the beads-on-a-string model.

counterintuitive manner: It distributes everything to everyone. Everyone knows everything about the routing of any PDU. And each PDU contains all the information necessary for any system to handle it.

In a very real sense, connectionless is *maximal* shared state, not minimal. (Hey, I was as surprised as you are!) The interesting difference is that by widely disseminating the information, the complexity (hardness) of the protocols required is reduced. The connection-oriented approach is forced to hard state protocols because it tries to minimize the information in each PDU and in each node in the virtual circuit, centralizing routing and resource-allocation functions elsewhere as much as possible. This forces the use of much more complex mechanisms to maintain consistency. Whereas connectionless puts as much information in the routers and the PDUs as possible, thereby being less affected by failures. From a historical perspective, this is also consistent. The connection-oriented PTT advocates were from an older, more Malthusian tradition that believed that everything must be used sparingly and tried to minimize resources in favor of increased (deterministic) complexity, whereas the connectionless advocates derived from a younger tradition of plenty where memory was cheap and getting cheaper, and they were more comfortable with stochastic processes that might consume more resources but were simpler and had better overall characteristics.

The concept of shared state has always included both the amount of state and the degree of the coupling. An idea of how inconsistent the shared state could be for some period of time, always hard to quantify. Initially, our focus had been on just the data transfer protocols, but the properties we saw there were more affected by the routing and resource-allocation functions of the layer than we cared to admit. We weren't looking at the whole problem. Once we do, it is apparent that connection-oriented protocols are trading off complexity to minimize resources (state) but making the system more brittle in the process, while connectionless protocols disseminate information (state) widely in favor of simpler more resilient characteristics.[17] Because everyone has been given sufficient information for routing to know what to do with any PDU, and because every PDU contains the necessary information for anyone who sees it to act on it, the loss of state by any one system has minimal impact. Consistency is still a concern. But we extend considerable effort on routing protocols to ensure that Routing Information Bases become consistent quickly. (Perhaps the dumb network "ain't so dumb" after all!) In a sense, we have orthogonal axis; connec-

---

[17] If there were a means to quantify "degree of coupling/complexity" with amount of shared state, I suspect we would find that, looked at from this perspective, there is not much difference in the total "shared state," although there is a difference in the characteristics of the result.

tionless represents maximal state in terms of space, while connections are maximal state in time.

The connectionless approach focuses entirely on routing and ignores the resource-allocation problem, whereas the connection-oriented approach centralizes routing (that is, forces it to the edge) and concentrates on resource allocation along the path.

So, how does this insight contribute to our desire to find a unifying theory that integrates connection and connectionless? We would like to be able to support flows with different characteristics (QoS) while retaining the flexibility and resiliency of connectionless. We have also noted that the proper place for connections is when traffic density is higher (more deterministic) and for connectionless when it is lower (more stochastic). We distribute connectivity information to everyone, but we have always insisted on only distributing resource-allocation information along the path. No wonder our attempts at providing QoS always turn out looking like connections; we are doing what they do! We were able to break with the past and not think that routing had to be associated with a path, but we didn't do it when it came to allocating resources! We need to treat resource allocation just as we treat routing: as distributed.[18]

Going back to the "other" characterization of the difference between co/cl: In connectionless, the processing of each PDU is independent of the processing of other PDUs in the same flow. With connections, the processing of each PDU in a flow is determined by the processing of the previous PDUs. Or to turn it inside out, with connection-oriented resource allocation, information (including routing) is only stored with nodes on the path of the connection; whereas with connectionless resource allocation, information is stored with every node. Let's consider *this* to be our continuum? The probability that this PDU is processed precisely like the last PDU in this flow varies between 0 and 1.

For routing, each router computes where it should forward a PDU based on information from other routers it receives. Let's take a similar approach with flows. Based on information from other routers, each router computes the probability it will be on the path for this flow and if so what resources should it "allocate." An aspect of the exchange might include an indication of the sender's intent to spread the resources over several paths.

This leads to a model where flows are spread across different paths and resources are allocated on the basis of the probability of their use. If we assume that there are m paths between A and B, a connection is represented by one path having the probability 1 of being used. For example, there might be 5 paths between two points with probabilities: 0, .2, .6, .2, and 0. Pure connectionless is

---

[18] Our attempts at QoS reflect this dichotomy. We have tried the connection approach ATM, MPLS, InfServ (RFC 1633, 1994), and so on, and the pure connectionless approach, DiffServ (RFC 2430,1998). RSVP (RFC 2205,1997) is essentially connection establishment for IP.

represented by each path being equally likely or 1/n. Distributions may be anything in between. The question is what resources should be allocated for these probabilities given the desired QoS. This reorients the problem to one of distributed resource allocation, not flow reservation. We have considered the problem as one of allocating flows, not allocating distributed resources.

Each node has resources to allocate. Each initiator of a flow requests distributed resources based on the QoS parameters of the request. Each member of the layer can then compute the probability that it is on the path and allocate resources accordingly. This gives us a model for doing quite a bit more than just integrating connection and connectionless under a single model. In a sense, this model extends Watson's "particle physics" model of connections. That is, all connections always exist; we just don't cache state for them, unless resources are allocated for them. Here we view flows as a probability distribution, or we might characterize a flow as smeared across several paths. Routers allocate resources based on the probability that they will receive PDUs for a flow. This allows routers to reserve resources to better respond to failures during the transients while resource-allocation information is updated in response to a failure.

This is not a "major breakthrough," nor is it intended to be. We were looking for a unifying model of connection and connectionless. This one seems to hold promise, and it is the only one we have found that does. This will give us a tool to aid our thinking. How does thinking in terms of this model change how we look at the problem? However, as interesting as it might be, this is not the place to pursue it. We need to continue our journey before we have all the machinery necessary to apply this approach to solving this problem. Although we can't say as yet whether this approach is tractable, we can certainly note that it does integrate connectionless and connection. In fact, one of the appealing aspects of this model is that it seemingly makes the distinction between connections and connectionless meaningless (although far from proof, this is definitely one of the trademarks of a "right" answer), similar to when a solution turns out to solve problems other than the one it was intended for.

Conclusions

In this chapter, we have found that separating mechanism and policy uncovered some interesting patterns in the structure of protocols and revealed that the plethora of data transfer protocols we have today actually have more similarity than differences. The data transfer protocols seem to divide into two kinds: relaying and multiplexing protocols and error- and flow-control protocols. We have found that the range of error- and flow-control protocols, from the weak UDP-like to the strong TCP- or delta-t-like protocols, can be simply accommodated by a single structure. We have also looked at the Thirty Years War over connections versus connectionless. We have been able to characterize the proper role of each and have made some surprising insights into the difference between connectionless and connections and made great strides in finding a synthesis that avoids the damaging schism they have caused in the past. But, we have gone about as far as we can looking at individual protocols. We need to consider the structures that result from assembling protocols with different scope. But before we can do that, we need to collect some more data to have a good understanding of the landscape. The next two chapters review the state of our knowledge of the "upper layers" and of addressing.

Chapter 4

Stalking the Upper-Layer Architecture

You have Telnet and FTP. What else do you need?

—Alex McKenzie, 1975

If the Virtual Terminal is in the presentation layer, where is the power supply?

—Al Reska, 1979

Introduction

Although there has been a strong interest in "the upper layers" over the years, as these quotes indicate, there have been differing misconceptions about them. Since the earliest days of the Net, the upper layers have been a bit mysterious and unclear. The early network software removed concerns of reliability and routing from the applications. And with only a couple of dozen hosts connected by what seemed high-speed lines, one had the illusion of having an environment for distributed computing. All of this sparked the imaginations of those involved to the possibilities as it continues to do today. It seemed that rather than merely an amorphous collection of applications, there ought to be some general structure for organizing upper-layer functions, as there was for the lower layers.

The lower layers had succumbed to organization much more quickly, at least on the surface. By 1975, it was fairly common to hear people talk about transport, network, data link, and physical layers. It wasn't until later that things got sufficiently complex that the rough edges of *that* model began to show. Even then, however, those four layers seemed to capture the idea that the lower two layers were media dependent, and the upper (or middle) two were media independent and end to end.

The upper layers (above transport) were a different story. No obvious structuring or decomposition seemed to apply. Part of this was due both to the lack of applications and, in some sense, too many. For some time, the network did seem to be able to get by with just Telnet and FTP (mail was originally part of FTP). To find applications on a host, "well-known sockets" were used as a stopgap measure. (There were only three or four applications, so it wasn't really a big deal). It was recognized early that there was a need for a directory, and there were some proposals for one (Birrell et al., 1982). But beyond that, application protocols were very much "point products." Protocols were unique to the application. There did not seem to be much commonality from which one could create a general structure that was as effective as the one for the lower layers, or that easily accommodated the variety of applications and at the same time provided sufficient advantage to make it worthwhile. Unfortunately, early in the life of the Net, upper-layer development was squelched before the promise could be explored. As we will see, it is this event that most likely contributed most to the arrested development of the Internet and left it the stunted, unfinished demo we have today.

The OSI work made a stab at the problem and for a while looked like it was making progress. But although they were able to uncover elements of a general structure, that architecture suffered from early architectural missteps that made application designs cumbersome and from overgenerality that required complex implementations for even simple applications, but mainly it was the internal divisions that killed OSI.

Over the past few years, there has been an opportunity to consider what was learned from these experiences and what they tell us about the nature of the upper layers. Consequently, a much better understanding has surfaced based on a broad experience not only with a variety of applications, but also recognition of similarities between the upper and lower layers. It is now much clearer how the lower layers differ from the upper layers, what the uppers layers do and do not do, how many layers there are, and what goes where. This chapter attempts to bring together these disparate results and put them in a consistent framework. Are all the problems solved? Far from it, but having such a framework will provide a much clearer picture of how we can go forward and will allow new results to be put into a context that makes them more useful. Upper-layer naming and addressing will be considered in the next chapter; here we are concerned with working out the structure. What we are interested in is understanding the relation of "networking" to "applications" or to distributed applications. Networking is not "everything" and cannot be considered to include all of distributed computing. We need to understand how and where one leaves off and the other starts and the relation of the two. We are not so much interested in being encyclopedic as considering what we have uncovered about "the upper layers" that is both right and wrong.

A Bit of History

The Upper Layer(s) of the ARPANET

It would be difficult to claim that the members of the early Network Working Group started with an idea of upper-layer architecture. Their focus was on building a network. Applications were primarily there to show that it worked! The group had its hands full with much more basic problems: How do you do anything useful with a widely different set of computer architectures? How do you connect systems to something that they were never intended to be connected to? (You made it look like a tape drive.) How do you get fairly complex network software into already resource tight systems? Just implementing the protocols was a major effort for any group. The early ARPANET had much more diversity in the systems connected to it than we see today. Just in the hardware, there were systems with all sorts of word lengths (16, 18, 24, 32, 48, 64, etc.) and at least two varieties of 36-bit words. There were at least a dozen different operating systems with widely disparate models for I/O, processes, file systems, protection, and so forth.[1] Or at least, they seemed to be very different. If there was an architectural direction, it was to provide over the Net access to each of these systems as if you were a local user. (Or as close as 56Kb lines would allow; and 50Kb seemed vast when most remote access was 110 or 300bps!). Furthermore, some of these systems were very tightly constrained on resources. The big number cruncher on the Net was an IBM 360/91, with an outrageous amount of memory: 4MB! (And the operating system was huge! It occupied half!) The general attitude was that an operating system ought to fit in a system with 16KB and still have plenty of room to do useful work. The primary purpose of these early applications was to make the hosts on the Net available for remote use. Thus, the first applications were fairly obvious: terminal

---

[1] Today, all these systems would be classed as "mainframes." But as one would expect, there were different distinctions then: A few machines were mainframes; number crunchers, systems to submit big batch computation jobs to. Some were timesharing systems whose users specialized in an area of research, in essence precursors to networked workstations. Some were access systems, dedicated to supporting users but provided no computation services themselves; they were early minicomputers. All of them would now fit in a corner of a cell phone.

access, transfer files, and submit jobs for execution. But once it worked (and it worked well), our imaginations ran the gamut of what could be done with a resource-sharing network. But from all of these problems and these initial applications came some very important architectural results in the design of application protocols that still serve us well today, and as one would expect there were also a few missteps along the way.

Early Elegance: Telnet, FTP, and RJE

The early NWG concentrated on three basic upper-layer protocols: a terminal protocol, a file transfer protocol, and a remote job entry protocol. Let's consider each one in turn.

Telnet was the first virtual terminal protocol. The first Telnet was sufficient to demonstrate that the network was usable; but because it reflected so many of the terminal characteristics to the user, it was less than a satisfactory solution. The NWG met in late 1972 and drafted the "new" Telnet.[2] The experience with getting Telnet wrong the first time paid off. With the experience gained from the first attempt, the NWG had a better understanding of what a terminal protocol needed to do and the problems Telnet needed to solve and how to do it effectively. Most important, Telnet was not a remote login application, but a terminal-driver protocol. Remote login is an application built using Telnet (again taking the operating system perspective). The new Telnet protocol had several attributes that are unfortunately still rare in the design of protocols.

The designers of Telnet realized that it was not simply a protocol for connecting hosts to terminals, but it could also be used as a character-oriented IPC mechanism between distributed processes: in essence, middleware. In particular, it could be used (and was) to connect two applications that had been written to interact with humans. Telnet defined a canonical representation of a basic terminal, the *network virtual terminal* (NVT). The NVT (Figure 4-1) defined a rudimentary scroll-mode terminal with very few attributes.[3] The model for a Telnet connection consists of two NVTs connected back to back: The "keyboard" of one is connected to the "screen" of the other and vice versa. The Telnet protocol operates between the two NVTs. The terminal system and the host system convert their local representation into the NVT representation and convert the output of the NVT to their local representation.

---

[2] At this point, calling it "new Telnet" is a bit like calling the *Pont Neuf* the New Bridge.

[3] There was an incredibly wide variety of terminals (probably more than 50) on the market at the time running the gamut from electric typewriters printing on paper, to displays that mimicked the paper printers, to fairly complex storage terminals that handled forms and could display text with bold or reverse video. The NVT did only the simplest of these, although options were created for more complex ones.

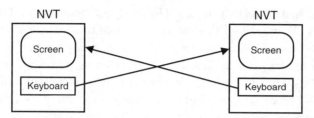

Figure 4-1 The Telnet NVT model.

Telnet defined an innovative symmetrical negotiation mechanism that allowed a request by one to be the response to the other. The mechanism is used by the two users to select and enhance the characteristics of the NVT, such as character echoing, turn off half duplex, message size, line width, tab stops, logout, and so on. The negotiation is structured so that when the connection is established each side announces what it intends to do or not do (by sending the commands WILL/WONT followed by the appropriate Telnet options) and what it intends the other side to do or not do (DO/DONT). The options were encoded such that an implementation that did not understand an option could refuse it without having to "understand" it; that is, just send a WON'T *x*. Each side's announcement becomes a response to the other side. If there is no conflict, one side will announce DO *x*, and the other will announce WILL *x* (the WILL becoming a response to the DO and vice versa). If a conflict occurs, each option defines a scheme for resolution. Telnet is one of the very few symmetrical application protocols. Notice that although the protocol is symmetrical, what is being negotiated is asymmetrical. Different systems did or required different functions. The Telnet negotiation gave them an elegant means to attempt to offload some functions if possible and still get done what was needed.

While of little interest today, the handling of half-duplex terminals shows the subtlety and elegance of Telnet. At the time, terminals that could not send and receive at the same time (that is, half duplex) were still common, in particular IBM terminals such as the 2741, a computer-driven Selectrix typewriter. Consequently, they had to be accommodated, even though most understood that full-duplex operation was displacing them and were much simpler to handle. Most protocol designers took the idea of "turning the line around" literally and assumed that

Why Telnet Is Important?

Most textbooks no longer cover Telnet (undoubtedly because they deem remote terminal support a thing of the past). This is precisely what is wrong with today's networking textbooks. The reason for covering Telnet is not because it provides remote terminal support, but because it teaches lessons in understanding networking problems.

Telnet takes a problem that everyone else saw as asymmetrical (terminal-host) and found an elegant symmetrical solution. That solution made Telnet much more useful than mere terminal support. Telnet also finds an elegant solution to a classic "oil and water" problem (the handling of half/full duplex) that makes both degenerate cases of a more general solution.

We consider Telnet because these concepts are important in the education of network designers (the goal of a university education), even though they might not be for the training of network technicians.

the protocol had to be half duplex. However, the designers of Telnet showed more insight. They realized that the protocol had to manage only the *interface* between the protocol and the remote user as half duplex; the *protocol* could operate full duplex. Hence, Telnet sends indications (Go Aheads) so that the receiver knows when to "turn the line around" (that is, tell the half-duplex terminal it could send). This allowed an application to simply send the indication regardless of whether the other side was full or half duplex, and the receiver either used it or ignored it. Half duplex was subsumed as a *degenerate* case and did not greatly distort the structure of the protocol (as it did with many others). Take, for example, the OSI Session Protocol, which made the protocol half duplex and made full duplex an extended service. Consequently, the minimal Session Protocol requires more functionality than one that uses the full-duplex *option*. Half-duplex terminals could use full-duplex hosts and vice versa. Neither really had to be aware of the other, and the application did not have to be aware of which was being used. As the use of half-duplex terminals declined, the use of the Go Ahead has quietly disappeared.

If Telnet got anything wrong, it was holding fast to a stream rather than record model.[4] The generally accepted wisdom in operating systems at the time was that the flow of data between processes should be streams. "Records" implied fixed-length records. However, the desire to hold to the accepted wisdom for Telnet meant that every character had to be inspected for the Telnet command characters. Telnet commands are a relatively rare occurrence in the data stream. A little record orientation (that is, putting Telnet commands and terminal data in separate "records") so that every byte did not have to be touched to find the relatively rare Telnet commands would have greatly decreased processing overhead.

But all in all, Telnet is a fabulous success both architecturally and operationally, as indicated by its continued use today. Telnet embodies elegant examples of efficient solutions to problems by making them degenerate cases of a more general model (rather than the more typical approach of simply shoving distinct mechanisms together to solve each case, which eventually leads to unwieldy implementations and to designs that are difficult to adapt to new uses).

File Transfer Protocol (FTP) was built on Telnet, partly for architectural reasons and partly for pragmatic reasons (Figure 4-2). FTP uses a Telnet connection to send its four-character commands followed usually by a single parameter

---

4   Well, maybe one other. There was a Big Bad Neighbor who insisted that the best way for remote terminals to operate was character-at-a-time transmission and remote echoing by the host across the Net. This proved to be very slow to the users (primarily because of operating system overhead). Although attempts were made to develop a Telnet option to improve efficiency, it never proved workable. But this really isn't an inherent part of the protocol, so it is a footnote.

terminated by CRLF (*carriage return, line feed*). The actual file transfer is done on a separate connection between data transfer processes. The architectural reason (and a good one) to separate the command and data streams is so that commands, especially aborts, do not get stuck behind large file transfers. This connection was generally a fixed offset from the Telnet connection, with one exception, the TIP.

The constraints of the TIPs had a major influence on the nature of FTP. TIPs were a variant of the ARPANET switch (IMP) that had rudimentary host software to connect users' terminals to hosts elsewhere on the Net. Users would open a Telnet connection and would act as the FTP client, typing in the commands directly. Then, using the SOCK (now PORT) command, the user would instruct the remote FTP server to connect to a socket on the TIP to send the file. Because the TIP had no file system, you might be wondering what was the point. Printers and other devices attached to the TIP were hardwired to certain socket numbers. Although this was done on occasion, it was not very popular. Because the TIP software ran as the low-priority task on the IMPs (after message forwarding), it often experienced significant delays.

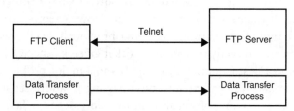

Figure 4-2 The ARPANET FTP model.

FTP defined a rudimentary *network virtual file system* (NVFS) and the basic commands to carry out file transfers and to interrogate a foreign file system. There was such a wide variety in file systems that the NVFS (like the NVT) was restricted to the bare minimum. The main emphasis was on the attributes of the file and saying as little about the nature of the contents as possible. There are basic conventions for the file format (characters, binary, and so on) and for the structure of the file (record or stream). The protocol allowed for checkpoint recovery and third-party transfers.

One Step Forward, Two Back

It is curious that although the original version of FTP (RFC 542) allowed checkpoint recovery and third-party transfers, when FTP was revised for operation with TCP, this capability was removed by what I am told were reactionary factions. An incredulous development to remove useful functionality! We can only hope that these kinds of reactionaries do not continue to put their imprint on an Internet that needs visionaries, not "stick-in-the-muds."

Initially, mail was two commands in FTP. It wasn't until later that it was separated into a distinct protocol (that bears the mark of its origins). Rather than attempt to impose common file system semantics (which would have greatly increased the amount of effort required and the degree of difficulty in implementing it in the existing operating systems), FTP transparently passes the specifics of the host file system to the FTP user. An intelligent method for encoding responses to FTP commands was developed that would allow a program to do an FTP but at the same time provide the ability to give the human user more specific information that might be beneficial to determine what was wrong.

It is hard to say there is anything wrong with FTP per se. One can always suggest things it doesn't do and could, but for what it does, it does it about as well as one could expect, and none of these really break any new architectural ground. More would have been done at the time if it had not been for the constraints on the TIP (there were complaints at the time that the tail was wagging the dog) and schedule pressures to have something to use. (There were small things wrong that illustrate how a temporary kludge can come back to haunt. For example, as noted previously, FTP was kludged to allow TIPs to transfer directly to a specific socket given by the SOCK command. Later, this became a Best Common Practice (!) and a major problem with NATs. The SOCK command was bad architecture; passing IP addresses in an application is equivalent to passing physical memory addresses in a Java program! It was known at the time and should have been removed when the last TIP was removed from the Net.)

Remote Job Entry (Figure 4-3) is an early application protocol that is today obsolete, but in the 1970s submitting a program to run on a remote machine and retrieving the output (usually a printer file) was a major application. This was also the downfall of the early upper-layer architecture. The designers started paying too much attention to architectural elegance and not enough to the users' pragmatic requirements and constraints. It was not hard to see that the job input (yes, the card reader input) and the printer output were files. It was very neat to build FTP on top of Telnet. NETRJE required the ability to send RJE commands and move files. What could be simpler than a Telnet connection for RJE commands and then use FTP to move things around? Simple to describe and easy to implement (if you don't need it). NETRJE put the greatest resource usage where it could least expected to be: the RJE client.

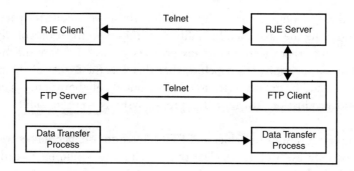

Figure 4-3 The ARPANET RJE model.

Consider a TIP, which did not have the resources to implement an FTP client, but only Telnet. To be a client RJE, a TIP would have to make a Telnet connection to an RJE server, which invoked its FTP client to create a FTP Telnet connection to the FTP server on the RJE client system. The TIP and most potential users of RJE did not have the resources to support an FTP server, which is why they were using RJE in the first place! Therefore, NETRJE never got much if any use. (A competing protocol, which did take into account the realities, did get considerable use. This protocol, CCN RJE [Braden, 1977], first proposed in 1971, puts the load where it belongs. It set up a Telnet connection and then opened data transfer connections for card reader and line printer transfers to sockets, a fixed offset from the Telnet sockets.)

What Was Learned

First and foremost, the upper-layer development of the ARPANET (Figure 4-4), as rudimentary as it was, proved that applications could be built and could be useful. Very useful. Technically, we gained valuable experience with distributed systems. We learned the difficulty of dealing with the subtle differences in the semantics that different systems had for what appeared very similar concepts. We even found some elegant solutions to some sticky problems that could serve as examples going forward. We learned the necessity of striking a balance between overspecifying and keeping it useful. And we learned not to get carried away with elegance: Our triangulation of Clauswitz and Mao struck home. But we also realized that we had chosen to solve specific problems. Although we had a good start, we did not yet understand the fundamental nature of the upper layers. What structure did a resource-sharing network require?

With these accomplishments came much enthusiasm among the people developing and using the early Net. In addition, to these specific protocols that everyone was using, there were numerous projects going on that went far beyond these three applications. To conclude that this was the extent of the use of the early Net would be grossly inaccurate. Distributed collaboration, hypertext systems, and production distributed database systems were all built during this period.

As implementations of Telnet and FTP came into use, people became excited at the possibilities. And it was clear that much more would be needed to make the Net a viable network utility. A group of interested parties formed a Users Interest Group (USING) to develop the necessary protocols. The group began to look at a common command language, a network editor, common charging protocols (not for the network but for using the hosts), an enhanced FTP, a graphics protocol, and so on. This group had an initial meeting in late 1973 to get organized, and a first major meeting in early 1974. However, ARPA became alarmed that this group would essentially wrest control of the network from them and terminated all funding for the work. (Hafner et al., 1996). ARPA would have benefited much more by harnessing that energy. Actually, ARPA had already, in a sense, lost control of the direction of the Net (short of shutting it down). The wide use of the Net might have come much sooner had ARPA encouraged, not squelched, the initiative the users showed.

Rerunning History

Of course, you can't do it. But, it is interesting to conjecture what might have happened had ARPA pursued development of the upper layers? Clearly, the direction USING had laid out to explore new applications should have been pursued. This was a major area, which had hardly been considered; there seemed many application protocols that could be useful. Given the capabilities of the systems, that direction most likely would have led toward something like a Novell NetOS environment. But the advent of the Web raises questions whether that path would have created or inhibited an environment conducive to the explosive growth of the Web and the immense benefits it has brought. (Although, a less explosive spread might have been had some benefits, too, a little less exuberance might have been wise.) It is easy

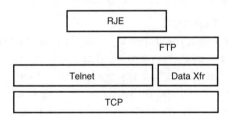

Figure 4-4 The ARPANET upper-layer architecture.

Upper-layer developments in the ARPANET halted for two decades. All subsequent developments have addressed specific protocols and have not considered how they relate to each other, what common elements there might be, or how it could be a distributed resource-sharing utility as early papers described it.

The early ARPANET upper-layer protocols made a greater contribution to our understanding of the design of protocols than to the architecture of the upper layers. But that was to be expected, given that it was a first attempt. There was only so much that

continues

could be done. Developing distributed applications was not the primary rationale of the project anyway. Unfortunately, the innovations in these early protocols were often promptly forgotten by future work: the importance of separating control and data, or the fact that terminal protocols could be symmetrical and more useful, was never utilized by any other protocol, and I suspect never realized by their designers. For example, the early OSI VTP was symmetrical, because of Telnet, but the U.S. delegates from DEC pushed it into a much more cumbersome asymmetrical design in line with their product.

The use of the canonical form (for example, the NVT) was a major innovation both theoretically and practically. It is the tip of the iceberg to understanding of key elements of the theory of application protocols. This was the so-called "n^2 problem." Potentially, hosts would have to support $O(n^2)$ translations from each kind of system to every other kind of system. On the other hand, to define a model that was the least common denominator would have been so limiting as to be essentially useless. A middle ground was taken of defining a canonical (abstract) model of the elements that were to be transferred or remotely manipulated (in this case, terminal or file system elements). For Telnet, this was NVT and for FTP, an NVFS. The definition of Telnet is strongly tied to the behavior of the NVT. Although the definition of FTP refers to its canonical model less frequently, it is no less strongly tied to the model of a logical file system. The concept was that each system would translate operations from its local terminal or file system in its local representation into the canonical model for transfer over the network while the receiving system would translate the protocol operations from the canonical model into operations on the local representation in its system. This reduced an $O(n^2)$ problem to a $O(n)$ problem. Of course, it also has the advantage that each system only has to implement one transformation from its internal form to the canonical form. It also has the benefit that new systems with a different architecture don't impact existing systems.

There are two unique characteristics to this approach that differed from other attempts. First, the model was taken to be a composite of the capabilities, not the least common denominator. Although there was no attempt to replicate every capability of the terminal or file systems represented in the network, useful capabilities that either were native capabilities or capabilities that could be reasonably simulated were included. Even with this approach, the wide variation in operating systems made it difficult to define every nuance of each operation to ensure proper translation.

continued

to see how a NetOS environment could lead to self-contained islands. On the other hand, by not pursuing upper-layer development, ARPA removed the driver that would have required richer lower-layer facilities, greater security, finishing naming and addressing, a much earlier impetus to provide QoS, and so on. This might have avoided many of the current problems of spam, virus attacks, mobility, scaling, etc. that plague today's Net). Without new applications as a driver, the only impetus the Internet had was to do what was necessary to stay ahead of growth, which through the remaining 1970s and early 1980s was relatively moderate. And most of that pressure was relieved by Moore's law. As discussed later, this turns out to be the critical juncture in the development of the Internet that allowed it to remain an unfinished demo for 25 years and is now the crux of our current crisis.

Translation is the operative word here. Contrary to many approaches, the implementation strategy was not to implement, for example, the NVFS on the host as a distinct subsystem and move files between the local file system and the NVFS (such approaches were tried and found cumbersome and inefficient) but to translate the protocol commands into operations on the local file system and the files from the canonical file format to the local file format. The least common denominator approach was avoided by the simple recognition that there did not have to be a 1:1 mapping between operations on the logical object and the local representation but that the operation in the world of the model might translate into multiple operations in the local environment. In addition and perhaps most significantly, it was also found that the process of creating the abstract model for the canonical form uncovered new understanding of the concepts involved.

The ARPANET application protocols required the use of a single canonical form. One of the widespread complaints about this approach was requiring like systems to do two translations they didn't need, along with the assumption that it is more likely that like systems would be doing more exchanges with each other than unlike systems. Accommodating this requirement, along with a desire to regularize the use of the canonical form, led directly to the syntax concepts incorporated into the OSI presentation layer. However, by the time OSI began to attack the problem, the problem had changed.

In the beginning, computers never "talked" to each other; and when they began to, they talked only to their own kind. So, when the ARPANET began making different kinds talk to each other, a lot of kinds had to be accommodated. As one would expect, over time the amount of variability has decreased; not only are there fewer kinds, but also systems tended to incorporate the canonical model as a subset of their system. Also, new network applications were created that had not existed on systems, so its form becomes the local form. Consequently, the emphasis shifted from canonical models to specifying syntax.

A Rose Is a Rose Is a Rose

This was further complicated by the fact that at that point everyone knew their system very well, but knew little of the others, and the systems often used the same terms for very different concepts. This led to considerable confusion and many debates for which the ARPANET and the IETF are now famous. This also made writing clear and unambiguous specifications for application protocols difficult. Even when we thought we had (for example, Telnet, 1973), we were often brought up short when a new group would join the Net and come up with an entirely different view of what the specification said. OSI tried to solve this with FDTs, which are daunting to many developers; the Internet, by requiring two implementations, tends to inhibit innovation.

Does this mean that the canonical model is no longer needed? We can expect other situations to arise where applications are developed either to be vendor specific or to be industry specific (groups of users in the same industry) in relative isolation that will later find a need to exchange information. The canonical form can be used to solve the problem. Today for example, the canonical model is used to create the *Management Information Bases* (MIBs) or object models for these applications or for interworking instant messaging models.

The ARPANET experience showed that there is some advantage to getting it wrong the first time. The first Telnet protocol was not at all satisfactory, and everyone believed it had to be replaced. But the experience led to a much better design where the conflicting mechanisms were accommodated not by simply putting in both (as standards committees are wont to do) but by creating a synthesis that allowed both to meet their needs without interfering with the capability of the other.

But it has to be very wrong. When FTP was completed in 1973, there was a general feeling that the problem was much better understood and now it would be possible to "get it right." However, it wasn't wrong enough, and it never went through the major revision, although some minor revisions added commands to manipulate directories, and so on.[5]

(While this is an example of the tried–and–true rule of thumb, that you "always have to throw the first one away," this may also be a consequence of "we build what we measure." Unlike other disciplines where the engineering starts with a scientific basis, we have to "build one" in order to have something to measure so that we can do the science to determine how we should have built it. No wonder we throw the first one away so often!)

With the early termination of research on applications in 1974, the early developments were limited to the bare-minimum applications. With the impetus removed to develop new applications that would push the bounds of the network, new insights were few and far between. Perhaps one of the strongest negative lessons from this early upper-layers work was that elegance can be carried too far. RJE using FTP and FTP and RJE using in Telnet led to an impractical solution. We will defer our consideration of applications in the Internet now (more or less keeping to the chronology), and shift our attention to OSI to see what it learned about the upper layers and then return to the Internet to pick up later developments there and see what all of this tells us about the fundamental structure of networks.

---

[5] It is painful to see kludges we put into FTP to accommodate constraints at the time now touted as "best practice."

The OSI Attempt or "Green Side Up"[6]

Session, Presentation, and Application

Beginning in 1978, OSI was the first of the standards groups intent on getting something out quickly and the first to learn that with a widely diverse set of interests that it could be difficult, if not impossible, to achieve agreement. At the first meeting in March 1978, the group adopted an architecture developed by Charles Bachman, then of Honeywell, that had seven layers. At that time, the characteristics of the protocols for the lower four layers were well-established. Although there was uncertainty about what went in session, presentation, and application (see Figure 4-5), the seven layers in the Honeywell model seemed to make a reasonable working model. It was clear there would be many application protocols. But for the time being, the terminal, file, mail, and RJE protocols formed the basis of the work. What parts of these protocols, if any, went into the session and presentation layers? Or did they all belong in the application layer? And, did other functions belong in session and presentation? For the next three years or so, considerable debate continued, attempting to work out the upper-layer architecture. The upper layers were pretty much a clean slate.

As with everything else in OSI, there was no consensus on the upper layers, and the disagreement was along the same lines as in the lower layers: the PTTs versus the computer industry. The European PTTs had two point products they wanted operating under the OSI name. And it didn't matter to them whether accommodating them left a path open for future applications. They were a monopoly. Customers had to buy whatever they offered. The computer industry, on the other hand, realized that the upper layers had to lay a foundation for everything to come. So as the computer industry faction began to try to make sense of the upper layers, the European PTTs inserted themselves into defining the session layer. They had been developing protocols for two new services to run over X.25: teletex and videotex. Teletex was billed as e-mail. It was actually telex with some memory and rudimentary editing capability, a far cry from the e-mail protocols

Speeding Up Standards

OSI intent on getting things done quickly! I know. Many will find this hard to believe, but it is the case. There has been a lot of talk about speeding up the standards process. From years of participating and watching the standards process, it is clear that the vast majority of the time is consumed by people becoming familiar and comfortable with unfamiliar ideas. There is little, if anything, that can speed up such a process. Building consensus simply takes time; and the greater the diversity of interests and the more people involved, the longer it takes. Rushing a consensus or trying to force a particular answer usually destroys the result (for example, SNMPv2). There are no shortcuts. When IEEE 802 started, they were going to produce Ethernet standards in six months; it took three years. The ATM Forum has a similar history. The IETF is a classic example. When it

continues

---

6   The punch line of a politically incorrect ethnic joke from at least the 1970s, possibly before. (I know of a tree nursery company that used the name). The joke is about some guys (insert politically incorrect ethnicity of your choice) laying sod and the foreman having to constantly remind them, "Green side up." The reader can fill in the rest.

that had been ubiquitous in the ARPANET and other research networks for almost a decade.[7] Videotex was more sophisticated: a terminal-based information system with rudimentary graphics capability. Although hypertext had been around for over ten years at that time, it was not widely available. Videotex was targeted at what could be done with the technology of the early 1980s.

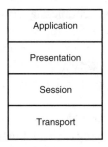

Figure 4-5 The OSI upper-layer architecture.

The PTTs, jumping on the OSI bandwagon of the early 1980s, wanted the teletex and videotex protocols (which were already designed and being built) to be OSI. OSI was just beginning to determine what the upper layers should be. The PTTs basically laid out their protocols and drew lines at various places: This small sliver is the transport layer; here is session layer, there is really no presentation, and the rest is the application layer. These were intended to run over X.25. Throughout the late 1970s and early 1980s, the PTTs argued in every forum they could find that transport protocols were unnecessary. However, OSI was coming down hard on the side of the debate that said X.25 was not end-to-end reliable and a transport protocol was necessary. The PTTs insisted X.25 was reliable. So, Class 0 Transport was proposed by the PTTs so that they would have a transport layer that didn't do anything. And then, when they got to the application layer and

---

[7] The PTTs have consistently proposed initiatives [videotex, teletex, ISDN, ATM, WAP, and so on] whose market window, if it exists at all, passes before they can create the standard, build the equipment, and deploy it. The sale of these is a credit to their marketing departments or the desperation of their customers.

continued

was reasonably small and its population fairly homogeneous and academic, it developed a reputation for doing things quickly. Now that it has a more diverse participation, it is taking longer than any other standards group has ever taken. (For example, IPv6 has taken 12 years for a small change.) The IETF's participation is still less diverse than OSI's was. It appears that other factors are contributing to the lengthy development time.

If We Build It, They Must Come.

The fundamental market strategy of a PTT. But in this case they didn't. People will not pay to get advertising. The primary, and perhaps only, successful example is the French Minitel. France Telecom justified giving away the terminals with phone service with the argument that between the costs saved in printing and distributing phone directories annually and the revenue from advertisers and information services, such as booking airlines or trains, more than covered the cost. As with the Web, pornography was the first to make money from videotex. However, giving away the terminals makes it hard to justify upgrading the hardware. The French PTT failed to see that technology would change much faster than phone companies were accustom. Although, the design was resurrected in the 1990s and called WAP.

thought no one was looking, they stuck in RTSE to provide end-to-end reliability and said they were doing checkpointing for mail. It was really quite amusing how many pundits and experts bought the argument.

The functions proposed for the session layer that fell out of this exercise were various dialog control and synchronization primitives. There was a strong debate against this. Most people had assumed that the session layer would establish sessions and have something to do with login, security, and associated functions. This came soon after the competing efforts were made a joint ISO/CCITT project. There was considerable pressure to demonstrate cooperation with the PTTs, even if it was wrong. So, the Europeans block voted for the PTT proposal.[8] (So, the OSI session layer was stolen by the PTTs and had nothing to do with creating sessions—something that took many textbook authors a long time to figure out.)

Meanwhile, the Upper-Layer Architecture group had continued to try to sort out what the upper layers were all about. It was fairly Stoic about what had happened with the session layer. Most believed that even if the functions were not in the *best* place, it was close enough for engineering purposes (an argument we hear often in the IETF these days). The session functions were needed, and when presentation and application were better understood, a way could be found to make the outcome of the session layer less egregious. (As it would turn out, the problems it causes are too fundamental, but this does serve a valuable lesson about compromising technical veracity to commercial interests.)

Early on (and almost jokingly), it had been noted that in the applications (or in the application layer) PDUs would have no user data. They would have all PCI, all header. In other words, this was where the buck stops. There was nowhere else to forward user-data. Or more formally, the PDUs contained only information (that which is understood by the protocol interpreting the PDU) and had no user data (that which is not understood by the process interpreting the PDU) for a higher layer. We will also find that this distinction still matters even in the application.

Because the upper-layer problem was less constrained than in the lower layers and clearly part of the more esoteric world of distributed computing, a more formal theoretical framework was necessary to understand the relations among the elements of the application layer. For this, they borrowed the idea of conceptual schema from the database world.

---

[8]   Interestingly, AT&T did not side with the other PTTs and argued that the functions being proposed for the session layer did not belong there but belonged higher up.

From this, it was clear that for two applications to exchange information, the applications needed "a shared conceptual schema in their universe of discourse."[9] If the other guy doesn't have a concept of a "chair," it is impossible to talk to him about "chairs" regardless of what language you use. As it turned out, this was a generalization of the concept of the canonical form developed for the ARPANET protocols, but now with greater formalism. The concept comes directly from Wittgenstein's *Tragtatus*. The conceptual schema defines the invariant semantics that must be maintained when translating between systems with different local schemas.

Database Schemas

In the database world, the conceptual schema was the semantic definition of the information, which might be represented by different structures or syntaxes for storage (called the internal schema) and for presentation to a user or program (called the external schema).

Clearly, if the applications had shared conceptual schemas (that is, semantics), the application layer must provide the functions to support the management and manipulation of these semantics. And wherever there are semantics, there must be syntax. So if the application layer handles the semantics, then clearly the presentation layer must handle the syntax! Wow! Now they seemed to be getting somewhere; maybe there was something to these upper three layers! On the other hand, one cannot manipulate semantics without its syntax. Consequently, one finds that the presentation layer can only negotiate the syntax used by the application. Any actual syntax conversions must be done by the application.

So, the common part of the application layer provides addressing and negotiates the semantics to be used, identified by the application context, and the presentation layer negotiates the syntax identified by the presentation context.

Thus, the presentation layer became the functions to negotiate the syntax to be used by the application. It was envisaged that a syntax language would be used to describe the PDUs used by an application. The syntax language was defined as an abstract syntax and a concrete or transfer syntax. The abstract syntax of a protocol refers to the data structure definitions specifying the syntax of the PDUs in a particular syntax language, whereas the concrete syntax refers to a particular bit representations to be generated by that abstract language (Table 4-1). By analogy, the data structure constructs of a language such as C or Pascal correspond to an abstract syntax language. The data structure declarations in a program written in such a language correspond to the abstract syntax of a protocol, while the actual bit representations generated by the complier represents the concrete syntax.

---

[9] There was a heavy contingent of logical positivists in the group. What can I say? At least they weren't French deconstructionists.

Table 4-1 *The Distinction between Abstract and Concrete Syntax Is Similar to the Distinction Between a Programming Language and Its Code Generators*

Programming Language		ASN.1
<integer> ::=INTEGER<identifier>;	**Language Definition**	GeneralizedTime ::= [Universal 24] Implicit VisibleString
INTEGER X;	**Statement Definition**	EventTime ::=Set { [0] IMPLICIT GeneralizedTime Optional
		[1] IMPLICIT LocalTime Optional}
(32-bit word)	**Encoding**	I | L | GeneralizedTime
$012A_{16}$	Value	0203000142_{16}

The presentation protocol provided the means to negotiate the abstract and concrete syntaxes used by an application. Note that presentation only *negotiates* the syntax. It does not do the translation between local and transfer syntax (what the ARPANET called the local and canonical form). OSI realized that such a clean separation between syntax and semantics is not possible. The translation must ensure that the semantics of the canonical model are preserved in the translation. This was referred to as the *presentation context*. Because an application defined its PDU formats in the abstract syntax, an application could use any new concrete syntax just by negotiating it at connection establishment. OSI defined *Abstract Syntax Notation 1* (ASN.1) as the first (and it would appear to be the last) example of such a language. Then it defined the *Basic Encoding Rules* (BER) (ISO 8825-1, 1990) as a concrete encoding. BER was a fully specified encoding of the (type, length, value) form and allowed the flexibility for very general encodings. BER proved to be inefficient in its use of bandwidth and a little too flexible for some applications. With impetus from ICAO, the International Civil Aviation Organization, OSI embarked on two other sets of encoding rules: one to be bandwidth efficient, Packed Encoding Rules (PER), and one to be more processing efficient, Light-Weight Encoding Rules (LWER). PER was done first and archieved both goals. It was 40% to 60% more bandwidth efficient, but surprisingly was roughly 70% more efficient in processing. No need was seen in pursuing LWER, so it was abandoned. Experimentation indicates that PER is about as good in encoding efficiency as is likely, indicated by the fact that data compression has little or no effect on it.

Initially, OSI embarked on developing a number of application protocols, some of which have been alluded to here: OSI variations on Telnet, FTP, and

RJE (JTM, *Job Transfer and Manipulation*). *File Transfer Access Method* (FTAM) and JTM were based on British protocols, and *Virtual Transfer Protocol* (VTP) was based on a combination of proposals by DEC and European researchers. Each had more functionality (to be expected since they came ten years later), but none show any new architectural innovations, including those incorporated in the early ARPANET/Internet protocols, nor were they designed so that initial implementations were inexpensive. The minimal implementation was always fairly large.

Later, OSI developed a number of important areas that the Net had ignored, such as *commitment, concurrency, and recovery* (CCR), a two-phase commit protocol intended as a reusable component; TP (*transaction processing*, which made apparent the limitations of the *upper-layer architecture* [ULA] structure); *Remote Database Access* (RDA); *Remote Procedure Call* (RPC), how to standardize 1 bit; and a directory facility, X.500; and management protocol, *Common Management Information Protocol* (CMIP), which is discussed later. CCITT (ITU-T) also took the lead in developing an e-mail protocol, X.400. The original ARPANET e-mail had been part of FTP and was later extracted into SMTP without major change. Mail was directly exchanged between computers (most were timesharing systems). By the time of the discussions leading up to X.400, most systems were workstations or PCs. Hence, this led to distinguishing servers that received mail on behalf of users: the concepts of message transfer agents and message servers. Initially, X.400 used only the session layer, but as the presentation layer was incorporated, unforeseen problems arose.

For the application layer, OSI recognized that a common connection-establishment mechanism would be required for all applications. One could not expect applications to be "hardwired" to network addresses. Without such a common mechanism, a host would have to be able to interpret all the initial PDUs of all the applications it supported to determine what application to deliver it to.

The common connection-establishment mechanism, *association control service element* (ACSE), provides mechanisms for application layer addressing, application context negotiation, and authentication. Thus, the applications defined by OSI (CCR, TP, file transfer, and so on) in essence only define the behavior of the data transfer phase. ACSE provides the establishment phase.

Well-Known Sockets

The ARPANET had also recognized the requirement for a directory early on, but the need to demonstrate that the network could do useful work outweighed all else, and so well-known sockets were created as a kludge to demonstrate the first few applications. "Doing it right" would have to wait. No one expected that there would be no new applications for 20 years and that we would still be waiting to "do it right." By the early 1980s, well-known sockets were an institution for a new generation, and amazingly enough, one still hears arguments that well-known sockets were an inspired piece of design. A sad commentary on the state of the field.

The other major contribution to the upper layers that OSI did seem to get right was the nature of the application process. At first glance, this looks like a standards committee compromise. Being part of ISO, as OSI began to consider applications, it ran into the problem of what was within OSI and what was the purview of other committees, such as database, programming languages, banking, and so on. While on one hand this was the usual turf battle, on the other it raised a very real question of where networking stopped and other aspects of computing started. This quickly devolved into a very esoteric debate over the nature of distributed applications and whether application processes were inside or outside OSI (that is, the communications environment). After much debate, the solution that was arrived at was that the application process was on the line (see Figure 4-6), yet another standards committee nondecision. But with consideration, one finds that it is not only the right answer, but that it is also a fairly powerful one.[10]

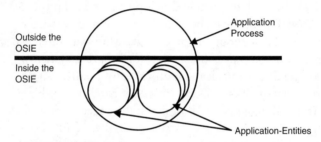

Figure 4-6 An application process consists of one or more application entities, of which there may be multiple instances of each.

What one finds is that it makes much more sense to treat the application protocol(s) as part of the application; or in OSI terms, application entities are part of the application process. If the application protocols are considered distinct entities used by an application, one gets into an infinite regress with respect to the shared state. The parts of the application process, not part of the application entity, are those aspects of the application not involved in communications. The *application process* (AP) consists of one or more *application entities* (AEs), which are instantiations of the application protocols. The application-entities are part of the communications environment (they called it the *OSI environment,* or OSIE) while the rest of the application is not. In other words, the top of the application layer includes the AEs but not the rest of the AP.

---

[10] Who would have thunk!

Consider an example: A hotel reservation application might use HTTP (an application entity) to talk to its user and one or more remote database protocols (different application entities) to actually make the reservations. The application process outside the OSIE moderates the use of these protocols, doing whatever processing is necessary to convert user input to database requests. Clearly, an application process can have not only different kinds of AEs, but also multiple instances of them, and there could be multiple instances of the AP in the same system. Not all applications would have the full complement of instances, but some would. The application naming must allow relating an application and its AEs (and their instances) to ensure that communication is associated with the correct application. This turns out to be a powerful and general model and easily describes and supports the requirements of distributed applications.

This also illustrates where the ARPANET approach of using operating systems as a guide turns out not to be sufficiently rich. From this perspective, we can see that all of our early applications (Telnet, FTP, mail) were special cases: The AE and the AP are essentially synonymous; there is little or no AP functionality distinct from the application protocol, and there is generally one per system. So, naming the application protocol was all that was necessary. It is not until the advent of the Web that there are applications in the Internet where the application and the protocol are not synonymous; that is, there is significant functionality clearly not associated with the application protocol. And there are many applications in the same host using the same protocol. One wants to access cnn.com (the AP), not HTTP (the AE). Relying on the operating system model had been a good first cut, but it was not sufficiently general. Again, we see evidence of the harm done by not pursuing new applications into areas that would have taken us beyond the operating system model. Given the nature of the discussions going on in the ARPANET in 1974, I have every confidence that had new applications been pursued, something equivalent to this model would have evolved. It is interesting to note that this distinction arises primarily when considering "user applications" and less so when considering system applications. We definitely had a systems programmers' perspective. Distinguishing application protocols from the application while at the same time recognizing that naming the application protocol first requires naming the application turns out to be a very powerful insight and has implications far beyond its immediate use in the application layer.

That Which Must Not be Named

Why is there no name for this "other part"? The part of the AP not in any AE. Good question. On the one hand, some member bodies insisted that we not describe or name anything outside the OSIE. This was the turf of other committees, and we shouldn't say anything about it. On the other hand, to not do so is just asking for trouble. To draw the distinction too closely would have some pedants insisting on some formal boundary, whereas good implementation would probably dictate a less-distinct boundary between the AE aspects and the AP aspects or even interactions of AEs. Later we will see that this was well founded.

The other aspect of the OSI application layer isn't so much new as just good software engineering. The OSI approach to application protocols allowed them to be constructed from reusable modules called *application service elements* (ASEs) see Figure 4-7. It was clear that some aspects of application protocols could be reused (for example a checkpoint-recovery mechanism or a two-phase commit scheme). Clearly, some part of the application protocol would be specific to the task at hand. As we have seen, a common ASE was required by all applications to create the application connection, ACSE. There was also a connectionless form of ACSE called A-unit-data that complemented the unit-data standards in the other layers. In OSI, an application protocol consisted of ACSE and one or more ASEs bound together by a *control function* (CF), which moderated the interactions among the ASEs. Because ASEs had inputs and outputs like any other protocol state machine, the CF was just a state machine that controlled the sequencing of their interactions. There is nothing unique about this approach. It is just good software engineering. But it is unfortunate that this approach was not pursued; it might have facilitated uncovering some interesting structures in application protocols.

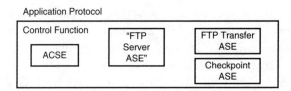

Figure 4-7 OSI application protocols were assembled from modules called application service elements bound together by a control function to moderate interactions among them. All applications protocols used ACSE to set up application connections and for authentication. (There was also a connectionless form of ACSE.)

But as this picture of the upper layers came together in the early 1980s, cracks began to appear in the structure, and as the decade wore on and the applications became more ambitious, the cracks became more severe. By 1983, it had become clear that each session and presentation connection supported a single application connection. There was no multiplexing above transport and no need for addressing in session and presentation. Consequently, there was no need for the session and presentation layers to set up connections serially, and it would incur considerable overhead if it were done that way. To some extent, OSI was even further down the path of too many layers causing too much overhead that had undermined the early ARPANET's attempt. But there was a way out.

Also, it was becoming more and more clear that the functionality of the upper layers decomposed not so much "horizontally" as the lower layers did, but more "vertically" into modules. (In the mid-70s, I had made this observation while investigating how to decompose protocols to improve their processing (others remarked on it as well), but there wasn't enough data to discern a pattern.) This idea was opposed by many who were intent on adhering to the seven-layer structure regardless.[11] It was clear that the implementation of the establishment phase of session, presentation, and application should be considered to be one state machine and the session functional units (that is, the dialog control and synchronization primitives) should be viewed as libraries to be included if required. In 1983, steps were taken by making slight changes to the protocol specifications to allow the connection establishment of all three upper layers to be implemented as a single state machine. This meant that the preferred implementation was to merge ACSE, presentation, and session into a single state machine. This created a much smaller, more efficient implementation, *if* the implementer was smart enough to see it.[12]

This clearly says that the layer structure might need modification. But in 1983, it was too early to really be sure what it all looked like. Just because the connection establishment of the upper three layers could be merged was not proof that the data transfer phases should be. And remember, the CCITT wanted the data transfer phase of the session layer just as it was for teletex and videotex. So, it was not going to support any radical reworking of the upper layers. It also opposed the use of the presentation layer (teletex and videotex were defined directly on top of session) and would not have agreed to a solution that made presentation a *fait accompli*. So in the end, it was felt that this was the best that could be achieved at the time. It was a small modification that made a move in the right direction and allowed much more efficient implementations to be done. It was hoped that it would be possible to work around what was in place, after there was a better understanding. Meanwhile, the upper-layer group continued to work out the details.

Standards Aren't Design Specs

This discussion leads to the oft-cited observation that an architecture does not need to bear a resemblance to the implementation. This is in some sense true. There *are* many "correct" implementation strategies for any given architecture or protocol standard. One should never treat a standard or any protocol specification as an implementation design. However, specifications should not stray too far from the more common implementation strategy. In fact, what one often discovers is that the optimal implementation strategy and the "correct" architecture are often quite close. If not, something is wrong. Of course, recently the tendency has been to do the implementation and then define the architecture. This is equally wrong. Doing the arithmetic before the algebra leads to inefficiency and dead ends, the contra-positive of our philosophical triangulation (Clausewitz and Mao). It is not only important to keep theory close to practice, but also to keep practice close to theory!

---

[11] It was amazing how quickly for some that the seven-layer model went from a working hypothesis to a religion.

[12] Most weren't. This became known as the "clueless test" for implementers.

Don't Feed the Animals

As we noted in the preceding chapter, OSI had two 800-pound gorillas in the room: IBM and the PTTs. Many were very concerned about giving either one the upper hand to push their "proprietary" approach. On the one hand, the PTTs had too much clout to reverse their position on session and presentation. Teletex and videotex were just entering the market. On the other hand, going to a five-layer model ran the risk of admitting that IBM's SNA had been right and having IBM force SNA on the committee—it chaired nearly every national delegation. And there was one attempt, known as the Br'er Rabbit episode, to replace the upper layers with SNA's LU6.2. Hence, the illusion of seven layers was maintained.

A Note on Committee Realities

Some readers will think the OSI people were pretty stupid for not seeing these problems coming. They did. Or at least some did. However, if you have ever participated in a standards committee, you know that taking the "right" technical approach seldom counts for much. What does count are implications for products and market position. At the time the structure was being set in the early 1980s, these objections were theoretical, of the form "this could happen." They could not point to specific protocols where it happened. This, of course, allowed so-called

continues

This would not have been too bad if it were the only problem, but other problems arose that indicated that there were more fundamental problems with the upper-layer structure

According to the theory, if an application needed to change the presentation context during the lifetime of the connection, it informed the presentation layer, which made the change by renegotiating it. Different parts of an application might require a different syntax to be used at different times on a connection. However, it quickly became apparent that because the application protocol could invoke session synchronization primitives to roll back the data stream, the presentation protocol would have to track what the application protocol requested of session so that it could ensure that the correct syntax was in use for the data stream at the point in the data when it was rolled back by the session protocol. This added unnecessary complexity to the implementation and was a strong indication that the session synchronization functions belonged above presentation, not under it.

Furthermore, as more complicated applications began to be developed, conflicts in the use of the session layer developed. For example, CCR was defined to provide a generic two-phase commit facility that used session functions to build the commit mechanism. Later, the transaction processing protocol, TP, used CCR for two-phase commits but also made its own use of session primitives necessarily on the *same* session connection. Session had no means to distinguish these two uses, and there was no guarantee that they would be noninterfering. TP would have to make sure it stayed out of the way of CCR, but that violates the concept of CCR (and all protocols) as a black box. In essence, session functional units were not re-entrant and really in the wrong place.

Also, there were the problems caused by relaying in X.400 email. Connections between applications were the ultimate source and destination of data. However, the RM explicitly allowed relaying in the application layer. X.400 (or any mail protocol) may require such relaying. This implies that while the syntax of the "envelope" has to be understood by all the intermediate application layer relays, the syntax of the "letter" needs only to be understood by the original sender and ultimate receiver of the letter, not all the intermediate relays. Because there are far more syntaxes that might be used in a letter, this is not only reasonable, but also highly desirable. However, presentation connections can only have the scope of a point-to-point connection under the application layer relay. It was not possible for the presentation layer to negotiate syntax in the wider scope of source and destination of the letter, independent of the series of point-to-point connections of the relays. The "letter" could be relayed beyond the scope of the presentation layer on another presentation connection to its final destination. The architecture required the relay to support all the syntaxes required for the envelope *and the letter* even though only the sender and the receiver of the letter needed to be able to interpret its syntax. SMTP avoids this by an accident of history. When mail was first done, there was only one syntax for the letter, ASCII. By the time there were more, *Multipurpose Internet Mail Extensions* (MIME) could simply be added for the "letter," with ASCII required for the envelope.

All of these indicated severe problems with the upper-layer architecture, but the problems were also an indication of what the answer was. And, although it might not be compatible with the seven-layer model in its purest form, it wasn't that far off from its original intent.

What Was Learned

OSI made major progress in furthering our understanding of the upper layers but ran into problems caused by conflicting interests: both from economic interests and in adhering to a flawed model.

Authentication, addressing the desired application, and specifying some initial parameters were generally the concepts associated with session functions. These were embodied in ACSE in the application layer. So without stretching things too far, the theft of the session layer for the PTT teletex and videotex protocols turned the OSI upper-layer architecture upside down. (Right, green side down!) Avoiding the problem, by saying that the use of session was a "pass-through" function, merely added unnecessary complexity to the layers that were passed through. It is hard to argue that there is never a situation where a pass-through function may be the correct solution. However, pass-through functions must be limited to those that do not cause a state change in an intervening layer. This severely limits the possibilities. Furthermore, in general one would want functions located as close to their use as possible. There would have to be a strongly overriding reason for locating another function between an application and a function it uses. Fundamentally, it appears that pass-through functions should never be necessary.

continued

pragmatists, those with a vested interest, and the just plain dull to counter these arguments as just speculative prattling. Or arguments of why go to the trouble of doing it right if we don't know it will really be needed. (Sound familiar?) It was not until the late 1980s that work had progressed sufficiently that there was hard evidence. This is often the case in all efforts, in standards and elsewhere. One does not have the hard data to back up real concerns. The demand to accommodate immediate needs regardless of how bad a position it leaves for the future is often overwhelming and much more damaging. Basically, don't violate rules of good design. It might not be clear what will need it, but one can be assured that something will.

The fact that there is no multiplexing in the session and presentation layers is a strong indication that although there may be session and presentation functions, they are not distinct layers. The presentation negotiation of syntax is best associated as a function of the application connection establishment mechanism, which practically speaking it is. The session functions are actually common modules for building mechanisms used by applications that should be considered, in essence, libraries for the application layer. This also satisfies the previous result and is consistent with the common implementation strategy. Assuming that there are other common building blocks for applications than those found in the session protocol, this would seem to imply that one needs an application layer architecture that supports the combining of modules into protocols.

So, if the architecture is rearranged to fit the implementation strategy, all the earlier problems are solved...except one: the syntax relay. The flow for relaying is independent of the flow of the data for what is relayed. To take the e-mail example, and applying what was developed in the earlier chapter, the letter from an e-mail is a connectionless higher-level flow that specifies the syntax of the data it carries and is encapsulated and passed transparently by the relaying protocol of its layer (with its syntax) via a series of relays. Essentially, we need two layers of application connections to separate the "end-to-end" syntax of the letter and the "hop-by-hop" syntax of the envelope. An interesting result but not all that surprising. We should expect that applications might be used as the basis for building more complex applications.

One might want to build application protocols from modules but also want to build application protocols from other application protocols. To do this about 1990, I proposed to revise ACSE, to make it recursive.[13] To do this required ACSE to also negotiate syntax of these protocols within protocols. As it turned out, the design of the OSI transaction processing protocol using session, presentation, and application layers in the traditional manner was cumbersome and complicated. However, with this extended application layer structure, the design was straightforward and closely reflected the implementation. This model could also solve the mail relay problem by simply making the letter an encapsulated connectionless PDU with its own syntax being sent among application relays with their own application connections and syntax for the envelope.

---

[13] Writing service and protocol specifications for a recursive protocol is a very interesting exercise. One learns how dependent one has become on thinking that the layer below is different.

OSI improved our understanding of the nature of the upper layers. The recognition of the roles of syntax and semantics in application protocols was crucial. The distinction between abstract and concrete syntax is equally important and allows protocols to be designed such that they are invariant with respect to their encoding. This means the encoding can be changed without rewriting the entire protocol in much the same way that a compiler can change code generators without changing the language. (Remember in Chapter 3, "Patterns in Protcols," this property was needed to further simplify data transfer protocols.) The recognition that application and presentation context were specific cases of a general property of protocols (that is, negotiating policy) was also important. The realization that the field in lower-layer protocols to identify the protocol above was really a degenerate form of presentation context (that is, identified the syntax of the data transfer phase), not an element of addressing, contributed to our general understanding of protocols. In the same way that the presentation layer proves to be a false layer, this too proves to be a false and unnecessary distinction. However, OSI became locked into a particular structure of layers too early (as did the Internet). If ACSE had been the session layer, which is what most had intended, it would be before it was stolen the result would still not be quite right, but it would have been much closer and possibly close enough to get the rest of the solution. However, it was a sufficiently large change that the majority of participants could not accept a shift from seven layers to five, primarily for political/economic reasons and because OSI would be turning its back on protocols that were dead ends anyway (for example, keeping checkpoint recovery out of FTP to protect ancient legacy equipment).

Network Management

As the number of private networks grew in the early 1980s, interest grew in how to manage them. The early ARPANET had an excellent network management capability, but it was internal to BBN (MacKenzie, 1975). The stories are legend: BBN calling Pac-Bell to tell them one of its T1 line from Los Angeles to Menlo Park was having trouble and PacBell not believing that the caller wasn't in either Los Angeles or Menlo Park but calling from Boston. The entire network could be observed and largely debugged from its management center in Cambridge, Massachusetts, as long as a switch (IMP) didn't suffer a hard power failure.

The Main Lesson of OSI

The main lesson of OSI is to never include the legacy in a new effort. We can see how OSI's attempt to accommodate ITU caused many bad compromises to be made in the upper layers and bifurcated the lower layers. ITU hijacked the session layer for services that were a dead end. This so contorted the structure of the upper layers that there was no means to correct the problems without considerable modification of the architecture and the protocols. The ITU insistence on X.25 in the lower layers split them in two. (How X.25 was supposed to accommodate applications of the 1990s is still a mystery.) OSI was two incompatible architectures. All these conflicts undermined the effort and confused its adopters. Every word and punctuation mark in every document was a point of contention. Every minor point was a compromise

continues

Then someone had to be physically there to run the paper tape loader to reboot it. IMP software downloads were distributed over the Net under BBN control. Existing network management was primarily oriented toward controlling terminal networks, and the management systems were very vendor specific (not at all suitable for managing multivendor networks). There was little experience with managing networks of computers.

The major difference in packet networks was one of moving from control to management. Early terminal (and voice networks) viewed these systems as network control, and they did. Most decisions about the network, including routing, were made from the network control center. However, a major characteristic of packet-switched networks was and is that events in the network are happening too fast for human intervention. A human in the loop will make the situation worse, working at cross-purposes to the routing algorithms and flow-control mechanisms. Hence, there is a real shift from "control" to *management*.

Starting in late 1984 under the impetus of the GM *Manufacturing Automation Protocol/Technical and Office Protocols* (MAP/TOP) effort, a major push was made to develop network management for factory and office automation. Coincidentally, earlier in 1984, I had worked out the basics of network management architecture for my employer. GM liked what we had done, and this turned formed the basis for the MAP/TOP network management effort. This early attempt was based on the IEEE 802.1 LAN management protocol (IEEE, 1992). The protocol was in use as early as 1985. The protocol had a simple request/response structure with set, get, and action operations and an asynchronous event. The operations were performed on attributes of objects in the device, the precursor of the MIB. While the protocol developed by IEEE 802 was intended to operate over a LAN, there was nothing about the protocol that was specific to LANs. Recognizing that the responses would likely span more than one packet, the request/responses used a transport protocol, while the asynchronous event was sent as connectionless.

IBM was between a rock and a hard place. SNA was a hierarchical network architecture intended to support the centralized mainframe business. SNA was perfectly positioned to complement and avoid the phone company market. But now the packet networks destroyed this division and put

continued

with the old model, consistently weakening any potential of success. There was never a consensus on what OSI was, making it two architectures for the price of three, when it should have been one for half the price.

On the surface, including the legacy seems reasonable and cooperative. After all, one must transition from the old to the new. And it *is* reasonable, but it is wrong. Contrary to what they say, the legacy doesn't really believe it is the legacy. They will point to successes in the marketplace. If people buy it, how can it be wrong? There will be considerable emotional attachment to the old ways, not to mention the vested interest in the many products and services to be obsoleted by the new effort. The legacy will continually be a distraction. Their reticence to change will cause the new effort to fall short of its potential and jeopardize its success. Death by a thousand cuts.

No matter how great the temptation to be reasonable and accommodating, this is one point that cannot be compromised.

IBM and the phone companies in direct competition. The computer industry was endorsing these packet networks with a peer architecture. IBM had 85% of the computer market, so the others were not an immediate threat, although minicomputers and workstations were coming on fast. However, the phone companies were big enough and powerful enough to be a threat. In 1982, IBM endorsed OSI and suddenly SNA had seven layers instead of five. But, the marketing hype said, while OSI was good for data transfer, it didn't do network management. It was well understood that it was impossible to convert a hierarchical architecture to be peer, but IBM wasn't ready to give up that quickly. It needed time to map a path through this two-front minefield. Not only did IBM build good hardware and have good marketing, they also were masters of electro-political engineering. It then embarked on a strategy of stonewalling the development of network management within OSI (which, given the complexity of the issues, was not hard).

It would be hard for anyone to get a management protocol effort started in OSI with the IBM delegates there to bring up all sorts of spurious details to debate. The IBM standards people were focused on OSI and mainframe networking. Their focus in IEEE 802 was 802.5 Token Ring. From their point of view, those software architect types in 802.1 didn't require a lot of attention. The physical layer was where all the action was. (At this time, a data-comm textbook would devote 300 pages to the physical layer and 50 pages to everything else.) It is not surprising that the IBM Token Ring guys weren't watching too close, if they even knew they were there. So what if there were these "kids" from a LAN company working on it. There were a lot of young engineers jumping on the Ethernet LAN bandwagon. Let them play around developing a LAN management protocol. (The IBM Token Ring guys attending 802 didn't make the connection that these "kids'" manager was the *rapporteur* of the OSI reference model and chief architect for a network management product in development and that most of what they were taking into 802.1 was intended for elsewhere. The IBM Token Ring delegates never mentioned the activity to the IBM OSI delegates. And of course, I was highly critical of the ongoing OSI network management work, seeming to support IBM's "concerns," which wasn't hard with IBM mixing it up, when in fact, it was intended to throw them off the scent. I knew that if I took the lead in the IEEE project and the OSI Reference Model, it would get IBM's attention. Hence, IBM was caught flat-footed when the IEEE management protocol was brought into OSI as a fully complete proposal. No development required. Ready to go to ballot. IBM tried all sorts of procedural maneuvers to stop the introduction, but to no avail. There was too much support for it. This broke the logjam on network management, after which the work proceeded at a good pace.

However, experience with the IEEE protocol in mid-1980s showed that although the obvious set/get approach was simple and necessary, it was not going to be sufficient. It was in some sense too simple. It could take a lot of request/responses to get anything done. So, there was already an effort to extend management protocols to do sequences of operations at once. When the IEEE protocol was introduced to OSI in 1985, object-oriented programming was just coming into wide use. The IEEE protocol was generalized to what became the *Common Management Information Protocol* (CMIP). The new features of CMIP were centered on making the MIBs object oriented and including the concepts of scope and filter. MIBs almost always have a tree structure, sometimes referred to as a "parts explosion" or "bill of materials" structure. Scope and filter allowed a request for attributes to specify how much of the tree to search (scope) and filter by a simple relational expression. With CMIP underway, work developing MIBs for all the OSI layers and protocols, as well as definitions for various management applications (such as configuration, accounting, performance, and so on), proceeded apace.

Initially, the intent was to apply scope and filter to both sets and gets. However, it was pointed out that the nature of applying scope and filter to sets was not invertible. (In general, there is no inverse for expressions of the form "for all x, such that <relation exp>, replace x with y.") Hence, scope and filter were restricted to gets only. This is much more powerful than SNMP's GetNext or GetBulk capability and takes less code to implement than lexigraphical order in SNMP.

Somewhat later but overlapping in time, the IETF began work on network management. There were two efforts in the IETF: SNMP, which was essentially equivalent to the IEEE 802 management protocol; and *High-Level Entity Management System* (HEMS), an innovative approach to management protocols that was object oriented and based on a pushdown automata model similar to Postscript (RFCs 1021,1022, 1023,1024; 1987). For some inexplicable reason, the IETF chose to go with the backward-looking SNMP, which turns out to be *simple* in name only. Both CMIP and HEMS implementations are smaller. In addition, SNMP adhered to the "everything should be connectionless" dogma. This decision limited how much information could be retrieved and made getting a snapshot of even a small table impossible. SNMP also limited the nature of the unsolicited event so that devices had to be polled. This decision is hard to explain. In the ARPANET, a proposal to do polling for anything would have been literally laughed out of the room as "old mainframe think." Why it was acceptable at this juncture given that it clearly doesn't scale and networks were growing by leaps and bounds is mystifying. Furthermore, it made little sense. One polls when there is a reasonable expectation of data on each poll. Terminals were polled because most of the time they had characters to send. If new data is infrequent, event driven makes more sense. Polling for network management would seem to imply that it was assumed most devices would be failing a significant fraction of the time or at least experiencing exceptions. A strange assumption! Dogma was allowed to ride roughshod over the requirements of the problem.

That was not the worst of it. Just as IBM had realized that network management was the key to account control, so did the router vendors. A standard network management protocol that could manage any device from any manufacturer would make routers interchangeable. Hence, some router vendors immediately said that SNMP was good for monitoring but not for configuration (because it was not secure). This was a curious argument. From an academic point of view, it was, of course, true. SNMPv1 security was weak. But practically, SNMP was encoded in ASN.1 (an encoding scheme its detractors delighted in pointing out was overly complex and in moments of exaggeration likened to encryption), whereas the router vendors did configuration over an ASCII Telnet connection protected by passwords sent in the clear! Almost no one had an ASN.1 interpreter, but every PC on the planet had a Telnet program. Practically, SNMP was far more secure than the router vendors' practice at the time. Oddly enough, the IETF and the customers were taken in by this ruse.[14]

This turn of events led to the hurried and botched development of SNMPv2. A small group tried to write the entire new version and then ram it through the IETF with little or no change. This is a well-known recipe for disaster in consensus organizations, and this was no exception. When it was all over, none of the original authors were speaking to each other. New factions had developed around different variations of version 2 (eventually, after a cooling off period, leading to SNMPv3). But by that time, the ruse had achieved the desired affect, and SNMP was viewed as being for monitoring, and the router vendors laughed all the way to the bank.

The other problem in network management was and is the proliferation of MIBs. One would think that each layer could have a MIB that is largely common across all protocols used in that layer. (Actually, it can be done.) OSI actually made a halfway attempt at commonality but did not go as far as it could have, and as it went down in the layers, the commonality disappeared quickly. In the IETF, it was a complete free for all, with a proliferation of MIBs for each technology, for each protocol, and in some cases for different kinds of devices, before they realized there was a problem. And although they did try to introduce some commonality, later the horse was out of the barn by the time the concepts were in place. It is clear that the key to simplifying networking must be in creating greater commonality and consistency across MIBs. What is also clear is

---

[14] This appraisal of SNMP is not based on 20/20 hindsight but of observations at the time of the events and, in some cases, the events were predicted.

that it is not in the vendors' interest to create that commonality and consistency, at least, as they perceive the market today. If it is going to happen, it is going to have to be built in to the fabric of the architecture.

All in all, the decision to pick SNMP over HEMS has probably set back progress easily by a decade, cost network providers countless millions of dollars in lost productivity and overhead, and slowed or prevented the deployment of new services and applications. By retaining account control and routers not being interchangeable has also increased costs of operations and of capital equipment (all in all, reducing competition). The shortsightedness of this decision ranks along side the decision to do IPv6 as clear steps backward rather than forward. The failure to explore the HEMS approach, especially considering possible cross-fertilization of ideas from CMIP, represents a major lost opportunity.

But what does network management tell us about upper-layer architecture? Actually, quite a bit. Prior to tackling network management, applications had been seen as requiring unique protocols for each application: Telnet, FTP, RJE, mail, and so on. Experience with network management showed us that the variety is in the object models. The range of operations (protocol) was actually fairly limited. Not only are the protocols for management applicable to other "network-like" systems (for example, electric grids, gas, water distribution, airlines), but also a host of other applications can use the same basic object-oriented protocol for performing actions at a distance. It was clear that most application protocols could be viewed as a limited number of operations[15] (protocol) on a wide range of object models (operands or attributes). (It appears that the application protocols come in two forms: request/response and notify/confirm.) Hence, the number of application protocols is really quite small. So in the end, it begins to look like Alex may have been pretty close on the number of application protocols after all; they just weren't Telnet and FTP!

But the problem of the protocol operations being too elemental is still with us. Scope and filter were found to be useful in practice. It is unfortunate that we were not able explore what might have come from using HEMS, which might well have represented that "middle ground" between the elemental "Turing machine-like" structure of protocols, such as SNMP and CMIP, and a language with a full control structure, such as Java, Perl, or XML. It may appear that not

---

[15] The operators seem to be set/get, create/delete, start/stop, and event, and the protocols seems to be of either a request/response form or a notify/confirm form, where the later could be symmetrical.

many situations fall into the middle ground of needing more complex management command sequences but being too resource limited to support a full language. But then, that might be what the problem is trying to tell us. On the other hand, having not really looked for useful models in that middle ground would tend to lead us to that conclusion. This is an area that deserves exploration.

HTTP and the Web

The development of SNMP took place in the late 1980s, but the application protocol that had the most impact on the Internet did not come from the IETF or from computer science research. HTTP and the development of the World Wide Web came from a completely different community. The history of the Web has been chronicled many times. Developed by Tim Berners-Lee at the particle physics center, CERN in Geneva, it languished for awhile as "just another Gopher" until Marc Andreesen at *National Center for Supercomputer Applications* (NCSA) at the University of Illinois had the idea to put a better user interface on it. A major effort at NCSA was developing tools to facilitate the visualizing of huge amounts of data generated by the center. The rest, as they say, is history.

The Web has been so successful that to much of the world, the Web is the Internet. Our interest here is in the new structures and requirements the Web brought to the Internet. There were basically three:

1. The necessity to distinguish the application from the application protocol

2. The effects of many short transport connections on network traffic

3. (and related to the first) New requirements for addressing deriving from the need to deal with the load generated by many users accessing the same pages

To a large extent, the Web caught the Internet flat-footed. Here was a fairly simple application (at least on the surface), but it was suddenly creating huge demand requiring more sophisticated distributed computing support, which the Internet did not have. The

The First "Web"

This was not the first use of hypertext for the Net. In the early 1970s, Doug Englebart had used the ideas in the *oNLine System* (NLS) for which he also developed the mouse. NLS was also used for the *Network Information Center* (NIC) and was in many ways more sophisticated than the Web, but it did lack graphics and required an entire Tenex to support it. In RFC 100, minutes of a 1970 NWG meeting, it mentions that NLS was ported to an IMLAC, an early graphics terminal. In other words, a personal computer with a mouse running the Web! Again, if ARPA had continued to pursue applications with Moore's law, we might have had the Web a decade sooner.

Web was put in the position a bit like an application finding that it has to do its own memory allocation. Let's quickly review how the Web works, what happens when there are lots of users and lots of pages, and then consider what this implies for the Net.

When a user wants to access a Web page, she types a *Universal Resource Locator* (URL) to her HTTP client (or browser), and it is sent using the HTTP protocol over TCP to the HTTP server. DNS is used to resolve the URL to an IP address. The response returns a page of formatted text and graphics and containing many URLs to other objects on the page. All of these URLs may point to information on different systems. The browser then accesses each URL with a separate request over a new TCP connection. The responses provide more objects to populate the Web page, as well as URLs, which can be selected to access new pages. The Web is a stateless (connectionless) application for accessing and displaying Web pages. Everything is driven by the client. While links may be to any server in the Internet, it is often the case that there is considerable locality in accessing a page. Clearly, as the number of users increases and the popularity of certain Web sites increases, the load caused by large numbers of TCP connections begins to take its toll on both the servers and the network.

The first thing we notice is that the Web user is accessing the Web application. There may be thousands of Web sites on the same host all using HTTP. This is not like Telnet, FTP, or mail, where there is only one application using one application protocol per host. HTTP is just the vehicle for the two parts of the application to communicate. Here we have the first example in the Internet of the distinction between AP and AE that OSI found was necessary.

The first problem confronting the Web was that there was no application name space for the Internet. It essentially had to create URLs. This was not difficult at first, because part of the URL corresponded to the domain name of the host. The browser would just extract the domain name from the URL and do a DNS lookup, get the IP address, and open an HTTP connection and send the whole URL to the HTTP server. But very quickly, things got more complicated. Suppose the owner of the application wants the Web server to be on a server somewhere else?

For example, suppose gaslesscar.com company wants to reserve its own server to support corporate activity and outsource its Web site for customers, www.gaslesscar.com, to a service provider. What does it do? Suppliers still need to connect to gaslesscar.com, whereas customers should be directed to the host of the service provider. The company needs to retain the name recognition. It can be kludged to work by letting the customers first connect to the corporate site and redirecting them. It works, but it is unnecessary load on the corporate server, it will cause delays seen by the customer, and it raises security issues and a host of other problems. Clearly, URLs had to be directly supported by DNS, and they were. But by the same token, DNS was not designed for this kind of usage.

Clearly, the Web is going to generate a lot of TCP connections and large volumes of data. TCP had been designed on the assumption that connections might be short, a few minutes or even seconds, to very long, a few hours, and that hosts might be setting up new connections on an average of every few seconds (at most, several hundred connections per hour). Connections lasting milliseconds and thousands per minute were not foreseen. This by itself was not a big problem, but the problem of balancing this with applications with much different usage patterns was.

HTTP opens many very short connections and sends only a few bytes of data, even though the total amount of data sent for a page is equivalent of a reasonably sized file transfer. Each HTTP connection never sends enough data to be subject to TCP congestion control, whereas other traffic with longer-lived connections is. This allowed HTTP traffic to unfairly grab an unfair share of the bandwidth, the "elephants and mice" problem. This was the first real encounter with applications that generated heterogeneous and incompatible traffic. The short connections also put a resource strain on TCP control blocks, which cannot be reused for a very long time relative to the time they are used. HTTP1.1 solves both of these problems with persistent connections. By using a TCP connection for more than one request/response interaction, it reduces the turnover in *traffic control blocks* (TCBs) and transfers enough data over the connection to ensure that TCP congestion control comes into effect and HTTP traffic only gets its fair share.

Because the Web page will follow Zipf's law, the same pages will be retrieved for many users. This leads to a requirement for Web caching, either within the client, within the client's subnet, within their ISP, or by a Web hosting service. The client HTTP is modified to send all requests to a cache site regardless of what is indicated in the URL. If it is not there, it may be forwarded to another cache or to the site indicated by the URL. The server can offload subsequent accesses to the page by returning a response with links relocated to another server.

In the case of the Web, a way was found to jury-rig existing structures with minimal additions to meet the Web's needs. Will it be possible to find a band-aid for the next application? How many applications aren't being developed because the structures are not there to support them? When do the band-aids begin to interfere with each other? This is all arithmetic. What is the algebra? What is the right way to accommodate load leveling and migrating applications in a network? All of these are problems we will encounter with other applications. We have solved the problem for the Web, but we have not solved them for the Internet. Or as the press believes, is the Web the Internet?

Directory- or Name-Resolution Protocols

Another interesting class of distributed applications is the directory- or name-resolution protocols. The need for these was recognized quite early. If one were building a "resource-sharing network," a phrase that appeared in many early networking papers, one would need a means to find the resources. Because operating systems were the guiding metaphor from the early 1970s, the obvious solution was some sort of "directory," a service that could tell the user where things were. The earliest attempt was the XNS Grapevine system (Birrell, A. et al., 1982) developed by Xerox PARC in the late 1970s and extended in Clearinghouse (Oppen and Dalal, 1983). Other commonly known, similar services include DNS, X.500, Napster, Gnutella, distributed hash tables, and so on. All of these have the same basic elements and the same structure with a few variations depending on size, degree of replication, and timeliness of updates. Basically, this is a distributed database problem (see Figure 4-8).

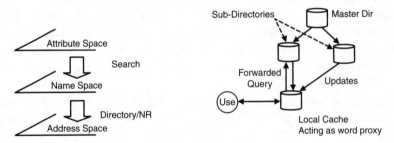

Figure 4-8 Elements of a directory- or name-resolution system.

Name-Resolution Systems

A *name-resolution system* (NRS) consists of a database, usually distributed, that is queried by the user. The database maintains the mapping between two name spaces: one that names what is to be located, and one that names where the object is. (To facilitate the description, I refer to the "what" names as "names" and to the "where" names as "addresses." We will consider names and addresses in more detail in the next chapter.) In some cases, a third name space of attributes and a mapping to the application names is used. This allows the user to query not just on the name of the object, but also on attributes of the object. In general, this is a separate NRS. This is what *search engines* do. Name-to-address mapping is what *directories* do. Some services replace the application name space with the attribute name space—in effect, treating a string of attributes as the name of the object. This is not always a wise decision. A string of attributes may identify one, none, or many elements, and furthermore, the object(s) ultimately referred to by the string may change with time. This yields a potentially large number of names for the same object. If the service needs to maintain accountability and track access to the objects (as may be required for security purposes), the attribute searches should resolve to a unique name so that accountability is maintained. (Because objects may move, it is necessary to resolve to a name rather an address.)

NRS Structures

The database for an NRS may be centralized, cached, hierarchical (that is, a tree), or a combination of the cached and hierarchical (usually depending on size and the degree of timeliness required). None of these needs to be mutually exclusive. It is straightforward and common for these systems to evolve from one form to another. For small or non-critical databases, there is often just a central database. Cached databases are introduced usually as a local cache to improve performance and reduce overhead at the cost of partial replication. The caches usually have a flat organization but can easily evolve into a hierarchy. With larger databases, the hierarchical structure of the name space is generally exploited to create subdatabases responsible for subsets of the database. The degree of replication (that is, caching) among the resulting tree of databases will depend on the application. For NRSs with significant load/availability requirements, the databases may be fully replicated. It is easy to see how some sites become known for keeping larger portions of the database. Over time, the structure may be regularized with known sites for subsets of the database. There is no requirement with a hierarchical structure that every node in the name space has a distinct subdatabase. These are usually based on size or organization boundaries. Flexibility is more important than following rules. Queries can be sent to the appropriate site with knowledge of the correspondence between the name structure and the appropriate subdatabase.

When Is a Name a Query?

This brings up an interesting convergence that makes distinguishing a query and a name difficult. And you thought they were clearly different! Let me explain.

The OSI Directory Service, also known as X.500, was probably the first to run into this conundrum. X.500 was initially intended to provide the mapping between application names and their network addresses. But as the work developed, it was made a more general-information repository for finding resources of almost any kind. They originally proposed the use of "descriptive names," which was an arbitrary sequence of attribute/values. This looked very similar to a query. A sequence of attribute/value pairs is nothing more than a query in disjunctive normal form. When it was pointed out that accountability was

continues

Two protocols are required for this service:

1. A request/response protocol for querying the database

2. A protocol for distributing updates to the database, if it is distributed

The user sends a query to a member of the NRS. If the member can satisfy the query, it returns a response to the user. If not, an NRS may be designed to respond to the user either by referring it to another database in the system or by forwarding the query to another NRS database. Depending on the level of reliability the NRS tries to maintain, if the query is forwarded, the forwarding database may act as a proxy for the user, keeping track of outstanding requests, or the database forwarded to may respond directly to the user. This latter approach may complicate security.

With a replicated distributed database comes the problem of updating the copies when there are changes. This may either be initiated by the copy (the request form) or by the member when a change occurs (the notify form). The frequency of updates varies widely depending on the frequency of change and the degree of timeliness necessary. Cached systems will tend to age and discard their caches, or perhaps distinguish often used entries and update them. Updates may be done periodically, or initiated by significant events (a new member or a member disappearing), or both. Hierarchical systems tend to periodically update in addition to responding more immediately to change.

required for application names, they retreated to an ordered sequence of attribute/values, called a "distinguished name," which satisfied the requirement of accountability. Distinguished names still have a strong similarity to queries and indicate that the traditional hierarchical pathname is merely a distinguished name where the attributes are "understood." None of the mathematical or philosophical work on naming addresses the difference between a name and a query and whether it matters.

This is one of the things that science and mathematics is supposed to do. When a close similarity is uncovered between two concepts that were thought to be quite distinct, it warrants a more careful consideration. It might turn out to be nothing. Or it may lead one to discover that we have been looking at a collection of problems in entirely the wrong way and lead to reformulation and simplification.

Table 4-2 *Characteristics of NRSs*

Database Organization	Centralized
	Hierarchical
	Cache
	Cache/Hierarchy
Query	Referral
	Forward
	Proxy
Update	Periodic
	Event-driven
	Combination

When new sites come up, they register their information with a local or near-local service, and it is propagated from there as necessary. When sites go down or a resource moves, the contents of the database change, and these changes must be propagated. This is generally accomplished by either the child services requesting an update periodically or by an affected database notifying its neighbors of the changes.

DNS, X.500, or Grapevine are structured like this, choosing specific policies for querying, database organization, and updating. They started from a centralized or cached service and grew to be more hierarchical. Napster (centralized) and Gnutella (cached) basically do the same thing for finding files rather than applications or hosts. Another P2P approach that curiously has gotten a lot of attention is based on *distributed hash tables* (DHTs). This approach differs from the earlier approach only in how a hierarchical application name space is generated. With DHTs, the name of the resource, usually the URL, is hashed. The hash creates a number of buckets where resources may be stored. The sites where resources are stored are arranged according to the subset of the hash space they are responsible for. The resource or information about the resource is stored at the site indicated by the hash of the name. The sites organize themselves in hash order. Using a hash means that the resources will be evenly distributed across the databases. The user accesses a resource by searching in hash order. This may be beneficial in terms of load leveling, but it destroys any locality that may have been embedded in the original name and would have allowed the sites to do some intelligent caching. To add insult to injury, attempts to address this shortcoming have been proposed by adding additional mechanisms to treat the hash value as a hierarchical name (!). A user uses a hierarchy imposed on the hash to find the site with the resource. Essentially the same way, a DNS lookup uses the structure of the domain name to find the correct DNS server. This somewhat begs the question, why not use the original name, which in most cases was already hierarchical and very likely reflected locality to a large degree. It would seem that if one wants to optimize the use of Web pages or files using such name-resolution protocols, one would have much more success using operating system paging as an analog.

What About Peer-to-Peer?

Indeed. What about peer-to-peer? There has been quite a fad surrounding P2P. Claims that it represents new ideas in distributed computing. Much of the hype has centered on its application to music "sharing," also known as intellectual property theft. P2P appears to be the poster child for just how far networking has fallen as a science.

First and least, *peer-to-peer* is bad English, equivalent to *irregardless* as words to show your illiteracy. Peer communication has always said it all. Communication is always with another entity. Peer denotes the nature of the relation. Peer-to-peer is simply redundant. Computer science has never been known for its writing, but there is no point making our illiteracy a neon sign.

"Okay, so you're pedantic," you say. "Whatever you call P2P, it introduces new concepts to networking: systems that are both client and server. Transfers don't have to go through a third party." This has been the case since the day the ARPANET was turned on. For more than a decade, until workstations and PCs became prevalent, most hosts on the Net were both clients and servers. Communication has never been required to go through a third party. One queries DNS and communicates directly, not through DNS. By 1973, even FTP supported third-party transfers! A could transfer a file from B to C without going through A. There is nothing in the protocols or the architecture that imposes such constraints. Any such limitations are only

continues

continued

in the minds of those using the Net. This has more in common with science in 17th-century China, where knowledge of previous discoveries was lost and rediscovered. It is easier to forgive them taking centuries to lose knowledge, whereas it takes only networking a few years.

"But there are these new algorithms for finding where things are." Go back to reading the text. They are just variations on the name-resolution and directory systems we have been proposing and building for a quarter century. To add insult to injury, none of the so-called P2P protocols are not peer (symmetric) protocols. They are client/server (asymmetric) protocols.

Why has no one pointed out that not only is there nothing new about P2P, but also what there is, isn't that good? As computer scientists, we should be quite concerned when the primary claim of a fad in our field is for illegal pursuits and is at the same time an embarrassment to our intelligence.

What Distinguishes the Upper Layers

On the surface, distinguishing the upper layers from the lower layers has always been easy. But when the details were examined, it was most often a case of "I can't tell you what it is, but I know it when I see it." It was difficult to find a set of characteristics that was better than "that which is above transport" (a definition used even recently). But as our understanding improved, it appeared that were two characteristics that distinguish the upper layers from the lower layers, regardless of what those layers are:

1. In the upper layers, processing is in units that have semantic significance to the application (that is, incur the least processing overhead/effort for the application); whereas in the middle layers, processing is in units best suited to the resource-allocation requirements; and in the lower layers, the characteristics of the communications media or network technology are dominant.

2. In the upper layers, addressing is location independent. In the lower layers, addressing is location dependent. Or perhaps more precisely, whereas lower-layer addressing is based on the topology of the network, upper-layer addressing is usually based on a sort of "semantic" topology (for example, all network access applications, all software development applications, and so on).

In a sense, the characteristics of the media percolate up, while the characteristics of the application seep down, and both are "filtered" along the way with the differences reconciled when they meet in the middle.

The overriding shift when we move from the lower layers to the upper layers is that semantics becomes important, whereas it was consistently ignored in the lower layers. This is not to say that upper-layer protocols deal only with the semantics and that user-data. (That is, data that is passed transparently without interpretation does not appear in the upper layers; it does.) It is just that the boundaries of the PDUs are not chosen arbitrarily with respect to the application but are chosen to be significant to the application. A couple of simple examples will help to illustrate the point.

Semantic Significance

In the lower layers, message or PDU boundaries are chosen to accommodate the constraints of the media or networking technology. The requirements of the application are rarely noticed (and even less the deeper in the layers one goes). This changes in the upper layers, where "record" and "transaction" boundaries of the application become important. Not only is everything done in terms of these boundaries, but also in most cases, nothing can be done if one does not have a complete "record" or "transaction." Thus, we find checkpoint-recovery protocols that work on records or two-phase commit protocols that work on record or transaction boundaries, determined by the application.

This lesson was learned early in the development of FTP. Checkpoints in FTP are inserted anywhere at the discretion of the host sending the file (the stream model asserting itself). One of the major dichotomies between host operating systems was (and still is) whether their file systems are stream or record oriented. It was noticed that when a stream-oriented host was transferring a file, it inserted checkpoints every so many bytes. If it were transferring to a record-oriented host, the record-oriented host could only recover a failed transfer on record boundaries. If the number of bytes between checkpoints were relatively prime with respect to the record length, the record-oriented host could only recover by transferring the whole file. Some early file transfer protocols made this problem worse by having checkpoint windows (similar to the window flow-control schemes in transport protocols). The sender could only send a window's worth of checkpoints without a checkpoint acknowledgment (not a bad idea in and of itself). The transfer then stopped until one or more checkpoint acks were received. In this case, it was possible for the file transfer to deadlock. The receiver couldn't ack because the checkpoints were not on a record boundary, and the checkpoint window prevented the sender from sending more data until a checkpoint was ack'ed. The fundamental difference was that for a stream-oriented host, the only semantically significant points in the file were the beginning and the end of the file. By inserting checkpoints arbitrarily, it was imposing a policy that was more lower layer in nature than upper layer. The NVFS failed to impose a necessary property on the checkpoint-recovery mechanism.

Similarly, problems could arise in performing mappings between different syntaxes if they were not isomorphic. To take a trivial example, consider the mapping of an 8-bit EBCDIC character set to 7-bit ASCII, a common problem for early Telnet. Early in the ARPANET, new translation tables were deployed in the TIPs, and it was found that it was not possible to generate the line-delete or character-delete characters for systems that used EBCDIC. Nonisomorphic translations must ensure that the semantics important to applications are preserved. While sometimes surprising, translations for character sets are relatively easy to accommodate and a simple example of the problem. However, when mapping operations on file systems or other such complex operations between different systems, ensuring the invariance is far more subtle. (The point is not so much that a file system is complex, but more that it doesn't take much complexity to create problems.) It can be much less obvious what effects of the operation on a particular system a program is relying on for its successful operation.

The canonical form provides the basis for addressing problems of this sort. The model of the application defines not only its structure, but also the operations that can be performed on that structure. The canonical form, in effect, defines the invariant properties of the operations that must be preserved when mapping from one local system to the canonical form. The canonical form defines the transfer semantics in much the same way that the concrete syntax defines the transfer syntax.

Today with the network being such an integral part of applications, it is less likely that these sorts of problems will occur as often. However, they will turn up as applications that were never intended to be networked (developed in different environments) find that they have to communicate. In these cases, it won't the simple applications, such as terminals and file systems, but complex business applications where teasing out the semantic invariances will be much more difficult.

Location Independence

The difference in addressing had been recognized since some of the earliest research on networking. Very early (circa 1972), it was recognized that it would be highly desirable to allow applications to migrate from host to host and to accommodate such migration would require applications to be named such that their names were independent of their location (that is, what host they were on) (Farber and Larson, 1972). There was a tendency to refer to this as upper-layer "naming" as distinguished from lower-layer "addressing" as recognition of this difference. However, this is not really the case.

Although an address is a name, a name is not necessarily an address. Addresses are assigned to an object so that the object is easier to find. The algorithm for assigning addresses to objects defines a topology (in most cases, a metric topology). Therefore, addresses always represent points in a topology, whereas names are merely labels. Rather than say a name space is a flat address space, In most cases, a flat name space is simply an address space out of context.

If one considers carefully the nature of "naming" as developed in meta-mathematics and mathematical philosophy as distinguished from addressing, one is led to the conclusion that in computer science and especially networking, virtually all names are used for *finding* the object. All of our naming schemes are schemes constructed to make locating an object easier (for some value of *easy*) in some context, whether spatial or semantic. (A file system path*name* is structured to make finding the file in our collection of files easy. We use directories to group related files under meaningful names. It isn't addressing in a spatial sense, but it is addressing, rather than just naming.)

In the lower layers, geographical or network topology characteristics are used as the organizing principle for locating objects. In the upper layers, other characteristics are used for locating applications that are seldom related to location. Unfortunately, unlike the lower layers, a crisp set of characteristics commonly used to organize the address space has not yet emerged for application addressing schemes. The most one can say is that characteristics of the applications are used. (One might say that application addresses are organized more by "what" or "who" rather than "where.") In some cases, schemes have reverted back to location-dependent characteristics. However, such schemes preclude any migration of applications being transparent to a user.

As mentioned earlier, directory schemes, such as X.500, in pursuit of "user-friendly names" initially proposed a "descriptive naming" scheme consisting of the intersection of an arbitrary list of attributes and their values. This characterization begins to confuse the difference between a query and a name. These attributes, in effect, define a topology within which the application is "located." Applications in the same part of the directory are in the sense of this topology "near" each other, at least from the point of view of the application naming space, while almost certainly not from the topology of network addresses.

Too Fine a Point? ...Maybe

In many cases, it will seem that I am merely splitting hairs, and that *is* always a danger. But in many aspects of network architecture, especially addressing, these subtle distinctions have a profound effect on the outcome, a sort of "butterfly effect" in logic. These distinctions can make the difference between a system in which it is easy and efficient to do things and one that is cumbersome and inefficient and even a dead end.

Conclusions

Although I cannot claim that there has been a thorough investigation of upper layers over the past 35 years, there has been a lot of work. Mostly, we have to draw our conclusions based on generalizing from specific applications, rather than attempts to construct a theory of the upper layers. We were able to show that the division of labor represented by the OSI upper layers works only for the simplest applications. On the face of it, this would seem to indicate that there is no upper-layer architecture, or if there are upper layers, they have nothing to do with what OSI thought session and presentation were. We can say that there is an application architecture, but there is no common *upper-layer* architecture.

While we can characterize the "upper layers," it does appear that the only structure common to all distributed applications is the distinction made by OSI between the application process and the application protocol. The requirement for a common establishment mechanism was an important step in replacing the stopgap left over from the ARPANET demo. Specific application domains will have more detailed structures, and there are probably common application protocol modules that can be used across application domains, but that is probably about it. We have uncovered some useful techniques for structuring application protocols, and as with anything, we have learned some things not to do. In addition, application protocols essentially reduce to defining the means to perform operations at distance on object models, and we can identify that the fundamental operations are read/write/append, create/delete, and probably start/stop. We only lack a model for the control structure that strings them together. Does this indicate that the essential distinction between upper and lower layers is the distinction between transparent (semantic-free) communication and distributed system structures and programming languages?

After looking at naming and addressing in the next chapter, we take a step back to see whether we can make coherent sense of all of this.

Chapter 5

Naming and Addressing

Did I ever tell you that Mrs. McCave
Had twenty-three sons and she named them all Dave?
Well, she did. And that wasn't a smart thing to do.
You see, when she wants one and calls out, "Yoo-hoo!
Come into the house, Dave!" she doesn't get one.
All twenty-three Daves of hers come on the run!

This makes things quite difficult at the McCaves'
As you can imagine, with so many Daves.
And often she wishes that, when they were born,
She had named....

[There follows a wonderful list of Dr. Seuss names she wishes she'd named
them, and then concludes with this excellent advice.]

But she didn't do it and now it is too late.

> —Dr. Seuss, Too Many Daves

Introduction

Many years ago when I started to work on the addressing problem, I remembered the opening lines to a Dr. Seuss story that I had read to my children far too many times. I thought it would make a good introductory quote for naming and addressing. So I dug into my kids' books to find it. Of course, I couldn't do that without reading the whole story through to the end for the great list of names she wished she had called them. But I had forgotten how it ended. I hit that last line and wondered whether Dr. Seuss had been sitting in all those addressing discussions and I just never noticed him! There was never more appropriate advice on naming and addressing than that last line.

The problem of addressing has confounded networking from the beginning. No other problem is so crucial to the success of a network; is so important to get right early and at the same time is so subtle, so philosophical, and so esoteric. No matter how you approach it. Once defined, it is difficult to change, and you may find yourself in the same situation as Mrs. McCave. If it is wrong and must be changed, the longer it takes to realize it, the more painful (and costly) it will be to change. If it is really wrong, the use of the network becomes cumbersome and arcane and eventually useless. Trying to fix it piecemeal as problems arise, only prolongs the agony, increases the cost, and increases the pain when the inevitable finally comes. But if it is right, many things become easier, and you scarcely realize it is there.

Why Do We Need Naming and Addressing?

The short answer is: to know where to send data. However, the more considered answer is a little longer (but amounts to the same thing). One of the major efficiencies of networks is that every source does not have to be directly connected to every destination. If they were, only the simplest networks would be feasible, and addresses would always be a local matter. But by allowing nodes in the network to act as intermediaries to relay messages from sources to destinations, we must at least distinguish them with names, and as the network grows we can greatly decrease the cost of the network at the "mere" expense of adding addresses to the protocols and routing to the network.[1] We need to distinguish messages from each other. For simple networks, the mechanisms are deceptively simple, and simply enumerating the nodes is sufficient. But as the size and complexity of the network grows, naming and addressing begins to show itself as a subtle maze with all sorts of traps, quagmires, and dead ends. The protocol designer begins to wonder whether he has unwittingly signed a pact with the devil. But it is too late to turn back. And one is left wondering how engineering suddenly became so philosophical.

There are basically two separate problems that we must consider: 1) What objects need to be named to effect communications, and 2) the nature of the names and addresses used to label these objects. But before diving into the theory of addressing, let's consider how we got here so that we have a better understanding of why the theory is being asked to answer certain questions.

---

[1]   The "multidrop" technologies accomplish a similar reduction in cost for "star" topologies and also require addressing mechanisms.

How the Problem Arose

Naming and addressing had never been a major concern in data communications. The networks were sufficiently simple and of sufficiently limited scope that it wasn't a problem. Most early networks were point-to-point or multidrop lines, for which addressing can be done by simple enumeration. Even for large SNA networks, it was not really an issue. Because SNA is hierarchical with only a single path from the leaves (terminals) to the root (mainframe), enumerating the leaves of the hierarchy (tree) again suffices.[2] In fact, addressing in a decentralized network with multiple paths, like the early ARPANET or even the early Internet, can be accommodated by enumeration and was. But everyone knew the addressing problem was lurking out there and eventually it would have to be dealt with.

The ARPANET was a research project that wasn't expected by many to succeed. No one expected the ARPANET to ever be large enough for addressing to be a major problem, so why worry about an esoteric problem for which at the time we had no answers. As it was, there were an overwhelming number of major technical problems to solve which were a lot more crucial. Just being able to route packets, let alone do useful work with it, would be a major achievement. After all, it was research. It was more important to be focused on the few specific problems that were central to making the project work. Addressing was distinctly a lesser issue. Of course, to everyone's surprise the ARPANET was almost immediately useful.

Because the initial design called for no more than a few tens of switches connecting a few hosts each, addressing could be kept simple. Consequently, there were only 8 bits of address on the *Interface Message Processors* (IMP). Host addresses were the IMP number (6 bits) and the IMP port numbers (2 bits). Each IMP could have a maximum of 4 hosts attached (and four 56K trunks). IMP numbers were assigned sequentially as they were deployed.

Although a maximum of 64 IMPs might seem a severe limitation, it seemed like more than enough for a research network. There was not much reason for concern about addressing. Once the success of the ARPANET was accepted, the address size of NCP was expanded in the late 1970s to 16 bits to accommodate the growth of the network. (*Network Control Program* implemented the Host-to-Host Protocol, the early ARPANET equivalent of TCP/IP.)

---

[2] SNA could even enumerate the routes, because the hierarchy kept the number from growing too fast. But if you don't understand why, it can lead to problems. There was a network company that many years ago tried to use the SNA approach for nonhierarchical networks (after all if it was used by IBM, it must be right!) and couldn't figure out why the number of routes exploded on them.

It was clear that the one aspect of naming and addressing that would be needed was some sort of directory. ARPA was under a lot of pressure to demonstrate that the network could do useful work; there certainly was not time to figure out what a directory was and design, and implement such a thing. And for the time being, a directory really wasn't necessary. There were only three applications (Telnet, FTP, and RJE), and only one each per host. Just kludge something for the short term. A simple expedient was taken of simply declaring that everyone use the same socket for each application: Telnet on socket 1, FTP on 3, and RJE on 5.[3] Every host would have the same application on the same address. This would do until there was an opportunity to design and build a cleaner, more general solution. Hence, well-known sockets were born. (Strangely enough, while many of us saw this as a kludge, discussions among the people involved revealed that others never saw it that way. An unscientific survey indicates that it may depend on those who had early imprinting with operating systems and those that didn't.)

If there was any interest in naming and addressing during that period, it was more concerned with locating resources in a distributed network. How does a user find an application in the network? By the mid-1970s, several efforts were underway to build sophisticated resource sharing systems on top of the ARPANET (the original justification) or on smaller networks attached to the ARPANET. David Farber was experimenting with a system at UC Irvine that allowed applications to migrate from host to host (Farber and Larson, 1972); and another ARPA project, the National Software Works, was trying to build an elaborate distributed collaboration system on top of the ARPANET (Millstein, 1977). These projects raised questions about what should be named at the application layer and how it related to network addresses, but outstripped the capability of systems of the day.

The problem of naming and addressing had been a factor in the development of operating systems. The complexity of process structure in some operating systems provided a good basis for considering the problem (Saltzer, 1977). Operating system theory at the time drew a distinction between location-independent names and the logical and physical levels of addresses. This distinction was carried into networking and generalized as two levels of names: 1)

---

[3] When "new Telnet" was defined, socket 23 was assigned for debugging and experimenting with the new design until the old Telnet could be taken out of service and new Telnet moved to socket 1. Telnet is still on socket 23.

location-independent names for applications and 2) location-dependent addresses for hosts.

The general concept was that the network should seem like an extension of the user's interface. The user should not have to know where a facility was to use it. Also, because some applications might migrate from host to host, their names should not change just because they moved. Thus, applications must have names that are location independent or as commonly called today, portable. The binding of application names to processes would change infrequently. These applications would map to location-dependent addresses, a mapping that might change from time to time. Network addresses would map to routes that could change fairly frequently with changing conditions of the network. That was the general understanding.

Using switch port numbers for addresses was not uncommon. After all, this is basically what the telephone system did (as did nearly all communication equipment at that time). However, although this might have been acceptable for a telephone system, it causes problems in a computer network. It didn't take long to realize that perhaps more investigation might be necessary. Very quickly, the ARPANET became a utility to be relied on as much or more than an object of research. This not only impairs the kind of research that can be done, it also prevents changes from being made. (On the other hand, there is a distinct advantage to having a network with real users as an object of study.) But it also led to requirements that hadn't really been considered so early in the development. When Tinker Air Force Base in Oklahoma joined the Net, they very reasonably wanted two connections to different IMPs for reliability. (A major claim [although not why it was built] for the ARPANET in those days of the Cold War was reliability and survivability.) But it doesn't work quite so easily. For the ARPANET, two lines running to the same host from two different IMPs, have two different addresses and appear as two *different* hosts. (See Figure 5-1.) The routing algorithm in the network has no way of knowing they go to the same place. Clearly, the addressing model needed to be reconsidered. (Because not many hosts had this requirement, it was never fixed, and various workarounds were found for specific situations.) Mostly, the old guard argued that it didn't really happen often enough to be worth solving. But we were operating system guys; we had seen this problem before. We needed a logical address space over the physical address space! The answer was obvious; although it would be another ten years before anyone wrote it down and published it. But military bases were rare on the Net, so it was not seen as a high-priority problem. Also, we all knew that this was a hard subtle problem, and we needed to understand it better before we tried to solve it. Getting it wrong could be very bad.

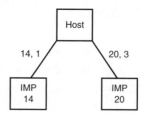

Figure 5-1 Because ARPANET host addresses were the port numbers of the IMPs (routers), a host with redundant network connections appears to the network as two separate hosts. Routing can't tell the two lines go to the same place.

Background on Naming and Addressing

The problems of naming and addressing remained an interesting side issue for the Net, not a problem crucial to survival for many years. There weren't too many places to learn about naming and addressing. In the early days of computer science, there was considerable emphasis on mathematical logic, the predicate calculus and related subjects. Some aspects of naming are taken up there in some detail. As previously mentioned, there had been some work done in the context of operating systems. The postal system and the telephone system solved this problem on a global scale; and although both are large systems, they are also simpler in significant ways. Most of the network is hierarchical, and the part that isn't was strongly geographical with a single provider. They didn't have to consider multicast, migrating applications, multihoming, or until recently, mobility.

Foundations of Mathematics and Naming

As we have said, the problems of naming and addressing have a tendency to get philosophical. What to name, the relation among various names and the objects they refer to, and the structure that such names should have and what constructs they can support are all issues to be considered. It doesn't take long before it can begin to sound like counting angels on the head of a pin. However, experience has shown that subtle distinctions can often make the difference between a simple but rich and efficient naming scheme and a scheme that becomes complex and cumbersome and may not even work. So, perhaps we should consider those aspects before we go too much further. Because we are concerned with naming and addressing in computers and networks of computers, we will not discuss the full scope of naming issues that have been taken up by philosophy. We will only provide a taste of these issues and limit ourselves to those aspects of the mathematics that apply most directly to our problem.

Modern considerations of naming derive from the work on the foundations of mathematics and symbolic logic. This work got significant attention in the late 19th century with the interest in the foundations of mathematics and the work of Gottlieb Frege, with major contributions coming from the work of Bertrand Russell and Alfred North Whitehead, Ludwig Wittgenstein, Rudolf Carnap, and others who became known as the Vienna Circle. Primarily, they were concerned with two problems: 1) creating a strictly axiomatic basis for all of mathematics and 2) the means to create purely logical language to describe the world. Both projects failed. The first because Kurt Gödel proved the "incompleteness theorem," or in essence "no matter where you start, there is some place you can't get to from here." And the second by Wittgenstein, who in his *Tractatus Logico-Philosophicus* made it clear that most of what philosophy had been talking about for the past 2,000 years could not be stated with sufficient precision to prove any conclusions. And all those things that could were tautologies, which say nothing. However, in the process of getting to these conclusions, considerable insights were made into the nature of language, the foundations of mathematics, symbolic logic, and so on.

Much of this work related to constructing a precise logical language. Consequently, one of the major considerations was precisely determining the relation of names to their meanings and how these meanings came about. Frege, in his essay "On Sense and Meaning" (1892) defined a name as follows:

A proper name (word, sign, sign combination, expression) expresses its sense, means or designates its meaning. By employing a sign we express its sense and designate its meaning.

Here and in the *Basic Laws of Arithmetic* (1884), Frege goes on to develop the concept of a name to correspond closely to what one intuitively thinks of as a noun clause. As alluded in the definition, a name can be an expression. Frege also introduced variables into these expressions and the concept of bound and unbound variables, although the use of these terms did not come until later. Frege distinguishes simple and complex complete names. Simple names are what we would term constants; complex names are expressions. A complete name has all of its variables bound to constants. For Frege, an incomplete name (i.e., one with unbound terms) is a function. Frege uses these concepts and a unique notation in an attempt to derive the fundamental rules of arithmetic. However, he only came close. As his book went to press, Frege received what is now a famous letter from Russell advising him of a problem Russell had encountered in his own attempt with Whitehead to put mathematics on a completely logical footing (the set of all sets that do not contain themselves, leading to the Russell paradox). Frege had missed the paradox that stumped Russell for quite awhile and whose solution is still debated by mathematicians. Although the damage was not irreparable, Frege never revised his book to fix the problem.

Twenty some years later, the young Ludwig Wittgenstein took issue with Frege and to some extent Russell in his work that revolutionized mathematics and philosophy, the *Tractatus Logico-Philosophicus* (1922). We have already touched on the *Tractatus* in Chapter 1, "Foundations for Network Architecture," but here let's look more closely at what it says about names. Right off the bat, Wittgenstein takes issue with Frege:

> **3.142** Only facts can express a sense, a set of names cannot.

> **3.143** Although a propositional sign is a fact, this is obscured by the usual form of expression in writing or print. For in a printed proposition, for example, no essential difference is apparent between a propositional sign and a word. (This is what made it possible for Frege to call a proposition a composite name.)

> **3.144** Situations can be described but not given names.

An early 20th-century flame, W goes on to give a much restricted definition of a name, which corresponds to what we will call here a *primitive name*:

> **3.202** The simple signs employed in propositions are called names.

> **3.203** A name means an object. The object is its meaning. ('A' is the same sign as A.)

> **3.22** In a proposition a name is the representative of an object.

> **3.26** A name cannot be dissected any further by means of a definition: it is a primitive sign.

> **3.261** Every sign that has a definition signifies via the signs that serve to define it; and the definitions point the way.

> Two signs cannot signify in the same manner if one is primitive and the other is defined by means of primitive signs. Names cannot be anatomized by means of definitions. (This cannot be done to any sign that has a meaning independently and on its own.)

W is nailing things down pretty tight, defining a name as essentially a label for an object. This is a denotative approach to naming. He goes on to point out that names by themselves say very little:

> **3.3** Only propositions have sense; only in the nexus of a proposition does a name have meaning.

3.314 An expression has meaning only in a proposition. All variables can be construed as propositional variables. (Even variable names.)

3.3411 So one could say that the real name of an object was what all symbols that signified it had in common. Thus, one by one, all kinds of composition would prove to be unessential to a name.

4.0311 One name stands for one thing, another for another thing, and they are combined with one another. In this way the whole group—like a *tableau vivant*—presents a state of affairs.

4.23 It is only in the nexus of an elementary proposition that a name occurs in a proposition.

So, W comes full circle or would seem to. The meaning of a name can only be determined when it occurs in a proposition (i.e., in context). Further, all expressions must reduce to a primitive name, and these expressions do not affect the name. Where is W headed with all of this? Right here:

5.526 We can describe the world completely by means of fully generalized propositions, i.e., without first correlating any name with a particular object.

6.124 The propositions of logic describe the scaffolding of the world, or rather they represent it. They have no 'subject-matter'. They presupposed that names have meaning and elementary propositions sense; and that is their connection with the world. It is clear that something about the world must be indicated by the fact that certain combinations of symbols-whose essence involves the possession of a determinate character-are tautologies. This contains the decisive point. We have said that some things are arbitrary in the symbols that we use and that some things are not. In logic it is only the latter that express: but that means that logic is not a field in which we express what we wish with the help of signs, but rather one in which the nature of the natural and inevitable signs speaks for itself. If we know the logical syntax of any sign-language, then we have already been given all the propositions of logic.

The hope had always been that logic could resolve important questions in philosophy. What W has done here and will wrap up between here and the famous statement 7 says that names are arbitrary labels and all statements in logic are tautologies. They say nothing about the real world.

What Happened Next? A More Organic View

For those who are curious, W did not rest with the *Tractatus*. He was still troubled by its implications. Twenty years later he published his thoughts again, and this time changed his view considerably, taking a more connotative model of language that is closer to how organisms seem to actually acquire language. Oddly enough, his point of departure was St. Augustine:

1. "When they (my elders) named some object, and accordingly moved towards something, I saw this and I grasped that the thing was called by the sound they uttered when they meant to point it out. Their intention was shown by their bodily movements, as it were the natural language of all peoples: the expression of the face, the play of the eyes, the movement of other parts of the body, and the tone of voice which expresses our state of mind in seeking, having, rejecting, or avoiding something. Thus, as I heard words repeatedly used in their proper places in various sentences, I gradually learnt to understand what objects they signified; and after I trained my mouth to form these signs, I used them to express my own desires." (Augustine, *Confessions,* I. 8)

These words, it seems to me, give us a particular picture of the essence of human language. It is this: The individual words in language name objects-sentences are combinations of such names. In this picture of language, we find the roots of the following idea: Every word has a meaning. This meaning is correlated with the word. It is the object for which the word stands.

38. Naming appears as a queer connection of a word with an object. And you really get such a queer connection when the philosopher tries to bring out the relation between name and thing by starting at an object in front of him and repeating a name or even the word "this" innumerable times. For philosophical problems arise when language goes on holiday. And here we may indeed fancy naming to be some remarkable act of mind, as it were a baptism of an object. And we can also say the word "this" to the object, as it were address the object as "this"-a queer use of this word, which doubtless only occurs in doing philosophy.

43. For a large class of cases-though not for all-in which we employ the word "meaning" it can be defined thus: the meaning of a word is its use in the language. And the meaning of a name is sometimes explained by pointing to its bearer.

275. Look at the blue of the sky and say to yourself "How blue the sky is!"—When you do it spontaneously-without philosophical intentions—the idea never crosses your mind that this impression of color belongs only to you. And you have no hesitation in exclaiming that to someone else. And if you point at anything as you say the words you point at the sky. I am saying: you have not the feeling of pointing-into-yourself, which often accompanies "naming the sensation" when one is thinking about "private-language." Nor do you think that really you ought not to point to the color with your hand, but with your attention.

293. If I say of myself that it is only from my own case that I know what the word "pain" means—must I not say the same of other people too? And how can I generalize the one case so irresponsibly? …

Not only has his thinking changed to such an extent that he now considered that names are conventions among people, not arbitrary labels that can be applied willy-nilly, but he is also considering that the senses that one applies a name to may be different for different individuals (something borne out by cognitive psychology and neurophysiology). The world is far less deterministic that even the *Tractatus* allowed.

Although there had been suspicions to the contrary before this point, mathematics had always been considered a science. There was a belief that it was a universal language with which the world could be completely and precisely described, which would in turn lead to answering many long-standing questions, including some outside the traditional realm of science and mathematics. After all, much of its use was in the service of science, and science made many statements and solved many problems about the real world with mathematics. W has now slammed the door on this view. Logic and, by the constructions of Frege and Russell, mathematics say nothing about the real world and can't. Mathematics is not a science. Mathematicians were operating in the world of Platonic ideals, believing that these truths that they derived were independent of human thought. Although refined by other logicians and mathematicians in the intervening 80 years, the structure and limitations erected by W have remained, circumscribing how far mathematics can go in answering questions that affect people.

But although this was a failure on one level, it was precisely what was required 30 years later when it became possible to build logic machines and get the fledging field of computer science off the ground. The concepts of primitive name, simple and complex, complete and incomplete names were precisely the foundations necessary for constructing the logical languages required for computers, where now these languages could be used in propositions that said something real about a virtual world. It also provides the basis for a theory of naming for networks and distributed system, but provides little help with any fundamentals for addressing. We need a mathematical characterization of "locating" objects.

Naming and Addressing in Telephony

Addressing in the telephone system developed from the bottom up. Initially, telephone systems were isolated islands. Telephone numbers corresponded to numbers on the switchboard, which corresponded to the wires that ran to the phones.[4] Enumeration worked again. The scope of the address space was limited to the island or central office called an exchange; that is, telephones in different exchanges might have the same number. When a phone system outgrew what could be handled by a single central office, trunks were used to link central offices. Each exchange was given a unique identifier, and this number was tacked on the beginning of the number for the telephone: the beginning of hierarchical addressing. Connections between islands required an operator.[5] With the advent of automatic dialing and long distance, it was necessary to add

---

[4] My first phone number was 61.

[5] Remember those old movies, *Operator, get me New York, Pennsylvania 6-5000.*

another level to the hierarchy, and area codes were created. But the fundamental semantics of the phone number never changed: It was the number of the wire that ran to the phone. There was really no attempt at structuring the assignment of numbers within an exchange, there might be some similarity in the exchanges used for a single city, but overall the structure of the address space was roughly geographical. This had more to do with conserving the amount of relay equipment than attempting to logically structure the phone numbers.

Over time, as telephone engineers found ways to hack the system to provide specialized services, the semantics of the telephone number got confused. There are strong indications that the phone companies didn't quite understand what they were getting in to. Although normal phone numbers were physical layer addresses, the label of a wire, the definition began to get confused: 800 numbers are application addresses being location independent, whereas 411 and 911 are simply well-known names for specific applications. (Most in phone company circles did not realized this, of course; they were still just phone numbers.) Initially, cellular phone numbers were network addresses, a good unique identifier as the phone was handed off from cell tower to cell tower. But as soon as roaming was provided, they became application addresses (because they were now location independent). Customers had become familiar that when they moved within a city their phone number did not need to change. Although exchanges had begun as exclusively geographical, this began to break down over time with improvements in switches and customer demand. Roaming just served to convince customers that they could move anywhere in the country and not change phone numbers. Because 800 numbers and initially cell phones were such a small population, the mapping from the application address to a network or physical layer address could be a special case. As Signaling System 7 was deployed in the 1980s, it enabled these changes during the 1990s, and the telephone system moved to rationalize its addressing architecture.

Naming in Operating Systems

Much more theoretical work has been done on naming than on addressing. As luck would have it, we are much more interested in addressing than naming. Almost everything in computer science is addressing of one form or another, not naming. There has been very little theoretical work done exploring the properties of addresses, no systematic exploration of addressing. Much of this was because computing systems were so resource constrained. Most of the work has been very pragmatic in the context of solving a specific problem. So, we have some idea of what works or under what conditions it works or what doesn't, but we have very little idea if this is the best we can do.

One of the few theoretical treatments of this subject tempered by implementation of a production system (i.e., it satisfies our philosophical triangulation) is the work of J. H. Saltzer on *Name Binding in Computer Systems* (1977).[6] This is what university-level computer science should be and isn't much of the time. This work develops the theory of naming and addressing in operating systems and programming languages in a general and implementation-independent manner. It is does the "algebra" first. Although space does not allow a detailed review of the paper, we do see that roughly three levels of naming are required in operating systems. Saltzer provides a framework for the sharing of data and programs in a computing environment. Although Saltzer does not consider the problems of naming and addressing in computer networks, many of the concepts that will be needed are discussed. These might be characterized as follows:

1. A name space that allows sharing among independently running programs

2. A name space that allows programs to logically refer to their variables regardless of where they are in memory

3. A name space that represents the program in memory

4. A path from the processor to the memory

The first has a "universal" scope of the whole computer system and encompasses all files (program or data) that are executing or may be executed on that system. This name space allows one to unambiguously refer to any programs and data files on the computer and in some systems, such as Multics, objects within these. The second provides a name space that allows the programmer to logically construct programs independent of memory size and location. This space creates a virtual environment that may assume resources that exceed those of the underlying real computer. This logical environment is then mapped to a real computer where the operating system provides the facilities that create the illusion of the virtual environment. (For example, virtual memory provides location independence and the illusion of greater memory than actually exists, and processor scheduling gives the illusion of a multiprocessor system.) The hardware then provides a path from the processor to the appropriate memory location.

For the naming of files and programs, a hierarchical approach was adopted rather quickly, consisting of a root directory, subdirectories, and finally primitive names. This was called a *pathname* because it defined a path through the directory structure. If a file was moved in this structure, its primitive name remained the same, but its pathname changed.

---

6 This might seem like ancient history here, but I highly recommend that you dig out this reference.)

X.25 and the ITU

In the mid-1970s, the PTTs rushed to get in the packet-switching business. Mostly to defend their turf because organizations that weren't telephone companies were building networks than because they thought it was a good business opportunity. After all, data traffic would never come close to the kind of volumes as voice traffic! The PTTs proposed a network design along the lines of the ARPANET or NPLnet using a new protocol, X.25, as their answer to the research networks. X.25 addresses have the same semantics as a telephone (no surprise). The structure of an X.25 address is similar to that for telephones, consisting of a country code, followed by a network number and DTE (host) number. But the allowances for growth were very small, allowing only ten networks per country. A distinct "group-id" field in the X.25 header identifies particular connections from this DCE. The address is the name of the interface over which all connections with that DTE pass.

The "East Coast elite" screwed up the ARPANET addressing because they were from Boston. In Boston, there is only one way to get anywhere, and so it is easy to confuse that a route and an address are the same thing. If they had been from the Midwest where everything is on a grid and there are many paths between two points, they would have known that a route and an address are two entirely different things.

It isn't true, but it makes a good story!

The Evolution of Addressing in the Internet: Early IP

Or Is it?

In New England, the way to get some place is to take out the map, find the destination, and trace a route back to where you are. Follow the path. Not unlike Internet routing.

In the Midwest, the address gives you a good idea where the destination is relative to where you are. You start in that direction, using addresses along the way to indicate whether you are closer or farther from the destination. Interesting. Forwarding without routing.

As previously discussed, the origin of the Internet's convention that addresses name interfaces derives from the implementation of the original IMPs. Although this was common practice for the small data networks of the time, it is basically the same as the telephone company. Using the telephone example was a reasonable first approximation, and it wasn't at all obvious how the street address example contributed anything to the solution (although there was a nagging sense that it should). Unlike telephone addresses, ARPANET addresses were only route dependent for the last hop. (In the phone system, there were multiple routes above the exchanges, although automatic rerouting is relatively recent.) It was clear that computers would have different requirements than telephones. We have already seen the problem of dual homing. But it was realized the problems of naming applications that were seen in operating systems would be more complex in networks.

The development of TCP and IP began in the mid-1970s to fix problems with the original Host-to-Host Protocol. As far as addressing was concerned, the only immediate problem that had to be dealt with was that there weren't enough of them. So, the IP specification expanded the address to 32 bits and slightly generalized the semantics of the address so that it named the "interface" rather than an IMP port.

The problem continued to be discussed. John Shoch published an important paper (Shoch, 1978). (Shoch's paper had been circulating within the ARPANET community for over a year before it appeared in print.) Shoch recognized (as so often scoffed at) that

Taxonomies and terminologies will not by themselves, solve some of the difficult problems associated with the interconnection of computer networks; but carefully choosing our words can help us to avoid misunderstanding and refine our perceptions of the task.

Shoch posited that three distinct concepts were involved: names (of applications that were location independent), which were "what we seek"; addresses (that were location dependent), which indicated "where it was"; and routes (which were clearly route dependent), which were "how to get there." Shoch made clear what many had been thinking but didn't know quite how to say. At the time, Schoch was working at Xerox PARC with Robert Metcalfe on the development of Ethernet and related projects. Shoch points out in his paper how the naming in networks parallels what is found in computing systems: Namely, that applications had names that were independent of memory location and made sense to human users, whereas programs used virtual memory addresses that allowed their code to be placed anywhere in memory and were mapped to the actual physical memory location (routing) by the hardware. It seemed to make a lot of sense.

A few years later (1982), the other most often cited paper on network addressing appeared, Jerry Saltzer's (RFC 1493) "On the Naming and Binding of Network Destinations." This is a most curious paper. Saltzer sets out to apply to networks the same principles he applied to operating systems and makes a major contribution to the problem. Saltzer notes that there are four things, not three, in networks that need to be named (just as there were in operating systems): services and users, nodes, network attachment, and paths. Saltzer carefully lays out the theoretical framework, defining what he means by each of these. After noting some of the issues pertinent to the syntax of names, Saltzer observes:

The second observation about the four types of network objects listed earlier is that most of the naming requirements in a network can simply and concisely be described in terms of bindings and changes of bindings among the four types of objects. To wit:

1. A given service may run at one or more nodes, and may need to move from one node to another without losing its identity as a service.

2. A given node may be connected to one or more network attachment points, and may need to move from one attachment point to another without losing its identity as a node.

3. A given pair of attachment points may be connected by one or more paths, and those paths may need to change with time without affecting the identity of the attachment points."

It would appear that Saltzer is suggesting that we name the objects and track the mappings (i.e., the bindings) between them. Notice the parallel between this list and Saltzer's list for operating systems earlier in this chapter.

Each of these three requirements includes the idea of preserving identity, whether of service, node or attachment point. To preserve an identity, one must arrange that the name used for identification not change during moves of the kind required. If the associations among services, nodes, attachment points and routes are maintained as lists of bindings this goal can easily be met.

Again Saltzer is pointing out a very important property (i.e., that the names given to objects must be invariant with respect to some property across the appropriate scope). In particular, service or application names do not change with location, node names do not change for attachment points within the scope of their location, and attachment points do not change as the ends of their routes.

This expands a bit on Saltzer's words, but it seems reasonable to assume that Saltzer recognized that names would not be assigned once and for all. And if they could change, there must be rules for when and how they could change. In fact, he states quite rightly that even if a name is made permanent, this "should not be allowed to confuse the question of what names and bindings are in principle present." He then reviews that "to send a data packet to a service one must discover three bindings" [given the name of a service]:

1. Find a node on which the required service operates

2. Find a network attachment point to which that node is connected

3. Find a path from this attachment point to that attachment point

From Saltzer's description, there is a name for each of these four and tables that maintain the bindings between the names:

1. Service name resolution, to identify the nodes that run the service

2. Node name location, to identify attachment points that reach the nodes found in 1

3. Route service, to identify the paths that lead from the requestor's attachment point to the ones found in 2

Saltzer then illustrates his points with a couple of examples that for Saltzer present problems in applying his model. He then concludes that regardless of what one may think of his analysis, "it seems clear that there are more than three concepts involved, so more than three labels are needed...." And finally, in his summary, he points out there is a strong analog between what he has described and the concepts found in operating systems.

This seems to answer our first question of what has to be named: Applications require location-independent names. This is Schoch's *what*. This allows the application to be moved without changing its name. That name maps to a node address that indicates *where* the node is and the application can be found, with each router maintaining a forwarding table that maps an address to a "next hop" (i.e., next node address). But then Saltzer lumps the next step in with routing. He clearly knows that a point of attachment address is needed, but he doesn't clearly distinguish how it differs from a node address. As noted previously, it was obvious that the solution to the multihoming problem was that a *logical* address space was needed over the *physical* address space. But then Saltzer follows the operating system model too closely and notes that there is a mapping of applications to nodes, a mapping of nodes to points of attachment, and then a mapping to routes as a sequence of points of attachments and nodes.

Saltzer misses a case that is unique to networks and key to understanding: In networks, there can be multiple paths (links) between adjacent nodes. Saltzer can't be faulted for missing this. Multiple paths to the next hop were rare or nonexistent when he was writing. Let's supply the answer.

After selecting the next hop, the router must know all the node address to point of attachment address mappings of its nearest neighbors so that it can select the appropriate path to send PDUs to the next hop.

Routes are sequences of node addresses from which the next hop is selected. Then the router must know the mapping of node address to point of attachment address for all of its nearest neighbors (the line in Figure 5-2) so that it can select the path to the next hop.

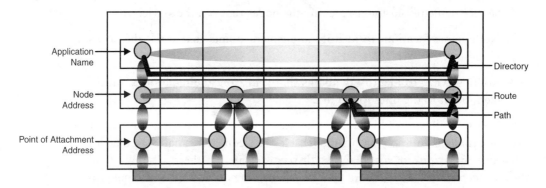

Figure 5-2 Addressing for a network requires at least an application name, a node address, and a point of attachment address. Directory maps application names to node addresses, routes are sequences of node addresses, and multiple paths between adjacent nodes require mappings between node addresses and point of attachment addresses.

"Routing" is a two-step process. A route is a sequence of node addresses. The next hop is chosen to the next node address. Then the mapping of local point of attachment addresses to the point of attachments of nearest neighbors for the next hop is needed to select which path to the next hop is selected. Looking at the figure, we see these bindings:

1. *Directory,* mapping of application names to node addresses to find where the application is. This is an example of the name-resolution or directory protocols discussed in Chapter 4, "Stalking the Upper-Layer Architecture."

2. *Routes,* as a sequence of node addresses calculated by the routing algorithms to generate the next hop

3. *Paths,* selected from the mapping node address to point of attachment address of the nearest neighbors (i.e., next hops)

Interesting! 1 and 3 are the same mapping! The path is also an example of a name-resolution service, just like the directory. The path database is smaller than the directory database, and the syntax of the names are a bit different, but the same mapping nonetheless. They both track name mappings that are "one hop" from each other (relative to their layer).

It was clear that a network address (i.e., node address) needed to be location dependent and application names should be able to be location independent. What about *point-of-attachment* (PoA) addresses? Traditionally, the PoA corresponds to the data link layer address. From the point of view of the nodes, it doesn't matter. All the nodes (routers) require is that PoA addresses of nearest neighbors are unambiguous. All PoA addresses don't have to come from the same address space and probably won't. Different protocols in different layers of less scope are possible and allowable. Any two connected nearest neighbors will have addresses from the same address space. (They have to because both ends of the communication use the same protocol, by definition.) But not all PoAs on the same router or host must be from the same address space. Whether a PoA address space will be flat or location dependent will depend on the protocols and scope of the PoA layers. Location dependence is a property that facilitates scaling within a layer by reducing the complexity and combinatorial properties of routing.

But what is curious about this paper is that Saltzer lays out the answer very clearly. When addressing is discussed in networking meetings, this paper is cited by almost everyone. The paper is almost revered. But the Internet architecture has no application names and no node addresses (a well-known socket is at best a suffix for a network address, and URLs show signs of backing into being a form of application name *within* http). The Internet has only PoA names, and routes. Saltzer says clearly that PoAs and routes are not enough. It is clear that the fundamental problem with Internet addressing is that it is missing half the necessary addressing architecture. Why then has the Internet not taken Saltzer's advice, especially given how Saltzer lays out the principles so clearly?

The XNS architecture developed at Xerox PARC for networks of LANs, and later used by IPX for Novell's NetWare product, had a network address that named the system, not the interface. This was the first commercial architecture to fix the addressing problem created by the IMPs. But, Xerox's decision to keep the specifications proprietary limited its early influence. At the same time, the decreasing cost and increasing power of hardware reduced the need to fix the problem in IP.[7] Later this same solution would be picked up and used by OSI.

The deployment of IP overcame the address space problems of NCP. Thirty-two bits of address space was more than enough. However, IP retained the semantics of the IMP port address and named the interface (see Figure 5-3). The primary reason for this is unclear. IP was first proposed in about 1975 and changed very little after that first draft. The only known problem at that time was with the semantics of the address, as exemplified by the dual-homing problem described earlier. The Saltzer analysis shows that multihoming isn't supported for routers, let alone hosts. But because the Net was small enough

---

[7] Once again, Moore's law perhaps causes more trouble than it helps by allowing us to ignore the scaling problems of the address space for so long that the network grew so large that solutions became more daunting. It is curious, given the DoD sponsorship of the early Internet, that there was not more pressure to fix such a fundamental capability. Worse, users had come to believe that addresses could be used as names. "Experts" demanded that IP addresses not change no matter where they were attached to the network: a fine property of names, but not of addresses.

without multiple paths between adjacent nodes, it wasn't a problem that Moore's law couldn't solve. (And when multiple paths did arise, it caused problems but band-aids were found for them.) The problems of multicast and mobility were many years off. It was understood that a change would be necessary, as was our repeated caution about the importance of getting addressing right. No one felt they really understood addressing well enough. It seemed prudent that a more complete understanding was necessary before making the change. We still didn't understand what location dependence meant in a network. It seemed prudent not to do anything until there was a better understanding of what to do. Even in the early 1980s, when NCP was removed and IP became the only network layer protocol, the Internet was still for the most part a network of universities and R&D organizations, so such a major change was still something that could be contemplated.

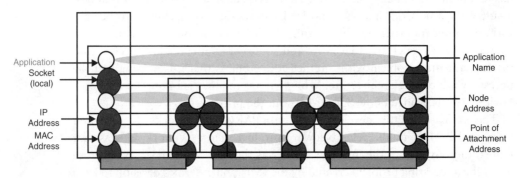

Figure 5-3 Mapping Saltzer's concepts to the Internet shows that half the required identifiers are missing (application names and node addresses) and one is named twice (point of attachment).

When IP was defined, some structure was imposed on IP addresses by dividing the address space into blocks of Class A, B, and C (Figure 5-4). (As other authors do, we will ignore the existence of Class D and E addresses for now.) The classes of IP addresses are intended to be assigned to networks with different numbers of hosts: Class A for the really big ones, Class B for the middle-size ones, and Class C for the really small ones. And of course, within a Class A network, Classes B and C can be used to provide a rudimentary form of location dependence.

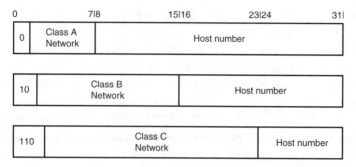

Figure 5-4 IP address format.

But these were allocations of size, and although they might be used to impose location dependence within a given network, no consideration was given to doing it across networks. Blocks of IP addresses were for the most part handed out in the order requested. 128.89 might be on the East Coast of the United States, and 128.90 might be in Hong Kong. So in fact, IP addresses were more like names than addresses. There was no structure or plan to assigning the network part of an IP address. It was assumed that addresses would be assigned in a location-dependent manner within the networks (an assumption made unnecessary by Moore's law) and that the number of networks would remain relatively small. There was no planning for tens of thousands of networks organized into tiers of providers.

As the problems of configuring networks for large organizations grew, subnetting was introduced. Subnetting takes part of the host-id portion of the address and uses it to represent subnets within the Class A or B address (or Class C, but they are pretty small for subnetting). This provides topological-dependent addresses within an organization; outside the organization, however, it is of no help.

OSI and NSAPs

Using the experience from the ARPANET and early Internet, OSI made some major strides in working out the theory of naming and addressing. It also made some major mistakes. (Although there are several interesting aspects to the OSI addressing concepts.) The amount written on it is fairly voluminous and impenetrable. We will consider the basics as briefly as we can and only elaborate on concepts or lessons that we need to carry forward. First, let's dispense with what OSI got wrong: The Europeans were intent on making X.25 the OSI answer to the network layer and not using any experience from the United States, even if it was improving on the lessons learned in the Internet. Consequently, they forced into the OSI architecture fundamental constructs to reflect X.25. As an example, in OSI an (N)-connection is defined to be shared state among (N+1)-entities, not the shared state among (N)-entities. But in spite of such fundamental problems, it was possible to resurrect the beginnings of a fairly reasonable addressing architecture, even if the errors did cause the definitions to get a bit convoluted at times.

OSI spent considerable time developing a theoretical framework for the architecture. This was not the "seven-layer model." But an earlier section of the reference model defined the common elements that all layers would have. The understanding was that there were common elements but different functions in each layer, in line with the Dijkstra concept of a layer. This effort was beneficial because it was an attempt at an "algebra" that clarified the nature of the problem provided insight into the solutions. It is unfortunate that politics could not be kept out of it. However, it seldom helped those who tried to use the standards because the standards seldom reflected the insights that had been gained. (The U.K. delegation insisted that any "tutorial material" should not be included. It seemed that they were intent on making the documents as difficult to use as possible.) There are two aspects of this theory: the general architecture as it relates to addressing and the specifics of addressing in the network layer.

Terms, Terms, Terms

Entity might seem like a pretty innocuous term. It was supposed to be. There was great fear that the *model* not specify implementation. Therefore, any term such as *process, program, task, procedure,* and so on that might be construed as specifying how it must be implemented was unacceptable. I have noticed recently that others have been driven to the same term.

The general OSI architecture consists of (N)-layers. (Of course, in the specific architecture constructed from this theory, the maximum value of N was 7.) Each system in the network contains elements of these (N)-layers, from 1 to 7. The intersection of an (N)-layer with a system is called an (N)-subsystem. Within each (N)-subsystem, there is one or more (N)-entities (Figure 5-5). An (N)-entity is the protocol machine for that layer. A (N)-subsystem could contain more than one (N)-entity (e.g., different groups of users) or (N)-entities of more than one kind (i.e., different protocols). In other words, an (N)-subsystem is all the modules in a system relating to a particular layer, protocol machines, management, buffer management, and so on. Having a term for everything in a system associated with a given layer proves to be quite useful.

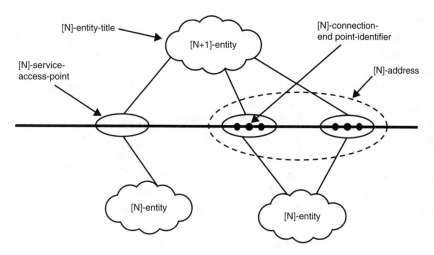

Figure 5-5 Entities, service access points, and identifiers.

As mentioned, an (N)-connection was defined to be "an association requested by an (N+1)-entity for the transfer of data between two or more (N+1)-entities." In other words, an (N)-connection went from one (N+1)-entity (in an (N+1)-layer) down to an (N)-entity across to an (N)-entity in another system and up to the (N+1)-entity in the remote system. (Pushing this definition were the Europeans attempting to legislate the X.25 view.) This tightly binds the shared state in the (N)-entities to the shared state in the (N−1)-entities. But it is important that it be possible to decouple the two, so that the shared state at (N−1) can be lost without affecting the shared state at layer N. This definition makes that difficult.

Later realizing that they needed a name for the relation between the (N)-entities (what the definition of a connection should have been), they defined an (N)-association as "a cooperative relationship among (N)-entity-invocations."[8] Yes! In OSI, associations were connections, and connections were what association should be. But then I have never known a standards organization yet whose arrogance didn't get it into this sort of doublespeak.

The (N)-connection crossed the boundary between an (N+1)-layer and an (N)-layer at an (N)-service access point or (N)-SAP. (N)-SAP-address identifies an (N)-SAP. (This is why one encounters the term *SAP* in other standards.

---

[8] Quite correctly, OSI tried to distinguish between type and instance. A protocol in a subsystem was the type, whereas a specific flow or connection using that protocol would be an instance or instantiation of the protocol. One connects to TCP (type), but each state machine along with its TCB represents an instance of TCP. So when the dust settled, the (N)-entity was the type, and the (N)-entity-invocations were the instances.

Notice how a SAP tries to be a port or interface.) An (N)-SAP was bound to one and only one (N)-entity at a time. If an (N)-entity needed to have an identifier, it was called an (N)-entity-title. (The pedants said it couldn't be called a "name" because addresses were also names.) An address was a location-dependent name. So, the term *title* was used for location-independent names. Associated with an (N)-SAP-address were one or more (N)-connection-endpoint-identifiers whose scope was the (N)-subsystem. An (N)-CEP corresponded to a single connection to an (N)-entity. The (N)-SAP-address was supposed to be an X.25 DTE address. The (N)-CEP-identifier corresponds to what many protocols or IPC facilities call port-ids, whereas for the PTTs it was the X.25 group-id. (Group-ids are similar to ATM virtual path-ids or MPLS tags. All three of these derive from the same telephony lineage). So, an (N)-SAP was really a port, an interface.

This constraint along with the definition of connection caused a number of problems. It implied that all the bindings between (N)-entities in a system had to be preallocated before a connection request was made. This, of course, makes dynamic assignment and resource allocation essentially impossible. By 1983, it was already believed that the reference model was too far along to be changed. So rather than simply fix the definition of connection and make the structure simpler, a level of indirection was created[9]: An (N)-address was defined as a set of (N)-SAP-addresses. But worse, the OSI "address" also identifies the interface. The one thing that most were trying to avoid. (In a committee, *consensus* never means that issues are resolved, only that progress can continue until someone finds a reason to raise the issue again.)

Another problem was discovered in how we thought we would build addresses. Initially, it was assumed that an (N)-address would be formed from an (N–1)-address and (N)-suffix, allowing addresses from a higher layer to infer addresses at lower layers. This was a fairly common approach found in operating systems. It can be found in early versions of the OSI reference model see, for example, ISO TC97/SC16/N117 (1978) or N227 (1979) and in the Internet today. It is a bad idea in networks. And why it is a bad idea is clear from its use in operating systems. Constructing names in this manner in operating systems has a name. They are called *path*names, and therein lies the problem. It defines a path. It defines a single static path within the system and then to the application when, in fact, there may be multiple paths that it should be possible to choose dynamically. It can be done, but essentially one must ignore that it has been done. Recognizing that it is a lot of redundancy for very little gain and may compromise security. It works in an operating system because there *is* only one

---

[9]   Yes, there is nothing in computer science that can't be fixed with a level of indirection. (sigh)

path *within* the operating system from one application to another. This is exactly what we wanted to avoid from our analysis of Saltzer. Hence, any addressing scheme that, for instance, creates a network address by embedding a MAC address in it has thwarted the purpose of the addressing architecture. There can be a relation, but the relation cannot be tied to the path. This is still considered a quite normal approach to take to forming addresses.

However, all was not lost. Or more to the point, the problems in the network layer were much more complicated. The U.S. delegation was insistent that there would be a connectionless network protocol that built on the experience of IP, and the Europeans were intent that the future of networking would be a connection-mode protocol (i.e., X.25) and that connectionless would as limited as possible. They attempted to work out an architecture of the network layer that could accommodate both. The resulting standard, called the *Internal Organization of the Network Layer* (IONL), shed considerable light on what the two warring factions were wanting and provided technical insights (ISO 8648, 1987). Although the language of the document can be quite impenetrable to the uninitiated, every configuration described in it has since turned up in one form or another. The IONL was a very useful exercise in working out how real-world situations would be handled within an architecture. The Europeans had to admit that X.25 was only an interface to the network (after all, it was the title of the Recommendation) and as such only provided access to a subnetwork. It was finally worked out that the primary function of the network layer was to make the transition between the subnetwork-dependent protocols and provide a service that was independent of the subnetwork technology. To do this could require up to three sublayers depending on the configuration and the underlying media:

- A *Subnetwork Access Protocol* (SNACP) is a protocol that operates under constraints of a specific subnetwork. The service it provides may not coincide with the network layer service.

- A *Subnetwork Dependent Convergence Protocol* (SNDCP) operates over a SubNetwork Access protocol and provides the capabilities assumed by the SNICP or the network layer service.

- A *Subnetwork Independent Protocol* (SNICP) operates to construct the OSI network layer service and need not be based on the characteristics of any particular subnetwork service.

Although a lot of this structure may seem (and was) politically motivated, there were several major technical insights. For our purposes, the most important of which was that there was a "subnetwork PoA" (an SNPA or "the wire") that had an address with a scope that had to span only the particular subnet. A system might have several of SNPAs that mapped to an NSAP address. The NSAP address as constructed by the IONL was, in fact, the (N)-entity-title. The (N)-directory, or in the this case the N-directory (N for network) (i.e., the routing information) maintained a mapping between the SNPA-addresses and the NSAP-address. This mapping provides a level of indirection between the physical addressing of the wire and the logical addressing of the network. This level of indirection provides the flexibility required for addressing to accommodate all the configurations and services necessary. This is repeated later, but it is worth observing now:

A network address architecture must have at least one level of indirection.

Like operating systems, there needs to be a transition between logical and physical addressing. As we have seen earlier from our interpretation of Saltzer in a network, two transitions are required: one in the network layer between SNPAs and NSAPs, between route dependence and route independence but both location dependent; and again between NSAPs and application entity titles, between location dependent and location independent.

The NSAP addressing structure attempted to solve two problems: accommodate a wide variety of existing address formats and set out a location-dependent address space. The address format of an NSAP is shown in Figure 5-6.

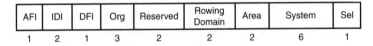

AFI	IDI	DFI	Org	Reserved	Rowing Domain	Area	System	Sel
1	2	1	3	2	2	2	6	1

Figure 5-6 OSI NSAP format for the United States

The address space is organized by countries. The country codes are assigned by an ISO standard. Each country is then allowed to organize its own space. In the United States, a rather elegant solution was found that avoids a requirement for an active centralized authority. There is an existing ANSI standard of organization identifiers. These are used after the country code. To get an assignment of NSAP addresses, one merely has to get an organization-id (which many companies would already have for other purposes), the organization-id goes after the country code the rest of address space can be used by the organization. This creates a provider independent address.

The AFI specifies the format of the IDI and the addressing authority responsible for the IDI. The AFI could select X.121, ISO DCC, F.69 (telex), E.163 (PSTN), E.164 (ISDN), ISO 6523-ICD, or Local. The DFI contains the country code; Org is the ANSI organization identifier. Routing Domain and Area are the topological routing information. The Reserved field was to allow for another level of the routing hierarchy if it was required. The System field is six octets so that an Ethernet address can be used. If this is interpreted too literally it will force the NSAP to name the interface, not the network entity as intended. (Groan. In a committee, it is sometimes difficult to keep people from wanting to do it wrong.) Although this format incorporates location-dependent elements, it does not indicate *where* in the topological structure of the network the address is. It doesn't help determine "which way" to send a PDU or if two destinations are "near" each other. This address is location dependent more in the sense of Boston than Chicago!

This address space reflects the growing understanding of addressing. The IP address space was mostly concerned about identifying networks and hosts without much concern for their relative position in a topology. At this point, although it was understood that something analogous to a "Chicago address" would be useful, no one had any idea how to do such a solution. It really wasn't understood that addresses needed to be topological (in the mathematical sense). With the NSAP address space, there is more concern that a topology is reflected in the address space by including the DFI or country identifier and organization identifier. However, this topology is not completely satisfactory either. This scheme assumes that the routing domains are below the level of organizations. This would be the case for large companies but hardly for smaller ones. Similarly, there are cases where being able to group several small countries under a single regional domain would be useful and conversely, breaking up larger countries into multiple domains would also be useful. Or was the address format the result of a compromise between the "X.25 faction" and the "IP faction"? This raises the question of what is the relation between provider-based addresses and provider-independent addresses. Clearly, provider-based addresses reflect the topology of the provider's network. What does a provider-independent address space reflect? The usual reaction is to immediately leap to a geographic approach. But is this the only one? Are there others that are not totally geographic in nature?

There were other minor problems: The format assumes that organizations are a proper subset of countries. (Although one could assume that a company's presence in another country has a different value for these fields.) The only other problem with the address format is the selector field, which supposedly identifies the protocol in the layer above. The OSI Architecture group had taken the position that it was counter to the architecture for an (N)-protocol to identify an (N+1)-protocol. A horrid layer violation. At the time, this was seen as relating to addressing. So rather than a field in the PCI, the Network Layer group made it a field in the address. Neither solution actually can be used to identify the upper-layer protocol, regardless of whether it is a layer violation. Such a field can only identify one occurrence of a protocol in the layer above bound to that address. (Admittedly, this does not happen often, but as with many other "rare" events, when it does it can make things cumbersome if the addressing has not been done right.) There are configurations where more than one instance of the same type of protocol bound to the same network address is necessary. As we saw in Chapter 3, "Patterns in Protocols," one could argue that we weren't seeing the problem correctly, that the field identifies the syntax of the protocol. However, we will find later that both interpretations are incorrect and such a field is unnecessary.

But all in all, OSI progressed the state of the art and tried to take Saltzer's advice, even if the ill informed stuck a MAC address in the NSAP. It recognizes PoA addresses, node addresses, and as we shall see later, application names extending Saltzer's scheme in an important way.

Communism is the longest most torturous path from capitalism to capitalism.
—Joke that circulated in Eastern Europe at the end of the 1980s

Addressing in IPv6

So let's consider the addressing architecture for this new IP in some detail. The IPv6 addressing specification is very emphatic: "IPv6 addresses of all types are assigned to interfaces, not nodes." However, it then observes that since any interface belongs to a single node, a "unicast address may be used as an identifier for the node"—a painful example of having heard the words but not understanding their implication. We will assume that a *node* is synonymous with a *system* and assume an interface is generalized from the IMP port from which it originated; that is, an interface is the path from the bottom of the IP layer through any lower-layer protocols to the physical media connecting to another system.

One exception to this model is granted to allow multiple physical interfaces to be assigned the same address as long as the implementation treats these as a single interface when presenting it to the IP layer. In other words, parallel interfaces or spares can be treated as a single interface. This would seem to indicate that this is a degenerate form of anycast address—and another kludge to make up for not having node and PoA addresses.

The Various Address Types

Although IPv6 supports a number of address formats, the format we are most interested in will be the Aggregatable Global Unicast Address. This is what most people will think of as an IPv6 address. But before we do that, let's dispense with anycast and multicast addresses and a couple of other address types that are unique to IPv6, the link-local and site-local addresses.

There are three types of IPv6 addresses (RFC 2373, 1998):

- **Unicast.** An identifier for a single interface. A packet sent to a unicast address is delivered to the identified by that address.

- **Anycast.** An identifier for a set of interfaces (typically belonging to different nodes). A packet sent to an anycast address is delivered to one of the interfaces identified by that address.

- **Multicast.** An identifier for a set of interfaces (typically belonging to different nodes). A packet sent to a multicast address is delivered to all interfaces by that address.

Anycast addresses. Anycast addresses are syntactically indistinguishable from unicast addresses. According to RFC 2373, a unicast address is turned into an anycast address by having multiple interfaces assigned to it. This is not quite the case. The nodes to which the interfaces belong must be explicitly configured to be aware of this. So, in fact, it is not multiple assignment that makes it an anycast address, but configuring the nodes to know that it is multiply assigned (an enrollment phase function). The RFC imposes two constraints on the use of anycast addresses: They cannot appear as the source address in any IP packet (reasonable); and they cannot be assigned to hosts, only to routers (less so). This latter constraint is perhaps the most odd because considerable use could be made of anycast addresses in applications. The subnet prefix of an anycast address is the longest prefix that identifies the smallest topological region of the network to which all interfaces in the set belong.

How this is supposed to work is not quite clear. For different nodes to be configured to be aware that multiple interfaces have the same address requires protocol to be exchanged. No such protocol has yet been defined. Clearly, any use of this facility must be stateless because successive uses may not yield PDUs being delivered to the same destination. This is another kludge to get around not having node and PoA addresses.

Multicast addresses. Multicast addresses include two subfields: A flags subfield that has 3 unused bits and a single bit that indicates whether this group address is permanently assigned; and a scope field that currently defines whether the scope of this group address is the local node, the local link, the local site, the local organization, or global. Permanently assigned multicast addresses have global scope; that is, the scope field is ignored. IPv6 defines a multicast address as "an identifier for a set of interfaces." There will be more to say on the nature of anycast and multicast "addresses" in Chapter 9, "Multihoming, Multicast, and Mobility."

Link- and site-local addresses. A link-local address essentially consists of the 10-bit format identifier in the high-order bits and a 64-bit interface identifier in the lower-order bits, and 59 bits of nothing in the middle. This address form is for "local" use only. The RFC suggests that link local addresses "are designed to be used for addressing on a single link for purposes such as auto-address configuration, neighbor discovery, or when no routers are present." The use of the term *link* implies that they are intended to be used on, for example, a single LAN segment (i.e., within a single subnet).

A site-local address, although similar to the link-local form, was to correspond to what private address space was in IPv4 (e.g., net 10). The subnet identifier distinguishes the multiple subnets within the same "site."

In 2003, there was a movement within the IPv6 working group, over considerable objections, to delete site-local addresses from the specification. There were strong feelings against the use of private address space within the IETF. Some believed that this "balkanized" the Internet, which it does, and contradicted some mythic ideal of the "spirit of the Internet." Engineering on belief rather than empiricism is always dangerous. As we have seen, NAT and private address space only break protocols in an incomplete architecture and primarily indicate bad design choices. Or to paraphrase Buckminster "Bucky" Fuller, NATS only break broken architectures.[10] As it turns out, private address space is a natural part of any complete architecture and poses no dangers and, in fact, has many benefits.

However, the removal of private address space from IPv6 would seem to represent a very large deterrent for corporate adoption. Although NATs do not provide complete security, they are an important element in securing and exercising control over a subnet. It is hard to imagine corporate IT directors giving up this simple measure to be replaced by elaborate and as yet unproven IPv6 security mechanisms. Once again, the IETF seems to have cut off its nose to spite its face.

In addition, address formats are defined for carrying NSAP and IPX addresses. (Although there is little expectation that these will ever be used.)

IPv6 also allocates two special addresses: 0 and 1 (or to be precise in the IPv6 notation, 0:0:0:0:0:0:0:0 and 0:0:0:0:0:0:0:1). The unspecified address is 0 and

---

[10] Bucky said, "Automation only displaces automaton."

"indicates the absence of an address." The unspecified address can never be used as a destination but may appear as the source address for a sender who does not have an address yet. (It is not clear what you do with such a PDU (you can't respond to it), but that is not important. The loopback address is 1 and is used by a system to send a PDU to itself. It may only be used as a destination address and then must be sent back to the sender. It should never be relayed to an address other than the sender, and the loopback address must not appear as a source address in a PDU.

IPv6 Unicast Addresses

It is the aggregatable unicast address over which there has been the greatest amount of debate. This debate has evolved around the decision that the IP address will continue to label an interface. This was complicated by the politics surrounding IP and OSI. By the time IPv6 was proposed, some had realized that addresses had to be topological. But they thought topology meant the graph of the network. Mainly, they were concerned that the addresses had to be aggregatable. As discussed in this chapter, the problem with the IPv4 address space is not so much the lack of address space but the growth of the routing tables. To reduce the number of routes that must be stored requires the ability to aggregate them. For example, the post office aggregates routes based on the hierarchy of the address (i.e., country, state/province, city, street, street number, and so on). When a letter is mailed, the first post office has to look at only the first couple of levels of the hierarchy to know where to send it. It does not need to figure out precisely where the destination is; it merely has to send the letter in the right direction. Similarly, some sort of hierarchy was required for IPv6 addresses. As we saw, CLNP adopted such a hierarchy based on countries and organizations within them.

The Internet had the same problem that had faced OSI: a flawed architecture and a reactionary group of traditionalists who opposed any change to the concept that an address labels an interface. However, the Internet architecture was also weak in another area. The Internet architecture really only covered the network and transport layers (or in terms of the seven-layer model, the top third of the network, SNIC, and transport and only had an address for the bottom third). Above and below network and transport, there was not really any structure, so there was no convention for names or routes, as proposed by Saltzer. This led to a tendency to try to solve everything in the network and transport layer.

Names and Addresses

Giving them the benefit of the doubt, it might be closer to the truth that people had become so used to addresses being names that they used them as names and expected that IP addresses could act like both names and addresses. After all, they had never been taught anything different. There are no textbooks in networking that cover what should be named.

The IPv6 effort determined the PDU header format and the size of the address field years before they determined what an address was to look like ("arithmetic before the algebra"). Also, most of the people involved in IPv6 were initially working under the misconception that the number of addresses was the major problem to be solved. There were some initial proposals that were similar to the NSAP address. But because the IPv6 address had to name an interface, to be aggregatable the addresses had to be provider-based. This had the unacceptable consequence that if one changed providers all hosts on your network would have to be re-addressed. (It is significant that the term commonly used in Internet circles is *renumbering* rather than *re-addressing*, which indicates that they think of it as enumeration or naming rather than addressing or changing location.)

As noted previously, a network architecture must make a transition from logical to physical at least once. The Internet architecture has no such transition. OSI had been "fortunate" enough that its traditionalist faction was X.25. That forced (or created the opportunity) to separate the physical address or subnetwork PoA from the network address. The Internet architecture did not really address the layers below network, and there was no X.25 faction. (Its traditionalists hung on to the IP of the "good old days.") Furthermore, the political climate was such that if OSI had done something, the Internet would either not do it or do the opposite and convince themselves there was a good technical reason to codify the old ways.[11]

This meant the possible solutions were severely limited. Therefore, any solution had to have an appearance of not doing what was most reasonable (i.e., a separation of logical and physical in different layers). Even though the idea and the solution had originated during the early development of the Internet and had been used by the, at least politically correct, XNS, it had last been used by OSI and was therefore unacceptable. (And yes, there are many rationalizations why this was not the reason.)

The developers working on the Internet had for many years realized that something needed to be done. But in the Internet, the "host" had always been the focus of attention. There had been several proposals (Curran, 1992; Chiappa, 1995) to name "endpoints." Chiappa defined an endpoint to be "one participant of an end-to-end communication, i.e., the fundamental agent of

---

11 This reaction has always been perplexing: Why react with "do anything but what the 'opposition' has done" and fall prey to "cutting off your nose to spite your face;" rather than "let us show you how to get it right"? Is this a characteristic of crowd behavior? Or is it something else? This is not the only example.

end-to-end communication. It is the entity which is performing a reliable communication on an end-to-end basis." Chiappa et al. saw this as mapping fairly directly to the concept of "host." However, the use of *one* and *an* in the definition would seem to imply more a single protocol machine than a collection of them. This was definitely on the right track. Replacing the traditional semantics of an IP address with the semantics of an endpoint in the protocol would have gone a long way to solving the problems confronting IP. However, this did not meet with much acceptance, probably because the implications of continuing to name an interface with an aggregatable address had not yet dawned on many of the members of the Internet community. To replace the semantics of an IP address with the semantics of an endpoint smacked too much of OSI. This situation existed for several years, and then Mike O'Dell (O'Dell, 1997) made a valiant effort to separate the IPv6 address into "routing goop," which would change when the host moved and an invariant globally unique "end system designator" that identified "a system invariant of its interfaces as *in the XNS architecture*" (emphasis added). This led to an addressing format (Figure 5-7) where the interface-id was the end-system identifier and the rest was the "routing-goop," as follows:

Where:

FP	The format prefix
TLA ID	Top-level aggregation identifier (13 bits)
Res	Reserved (8 bits)
NLA ID	Next-level aggregation identifier (24 bits)
SLA ID	Site-level aggregation identifier (16 bits)
Interface ID	Interface identifier (64 bits), probably an EUI-64 identifier

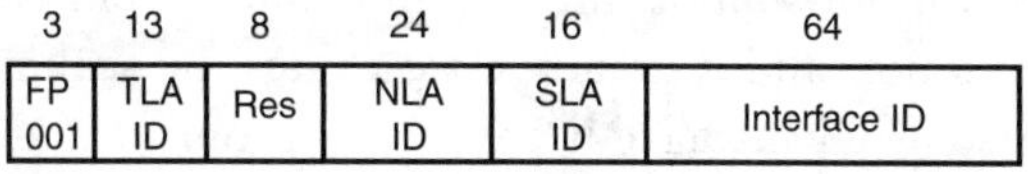

3	13	8	24	16	64
FP 001	TLA ID	Res	NLA ID	SLA ID	Interface ID

Figure 5-7 Format of an aggregatable IPv6 address.

The TLA, NLA, and SLA form the routing hierarchy of the address to the level of subnet, and the interface-id represents a completely independent globally unambiguous identifier. But, it does precisely what we found earlier that we didn't want to do: make it into a pathname.

This proposal came four years after the initial decision to develop IPv6 was made. By this time, memories had faded, there had been considerable turnover in the people involved, and the ramifications of the decision had finally become clearer to many. So with a little artful prose that did not open old wounds, O'Dell's proposal was able to thread the needle between the technical requirements and the political climate for a solution with only a moderate level of additional complexity. However, this was also unacceptable. The routing part of the IPv6 address is a path through a hierarchy of subnets, while the end-system designator has the same semantics as an IPv4 address. It names the interface (or to put it in other terms, the data link protocol machine). Here again, the IPv6 group found a way to take on the trappings of the solution without taking its substance to solve the problem. So although the form of O'Dell's proposal may be discernable in the IPv6 address format, the substance of it is not, and the problems remain.

At arm's length, an IPv6 address is similar to an NSAP in form. (...the longest, most torturous path....) It was common with NSAPs to use an IEEE 802 MAC address as the system-id, analogous to the use of an EUI-64 address as the interface-id. This was a case where the OSI architecture figured out something but the OSI Network Layer group, in a different committee, stayed with their intuitions. And as so often is the case in science, our intuitions were wrong. The NSAP format had four levels of hierarchy, whereas the IPv6 has three levels. OSI did not require "endpoints" or anything like them because it had application names. Because the IETF had no common application naming, it had, or thought it had, to solve everything in either the network or transport layer.

With IPv6, the routing part is not sufficient alone to distinguish a node. It can only distinguish the subnet but requires the interface-id to distinguish the node, whereas the interface-id alone can distinguish the interface. There are roughly 32 bits of redundancy in an IPv6 address (or enough for a couple of more levels in the routing hierarchy).

This approach will not support multihoming and mobility for the same reasons that IPv4 does not, and it greatly exacerbates the scaling problems in IP. The impact of these problems have been known about for a decade and a half, and now at this writing, with IPv6 barely deployed, they are already showing signs that are causing problems that are somewhere between severe and catastrophic. ("But she didn't do it and....")

Looking Back over IPv6

IPv6 has not instilled a lot of confidence among the cognoscenti. In fact, fear and trepidation is closer to the case. But deployment is beginning in fits and starts. There are still strong debates going on relating to the architecture of its addressing. For example, until very recently, some still argued that multihoming is being overly stressed. They contend that only a few hosts will need it and that a solution to multihoming is not really required; or because so few hosts need it, its cost should not be incurred by those who don't. This essentially ensures that any solution will be asymmetric and consequently will appear and be cumbersome and hence unacceptable.[12]

Superficially, it might appear that only a small percentage of all hosts require multihoming; that is, there are many more individuals connected to the Net than servers. However, even a small percentage of a large number can be a large number. But the real reason is that the ones that do need multihoming are very important to all the others. This is changing. As more companies come to rely on the Internet, the more they see multihoming as a necessity, and it is becoming more of a problem. Why is there an assumption that a solution must cost more, when in fact it actually costs less? It makes one wonder why people would argue that it is not very important. Why should there be so much debate over not doing multihoming? Redundant connections to the network would seem to be an "apple pie" issue. Of course, redundancy is a good thing, but not for the traditionalists. A simple solution to multihoming requires changing the semantics of the address. If multihoming is not important, there is no need for a change. So, the argument that multihoming is not important is actually more political than technical.

The concern over the addressing situation was sufficiently great that in 1999 that the IAB created an *Internet Research Task Force* (IRTF), the research side of the IETF) working group independent of the IPv6 work to consider namespace issues. This group met several times. There was a lot of discussion of endpoints as opposed to naming, but without a strong architectural model it was impossible to establish precisely what was required. Consequently, there was no consensus on the conclusions. But this effort seemed to focus the discussion on what has become known as the locator/identifier split. Many see the problem with the IP address is that its semantics have been overloaded with both locator meaning and identifier meaning, and if we simply separate them all the problems will be solved. Notice that they do not see that the IP address naming the interface is naming the same thing the MAC address does, but they also rely on the fact that the MAC address has greater scope than the IP address to make certain mobility-related capabilities work.

However, referring back to the Saltzer paper, this approach will give us an application name and a PoA address. Once again, it addresses the symptom but

---

12 This is a nice piece of electro-political engineering: Come up with very reasonable criteria that can only be met by an unacceptable proposal. This one is even better than the "lightweight transport protocol" red herring.

How Bad Could It Be?

The designers of IPv6 have blithely increased the size of the address without really considering the scaling implications of a full-blown IPv6 flat network. For several years, they ignored the router table expansion problem. They have continued to kludge the multihoming problem until the fall of 2006 when recognition of a looming crisis predicted dire consequences. After about ten days of considering that a more in-depth investigation was warranted, they fell back into the artisan response of looking for another band-aid.

In addition, some experts are concerned that router table calculations for the much larger v6 address will take much longer, greatly shortening the period between calculations. There is some question as to whether the effects of new forwarding tables once calculated would have time to take effect before it was time to recalculate. If the effects of the new forwarding table have not had time to "settle" before a new calculation begins, the input for the new calculation will be based on transient conditions, increasing the likelihood of unstable behavior.

Or more starkly, when a failure in the Net causes a router table computation, the Net will continue using the old tables while the calculation is made. The longer the calculation takes, the longer traffic is *not* responding to the failure, compounding the situation so that by the time the new forwarding tables are available, they have been computed for a situation that no longer exists and may make the response to the failure worse, not better.

The rationale for automatic routing has always been that events are happening too fast for a human to be in the decision loop. It may be that events are happening too fast to have v6 in the loop.

not the problem. The Internet's focus on the transport and network layer has led to attempts to solve these problems in one of those two places. But, there is no such thing as a transport address. This is creating a "beads-on-a-string in disguise" model, not an operating system or distributed systems model. Consequently, efforts such as *Host Identifier Protocol* (HIP) (RFC 4423) and SHIM6 (Nordmark and Bagnulo, 2006) are simply more stopgaps that fail to address the whole problem and apply yet another band-aid to one aspect of the problem. As many in the Internet rightly realize, all of these myopic band-aids are creating a system that is more and more unwieldy.

Many prominent members of the Internet technical community have not expected wide deployment of IPv6. The biggest problem is that IPv6 offers very little to those who have to pay for its adoption. The removal of link-local (private) addresses provides one more reason not to adopt IPv6 in the enterprise, but to only use it externally. All new facilities, such as security, multicast, QoS-related developments, and so on, are designed to work equally well with IPv4 or IPv6. Thus, all statements in the recent trade press that IPv6 is necessary and has better QoS, security, and such are simply spin. The only new capability provided by IPv6 is a longer address, and that in and of itself may create more problems than it solves. In early 2003, figures were published that around 50% of the IPv4 address space had been assigned and less than 29% was actually being used (Huston, 2003). A cursory inspection shows that between 25-30 Class A address blocks could and should be re-claimed. This would seem to indicate (and is supported by recent government reports) that there is no rush to move to IPv6.

The only advantages to IPv6 are the bigger address space, the loss of isolation with no equivalent to private addresses, and the knowledge that you are a good network citizen—hardly the basis for a large capital expense to make the transition. This is not going to impress corporate budget committees. However, the possibility of IPv6 failing to be adopted has so alarmed certain factions that an immense PR campaign has been initiated to drum up interest in IPv6. (The possibility that IPv6 may fail for technical reasons does not seem to bother them.) An IPv6 forum was created and many trade journal articles written advocating advantages to IPv6 for security, QoS, and so on, which, in fact, are unrelated to IPv6. Trade journals go out of their way to put a positive spin on even the bad news. The European Union and the U.S. government have endorsed IPv6 in much the same way they endorsed OSI two decades earlier. IPv6 advocates point to this as proof of IPv6's pending success, just as they ridiculed the same statements by OSI advocates. Others see this as the kiss of death as it was for OSI. India, Japan, and China have embraced IPv6 mostly because they cannot get large IPv4 address blocks from IANA to support their huge populations. However, as we have seen, more than enough v4 address space exists. IPv6 may happen as much because the IETF has not been able to come up with anything that solves real problems, rather than on its own merits. This does not bode well.

But what contribution can we say that IPv6 has brought to our problem of trying to gain a deeper understanding of the nature of addressing? Unfortunately, not much. There is really nothing new here that has not been done before. As we have seen, IPv6 is simply a more cumbersome form of IPv4.

However, it does provide further confirmation of the social behavior of standards committees. (OSI provides earlier confirmation.) Another example of how a vocal conservative (dare I say ill-informed) faction can slow progress, and the lengths that a minority with greater technical understanding must go to find a way to bend the position of conservatives to get some sort of solution that solves real problems,[13] not to mention that this direction benefits the vendors: Not only does the iterative increase in complexity keep a steady stream of new products to buy, but it also serves as a barrier to entry to new competitors and keeps customers tied to the vendor because their personnel can't understand the interactions of all the incremental improvements. CLNP had been only a slight improvement over IPv4. But it had been a bigger step than IPv6 represents and had been at least a move in the right direction. All of this contributes to the feeling that the concepts had run out of steam. After about 1975, there was very little new or innovative thinking going on. The only significant development one can point to is the development of link-state routing algorithms, which primarily was done in OSI, which stimulated similar efforts in the IETF.

If there is anything to learn from the IPv6 experience, it probably has more to do with the dynamics (or lack thereof) of consensus. It was James Madison (1787) who was the first to realize the inherently conservative nature of such groups. And human nature hasn't changed in 200 years. In his case, it led to the creation of mechanisms to stabilize an otherwise unstable system. In this environment, the lack of understanding of this dynamic has merely undermined innovation in a fast-moving technology. OSI started out as a "revolutionary"

---

13 The similarity to controversies in other areas of science are striking.

group intending to promulgate the packet network connectionless model. But the European tendency toward centralism and fear of the PTTs expanded the participation in the effort to include the opposition that saw X.25 as the answer to all network layer issues. This irresolvable conflict so severely split the OSI attempt that it ultimately failed. We have already discussed how the minority had to contort that architecture to achieve a semblance of a reasonable addressing architecture for the network layer, only to have it botched by the implementers. The fundamental lesson here is that the old paradigm can never be invited to collaborate with the new paradigm.

In the IETF, the conservatives have been a similar drag on innovation and good engineering. But here the stakes are much higher. OSI basically never had wide deployment. Businesses the world over now depend on the Internet. The IETF is now more concerned that the Internet architecture should not deviate from the old ways—that the architecture of 1972 has been given to it on stone tablets handed down from on high. When in reality, it was done by a group of engineers who were struggling to understand a new field and just to get something that worked. The conservatives now read deep meaning into what were expedient hacks, the authors of which knew they were hacks and knew they would need to be replaced "when there was time." The keepers of the flame are protecting an unfinished demo, rather than finishing it in the spirit in which it was started.

So if we have learned anything from IPv6, it is that all committees behave pretty much the same and will try to avoid deviating from the status quo. The problem within the IETF is compounded by the "democratic" organization, rather than a "representative" or republican organization. It has been well understood for 250 years that democracies don't work and are susceptible to just this kind of long-term behavior. But, mechanisms can be created in a republican form of organization that will work; this was Madison's innovative discovery in system design. Representative forms have the potential to adopt new results not yet fully understood by the larger group. However, it remains that the only time a committee will do something innovative is when the majority perceives it as unimportant. Not exactly a result that is terribly helpful or encouraging.

"Upper-Layer" or Application Addressing in OSI

From our previous discussion, we would expect addressing for upper layers to involve some unique problems. According to Shoch and Saltzer, applications are supposed to have names, whereas lower-layer protocols have addresses. We must consider the problem of naming applications and relating that to addressing. Let's consider how the Internet and OSI dealt with upper-layer addressing.

As noted earlier, the early ARPANET had its hands full demonstrating a resource-sharing network and created "well-known sockets" as a stopgap so that it could demonstrate the usefulness of the network. The need for a directory was well understood at the time, but there were other priorities. Because there were no new applications in the Internet for another 20 years, there was no reason to change. (And by this time, there was a new generation of engineers who now argued that well-known sockets were a gift from the gods, divine insight, not a kludge that should be fixed.)

The first impetus for change was not required by applications and all the resource sharing that had been expected, but by the proliferation of hosts. Since the beginning, each host had maintained its own table of hostnames and their corresponding network address (NCP or IP). Only a few hosts might be added per month, and not all hosts found it necessary to keep a complete table. However, as the rate of new hosts increased in the late 1970s, this fairly informal approach was no longer practical. The result was the development of DNS or the *Domain Name Server* (RFC 881, 882). DNS defined a database structure not only for mapping hostnames to addresses, but also for distributing the database to servers around the network. Later, DNS was used to also distribute URLs for HTTP.

URLs are not the same as well-known sockets. A well-known socket identifies a special transport layer port identifier that has a particular application protocol bound to it. There is an implicit assumption that there is only one instance of this protocol per host. A connection to a well-known socket will create a distinct connection or flow to the requestor. A URL identifies an application (i.e., a particular Web page that uses that protocol [HTTP]), and an arbitrary instance of that application is created. We must be careful when talking about URLs. What they were defined for and how they are used in combination with other conventions make them several things at once. This is fine and perhaps even advantageous for human use, but for architecture we need to understand the different objects being named and their relation.

As discussed in Chapter 4, OSI created problems for itself by getting the upper layers upside down. Applications sat on top of two layers (session and presentation) that had addressing (a general property of a layer). These layers were constrained to not allow mapping between connection and connectionless and to have no multiplexing. Consequently, mappings between two layers were required to be one-to-one. There was no need for addressing in these two layers. Another indication that these were not layers.

We saw that for the lower layers it was not a good idea to create addresses for a layer by concatenating it with the address of the layer below because it formed a pathname. For the upper layers of OSI, there was no multiplexing and, hence, no multiple paths. However, this would create very long addresses with considerable redundant information as one moved up from the network layer. For example, because a transport address would be NetAddr.suffixT, the session address to be carried in protocol would be TrptAddr.suffixS or NetAddr.suffixT.suffixS, and the presentation address would beNetAddr.suffixT.suffixS.suffixP. This creates a lot of unnecessary overhead in the PDUs. To avoid this, an (N)-address for the transport, session, and presentation was defined as a tuple consisting of a network address and the appropriate number of (N)-selectors. Thus, a presentation address was defined as follows:

(Network address, T-sel, S-sel, P-sel)

The PCI in each layer above the network layer only carried the selector. If an implementer was smart, the P-selector and S-selector were null. Consequently, the only addressing above the network layer was that transport protocol had to carry a T-sel of 16 bits.[14]

Because there was no addressing in the session and presentation layers, the interesting aspect of OSI addressing for the upper layers was the addressing architecture of the application layer. In Chapter 4, we saw how the distinction between the application process and application entity came about. Now we have to consider how the naming of them works.

Table 5-1 *Summary of OSI Application Naming*

Item (Identified by AE)	APT	APII	AEQ	AEII
Appl Process	+			
Appl Process Invocation	+	+		
Appl Entity	+		+	
Appl Entity Invocation	+	+	+	+

	Scope
APT = Application-Process-Title	Application layer
APII = Application-Process-Invocation-Identifier	Application process
AEQ = Application Entity Qualifier	Application process
AEII = Application Entity Invocation Identifier	(API, AE)

---

[14] Somebody in a NIST workshop thought the maximum size of T-sel should be 40 octets. Now I believe in large addresses as much as anyone, but even I thought 2^{320} application connections in a single host at the same time was a little excessive! Another indication that separating designers and implementers is not a good idea.

To recap from Chapter 4, OSI distinguished the "application entity" (AE), which was within the OSI architecture and consisted of the application protocols. Databases, file systems, the rest of the application, and so on were outside of OSI. (This was somewhat political because it meant that the OSI committee was not going to tread on the turf of other committees.) Thus, the protocols an application used were part of the network architecture but everything else was outside. This is exactly the distinction we noted in the Web page example earlier. The application that constitutes the Web page and everything it needs is outside the communication architecture, but the HTTP protocol (and any other application protocols it uses, such as FTP or a remote query protocol) is within the architecture.

Thus, the Web application is an AP, and HTTP is the AE; and in this case, the AP may have several AE instances, for the simultaneous HTTP connections. Each must be distinctly identifiable. An application could have multiple protocols associated with it. For example, a hotel reservation application might use HTTP to talk to the customer and a remote database protocol to make the reservation. Similarly, an application could have multiple instances of each protocol and different dialogs with different customers. So, there could be application entity instances. Of course, the designer might choose to instantiate a different process for each customer so that there are multiple instances of the application process but single instances of the AEs. Clearly, there could be applications where there were instances of both processes and entities. The AEs were the only part of the application process inside the OSI architecture.

We can see in hindsight that the early Internet applications were special cases and hence not good examples to generalize from. Not only were the protocol and the application essentially synonymous, but there was only one per system. This is where our operating system experience was not sufficiently rich and we needed insight from the users' world. Our first real-life example of this application structure was the Web.

Once this structure was recognized, the application naming architecture was straightforward. OSI defined naming that allowed AEs and their instances as well as APs and their instances to be addressed. Addressing in the lower layers had never bothered to address to the level of instances. There is no reason to connect to a specific transport or TCP connection. They are all the same. However, for applications this is not the case. Recovery and other mechanisms would need to be able to establish or reestablish communication to an existing invocation of a protocol (AE) or to the invocation of an application (AP) using it. This leads to the addressing structure shown in Table 5-1.

Before one balks too much at the apparent complexity of this naming structure, a couple of things need to be observed. First of all, most applications don't need most of this. But the ones that do, really need it. Second, the complex forms, when they are needed, are generally needed by processes, not humans. Third, it is not at all clear that any "naming" at this level should be intended for human use. In the days of command language–driven operating systems, application names and filenames were intended for human use. However, today this is much less clear. What we used to think of as "user-friendly" (e.g., www.cnn.com) is not considered so today.

In the early days of networking, it was believed that applications had names and hosts had addresses. But this was an artifact of the implementation (and sloppy thinking); it turns out that when one carefully analyzes the problem, the host never appears (another surprise). Processes on a host appear but not the host. As we saw, this concept was brought over from operating systems. As understanding improved, it became clear that the important property of addresses is that they are used to "locate" objects; that is, that they be topologically significant. But application "names" are not just labels. They are used to locate applications and are just as topological as addresses, although admittedly in a very different topology. The structure of application names is used just as much to *locate* the application in the space of applications as the structure of network addresses locates in the space of network nodes. (This might be close to what some call the "semantic Web.")

In most incarnations, this leads to proposals for a hierarchical name structure. However, more recently this has been challenged by a more brute-force approach relying on searching. The role in the 1980s and early 1990s that many saw a system like the X.500 Directory or URNs playing now seems to be supplanted by Google, Yahoo!, and so on. Even within our systems, we have relied on search rather than richer structures. It remains to be seen whether searching can scale or whether other mnemonic or more structured methods may be necessary. But the question remains, that some form of common name that humans can exchange among themselves for use with computers is needed. How do we make this user friendly when a *Macintosh* might be a red apple, a computer, a stereo amplifier, or a raincoat. Or do the humans have to learn how to be friendly with the names computers use? For our purposes, we are less concerned with how these interface to people and are more concerned with what needs to be named, the properties of the names, and their relation.

URI, URL, URN, and So On: Upper-Layer Addressing in the Internet

As noted in Chapter 4, there has been very little work in the Internet space on upper-layer architecture and consequently also on naming and addressing issues in the upper layers. Everything derives from the host-naming convention. Originally, the convention was simply <hostname>, as the number grew it became necessary to move to a multilevel structure:

<local domain-id>.†<host/site name>.<TL-domain>

This structure was generally used to name hosts within a site or subnet. In fact, if one looks closely at the URL syntax, one gets the impression that it is more a character-oriented syntax for specifying network layer constructs or a one-line macro facility not unlike the UNIX or Multics command line.

The work on the Universal Resource Name moves to a more sophisticated level of directory functions but does not really give us any insight in to the architecture of application naming requirements. The URN work in essence defines a syntax for names of resources and its interaction with a database defining various mechanisms to search the database and return a record. What the record contains is left to the designer of the specific URN. The URN syntax defines the top level of a hierarchy and conventions of notation and then allows specific communities to define the specific syntax to fit their application.

This would lead us to look at the applications to perhaps find some insights into application architecture naming issues. Unfortunately, most applications have not reached a level of complexity that requires more structure than a simple pathname hierarchy.

Conclusions

As we have seen, addressing is a subtle problem, fraught with traps. Early in the development of networks, simple solutions that ignored the major issues were more than sufficient. But as networks grew, the addressing problems should have been investigated. With the exception of two seminal pieces of work, however, they were largely ignored. However, the very long incubation period as an R&D effort (more than 20 years) removed from the pressures of business and used primarily by experts allowed people's ideas to calcify. The effect of Moore's law, increasing power, and decreasing cost of equipment made it possible to ignore the problems until long past the point when they should have been resolved (making it very painful to fix them). Early on (in CYCLADES), it was understood that it was necessary to make a transition from physical to logical address at least once (and even better if more than once). This was supported by Shoch's and then Saltzer's view that applications, nodes, points of attachment, and routes were the fundamental elements of addressing that had to be distinguished. From this and early distributed computing experiments, we recognized that application names were location independent, whereas nodes were location dependent but not route dependent. Although nodes seemed to be synonymous to hosts most of the time, there were counter-examples that showed that this was another false intuition. Oddly enough, it turns out that the only requirement to name a host or a system occurs in network management. Naming hosts is irrelevant to communications.[15]

This was later refined as topologically dependent. It was still unclear how these properties should manifest themselves. Given how network topologies can change, it was often unclear how this could be accomplished without being too tightly coupled to the physical topology of the network. It even took some time to realize (and is still unlearned by many protocol designers) that the limited scope of some layers meant that not all addresses had to be globally unambiguous. It is a sorry state of affairs that there has been almost no progress in understanding addressing in the past 25 years.

It should also be pointed out that although one can point to these facts in the literature, they were generally not understood by 99% of the engineers involved in networking. Very few, if any, textbooks in the field teach general principles of networking; they generally only teach current practice.[16] By the 1990s, current practice was the only general theory most engineers knew. There had always been a tendency to concentrate on research directly applicable to the Internet, instead of understanding the field of networking as a whole. Such general research had always been a fraction of the total, as one would expect, but by the mid-1980s it had pretty much died out entirely. Has the field begun to more resemble an artisan guild than an engineering discipline? This was compounded by no new applications to drive new requirements. The three applications that existed were all special cases that did not expose the full structure. This was not helped by the fact that addressing is a hard problem. Saltzer gave us the basics of what needed to be named, but finding a meaningful interpretation to location dependence was a major stumbling block. Both IP and CLNP made attempts, but both were rooted in the past. Now with all of this background, we are ready to consider how to assemble larger architectural structures.

---

[15] Yes, it is often the case that *node* and *host* are synonymous, and it may be convenient in informal conversation. But as Shoch's quote we referenced earlier indicates, professionally we must be precise in our use of terms, or we will get ourselves in trouble.

[16] Every so often, on one of the IETF discussions lists, some young engineer or professor gets a glimmer of these general principles that often contradict what we currently do. Instead of being told that "yes, those are the principles but we did not know that at the time," he is quickly led back to the party line using varying degrees of coercion.

Chapter 6

Divining Layers

In anything at all, perfection is finally attained not when there is no longer anything to add, but when there is no longer anything to take away....

—Antoine de Saint Exupery, Wind, Sand and Stars[1]

Networking is interprocess communication.

—Robert Metcalfe, 1972

Introduction

In the previous chapters, we have reviewed our experience with networking systems and uncovered some of the architectural structures of protocols. Along the way, we identified invariant properties and common components. Now, we are ready to consider what these patterns tell us about assembling them into larger structures. Traditionally, we have assembled them into layers, but layers have proved problematic. Are layers even the right organizing principle for networks? Let's consider the problem of defining what a layer really is. We will again look to our experience for guidance. Not to presage the outcome too much, but finding little help there, we will consider what the problem tells us.

---

[1] Kudos to Noel Chiappa for finding the first quote. Noel uses them for the same reason as I do. When someone says it well, there is no point trying to improve on it; just use it and give copious credit.

Putting Protocols Together

What We Have Seen

First let's consider where layers came from. The use of layers is relatively new to the field of communications. For more than 100 years, the beads-on-a-string model had worked adequately and had been sufficient for early data communications, too. During this period, networks were almost exclusively a matter of electronics. Creating black boxes and levels of abstraction is not something one finds much need for in wiring. Even for early message-switch networks, it was fine. Early message switches were considered "hosts" in the sense that once a message was received and written to disk, the communication was complete. Message switching was seen as a sequence of complete communications.

With the advent of packet switching, however, all of this changed. This new kind of network had more software than anything that had gone before, so it was natural that those building them had considerable software experience. In the late 1960s and early 1970s, that meant operating systems experts. At the time, the need for managing complex operating system software by hiding the complexity behind abstractions, such as layers, had gained considerable popularity. In these networks, the communication of a message was not complete until the packets had wound their way through the network, being relayed at various points to be reassembled at the destination. Hence, layering was introduced from operating systems.

If one reads the early papers, one can see a phenomenon not uncommon in the history of science: As researchers struggled to solve the problems of making networks that worked, while trying to understand what the underlying theory was, some had both feet planted firmly in the old model, some were on the fence, and some had made the leap to a new model. The model in use strongly impacted how one attempted to solve the problem. Many never gave up the beads-on-a-string model and only paid lip service to layers, just as some programmers pay lip service to modularity, objects, and the discipline of software engineering. That confusion continues to affect our perception of problems to this day.

Quite simply, most architectures considered a protocol and a layer to be synonymous. Each protocol constituted a black box, and the interface to that black box was the layer boundary. It was just assumed that this was the case. The emphasis was on the data transfer part of the problem. Less attention was given to how the necessary "support" fit into the model (e.g., routing and management).

The OSI reference model was the first to attempt to more rigorously define the elements of an architecture, but the definitions were somewhat circular:

"A layer is the collection of subsystems of the same rank."

"Subsystems are the intersection of a system and a layer."

—(ISO 7498-1, 1984, 1994)

The implication being that a layer was the set of all protocol machines at the same level across a set of systems: one protocol, one layer. But there was nothing that put any bounds on the set of systems in a layer. In some places, the language seemed to indicate that layers went on forever; in others, definite bounds existed. It was clear that at least some layers had limits. The limit of a layer was termed its *scope*. From the usage, we infer that the scope of a layer was determined by the PMs in the same layer that a protocol could communicate with directly without requiring a relay at the layer above. There is little if anything in the OSI reference model that indicates what is and isn't in a layer.[2] The use of the term *subsystem* intimates that there might be more than just the protocol; otherwise, the term *entity* would have been used.

If consideration of the definitions doesn't shed any light on the problem, perhaps looking at what has been proposed will. At first (the early to mid-1970s), a fairly simple structure seemed to worked fairly well (see Figure 6-1):

- There was the physical layer, with all the electrical signaling conventions.

- Then a data link layer, usually considered to be something like HDLC, that did error control and flow control over relatively slow and lossy point-to-point links connecting the packet switches. The characteristics of the data link layer were tailored to the media.

- Then there was a network layer, primarily responsible for resource allocation (i.e., relaying and routing).

- Then there was the end-to-end transport layer that ensured that data was not lost between the hosts and provided flow control between the communicating applications.

- And on top of the transport layer, the application layer.

---

[2] There is a list of supposed criteria for the layers. However, this list was added long after the layers had been set. (In fact, their inclusion was a last-minute condition for progressing the document to approval in 1980.) They were not used to arrive at the layers; and as homework problems in more than one textbook show, these can be used to justify any number of layered architectures. So, they can't really be seriously applied to our problem.

Nice and neat. It was presumed that there were more layers associated with the applications, but no one was quite sure what they might be.

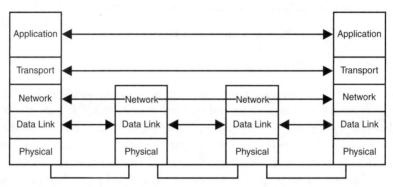

Figure 6-1 Early network architecture.

It was recognized that routing protocols were somewhat special protocols in the network layer that operated in the background to maintain the routing tables and information on network loading. The routing protocols were clearly out-of-band and not part of the data flow associated with user applications (but, instead, competed with it). By the 1980s, it was recognized that something called *layer management* in each layer allowed a network management system to observe protocol behavior and modify configurations and so on.[3] Routing was viewed as network layer management. However, given that the data link and transport protocols did not require anything remotely as complex as the routing protocols, it seemed a bit odd that the network layer should be so much more complex than the others. Simply labeling everything else, layer management had the sense of sweeping things under the rug. But, there were no other suggestions. In the OSI effort, no serious attempt was made to characterize the modules within a layer. This was to some degree on purpose. There was great concern that standards documents describe only what has to be standardized. Describing other aspects, it was believed, would constrain implementations. (And there was much greater variation in implementations than today.) So for example, how protocols interact with the operating system could not be discussed, nor could a protocol machine be described as a process. (What some systems called a process was not what others called it.) In addition, some believed that the inclusion of more detail would result in some sort of advantage

---

[3] Reminds one of the sphere visiting Flatland (Abbott, 1899).

for its advocates; therefore, those who didn't advocate it or didn't understand the value of including it opposed it.[4]

Then the world started to get a bit more complicated. LANs came along, and suddenly there were two protocols in the data link layer: a *Media Access Control* (MAC) protocol and a *Logical Link Control* (LLC) protocol.[5] LANs were not a simple point-to-point medium, but multiple access and introduced repeaters and bridges. And if that wasn't enough, the PTTs were pushing the beads-on-a-string model with X.25 and X.75. X.25 and X.75 were not peer network protocols, but "interfaces"—in the case of X.25, an interface between a host and a network or between a packet-mode *Data Terminating Equipment* (DTE) and *Data Communications Equipment* (DCE) in their language (i.e., between a host and the first router). The PTTs argued that X.25 was all that was needed (i.e., no transport protocol). They claimed their networks were reliable.

The PTTs realized that the transport layer sealed them off from the lucrative high-margin services and relegated them to a commodity business. (It wasn't so much that the PTTs couldn't develop services above transport as they couldn't do it without competition. They were very comfortable with being a monopoly.) The networking crowd argued that no network was perfectly reliable and that it would be negligent for hosts to assume they were. Consequently, to ensure sufficient reliability, a transport protocol was always necessary, so a transport protocol over X.25 was needed, too. This led to calls for supposedly simpler, lightweight transport protocols to operate over more reliable X.25

---

4 This does not mean that the opponents thought these proposals were wrong. They just did not want to give the advocates any advantage. Because, clearly, one does not propose things just because they are correct, but only to gain a market advantage. Once again, the tension between acting on principle and on self-interest raises its head. The United States tends to split 50/50, but Europe always acts on *raison d'etat*. One must recognize that a standard is never a purely technical document, but more a set of political and economic agreements.

5 This created multiple problems. First, most LANs are sufficiently error-free that an LLC is unnecessary. LLC was a purely political expediency forced on LANs by those who could not imagine a link layer protocol that did not look like HDLC. However, with the advent wireless LANs (talk about coming full circle), more lower-layer error control is sometimes necessary (see Chapter 2), so there is actually a reason for more error control and an LLC-like function.

Politics

There has been a lot of discussion in this book about the political issues that have affected the state of network architecture. Many readers will find this distasteful and irrelevant. It is the unfortunate reality that politics can never be eliminated from these processes. One might think that the basis in science would allow some rationality to prevail, and once in a while it does. However, one seldom has the irrefutable data required at the time of the debate to silence the opposition. Contributing to this is the problem that with today's rate of development, standards must to some extent shoot for a point in the future. If they merely codify current practice, by the time the agreement is reached, there is a very good chance that the standard will be irrelevant. On the other hand, there is also a significant chance that aiming at a point in the future, the group will guess wrong.

Many groups have tried to speed up the process. This is essentially impossible. The time a standard takes is in direct relation to the breadth of the group doing the work. Consensus is based on the members coming to an understanding. The broader the group, the longer the time; and there is very little that one can do to speed it up that does not endanger building a consensus.

networks, rather than the more complex, higher-overhead protocols required for connectionless networks. For them, X.25 might be used as the access protocol between the host and the network, but the network should be connectionless with an end-to-end transport protocol over the network. It was recognized that some (sub)networks might have poor quality and thus require an error-control protocol of some sort over them to bring the level of service up to the level of the networks on one or both ends. It seemed there were more protocols than layers!

Case in Point

A good example of the point just made. As one would guess, the "complex" transport protocol is as efficient as "lightweight" ones under the same conditions, and the difference in code size is not great. While there were implementations of the "complex" ones—CYCLADES TS, TCP, SeqPkt, and delta-t—there were no implementations or hard evidence to refute the arguments. And of course, all programmers *know* that they can write much tighter, smaller designs than anyone else and in most cases, they don't. Remember the PTTs wanted no transport protocol. Given there was going to be a transport layer, this was the contingency to further confuse the issue. By the time there was data to refute the argument, there were commitments to use them no matter what.

If the definition of a layer is one protocol per layer, then with LANs there were six layers: physical, MAC, LLC, network, transport, and application. If you believed the PTTs, there were four layers: physical, LAPB, X.25, and application. But if you were more skeptical, then for X.25 networks, there were five layers: physical, LAPB, X.25, transport, and application. And for others, there were six or seven layers: physical, LAPB, X.25, IP, TCP, and application. Architectures like this were seldom proposed outright; instead, proposals kept the basic four lower layers and proposed sublayers.

The ARPANET/Internet community responded by throwing up their hands and saying TCP and IP were on top of whatever was below IP and the applications were whatever was above TCP. As we saw, this had other consequences. OSI, dominated by the European PTT interests, didn't want to admit LANs existed (or any form of network that could be purchased from someone other than a PTT), so never said anything about the data link layer that wasn't HDLC-like, but they were forced to recognize the distinction between LLC and MAC. (Note that the debate between the PTT faction and the networking crowd was essentially a difference between deterministic and nondeterministic systems design.) However, with the network layer being the focus of the connection/connectionless debate, they grudgingly had to agree that connectionless network protocols were being used over X.25, and X.25 was by their own admission only a network layer access protocol. So, the network layer was sublayered[6]: subnet access protocols, subnet-dependent convergence protocols, and subnet-independent convergence protocols. As discussed in Chapter 4, "Stalking the Upper-Layer Architecture," the upper three layers were actually one (see Figure 6-2).

---

6   The three sublayers did not occur in all configurations. All of this was described in a document called the "Internal Organization of the Network Layer." Notice that it is called *organization*, not *architecture*.

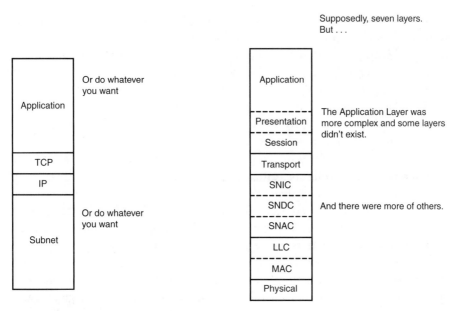

Figure 6-2 The Internet and OSI models.

As time went on, things got messier and messier. First, LANs did relaying with bridges, then bridges started generating spanning trees (sounds like routing), and more recently all pretense of not doing routing in the data link layer has disappeared. New technologies such as ISDN, ATM, and MPLS have introduced additional gyrations. There was even a DSL-related proposal that had seven layers *below* the transport layer. It starts to get a bit bewildering. What is going on? Just how many crystalline spheres and epicycles...oops! Wrong century...errr...layers are there?

And it wasn't just the arrangement of the protocols that was making layering a problem. The implementations had performance problems, too. The theory of layering supposedly requires each protocol in each layer to be a distinct state machine (i.e., a distinct process). A protocol state machine in layer N sends or receives PDUs by passing them across the layer boundary to the protocol machine in the layer below.

Crossing a layer boundary generally involved an API, which in the worst case was a system call and in the best case just a procedure call. If the implementation follows this theory closely, it will produce a considerable number of data copies and context switches and be very slow. By the early 1970s, everyone had learned this lesson. But even with minimal data copies, there is still a lot of overhead in context switches. To reduce context switches essentially requires merging the state machines of protocols in adjacent layers within a system. Although in theory this is possible, in practice there are factors that make it unwise.

Because most protocols are relatively complex and different, merging their state machines was prohibitive. (One reason for layering is, after all, to manage the complexity.) The differences in protocols (or more precisely, the lack of consistency between them) and the tendency to include options further complicate the task. And, maintaining the order of the processing required by the protocols works against merging. Protocol state machines share state with an apposite in a remote system. But all protocols state machines in the same system are not sharing state with apposites in the same remote system.

This further complicates merging the state machines, because adjacent layers in different systems will have different protocols. Following from this, one of the reasons for layering is that a protocol in a layer can be changed without affecting the protocols in adjacent layers. However, it is not often that a protocol design actually follows these principles closely enough that this can actually be done.[7]   To make matters worse yet, there seemed to be more and more reasons for protocol processing at layer N to look into headers at higher layers. Perhaps this layering idea wasn't such a good one after all. Its use in operating systems had undergone considerable change since Dijkstra's original paper. Maybe this is one of those concepts that if the world were well behaved it would be a good idea, but the world is messy. One thing is clear, however: The traditional layers we settled on in the early 1970s aren't showing us the way. There is something we aren't seeing. What does the problem say?

Listening to the Problem

Introduction

Are layers a good idea? Is this an early idea that belongs on the dust heap of history? Many think so.

Going back to fundamentals, what can we say about this problem? We have a collection of communicating finite state machines. As we saw at the beginning, all communication requires a shared schema, some shared state. The communicating parties must have some common ground, however minimal.

For our finite state machines to communicate, they must not only have a common language (i.e., the format of the PDUs) but also some shared expectation of what will be done with them. The collection of communicating machines

---

[7]   If it were, there wouldn't need to be all those standards titled "Mapping the X Protocol into the Y Protocol," or they would be a lot shorter: "The X PDUs Are Mapped to the Y PDU Data Field." Also, much of the IPv6 work modifying more than 100 existing RFCs is a consequence of this lack of discipline.

must have some common shared state. For the communication to take place, we have seen that certain mechanisms are also required to maintain that shared state. We have also seen that we need to hide the complexity of these functions as a black box to make it possible to build more complex functions on top. This gives us shared state, maintained by multiple protocol state machines, spread across different systems, treated as a black box. No matter how one describes it, something like a "layer" seems to be even more inherent in the problem of networking than it was in operating systems.

If that is the case, there must be something wrong with how we have been thinking about layers. But what? It is not like we have loaded the concept down with a lot of machinery. Perhaps if we just look at the communications problem *very* carefully, we will find something. But we have done this exercise thousands of times. We have been over it and over it; what can come out of this? We have analyzed analogies with sending a letter, making a phone call, ad nauseum. Yes, we have. But let's do it again.

Here we will adopt an approach in the spirit of Imre Lakatos's *Proofs and Refutations* (1976). However, instead of proposing a theorem, and then finding exceptions to it and successively refining the theorem, we will take a different but analogous path. We will start with the fundamental elements of computer communication: two application processes attempting to communicate, and a mechanism for achieving the communication within a *single* processing system. Then, we will successively expand the problem domain to communication between two systems, more than two pairs of applications, more than two systems, and so on.

Before the reader throws up his hands, thinking he knows all of this[8] (and he probably does), bear with me. I thought the same thing and was quite surprised not only in what I learned, but also in the order that things appear. Some things appear later than one expects, some earlier. The thoughtful reader will hopefully find some new insights and new understanding. I will try to maintain a balance between readability and sufficient formality that it isn't too painful for the reader and at the same time convincing that it could be made formal if necessary. We will find it useful to apply some of the results we have come across in previous chapters. We show that communicating application processes and a distributed IPC facility consisting of a protocol that provides an IPC mechanism and a protocol for managing distributed IPC are all that is required. From these few elements, everything else can be constructed.

---

[8] This sentence isn't sexist. Women have much more patience and wouldn't react this way.

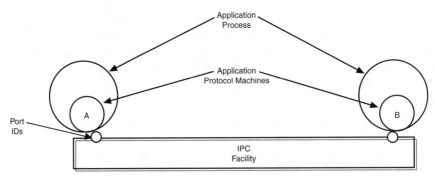

Figure 6-3 Communication within a single processing system.

Communications Within a Single System

The Operation of Communication in a Single System

In a single processing system, two application processes communicate by invoking the operating system's IPC facility (see Figure 6-3). As discussed in Chapter 4, it is useful to make a distinction between the *application process* (AP) and the part of the application actually involved in communications, the *application protocol machine* (APM). Although there are cases when the AP and the APM are synonymous, it is not always the case, and it is better to introduce it now. So, we will assume that all the interactions with IPC are performed by the APM on behalf of the application.

Furthermore, let's assume a very simple and generic set of system calls (API) that are available for the APM to use when making requests of IPC:

> <result> ← Allocate(<destination-application-name>, <port_id>, <properties>)

> <result> ← Send(<port-id>, <buffer ptr>)

> <result> ← Receive(<port-id>, <buffer ptr>)

> <result> ← De-allocate(<port-id>)[9]

The APM initiates communication with an Allocate primitive specifying the destination application process name. (The operating system knows who is making the request and its access permissions, so the source application name does not need to be passed explicitly.) The Allocate blocks and will eventually return with a port-id and a result (success or reason for failure). The port-id is unique only within the operating system. The properties field indicates parameters that

---

[9] I have never forgiven ANSI for taking "left arrow" out of the ANSI character set. ← and = are not the same operation, and := and all of its variants are ugly!

might affect how the IPC mechanism handles its resources relative to others (i.e., QoS). Once created, the application protocol messages are sent and received by invoking the Send and Receive primitives. After the initial Allocate, all interactions with the IPC facility use port-ids to refer to the flow. Successive invocations of Allocate with the same (source, destination) pair will yield distinct port-ids being assigned. We consider this case in more detail later:

1. The calling APM, **A**, invokes an Allocate request specifying the destination application name of the application process, **B**, along with other parameters about the characteristics of the communication.

   result ← Allocate (**B**, my-port, properties);

2. The IPC facility assigns a port-id to this instance of communication with **A**. This is the identifier that **A**, and the IPC facility will use to refer to this instance of communication.[10] If the request is well formed and the IPC has the resources to honor the request, it will allocate resources for this IPC connection.

3. If so, IPC uses the operating system's "search rules" to find **B**. IPC will use the operating system access control to determine whether **A** has access to **B**.

4. If **B** is not executing, IPC may cause **B** to be instantiated. **B** is notified of the IPC request from **A** and given a port-id, **b**.

   result ← Allocate (**A**, **b**, properties);

5. If **B** responds positively, and IPC notifies **A** with a different port-id, **a**.

   result ← Allocate (**B**, my-port, properties);

   Note that **A** and **B** have different port-ids for the same connection. The port-id identifies a connection endpoint.

6. Through **n**). Then, using system calls, **A** may send PDUs to **B** by calling **Send(a, buf)**, which B receives by invoking **Receive(b, rcv_buffer)**, and B can send to **A** in an analogous manner. The IPC facility manages the passing of data between the two processes. The processes would use a Receive primitive to have PDUs delivered. The exchange of messages between **A** and **B** will create shared state between **A** and **B**.

   Then, when they are done, one or both invoke De-allocate with the appropriate parameters (at what would be Step n+1).

---

[10] A variety of terms have been used for port-id. Any could be used. Its only significant property is its scope. Similarly, *instance of communication* could have been called flow, association, channel, connection, pipe, or any number of other terms for similar metaphors (although I have never seen *culvert* used). We will use *connection* here as a shorthand for all of its forms.

This shared state between the application processes is often called a *connection*. We will use this term but assume it includes all forms of association, flow, and connection.[11]

Properties of Major Elements

Naming for IPC. The application names are unambiguous within the system as a whole. Application names are used between applications and by IPC to identify destinations.[12] Port-ids have much less scope and are only unambiguous between an AP and IPC facility. It is important to be aware that this is the minimal requirement. Most systems will, for practical reasons, define the scope as unambiguous within the processing system because it is simpler to implement.

In general, an application name will refer to a program to be run, not to a specific instantiation of the program. However, sometimes it is necessary to refer to a specific instance of an application. Therefore, the name space should be able to accommodate this requirement. Later we will consider expanding this to accommodate multiple APMs and multiple instances of the same APM (as well as multiple instances of the same AP).

The application process and application protocol machine. In general, the purpose of an AP is not just to communicate with another process (although we have encountered some for which that is the case). The primary purpose of an AP is to accomplish some task for which communication is necessary. As argued earlier, the communicating APs or a third party that caused them to communicate must have the knowledge, however implicit, that if **A** passes messages to **B**, **B** will know what to do with them and vice versa. For two processes to communicate, there must be some common agreement on the "language" used and its semantics (or, to put it another way, the format of the messages exchanged, the conditions for when to send them, and the action to be taken when they are received). This common agreement is called an *application protocol*. The protocol for two processes to communicate for a particular task is recorded in a specification that details the syntax of the information exchanged and the procedures to be executed. The handling of the "common language" and the interface to the IPC facility represent a distinct substructure within the AP.

The IPC facility. This establishment sequence is assumed to be asymmetrical, in that if **B** initiates at the same time, it will communicate with a different instance of **A**. The initiation of most communications is by one party or the other. Later, we

---

11   Most of the words used to denote this shared state have become highly charged over the years thanks to the connectionless/connection debate. When necessary, I will use *flow* to designate weaker form, but will use *connection* as a generic term, seeing *flow* as a degenerate case. Part of our goal here is to make the distinction moot.

12   Later we will develop the requirements for application naming in greater detail. For now, we will keep it simple because this issue is tangential to our primary purpose. How this might be done was discussed in Chapter 4.

will consider the circumstances under which this case occurs and learn that an asymmetrical interface does not imply an asymmetric mechanism, and in a well-formed IPC, symmetric synchronization is a moot point. The IPC facility reliably moves messages from the memory space of one AP to the memory space of another. Operating systems accomplish this function by a variety of means. Most use message-passing semantics that rely on shared memory constructs of one form or another.[13] The actual mechanisms are not of interest to us here. However, the properties of the mechanism are. Successive invocations of Allocate with the same (source, destination) pair will yield distinct port-ids being assigned.

The IPC facility maintains an association between the port-ids of the two ends of the flow. Messages are delivered in the order they are sent. (It, of course, takes extra work not to.)

In most cases, flow control is implicit in an IPC facility. The sender may block until the receiver reads the message or alternatively, block only after some number of messages have not been read by the receiver. More elaborate flow-control schemes have been implemented, but this will do for this exercise.

Similarly, error control is not a major concern. Lost messages are unlikely and equivalent to memory leaks, which are bugs to be fixed quickly.[14] The only sources of data corruption are the same as memory corruption; and the same safeguards used to detect memory corruption protect messages "in transit," because they never leave memory.

Definitions of the Initial Elements

- **Processing system, System.** The totality of elements within the scope of a "test and set" instruction[15] consisting of the hardware; operating system, consisting of processor scheduling, memory management, and IPC; and application processes.

- **Application process.** The instantiation of a program running on an operating system in a processing system.

- **Operating system, OS.** A specialized application process consisting of three functions for managing processing, storage, and communication resources, and some number of "user" tasks, one of which is a task for managing the application.

---

13   Mechanisms that do not use shared memory are possible but will involve considerable data copying and perform poorly. But, even these will use shared memory for synchronization; so all in all, shared memory is required.

14   I am old fashioned and believe that memory leaks result from sloppy programming. These are bugs to be fixed.

15   Over the past 30 years, this seems to be the best definition of a processing system that is the least dependent on technology.

- **Application process name, application name.** A name taken from an operating system name space and bound to an application process.

- **Application name space.** The set of all possible strings that can be bound to APs and other objects associated with this operating system. The scope of this name space is the set of all possible application processes that can be named and can communicate via IPC.

- **Application protocol.** The set of conventions comprising the syntax of the input and output messages or PDUs and the associated procedures for transmitting output and action to take on input that must be in common between communicating APs.

- **Application protocol machine.** A component structure of an AP that implements the application protocol and manages interaction with the IPC facility for the instantiation of that application protocol within the AP.

- **IPC facility (interprocess communication).** An operating system facility available by a set of local library calls that is used by APs to communicate with each other.

- **IPC mechanism.** The internal mechanisms used within the IPC facility to effect interprocess communication.

- **Port-id.** An identifier that is unambiguous within the scope of the IPC facility and used by an AP and the IPC to distinguish separate instances of communication.

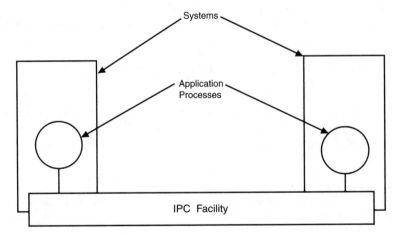

Figure 6-4 Communication between two systems.

Communications Between Two Systems

Now let's suppose that our two applications are in two different systems. As a first step, we will assume two systems connected by some form of wire. (Two systems with a wireless connection bring up extraneous issues that are best considered later.)

The Operation of Communication Between Two Systems

Figure 6-4 shows the new configuration. Let's just start through our sequence of steps and see where we run into trouble. Communication between two APs in two different systems operates in much the same way as communication between two APs in the same system, at least on the surface. We will find that it is within the IPC facility that there is a major change. The IPC facility can no longer be represented by a single process managing the IPC but must be modeled as two communicating, loosely coupled processes. These IPC processes are simply "lower-level" APs within the systems. Let's see how it works:

1. The calling APM, **A**, invokes an Allocate request specifying the application name, the destination name of the application process, **B**, along with other parameters about the characteristics of the communication.

   result ← Allocate (**B**, my-port, properties);

   Clearly, the application name space would have to be modified to ensure unambiguous names of all applications in both systems. Because we want the resulting system to appear to the greatest degree possible as a single system to its users, the definition of an application name is now changed as follows:

   Application name. A name taken from an application name space whose scope includes both systems and is bound to an AP.

   Application name space. The set of strings constructed to be location independent that can be bound to APs and other objects associated with the systems within the scope of this name space. The scope of this name space is the set of all possible APs and other objects that can be named and referenced across applications. Objects only referenced within an application are not in the scope of this name space.

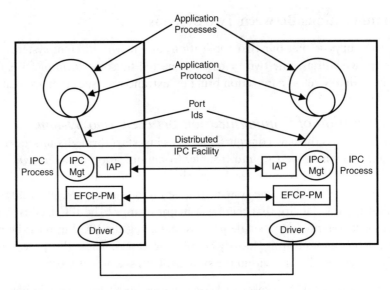

Figure 6-5 New elements required for communication between two systems.

2. The IPC facility assigns a port-id to this instance of communication with **A**. If the request is well formed and the IPC has the resources to honor the request, it will allocate resources for this IPC connection.

3. If so, IPC uses the operating system's "search rules" to find **B**. IPC will use the operating system access control to determine whether **A** has access to **B**. The IPC facility looks up the application name. If it is on this system, the communication proceeds as in the single-system case discussed earlier. If it is not on this system, the IPC facility must look on the other system.

We also need to determine whether the application is on this system or on the other one. In general, application names alone do not indicate on which system they are. This allows APs to be moved from one system to another without changing their names. Because we only have two systems, if the operating system search rules do not find the requested application in this system, it must be in the other one or not exist. Now we have a problem: We need to determine whether the application is on the other system and whether the requestor has permission to open a connection with it.[16]

---

[16] It was not necessary to consider this issue in the previous section because it was part of the local operating system. Now we need to communicate the process we need to establish communication with as well as determine whether the requestor has permission to communicate with this process.

We need a mechanism to ask the remote IPC process whether an application exists on its system and give it sufficient information about the source application to determine whether to allow the communication. This requires a protocol for carrying the names of the applications and other information. For the purposes of this discussion, we will refer to this as an *IPC access protocol* (IAP). We will also require a management task within the IPC facility to handle this IAP request and interface into the access control and search rules of the local operating system.

IAP would be a fairly simple request/response protocol that would have to carry the source and destination application names and access control information (probably using capabilities). Should IAP include authentication? No. Authentication must be part of the application. Only the source application can confirm that the destination application is who it claims to be. Hence, authentication must be done directly between the source and destination applications. Access control in an operating system (and by extension IPC) can determine only whether the source application has access to a destination application that "to the best of its knowledge" it believes to be the one being requested. Only an exchange between the applications themselves can confirm that that is the case. But this does bring up another requirement of the IAP. Before the request can be sent, the local IPC management tasks must establish an application connection with each other and authenticate that they are who they say they are. Once this is done, they can exchange IAP requests. Note that this application connection is part of what we called the *enrollment phase* earlier.

It is interesting that the first new mechanism we encounter is for management. We have an idea what IAP might look like. But this raises a question: How do we deliver IAP reliably?

Moving to two separate systems has invalidated many assumptions we had been able to make. We no longer have a shared memory to mask a multitude of problems. Perhaps first and foremost, our means of communication is now error prone and requires explicit synchronization and flow control. Therefore, we must have an error- and flow-control protocol operating between the two systems to guarantee reliability and to ensure the sender does not overrun the receiver (see Figure 6-5). This problem is well understood and was discussed in Chapters 2 "Protocol Elements," and 3, "Patterns in Protocols." The IPC facility creates shared state with a correspondent on the other side and uses mechanisms such as CRCs, FECs, sequence numbers, and a sliding window to provide reliability and flow control. Note that the IPC facility is now using a mechanism with less tightly shared state than in the previous case. The EFCP operates between the IPC processes in the source and destination systems. This solves the problem of getting messages reliably from one system to the other. The EFCP produces protocol messages that are given to the driver to send on the physical media.

"Shouldn't IAP be part of EFCP? Why have two protocols? It is simple. Combine them." On the face of it, it is tempting. However, note that the two protocols are doing very different functions for very different interests. One is managing IPC between two APs, including whether they are allowed to communicate at all. The second is purely concerned with providing a communications channel with certain properties. There are advantages to separating the purely data transfer function from the management and access control functions. It is true that IAP must use the EFCP. But note that the purpose of the management task that uses IAP is to manage the IPC resources. This management task will use IAP and then bind an EFCP channel to a port-id for use by the application. However, we can have our cake and eat it, too. As a degenerate case, we can send the IAP request as part of the EFCP establishment, should we so desire. However, we will see later that there are certain advantages, certain flexibilities that arise from keeping them separate.

With the IAP and the IPC protocol (EFCP) in place, we can proceed. Now the sequence works just as before, with the IPC facility assigning a Port-id to the instance of communication with the AP **A**. Now to revisit Step 3 (from earlier in this section):

3. If so, IPC uses the operating system's "search rules" to determine whether **B** is local. If **B** is not found, IPC sends an IAP request to the corresponding IPC process in the other system. An EFCP connection is created with the properties required for an IPC process-to-IPC process internal management connection. The IAP management PDUs are encapsulated in the EFCP connection assigned to it. The IAP connection is created, and the participants authenticated, and the request is sent. Interpreting the request, the remote IPC process uses its local operating system search rules to find **B**. If it fails, it returns that result. IPC will use the operating system access control to determine whether **A** has access to **B**. If it is on this system, the communication proceeds.

4. IPC may cause **B** to be instantiated. **B** is notified of the IPC request from **A** and given a port-id, **b**.

   result ← Allocate (**A**, **b**, properties);

5. If **B** responds positively, and IPC notifies **A** with a different port-id, **a**.

   result ← Allocate (**B**, my-port ← **a** properties);

   Note that as before, **A** and **B** have different port-ids for their respective endpoints of the connection. The distributed IPC facility allocates and creates an EFCP flow. (It is entirely possible for the distributed IPC facility to leave an "unused" EFCP flow in place on the assumption that it will be used soon.) It then sends an IAP message to carry the source and destination application names and the capability and other information. The receiving IPC process looks at the fields of the IAP PDU and determines what application is required and whether **A** is allowed to initiate communication with **B**. Once the IAP management exchange is successful, the EFCP connection is bound to the port-ids, and the applications may proceed with their dialog.

6. Through **n**). Then, using system calls, **A** may send PDUs to **B** by calling **Send(a, buf)**, which B receives by invoking **Receive(b, rcv_buffer)**. The IPC facility manages the passing of data between the two processes. The processes would use a Receive primitive to have PDUs delivered. The exchange of messages between **A** and **B** will create a shared state between **A** and **B** that is more loosely coupled than the shared state in the IPC facility.

Then, when they are done, one or both invoke De-allocate with the appropriate parameters (at what would be Step n+1).

Note that although the mechanism is a bit more complicated, it is really no different from what was required in the single-site case. The difference here is that coordination between two IPC processes is necessary. Note also that we have significantly decoupled operations at the API from the behavior of the traditional communication protocol.

Invalidated Assumptions

To recap, with the communicating APs in different systems, several assumptions we had previously made were invalidated. It is worthwhile to review what they were and how we compensated for their loss:

1. The management of the name spaces is no longer under the control of a single system.

2. The same program may exist on both systems, so the names must be unambiguous.

   We created a global application name space so that all applications in both systems have unambiguous names.

3. The operating system does not know all the applications that may exist on the other system, nor the permissions associated with it, so a mechanism is required to provide this information.

4. The local operating system access control mechanisms can no longer be relied on to provide adequate authorization and authentication.

We created an internal IPC management protocol to accommodate these requirements.

5. Explicit synchronization is required because there is no longer a test and set instruction or shared memory available.

6. The IPC mechanism can no longer use a common memory. Consequently, the data may be corrupted or lost entirely.

7. For the same reasons, flow control must now be explicit, not implicit. This is both to avoid the sending application overrunning the receiving application process and to avoid overrunning the capabilities of the supporting IPC facility.

We created an error- and flow-control protocol to accommodate these requirements.

New Elements Required

- **IPC access protocol (IAP).** The protocol used to communicate the names of the source and destination applications and other information (see Figure 6-6) necessary for determining whether the communication can be established.

Op	Dest Appl Name	Src Appl Name	QoS	Capability

Figure 6-6 Idealized PDU format of IAP request.

- **IPC process.** A process in a system that implements and manages IPC. This may entail coordinating with other IPC processes in another system, both to effect the communication and to manage the distributed IPC facility. (An IPC process is just a process like any other.)

- **Distributed IPC facility.** An IPC facility spanning two or more systems with at least one IPC process in each participating system.

- **Error- and flow-control protocol (EFCP).** A protocol (see Figure 6-7) necessary to replace the shared memory mechanisms of the single system to ensure reliability and to provide flow control of the IPC facility to the environment of communication between two systems. An EFCP PM is a task of the IPC process.

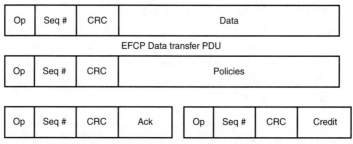

Figure 6-7 Idealized PDU formats for the error- and flow-control protocol.

- **IPC management task.** A task of an IPC process that manages IPC and interfaces into the search rules and access control of the local operating system. It also manages IPC resources.

- **Driver.** An application or library of procedures in the operating system that interfaces to physical media. Although both communicating systems have drivers interfacing their physical media, the drivers are not protocol machines because they share no state.

Simultaneous Communications Between Two Systems

In the preceding section, we considered the complications introduced in providing IPC between two applications in two different systems. Now we must expand our concept of IPC between two systems by allowing multiple simultaneous communications between the two systems. For this case, we need to determine at each step whether we can support multiple simultaneous IPCs where we need to.

Operation of Simultaneous Communications
We will start at the top with the applications and work our way down to develop the new concepts required for simultaneous operation:

1. The calling APM, **A**, invokes an Allocate request specifying the application name, the destination name of the AP, **B**, along with other parameters about the characteristics of the communication.

   result ← Allocate (**B**, my-port, properties)

2. The IPC facility assigns a port-id to this instance of communication with **A**. If the request is well formed and the IPC has the resources to honor the request, it will allocate resources for this IPC connection.

Multiple Pairs of Applications Communicating

We need to be able to allow more than one pair of APs to communicate at the same time. Having different application names for different applications is straightforward. And, we have already indicated that each Allocate request is assigned a different port-id within its system. Nothing new is required there. That leaves creating support in IPC:

3. If so, IPC uses the operating system's search rules to determine whether **B** is local. If **B** is not found, IPC sends an IAP request to the corresponding IPC process in the other system. An EFCP connection is created with the properties required for a IPC process-to-IPC process internal management connection. The IAP management PDUs are encapsulated in the EFCP connection assigned to it. The IAP connection is created, and the participants authenticated, and the request is sent. Interpreting the request, the remote IPC process uses its local operating system search rules to find **B**. If it fails, it returns that result. IPC will use the operating system access control to determine whether **A** has access to **B**. If it is on this system, the communication proceeds.

Multiple Instances of the EFCP

If the corresponding applications were in the same system, we would merely create multiple instances of the IPC mechanism, one for each dialog. For two systems, we do the same. The IPC facility must be able to support multiple instances of the EFCP at the same time. The EFCP is maintaining separate state information about each communication that is updated as PDUs are sent and received. (The amount of shared state and the frequency of update will depend on the nature of the policies in effect on the connection.) To support multiple pairs of communicating applications will require separate instances of this state and hence multiple instances of EFCP. Because we are going to be sending messages from different instances over a single physical media, we need to be able to distinguish which PDUs belong to which instance of IPC or which connection. The PDUS need a connection identifier.

The biggest hurdle is that because either side can initiate communications, we have to ensure that they don't both assign the same connection identifier. There are a variety of ways of doing this: A unique range of port-ids could be assigned to each system. Each side could start allocating from either the high or low end of the field, but then a rule is required to determine who starts at which end. All of these are a bit cumbersome. Traditionally, the solution to this has been just to make the connection-id the concatenation of the local port-ids. Because each port-id is unique within its system, the concatenation is guaranteed to be unambiguous between the source and destination. Is this all we need? This is all the identifiers we need because there is only one system to send it to. We will have to make a slight modification to our EFCP so that all PDUs carry this connection-id. Consider, for example, the Data Transfer PDU (see Figure 6-8):

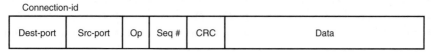

Figure 6-8 A connection-id must be added to support multiple simultaneous instances of communication.

There is an added level of capability we can consider at this point. Each Allocate API request will cause an IAP request to be generated. Note that the IAP request could also carry the port-ids to be used for this connection and carry the destination port-ids in the response. This would allow several possible actions by the IPC process:

- Initiate the creation of a new EFCP instance with the appropriate policies binding to the port-ids, the equivalent of setting up a TCP or HDLC connection.

- Allocate resources and create bindings to the port-ids, the equivalent of UDP.

Or

- The two systems maintain a pool of EFCP connections already created and simply bind the allocated ports. (Of course, if we use a "delta-t like" protocol, this is always the case.)

Managing the Single Resource

However, we are not done. We now have several EFCP instances attempting to share a single physical medium between the two systems. We need a new application to moderate the sharing of the single resource (i.e., the wire). The classic definition of an operating system. This application will need to maintain a table of the currently active port-ids, accept PDUs from the EFCP instances, and determine what order to send them on the physical medium. Its primary function is to manage the sharing or to multiplex the physical medium.

This multiplexing task may also optimize the use of the physical medium by concatenating PDUs and so on. If the use of the physical medium is heavy, the multiplexing task may additionally be required to provide priority to certain classes of users or special processing among the flows. The application requests these QoS parameters when it requests allocation of communication resources.

Let's assume that there are a list of QoS-related parameters that are available, such as bandwidth, delay, jitter, bit-error rate, and so on—the usual cast of character(s)-istics. Basically, we have two "knobs" we can use to achieve these characteristics and balance this with demands by other allocation requests: the mechanisms of EFCP or the resource allocations of the multiplexing task. The EFCP mechanisms are well understood, and policies are chosen for bit-error rate, flow control, and so on. The multiplexing task basically has two resources it can use to affect the characteristics of the traffic it is sending on the physical medium:

1. The order and rate of queue servicing (sometimes known as processor scheduling)

2. The management of queue lengths (sometimes known as memory management)

The EFCP instances and other applications are its tasks. This handles the real-time performance-sensitive task of moving traffic within the desired QoS. But....

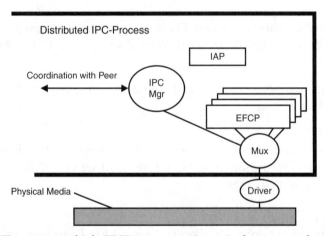

Figure 6-9 To manage multiple EFCP instances using a single resource, the media requires a multiplexing task and a manager to set policy with its peer.

The IPC management task (see Figure 6-9) will manage the interactions between this multiplexing task and the EFCP instances that feed it. It will need to translate application Allocate requests into policies and balance these with the operational policies of the system. Effective operation will require the IPC management task to coordinate in the other system. Because the systems are peers and we must assume that one will be requesting applications on the other system and vice versa with roughly equal frequency, the systems will have to exchange resource management information to coordinate their use of the common resources. In this case, that might be as simple as refusing an IAP request. The IPC management task manages the use of the single resource in coordination with the flow-control policies of the EFCP instances to provide the requested services and to keep them from overrunning the application.

4. IPC may cause **B** to be instantiated. **B** is notified of the IPC request from **A** and given a port-id, **b**.

result ← Allocate (**A**, **b**, properties);

5. If **B** responds positively, and IPC notifies **A** with a different port-id, **a**.

result ← Allocate (**B**, my-port ← **a** properties);

6. Through **n**). Then using system calls, **A** may send PDUs to **B** by calling **Send(a, buf)**, which **B** receives by invoking **Receive(b, rcv_buffer)**. The IPC facility manages the passing of data between the two processes. The processes would use a Receive primitive to have PDUs delivered. The exchange of messages between **A** and **B** will create shared state between **A** and **B** that is more loosely coupled than the shared state in the IPC facility.

Then, when they are done, one or both invoke De-allocate with the appropriate parameters (at what would be Step n+1).

New Elements Required

- **Connection identifier**. An identifier used to distinguish one IPC instance (connection) from another.

- **Multiplexing task.** An application to manage the utilization of interfaces by multiple IPC protocol instances and other applications.

Let's stop here and take stock of where we are. We first developed the concepts we needed for two applications to communicate within a single system. This requires the means to name the applications and an IPC facility usually based on shared memory. Then we expanded our scope to consider communication by two applications on two distinct systems. The primary change to support this configuration required replacing the IPC facility with an error- and flow-control protocol to overcome the problems of no longer having shared memory as a medium for communication.

We also had to provide a management function so that the IPC process on one system could request on behalf of the requesting application access to an application on the other system. Next, we allowed multiple applications to have simultaneous communication between the two systems. Now we need an instance of EFCP for each communication flow an application has and the ability to distinguish these flows. But more significant, we now have multiple EFCP instances contending for the use of a single common resource (i.e., the physical media). Hence, we require an application to manage the use of this single resource. Now we are ready to consider what additional facilities are required for communication with multiple applications on multiple systems.

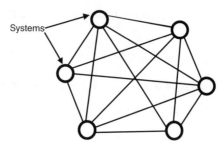

Figure 6-10 Communication with N systems/

Communications with N Systems

Operation of Communications with N Systems

Having now constructed how two systems communicate, we now need to generalize this to N systems. Figure 6-10 shows the connectivity of N systems using a somewhat brute-force approach. (Remember we are taking this slowly, step by step with patience we will get there.)

The major change for this case is that it is more of the same, much more. In the two-system case, we could assume that if the requested application wasn't local, it was in the other system. Now we have lots of other places to look. For small Ns, we could simply send $N-1$ requests and see who answers positively; but this is wasteful and isn't going to scale. For some value of N (and might even have been $N = 2$), it is more efficient if we keep a database of what applications are where, usually called a *directory*.

The directory is the extension of the operating system search rules to cover the other systems. The directory function may be accomplished by a variety of means: Each system can send to the others a complete list of all potential applications it contains and then update any changes (although this becomes a bit burdensome); one system searches for the application name locally and if not found, queries the other system; or something in between (i.e., cach and query). For large values of N, some organization may be imposed on the naming and/or the directories themselves to facilitate searching or the order of searching or the implementation of a caching strategy. (In general, the names should remain location independent unless the application is, in fact, location dependent.)

The directory function will have to use the IPC facility to accomplish its task. We will need a protocol for updating and querying the directory database. Without doubt, there will be other resource-related information that we will want to keep and other systems might want to query.

Basically, we need to maintain a database of IPC-related information that can be queried by other IPC processes in other systems and a management task that may for some of it notify other systems of important changes. As a placeholder let's call this protocol the *Resource Information Exchange Protocol* (RIEP. Maintaining this information will be based on a managed-object model. As shown in Chapter 4, it appears that application protocols in general consist of a small number of operations (read, write, create, delete, and so forth) on managed objects. The only aspect to be determined is how to manage parallel or sequences of operations.

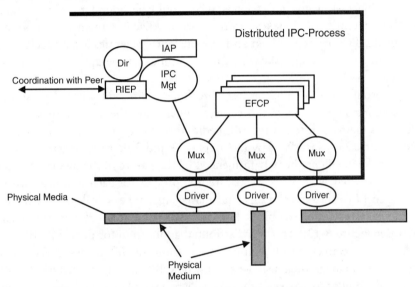

Figure 6-11 Each interface is managed by a multiplexing task and IPC management task.

A destination can be chosen by simply choosing the appropriate local physical interface. (Because everything is directly connected, every application is simply at the other end of one of the wires) Each system will have one interface for each destination. Each system will need to associate a *local* identifier with each interface.[17]

---

17 There is no requirement for these identifiers to be the same across all N systems. They are only used locally. For example, it is not uncommon for the road joining two towns to be named by its destination. So, the road between Kinmundy and Patoka is the called the Patoka Road in Kinmundy and the Kinmundy Road in Patoka.

For example, it might be the application name of the multiplexing application for that interface. There is no need for this identifier to be known outside this system. Because this has the role of what we normally view as a kernel application, it generally would not be known in a wider context. When directory information is received from a particular system, the information is just associated with the identifier for that interface. When the destination application name is looked up in the directory, the local identifier for the appropriate interface/destination is returned. There is a separate multiplexing task (see Figure 6-11) for each interface. In essence, these local identifiers identify which multiplexing task a given EFCP instance would be bound to. Or to state it slightly differently, the indexes are the port-ids. Each of them would be managed by an IPC manager. When an EFCP instance generates a message to send, it calls the multiplexing task, which has the index of the appropriate physical interface.

This proliferation of IPC processes to handle different wires does seem to warrant some rearranging to more effectively manage them. Because each interface may support a different type of media, this would imply protocol instances with different policies. (We saw in Chapters 2 and 3 that the policies of protocols near the media are heavily influenced by the nature of the media.) It would appear that what we have is a separate IPC process for each interface, with its associated EFCP instances if any and management. Let's collect each of these into a separate module or black box and call them a *distributed IPC facility* (DIF) (see Figure 6-12). This is a distributed application for providing IPC.

To more effectively insulate applications from the differences in these interfaces and to manage their use, let's put a new IPC management task "above" these DIF modules to processes the API calls from applications, look up application names in the directory, and select the appropriate DIF for that interface. This forms a simple higher-level IPC management process.

It would be straightforward to adapt this structure to multiple lines between the same two systems. This would require multiple distributed IPC facilities between them, and this new IPC management process would manage allocating the load among them. This new "higher-level" IPC process we have just created might communicate with their peers about resource allocation in the case of multiple paths to the same remote system. However, resource allocation on a specific path is properly the responsibility of the DIF managing that path and probably specific to the characteristics of that physical media.

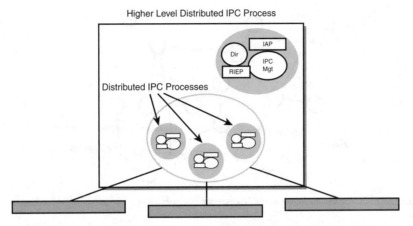

Figure 6-12 Different physical media may require very different management, so distinct DIFs are tailored to their operating parameters. Then a higher-level IPC process is created to manage the assignment of IPC requests to the appropriate interface and create a virtual media-independent view to the applications.

However, this does not scale well and would quickly become prohibitively expensive and impractical for even fairly small values of N. This leads to making the network more complicated, but cheaper.

New Elements

- **Directory.** A database that resides in each system that maintains a mapping of application names to the interfaces over which they are available (i.e., which remote system they are on).

- **Resource Information Exchange Protocol (RIEP).** A protocol used for updating the directory and other information maintained by the IPC facility on the status of its connections, resource allocations, and so on. It may be queried by other systems or subscribed to for updates.

- **Distributed IPC facility (DIF).** The collection of IPC processes cooperating to provide a distributed IPC service to applications. In most cases, the IPC processes comprising the DIF are in different systems.

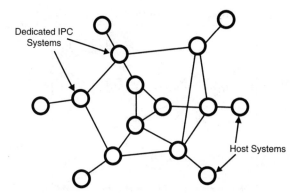

Figure 6-13 Communicating with *N* systems cheaply.

Communication with N Systems on the Cheap

In the preceding section, we expanded our use of IPC from communications between two systems to communication between *N*. However, we found that the brute-force approach does not scale, is inefficient, and introduces huge costs. To enable IPC cheaply, we take advantage of the fact that systems will not access all destination equally, and therefore some lines will be underutilized. So, we allow systems to relay PDUs to other systems and in some cases have systems dedicated to doing only this relaying (see Figure 6-13). This dedicated IPC system will optimize the use of the physical media by multiplexing traffic over far fewer lines.

For this case, it will be clearer if we keep the dedicated relays (routers) distinct from the systems acting as the source or destination of the PDUs (i.e., hosts). Clearly, a system could act as both, but for clarity of the discussion, let's keep them distinct.

Operation of Communication with N Systems on the Cheap

Each of these dedicated systems has two or more interfaces to physical media (see Figure 6-13). As shown earlier, we had to introduce a new application to do multiplexing and to manage multiple flows over the single resource, a physical media. We also saw how having multiple physical interfaces led us to organize communication for each interface with its peer with a higher-level management function to assign requests to interfaces.

For this configuration, we not only need to manage locally, but also to pass PDUs through a series of dedicated IPC systems (see Figure 6-14) to their destinations. Because the originating systems would be multiplexing, the dedicated systems would need to multiplex/demultiplex as well as relay. Because messages would come in one interface and leave on another, there is another opportunity to optimize the use of the outgoing media. These relays do not support anything above them. The relay is a variation on the multiplexing task, ultimately delivering messages to a multiplexing task in a remote system. To use the model we have been developing, we are going to have to expand the higher-level IPC management process from the last section. The relaying application has N instances of an application protocol, one for each interface (lower-level DIF) on which it sends or receives data. The relaying application receives PDUs from instances of the application protocol, makes the forwarding decision (choosing the application protocol instance to send the PDU on), and delivers the PDU to that instance.

Previously, identifying the local end of the "wire" was equivalent to identifying the destination. This is no longer the case. The relays have created a virtual space that creates a multipoint view of communication over a physical network, which is point to point. All applications sitting on top of this structure appear directly connected, as if it were some form multiaccess media.

Now we can no longer use the local names of interfaces to indicate where applications are. We need to assign identifiers to all of these IPC processes that are unambiguous among the members of the DIF. Clearly, we need to name the destination IPC processes (in the hosts) because that is where we are sending it. But why do the relay applications need to be named? Given the conclusions we worked out in Chapter 5, "Naming and Addressing," expanding on Saltzer's paper, there are two reasons: First because there can be more than one path to the next node, we need to distinguish interfaces and nodes. Second, the relays must know whom their neighbors are to know where to send a PDU next. Each PDU will need to carry the identifier of the destination IPC process. We need some additional PCI to carry these names to be added to all PDUs generated by the multiplexing task at the source and interpreted by all the relays and the destination. In Chapter 3, we referred to this class of protocols as RaMP (*Relaying and Multiplexing Protocol,* an example of which is IP). RaMP is the PCI for the data transfer phase of a multiplexing application. But we find that it isn't so much a protocol in the usual sense, but simply a piece of common Data Transfer PCI (i.e., a common header used by multiplexing and relaying applications).

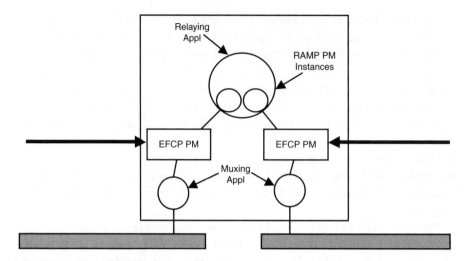

Figure 6-14 Diagram of a dedicated IPC system.

If it is the data transfer phase, what was the establishment phase? Are we building an inherently connection-oriented model? No. Take a step back and consider what it means for an IPC process to open a "connection" to another IPC process that is already a member of a DIF. We already saw this earlier: It is joining the DIF. This application establishment, with some related authentication and other initialization, is what we had previously called the enrollment phase.

Previously, enrollment had always been a collection of ad hoc procedures we frankly preferred to ignore. In this model, it is an integral and natural part of its operation. The application establishment would provide the other IPC process with the name of the requesting process along with access control information to be used to determine whether the requestor is allowed to join.

There will then be an exchange of the information required to allow this new member to operate in the DIF. In particular, the new IPC process is assigned an identifier by the DIF. This identifier is only unambiguous within the DIF and is used for moving EFCP PDUs among themselves. This is often called an *address*. Addresses are identifiers internal to a DIF. There is no reason for them to have any external visibility (more on this later). This is synonymous with the scope of the layer.[18]

---

[18] An alternate view is to see the collection of multiplexing and relaying applications as a single distributed application. In this case, the names described here are entirely internal to this application. In fact, this is the case with another distributed relaying application we are all familiar with: mail. This view has the advantage of easily supporting multiple distributed relaying applications of the same rank (e.g., VPNs or similar constructs).

We also know that in this configuration with multiple paths between the same points that PDUs may arrive out of order and that relays may experience congestion and discard some PDUs. Consequently, the source and destination systems would be wise to use an EFCP protocol to ensure the QoS and provide flow control between the source and destination. The policies used by the EFCP will depend on the QoS required by the requesting application. Note that the set of policies used for EFCP operation over this virtual link can affect the policies required for EFCP used on the physical network.

At the source, EFCP messages will be encapsulated in the Common Data Transfer PCI and passed among the relays to the destination multiplexing task. At the destination, they will be de-encapsulated and then, using the port-ids, delivered to the appropriate EFCP instance.

This will require that each PDU traverse more than one and perhaps many physical media. Because the media will tend to be the source of most errors, we need to take those into account early. Years of experimentation has shown that it is best to correct some errors early, but because the user application support will want to check to make sure everything is right, the dedicated systems need only perform enough error recovery to ensure that "user-level" error recovery is cost-effective. For some configurations, this will mean that for some types of these media-specific DIFs, the EFCP instances will not do much. For others, it will need to do a lot. This leads to our dedicated IPC systems having a configuration as in Figure 6-14.

It should be fairly clear by this time that our higher-level IPC management function has taken on all the trappings of being a full-fledged DIF, where the lower-level DIFs are its "wires." With the relaying functionality and its associated support functions, we seem to have most the elements of a DIF.

Do we need to identify the IPC process of the physical network that the relay will send it to? Not as long as the physical media is point to point. That question is equivalent to the configuration in the previous section; that is, identifying one end of the "wire" is sufficient. However, if it is a form of multiaccess technology, such as a LAN or wireless media, the multiplexing tasks in these DIFs will need to have addresses, too. And a Common Data Transfer PCI associated with that multiplexing task will be needed to carry them. (Some would call these MAC addresses.) However, these names will have less scope because they only need to unambiguous within the span of the physical media (or lower layer). It is sometimes argued that a large flat address space for these media-specific DIFs makes address assignment simpler, which it does. However, the cost of determining whether this device is allowed to join the network dwarfs any savings.

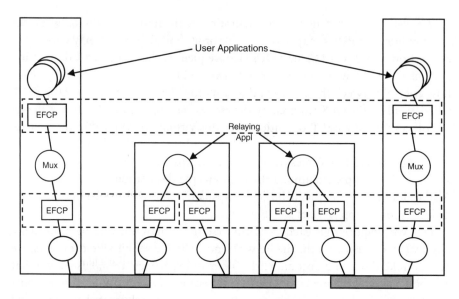

Figure 6-15 Three layers of IPC consisting of hosts with user applications and IPC subsystems.

These dedicated systems communicate with systems running the user applications and so must have at least a degenerate form of the IPC support. The host systems use the port-ids to keep track of PDUs between the EFCPs and the applications, whether the user applications or the relay and multiplexing tasks. The DIF may use port-ids to distinguish classes of traffic.

It is at this stage that the number of applications that can communicate can become quite large. Greater efficiency will result if caches maintained for the directory begin to reflect the locality of the systems they are responsible for. If the application names have a hierarchical organization, the caches may start to reflect that. With only a slight extension of the IAP function, it can be used to both find the address of an application and determine whether the requestor has access and the system hosting the application is willing to support the connection/flow. We will consider in a bit greater detail what this might look like in the next chapter. For now, let's just say that IAP will be found to extend the functionality of a DNS lookup.

The only problem we have not addressed is how the dedicated IPC systems know how to get PDUs to their destination. This requires that we introduce a new function into the IPC management task that generates routing information. This is a distributed function, which resides in each system where it has a multiplexing or relaying application. We have already indicated that the IPC management tasks exchange information on resource allocation, and in this configuration this function has greater importance. We can augment the information exchanged to include connectivity and resource loading of the relays.

Part of the information exchanged by the IPC processes in the DIF is about to whom they are directly connected. This allows the dedicated IPC systems to derive, using well-known algorithms, the necessary information about where each message is to be forwarded. Routing uses the names of the peer multiplexing and forwarding applications to derive routes (from which a decision can be made to choose the next hop). It also maintains information on all the forwarding applications of its nearest neighbors and which interfaces can be used to reach that next hop. This yields Figure 6-15. Note that routing is grayed out in the bottom layer because for most physical media it is not needed, although it might be present for some types of media.

The observant reader will have recognized that we have drawn the traditional picture of a layered network architecture. But the lines are in somewhat different places. We created a three-layer system of repeating elements, where the repeating unit is a distributed IPC facility. At this point, we should generalize the definitions given so far, drop the subterfuge of calling these "dedicated IPC systems" and instead call them "routers," and explore in more detail the properties of such a network architecture. We do this in the next chapter. We will now just be applying these basic concepts over and over in different places.

New Elements

- **(N)-layer.** A distributed IPC facility at a given rank

- **(N)-subsystem.** The instantiation of a layer in a system, an IPC process

- **Scope of an (N)-layer.** The set of all application processes able to communicate directly without relaying by a DIF of a higher rank.

Initial Conclusions

This exercise was begun purely to see whether stripping the problem down to its barest bones could shed light on the characterization of a layer. It has yielded much more than we had reason to expect. We can now see that the fundamental structure derives from applications and their supporting IPC (and now it looks so obvious). We now see how IPC between systems requires supporting applications and, in some cases (the ones we are most interested in), supporting systems dedicated to IPC.

Networking is distributed IPC and only IPC.

Remembering Advice to Freshman Engineers

We tell freshman engineers not to skip steps: Write each step down in full. When steps are skipped is when mistakes are made, when signs are dropped, when wrong answers are made.

In the days after I first did this exercise, as its implications began to sink in, I began to realize that it is much more than just a nice teaching tool. I became very annoyed with myself. This is an exercise that any of us could have done anytime in the past 30 years. We have all written analogies for how networking is similar to sending a letter through the mail or making a phone call, but we had never done it for computers! Or if we did, we had skipped steps and missed some important things.

We had all been guilty of not doing what we had warned freshman engineers of. I always enjoy these moments when the problem hoists us on our own petard. To quote the old radio show, *The Life of Riley*, "What a revolting development this is!"

I can hear the reader now, "Yeah, we knew that." And we did ...sort of. Metcalfe had it right 35 years ago. Not to put words in Bob's mouth, though, he would probably say he was just echoing what "everyone" believed in 1972! But we didn't act like it. We have treated these elements as very different and have been sloppy about including functions that don't belong and not including functions that did belong. Adhering more closely to "It is *just* IPC," maintaining a clear distinction between IPC and managing IPC, will yield considerable advantage. If it isn't directly part of IPC, it belongs elsewhere.

These IPC processes also follow the same structure of being applications using a supporting IPC and so on until the IPC is a physical wire. Although it might seem there are essentially two kinds of layers (i.e., those that contain only applications and those that support IPC), closer inspection reveals that the former is simply a degenerate case of the latter. A layer is the distributed IPC facility. The IPC facility is composed of IPC processes in usually different systems. But IPC processes are just applications using the layer below. An IPC process consists of a set of tasks along with the other applications below using the lower IPC facility and so on. So-called user applications exist on top of any IPC facility, which has sufficient scope to reach the desired corresponding application and alongside applications that are IPC processes for higher-ranking DIFs.

This makes clear that many things that have been considered quite different are, in fact, the same. As shown in Chapter 5, the "directory" is essentially a local query of the routing and naming functions for information on nearest neighbors. Relaying and routing for mail, for transaction processing, and for peer-to-peer (sic) applications are simply different forms of the routing we find in the network layer and so on. Differing demand patterns merely lead to different distribution patterns of the information and different policies. The need for both point-of-attachment (PoA) addresses and node addresses is far clearer. We see that the relation is relative. The node addresses of a DIF are the PoA addresses of the DIF above. All of the required naming and addressing from Saltzer turns out to be a natural consequence of the fundamental structure, as it should. While in one sense, the distinctions lose some of their importance, in another sense, it greatly strengthens them. And another ladder gets thrown away.

This exercise has revealed relations that were not foreseen at the outset. The relation to operating systems, while apparent from the start, has turned out to be much stronger than previously recognized. Although we "knew" it, this emphasizes much more strongly that "networking" is very much a distributed resource allocation, a distributed operating system. In other words, we must treat the collection of subsystems of the same layer, as a single system, sometimes much more loosely coupled than we think of a traditional operating system, but a system nonetheless. Each IPC process is, in essence, an operating system with distinct subtasks (or threads) for the EFCP and support functions such as routing and management.

Although strictly speaking, a layer is a distributed IPC facility, we must consider it in the context of the set of applications that can access it. The distributed IPC facility is a collection of applications that are multitasked, consisting of multiple instances of an error and flow-control protocol, a resource management function (i.e., relaying and multiplexing), and supporting tasks.[19] This section has made an argument for at least two layers: a layer dedicated to the media, a layer managing physical resources and a layer managing logical resources, with applications operating above them. This is not very different from the configuration described at the beginning of this chapter. But as we saw, things seemed to get more complicated. The repeating structure of DIFs accommodates and organizes that complexity by simply creating more DIFs.

There has always been some question as to whether we split TCP and IP in the right place. This analysis says we got it right. It confirms the separation of TCP and IP, CYCLADES TS and CIGALE, of OSI TP4 and CLNP, or of XNS SeqPkt and IDP was correct. The first is the protocol that provides basic IPC connection/channel/flow on a per-instance basis; the other is the common PCI for relaying and multiplexing of what is really a distributed application. However, this same analysis indicates that it was a mistake to separate the network and transport layers, because they are integral parts of the *same* distributed IPC facility.[20] The network layer has always been a stumbling block. On the one hand, the name implies that it is just the network and not the hosts (and we have a tendency to try to treat it that way). But it *is* in the host, too; it has to be. The concept of the network layer is a last vestige of the bead-on-a-string mindset (a view we were pushed into by the battle over the transport layer that was described earlier). The network layer must go. It is making us think like bellheads.

When IPC processes move to their "data transfer phase," they use common PCI, of which IP/CLNP/IDP/MAC are examples. But more interesting is how

---

[19] Don't take this too literally as an indication of an implementation strategy.

[20] I remember in a network layer meeting Dave Oran exclaiming in frustration that there were all these hints that transport and network should be closer together for things to work well. At the time, we could not see the argument that would allow us to do it. We now have the argument.

they get to the data transfer phase. Enrollment, something we wanted to ignore because it was messy (like writing boot loaders) is nothing more than normal application connection establishment with optional authentication and some initialization, including address assignments.

We find that names required for routing (i.e., addresses) are not just names of specialized applications called protocol machines, but are names *internal* to a distributed IPC facility for the internal coordination of IPC. This is a subtle but significant difference from our past understanding of addresses. These internal names are coordinating resource management as well as routing and relaying in a distributed IPC facility. They are used only by IPC processes for their own purposes. Any other properties we might consider ascribing to them are overloading the semantics of the identifier. No other applications have any need to ever know their existence. Every IPC process has an *external* application name and an *internal* address. How do you get to something before it has an address? By its external application name using the underlying IPC.

Why had we not seen this? When the original layered model was proposed, networks were very small and slow: Bandwidth was on the order of $5 * 10^4$ or less; processor speed, $\sim 5 * 10^5$; number of users was on the order of 10^3. Today, the numbers are very different: on the order of 10^{12}; 10^{10}; and 10^9, respectively. We had imposed a structure on a problem after seeing only a *microscopic* piece of the landscape if we graphed this with 10-meter axes, we would have a box 100nm by 100 microns by 10 microns!, and after trying only three or four relatively similar possibilities. Compared to operating systems where we had tried 20 or 30 different operating systems before we began to settle on a common model. These constraints tended to focus us on the differences and made the similarities hard to see. As the bandwidth of the media increased, the *range* of resources to manage did not remain constant (everything did not just move up), but the *range* increased,[21] making it more and more difficult to effectively manage and optimize resources over what is now a range of 6 or 7 decimal orders of magnitude and growing. There are still major applications that generate data at low rates and operating constraints that require lower-speed processors. It is well understood that resource-allocation algorithms and error-prevention/correction methods work best within a particular range, a range that is much smaller than the 6 or 7 orders of magnitude we are confronted with.

---

21   With bandwidths now at 10^{12}, applications do not operate nearly within an order of magnitude of that number as they did at the beginning, where all applications operated between 1K and 56K. Now applications operate any where from 10^3 to 10^{12}. This is a much different resource-allocation problem. Managing ever-higher bandwidth is a hard problem, but managing growing bandwidth in reasonably constant range (i.e. the minimum bandwidth rises, too) is an easier problem than managing increasing bandwidth *and* increasing range.

But we failed to act like scientists and continually question our fundamental structures. Economic and political forces outside our influence are as much to blame for this as our own failures. The bunker mentality created by the intense debates over connections and connectionless. We concentrated on the immediate and failed to delve more deeply to see what was really going on and look to the long term. And worse, we allowed Moore's law to corrupt us and make us sloppy.[22] And even worse, our academics failed us by only reporting what was being deployed instead of analyzing, critiquing, and distilling principles. The vast majority of our textbooks are vocational, not university-level textbooks.

Engineering must always make compromises. But engineering is predicated on science providing the principles of what is "right," so that engineering can make intelligent compromises. We have fallen into engineering without science.

Taking Stock

Let's step back for a moment and take stock of where we are. What are layers for? As always, there are two distinct purposes for black boxes or layers: the benefit it provides to the user by hiding complexity, and the structuring it provides for organizing the functions to accomplish that service (i.e., both external and internal benefits).

For the user or application, the layer provides an abstract hardware/media-independent interface to IPC, pure and simple. Communicating with a process on the same system or a different system should be as nearly the same as possible. The goal has always been to make the network as invisible as possible to the applications.

Furthermore, the use of layering in creating that illusion has provided a means for decomposing the problem, managing complexity, and achieving the abstraction (sometimes in stages) to isolate the application from the specifics of the hardware: the classic functions of an operating system, but focused on IPC. There have been basically two reasons for using layers for decomposition: functionally to control complexity and isolate like functions, and logically or organizationally to circumscribe the problem. For example, the data link layer isolates the media-specific functions from the more general resource management functions of the middle layers. Although multiple data link segments may be limited to specific areas (buildings, floors of a building, and so on) to constrain the management task to a given area and allow different media without affecting the resource management functions. Layers may be created for either rationale,

---

22 It is interesting that Moore's law can be a driver for innovation in hardware but have precisely the opposite effect on software.

either horizontally or vertically. In this example, layers were created vertically to isolate different functions and horizontally for logical separation. But there are reasons for which we would create layers horizontally to isolate different functions and vertically for logical separation.

In the previous chapters, we did get a glimpse of a few patterns or invariances in the organization of protocols:

1. The scope of "layers" tends to increase as one moves up.

2. The same protocol functions keep recurring with different policies all the way from the media into what is considered the "applications" and not arbitrarily, but in repeating patterns.

3. There is a requirement for common PCI, at least for addressing, both in the lower layers and in the applications.

4. Connection and connectionless can be achieved with a common model.

Experience had indicated that there were often advantages in managing resources if the error-control protocol and the relaying and multiplexing task could share information about the conditions they were observing. However, having these protocols in different layers (using the "one protocol per layer" rule) forced complete isolation between the relaying and error-control functions so that the sharing of this information was not possible. This model solves that and eliminates some duplication. But our "derivation" of networking as IPC shows conclusively that they are part of the same IPC facility and therefore should be part of the same layer.

A layer is a distributed IPC facility.

Not recognizing the need for the "IAP-like" protocol and seeing its role in resource allocation was another factor in not seeing the structure. Furthermore, as one moves in toward the backbone as more and more traffic is multiplexed, bandwidth tends to increase. The bandwidth range of applications in a single host is seldom as great as seen over the whole network.

All of these are indications of what should constitute a layer, of what the organization of layers should be, and to some extent how many layers an architecture should have. But we also realize that layers are not so much isolating different functions as different ranges of the resource-allocation problem. If we consider all of this, and keep in mind that we are looking for patterns, doing so will lead to an architecture that scales and that does not require new constructs for every new technology or capability that is invented.

This gives us a good idea of the structure we have been looking for: applications operating over an IPC facility, which then repeats, subdividing the problem. Each layer has the same functionality, but that functionality is optimized to deal with a subset of the range of the whole resource-allocation problem.

The Network IPC Architecture (NIPCA)

All of this leads us to one of those odd shifts in thinking, where a significant change in the *why* at first seems to have little affect on the *what*.

We have always viewed different layers as performing different functions. And we have had lots of arguments in design sessions and standards committees about which functions go in which layers or protocols (hoping that most functions would not be repeated in multiple layers). This was in no small part driven by the severely limited resources of the early hardware and Dijkstra's definitions, which may have been influenced by the same limitations: It would have been more efficient if functions could be done once and not repeated. But there were always conditions that seemed to warrant the inclusion of the same functions in different layers for various circumstances, primarily because of layers with different scope. For example, the view that segmenting should occur in transport but not in the data link layer, but there are cases where it is needed. Routing was in the network layer; LANs shouldn't do routing, but they do. Data corruption detection (CRC) is necessary in the data link layer, so why is it needed in transport? But it is. And so on. There were also circumstances when applications required fewer lower layers (e.g., LAN-based applications). And as the availability of resources has swamped those old systems, the emphasis has gone entirely the other way: Now we need to subdivide the resource-allocation problem to be effective, thus leading to repeating functions for different ranges of the problem.

The shift in thinking we have uncovered is this (throw away another ladder):

All layers have the same functionality. They differ in the scope and in the range of bandwidth and QoS they support. So, although the protocols in these different layers are the same, they have different policies and possibly syntax suited to that scope and range of bandwidth and QoS.

In one sense, nothing has changed. In the traditional range of operation, the layers are still pretty much what they were. In another sense, a lot has changed. We no longer have an architecture of individually crafted protocols, but an architecture of common repeating units. This takes network architecture from craft to rational discipline.

Fundamentally, networking is concerned with application processes communicating via a distributed IPC facility. (We will use *IPC facility* interchangeably with *distributed IPC facility,* just to keep things from getting to cumbersome.) That IPC facility is itself composed of APs in different systems, whose coordinated behavior creates a distributed application for allocating IPC resources. Each component application consists of error- and flow-control protocols, multiplexing and relaying functions, which implement the resource allocation, and are supported by various routing, resource monitoring, and management tasks. These applications in turn use an IPC facility and so on until the IPC facility is the physical media.

A layer has a rank (its position relative to other layers) and a scope (previously we would have said, reachable without relaying at a higher layer, which is still true; now the collection of IPC processes that coordinate to provide a distributed IPC facility). As rank increases, scope tends to increase, too. The number of elements in the layer increases, but the degree of coordination tends to decrease. A layer (a distributed IPC allocation application) consists of those protocols and internal applications necessary to allocate, maintain, and manage those resources. However, the layer is not necessarily the unique provider of IPC facilities as we have traditionally conceived it. For example, relaying of mail constitutes a specialized "layer." This would seem to indicate the following:

A layer is a collection of cooperating IPC processes. IPC processes are simply applications with application name taken from a name space sufficient to unambiguously identify all the applications reachable via the supporting distributed facility. An address space internal to the distributed IPC facility is used among the IPC processes to coordinate and manage IPC (i.e., data transfer).

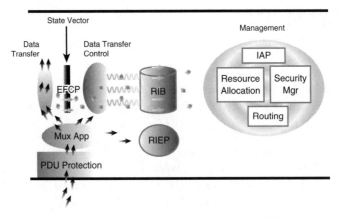

Figure 6-16 The elements of a layer have three parts: data transfer, IPC control, and IPC management, where "control" is short-cycle time management.

An IPC process, and by implication a DIF, consists of three distinct loci of processing (see Figure 6-16) loosely coupled through an information base/state vector:

1. **An IPC data transfer protocol.** A PDU "scheduling" function, which appends the Common Data Transfer PCI and provides multiplexing and relaying with any necessary policies to manage the buffers and queues; and a per-flow data transfer task that only handles Transfer PDUs (i.e., tightly coupled mechanisms) and associated with it an instance of ....

2. **An IPC data transfer control protocol.** To provide any loosely coupled mechanisms necessary with the appropriate policies instantiated on the basis of the requirements of each allocation request by the requesting application. The EFCP is present to the degree that the difference in QoS requested by a user above and the QoS provided by the layer below is sufficiently different to require additional measures.

3. **The IPC management.** A *Resource Information Exchange Protocol* (RIEP) that provides *Management Information Base* (MIB) query and update services to a set of resource management tasks for routing, security resource management, address assignment, and so on needed to manage and maintain the distributed IPC.

It is this unit that repeats in an architecture.

Although there are many interesting properties of this architecture, some of which we will get into in more depth in the remaining chapters, one aspect deserves further comment now. For any communication, the only information that a user application ever has or needs is its local port-id the destination application name and. It never needs nor has access to know addresses, well-known ports, and so on. With recursion, the network infrastructure is impervious to attack by hosts, because hosts simply can't address them. The trust required by a distributed IPC facility of a supporting IPC is very little: Only that the supporting communication will attempt to deliver PDUs to something.

It need not rely on it for anything more. It can, but it need not. It is entirely the DIF's responsibility during enrollment to determine that other IPC processes are valid members and its responsibility to protect its communication from tampering or eavesdropping. To join a DIF, the new IPC process must be authenticated and assigned an address. Of course, the strength of this authentication and the stringency of the policies will depend on the DIF. One can imagine that more public DIFs may be very loose, while more private ones will be fairly strong. However, the difference here as opposed to the current architecture is that there is a choice.

Organizing Layers

As with any architecture, there are two ways that it can be used: as a guide to existing protocol structures to gain a better understanding of what was done and why and how to do things better in the future; and to define a new set of protocols and architectures to solve problems. We are going to consider this architecture in both senses. The reason for doing this is to gain a better understanding of what we have done in the past and to construct a clearer picture of where we might go in the future,[23] recognizing that many engineering steps and compromises may be needed between the two and that absolute purity may never be achieved,...no, never will be achieved.[24] It has been claimed that we have all the pieces. This chapter has shown that we don't. However, the missing pieces, while not in some sense huge, they are key to transforming an unfinished demo into an elegant and powerful complete architecture.

The only issue that we have not dealt with is the organization of multiple layers. We have already seen hints of the solution to this. But, it does take another shift in thinking.

The trade press always likes to ask, "How many layers are there?" Clearly, there has to be at least one layer of IPC. This corresponds to applications running over what has traditionally been called the data link layer or a LAN. Nice, but not much scope. And we know that as LANs get larger they become more difficult to manage. In our derivation, we stacked two of these layers, the first representing the traditional physical/MAC and LLC; the second, network and transport. As previously noted, the problems of handling congestion and resource allocation have been difficult. Not surprising. We have been trying to manage a range of bandwidth that spans six orders of magnitude with the same protocols and policies! The only solution has seemed to be to throw hardware at it. Everything else not only increased complexity, but also it just patched a particular problem and didn't contribute to a solution that scaled. We can't expect this to work forever, and there are signs that it isn't.

---

23   The idea of progression by small incremental changes is good only if you know where you are going. If you don't, it is worse than being lost.

24   This architecture has a chance of maintaining more "purity" than most, because most of the usual threats to its "purity" are either aimed at policies that don't affect the purity or will impair the ability to maintain repeatable units, which is the source of much of its advantage.

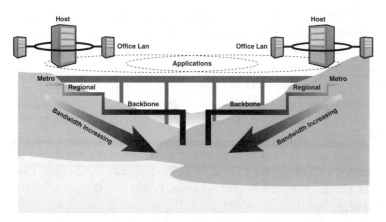

Figure 6-17 A highly stylized example of the hill and valley metaphor, showing only half of the valley. (Strict hierarchy is not required.)

Although very large LAN networks can be built using bridges, as just noted it has been found that such networks are "difficult" to manage. If routers are used to break up the LAN segments, many management advantages result. The problem is not bridging per se, and the advantage has little to do with routers per se. The advantages accrued from the decomposition caused by relaying at a higher layer allows management functions and the effects of failures to be contained to domains of manageable sizes where similar management policies can be applied. The same phenomena will be true of any large network. Another example is seen in routing. The original reason for distributed routing was that events happen in a network too fast for a human to be in the loop. Now there are indications that our routing calculations for large flat internets may be long enough that the same will soon be true of them. Our networks are becoming too large to *"manage,"* whether the global public network, large corporate networks, or networks supporting applications with a wide range of bandwidth requirements. Our current approaches provide nothing to contain the management of these large systems. They require further decomposition to be manageable. It is easy to foresee that more layers would improve the ability to manage resources. We are merely resorting to the old architectural strategy of divide and conquer. Resource management can be much more effective, and less suboptimal, if it can be applied to a relatively narrow range.

Arrrgh! More Layers!

I can hear it now! After the recent counterattacks by the beads-on-a-string faction, the fad has been that fewer layers must be better; they have even gone so far as to argue that all layers are bad. Although the architecture of the whole network has more layers, no single router in the network will implement any more layers than a current router does. Clearly, more layers could incur more overhead. But by the same token, attempting to manage an ever-larger range of bandwidth and a growing number of elements in one layer is ineffective and even more inefficient, and we are seeing that it has its limits.

Does more layers mean more relaying? How does this affect the global efficiency and the efficiency of packet handling in a single router? There are basically two issues: First, the number of hops between two points should be no different. More layers does not increase the number of relaying points, it only increases the units of switching; that is, lower layers should switch more data less frequently. If anything, a regular architecture may impose more hierarchy than a flat network, which will reduce the diameter of the network.

Calculations show that concatenation and decreasing address length in lower layers causes the fraction of the PDU consumed by the headers to

continues

continued

remain constant or decrease. Similarly, the number of PDUs switched drops dramatically. The only additional overhead to be considered is longer headers from encapsulation. But lower layers have less scope and hence shorter addresses, which account for most of the header.

Given that header size of lower layers is smaller and that lower layers will be aggregating (N+1)-PDUs into larger (N)-PDUs means the relative overhead is either constant or lower, sometimes much lower. In fact, even with four layers of relaying and at least two (N+1)-PDUs per (N)-PDU, the header overhead would be less per packet than a typical TCP/IP packet and five times less than ATM. It is important to stress that one only has as many layers as needed.

This also allows a better fit for the size of address and makes the fixed-length versus variable-length address argument moot. (Yet another case of designers understanding implementation better than implementers.) High-performance switching layers will be lower and thus have less scope and therefore shorter (likely) fixed-length addresses, while higher layers with greater scope will have longer addresses. However, these might be variable length; because they are only used in this much greater context, the requirement for variable length is less.

continues

Tunneling treats the symptoms but not the substance of the problem. The scaling issues we have with network architecture are not with data transfer but with management. Therefore, if instead of just recursing the relaying protocol, we recurse the *layer*, we would have the machinery in place to manage the resources of the recursion itself. A layer manages a given range of bandwidth and QoS parameters: a manageable range, not 6 orders of magnitude.

As a useful metaphor, consider a terrain of valleys (see Figure 6-18). The deeper the valley, the greater the bandwidth. Layers are built up to bridge between points on the sides of the valleys. Applications occur along the slopes or at the top of the valleys. (There may be small hills within a valley.)

Think of the top layer as having sufficient scope to connect to all destinations that a set of applications need to reach as a bridge across a valley from the top of a bluff on one side to the top of a bluff on the other. The depth of the valley is bandwidth; and the topography between the bluffs undulates (intervening subnets of differing physical bandwidths). The bottom layer (of which there are many, because they have limited scope and are tailored to various media) provides the basis for communication. The greater the range of bandwidth between the applications and the backbone, the more layers; the less range, the fewer layers. These intermediate layers are created in increments of bandwidth (a range that to be determined experimentally). Data from applications with low bandwidth would go through more layers than data from applications that required higher bandwidth. A layer would take a set of flows from above in a particular bandwidth range and multiplex them together to be a flow in the bandwidth range of its layer and so on, concatenating PDUs as they move toward the core of the network and thus reducing the switching overhead.[25] Notice that some of these intermediate layers might be provider based and represent a scope managed by a single provider, while a broader public or virtual private network floated on top of the provider subnets. To summarize:

---

[25]   There is a commonly held belief that there is too much time between PDUs to do concatenation without incurring significant delay. Given that current Internets are operated well below 30% to 40% loading where congestion appears, this would appear to be an artifact.

How many layers are there?	As many as you need	*continued*
How many kinds of layers?	One, a distributed IPC facility	Unlike most architectures, this approach does not require the use of layers that are not needed and local traffic will encounter fewer layers. Interestingly enough, the implementation of this structure avoids the problems found in traditional layered implementation of hand-crafted protocols by improving opportunities for pipelining and eliminating the need for data copies and task switching. Although unnecessary proliferation is always possible, it is by the same token self-limiting. As with any architecture, it does not prevent you from shooting yourself in the foot.
What does it do?	Transfer data for a set of users within a distributed IPC facility with a given QoS	

A network architecture consists of applications and is supported by an IPC facility configured appropriately on top of as many distributed IPC facilities, as needed.

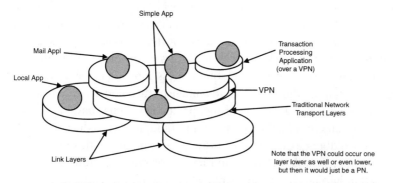

Figure 6-18 An example of six RIPCA layers (DIFs) stacked four high to achieve different host-related functions.

So, is the application the top layer? It is for that application. There may be applications that require greater scope that are above this one, and applications that require less scope operate on layers below this (see Figure 6-18). How much scope must the application have? Enough to communicate with everyone it needs to.

Where are network management applications? On top of any layer that has sufficient scope to access the *systems* (not necessarily layers) being managed. One might be tempted to make management domains and the scopes of the layers on which the applications run coincide. We could imagine that more "public" layers would have looser controls, including security, while more private ones would have tighter controls.

Conclusions

In this chapter, we have uncovered larger structures or patterns that were made apparent by finer structures we had found in the previous chapters. It would seem that we have achieved the goals of Newton's properties of a good theory. This is a model that requires a few simple concepts to generate the characteristics of networking as we know them and at the same time shows how many aspects of networking are accommodated as a consequence of the structure that today requires whole specialized mechanisms.

The concept of a single, repeating layer has been staring us in the face for quite some time. Now that we see the pattern, we can look back and see that many of the approaches to problems and some recent papers (Touch, et al. 2006) had been nosing around the answer, but none had actually seen the larger pattern or its implications. The advantage of this model is not that it solves any one problem. The plethora of existing hacks may each address its problem within the tolerance of engineering costs. But they seldom address more than one, and they generally make others more difficult. The advantage of this model is that it solves these problems without myriad mechanisms, protocols, shims, band-aids, and kludges, and without increasing the "parts count" (and, in fact, reducing it from the current Rube Goldberg assemblage). Further, the structure of this model creates a much more predictable behavior and has on several occasions proven to solve problems that had not been considered when assembling it.

As should already be apparent, and as shown in more detail in subsequent chapters, many current problems in networking are now easily addressed in some cases with no additional effort and in others with just a judicious choice of policy. As we will see, problems such as multihoming and mobility simply fall out for free. We will find that the IPC model and the compartmentalization it creates has security benefits, too. And a common structure that enforces much more consistency of behavior will allow much more efficient implementation strategies, and greatly improve the manageability of networks and reduce the skill level required. First, we need to consolidate our gains by defining the basic elements of the architecture and how fundamental processes work. Then, we will consider one unsolved question, that of the meaning of location-dependence in an arbitrary graph. Next, we will explore the implications of this architecture for a variety of topics such as multihoming, mobility, multicast, and so on, as well as conjecture about the nature of a synthesis of connection and connectionless that achieves the best of both. We will also consider the architecture of private and public Internets organized using these principles.

It does seem that one conclusion we can reach is that there is no general "upper-layer architecture," only the distinction between the application and application protocol machine. As shown in Chapter 4, the OSI upper three layers collapse into either aspects of application connection establishment (i.e., the presentation layer) or common building blocks for application protocols (i.e., the session layer). This seems to be the limit of the general "upper-layer architecture." It does appear that if we build distributed applications on top of distributed applications, that anything we build on will be a variation of a DIF, whether we call it a layer, mail relay, transaction processing, P2P, VPNs, or so on. It is a DIF with most of its elements. However, this is not to say that there are not more elaborate common structures for specific application domains.

Similarly, we see that the "protocol field" found in IP or the CLNP selector is unnecessary. Earlier I argued that this couldn't be addressing because it didn't distinguish all the necessary cases. We conjectured that it identified the syntax and was a special case of the function provided by presentation layer, as strange as that might sound. Perhaps a general property of protocols. But, we also found that everywhere it occurred was a false layer boundary. What we found is that the nature of boundary between layers is through a construct equivalent to the port-id. OSI had this concept but got it wrong by forcing its "port-id" to be the (N)-SAP-address (although the OSI Network Layer group got it right by seeing the network address carried by CLNP as the network entity title).[26] The conclusion is that there is never any need for an (N–1)-protocol to identify the (N)-protocol. The equivalent of a port-id is all that adjacent layers should have in common. Because the application requested communication with the peer using the same protocol among themselves, it must know what the syntax is. It is certainly no business of the DIF or layer to have any knowledge of what it should be. An application requests the allocation of IPC with a destination-application name. If that is ambiguous because the application uses multiple protocols, the request must include the application protocol machine name. This is the split between application process and application entity that we saw in Chapter 4.

Now that we have roughed out what the structure is, we need to do some serious work. In the next chapter, we try to put down in fairly precise definitions the elements of this architecture. This is a hard trek to make. There aren't many ways to make it easier without sacrificing precision, but I try to intersperse it with interpretations to relate it to real-world problems and interesting properties as we go along. Then we move on to an even harder topic of trying to increase our understanding of what is meant when we say that an address is "location dependent" and how this may benefit an architecture. Then, we return to applying this model to the problems of multihoming, mobility, multicast, and private networks.

---

[26] Strictly speaking, while very close this is still not quite right in that the Network Entity Title was the external name of the IPC process, whereas as we have seen the address is a name internal to the DIF.

Chapter 7

The Network IPC Model

I am far from thinking that nomenclature is a remedy for every defect in art or science: still I cannot but feel that confusion of terms generally springs from, and always leads to, confusion of ideas.

—*John Louis Petit,* Architectural Studies in France, *1854*[1]

A problem well stated is a problem half solved.

—*Charles Kettering*

Introduction

Now that we have concluded that networking is best modeled as a single repeating layer and reviewed some of the results we have arrived at over the past 30 years, we can construct the elements of a general model of networking, a Platonic ideal, that we can use both to analyze our previous work and to use as a guide going forward. Over the past decade or so, we have seen a growing attitude that the only criteria for measuring a solution was whether it could be made to work. The trouble is that with software anything can be made to work. This may be acceptable in some engineering domains, but this doesn't really tell us much about the nature of the problem. It isn't *science*. In science, the solution to any problem must always be evaluated in terms of "the theory." It is either consistent with the theory or it is not. And if not, we must determine what is wrong with the solution or what is wrong with the theory.[2] The task of science

---

[1] Noel Chiappa found this one, too!

[2] Of course, there is no *ex post facto*. Solutions developed before the theory can't be blamed for not following a theory not yet recognized. But these solutions often shed light on what we were struggling with and contribute to the theory.

is constructing and testing theories. The task of building things from those theories is engineering. The question then is how do we evaluate theories. In most sciences, theories attempt to describe and predict observations of important aspects of Nature and come as close as possible to achieving Newton's *Regulae Philosophandi*. In computing systems, there is not much Nature we can draw on, so we must rely more heavily on Newton.

Over the past six chapters, we have uncovered several elements of the model we came to in last chapter. Now we need to assemble the elements of the model and describe its operation in one place. As we saw in the preceding chapter, a layer is a distributed IPC application, embodied as a collection of processes cooperating to manage a particular range of bandwidth and QoS. Not all layers will require the full complement of functionality and, in some cases, will require only minimal functionality. The components outlined here should not be taken as an implementation strategy, but a logical model. Although the model will be described in terms of a single layer, the reader should be aware that this is probably not the preferred implementation strategy (at least not how I would do it), and as always there will be advantages to different implementation strategies for specific environments. For now, you should concentrate on shifting your mindset from the traditional networking model of custom static layers to thinking in terms of distributed applications that provide IPC recursively. This isn't as easy as it sounds.

We need to introduce terminology for various common elements. This will facilitate describing the behavior of a single layer and the operation of multiple layers. We start by introducing this terminology, then progressing to a description of the components, and then how layers are assembled. We will consolidate our gains from the first six chapters taking the opportunity to throw away a few more ladders. Many of these functions have been described elsewhere, and forms of them exist in conventional systems, although not necessarily arranged in this manner. This can be a rather mind-numbing exercise. On the one hand, we want to be reasonably precise and abstract to capture the invariances in their full generality. On the other hand, it needs to be readable and understandable. This is a hard balance to achieve.

One small contribution to readability is to drop the (N)- notation except when it is required to relate to a layer above or below. We will leave the (N)- notation in the definitions to indicate which elements are part of the repeating structure. Some might find the introduction of definitions at the beginning of each section disconcerting. Please bear with me. This avoids having to say everything twice: once to describe it and once to define it. Think of this as defining a family of implementations.

Basic Structure

Definitions

Defining *Computer*

These definitions attempt to capture the essence of a single "computer." Recognizing that peripherals are no longer electronics "bolted to the side of the machine" but specialized computing systems in their own right, "a computer" is today inherently a distributed system.

- **Processing system.** The hardware and software capable of supporting tasks that can coordinate with a "test and set" instruction (i.e., the tasks can all atomically reference the same memory).

- **Computing system.** The collection of all processing systems (some specialized) under the same management domain (with no restrictions of their connectivity, but recognizing that for a significant portion of this population the elements of the management domain are directly connected (i.e., one physical hop).

- **(N)-layer.** The collection of application processes cooperating as a distributed application to provide interprocess communication (IPC) (see Figure 7-1).

- **(N)-distributed-IPC-facility (DIF).** A distributed application consisting of at least one IPC application in each participating processing system. The (N)-DIF provides IPC services to applications via a set of (N)-API primitives that are used to exchange information with the application's peer. The corresponding application processes may be in other processing systems. This definition makes IPC in a single processing system a degenerate close.

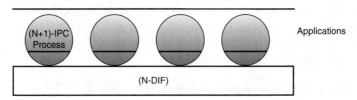

Figure 7-1 A distributed IPC facility is a layer.

Layer Versus DIF

A layer is a DIF. To facilitate the break with old ways of thinking, we will try to avoid the use of the term *layer* and use *DIF* throughout.

- **Application process, AP.** The instantiation of a program executing in a processing system intended to accomplish some purpose. An application contains one or more application protocol machines.[3]

---

[3] All of the terms associated with this concept are heavily loaded. We have chosen to use application process in the sense of processes used in most operating system textbooks. The (N)- notation is not applied to applications since they are in the system and not part of the IPC.

- **Distributed application.** A collection of cooperating APs that exchange information using IPC and maintain shared state.

- **(N)-IPC-process.** An AP that is a member of (N)-DIF and implements locally the functionality to support IPC using multiple subtasks.

- **(N)-protocol.** The syntax of PDUs, and associated set of procedures, which specifies the behavior between two (N)-PMs for the purpose of maintaining coordinated shared state.

- **(N)-protocol-machine, (N)-PM.** A finite state machine that implements an (N)-protocol, which exchanges PDUs with a peer to maintain shared state with a corresponding (N)-PM, usually in another processing system.

- **(N)-API-primitive.** A library or system call used by an application or an application-protocol to invoke system functions, in particular IPC functions, such as requesting the allocation of IPC resources.

- **(N)-service-data-unit, (N)-SDU.** A contiguous unit of data passed by an APM in an IPC API primitive whose integrity is to be maintained when delivered to a corresponding application protocol machine.

- **(N)-protocol-data-unit, (N)-PDU.** The unit of data exchange by (N)-PMs consisting of (N)-PCI and (N)-user-data.

- **(N)-protocol-control-information, (N)-PCI.** That portion of an (N)-PDU that is interpreted by the (N)-PM to maintain shared state of the protocol.

- **(N)-user-data.** That portion of an (N)-PDU that is not interpreted and is not interpretable by the (N)-PM and is delivered transparently to its client, as an (N)-SDU. (N)-user-data may consist of part of, precisely one, or more than one (N)-SDU. If more than one (N)-SDU, then SDUs in the (N)-user-data are delimited by the (N)-PCI.

To PDU or Not to PDU

PDU is used for the myriad terms for *packet, frame, cell, message,* and so on because I abhor having multiple names for the same concept, and PDU has been fairly widely adopted. PCI and user-data are used for header and user-data to emphasize the distinction between information as what the protocol understands and the data as what it doesn't.

- **Application protocol.** A protocol that is a component of an AP, characterized by modifying state external to the protocol.

- **Application PM, APM.** The instantiation of an application protocol within an application. Even though the communicating applications may be different, communicating application PMs must support the same application protocol.

- **(N)-data-transfer-protocol.** An (N)-protocol used by an (N)-DIF to transparently deliver (N)-user-data with specific characteristics; except for the transparent sending or receiving of (N)-SDUs, all operations of the protocol are internal to the state of the protocol.

Description of the Basic System

Fundamentally, we are concerned with applications communicating via an IPC facility. The case we will be most interested in is when the applications execute on separate processing systems. The case of applications communicating in the same system is a degenerate case of this description. The external behavior of the system is precisely the same, and the functions required are for the most part the same,[4] only the internal mechanisms to accomplish the functions differ.

Processing Systems and Their Operating Systems in Brief

Although not the primary a subject of this book, it is necessary to say something about the abstract environment that this architecture lives in. Networking is distributed IPC. A distributed IPC facility consists of a collection of two or more (N)-IPC processes.

In this model, we distinguish a processing system and a computing system. This distinction recognizes the inherent distributed-ness that systems are moving toward (and to a large extent are already there).[5] A processing system is represented by all computing resources within the scope of a "test and set" instruction.[6] All peripherals are viewed as specialized processing systems (e.g., disks, screens, keyboard, printers). All communication is accomplished by IPC.[7]

In this model, an operating system consists of three fundamental components: processor scheduling, memory management, and IPC. "Device drivers" are applications, kernel applications, but applications nonetheless.[8] Drivers exist only to manage the various hardware media interfaces (e.g., modem, bus, FireWire, USB, wireless). Interface drivers map the hardware to a logical communication model for the applications running on the hardware. Communication media should be distinguished only by their QoS and bandwidth

---

[4] There are some error conditions that must be accommodated in the distributed case that do not occur in the single system case.

[5] However, most operating systems and processor architectures are still firmly entrenched in the traditional model.

[6] I have used this definition for nearly 30 years, and it seems to get at the crux of the matter without having to reference specific configurations of processors and memory. If two processes can't coordinate with a test and set, they are in different systems. (An atomic swap is equivalent. Some authors seem to define a swap as a test and set.)

[7] Obviously, IPC is a form of I/O; however, the term *I/O* has been associated with the hardware arrangement where devices were essentially "bolted" to the side of the computer by highly specialized electronics. This is quickly becoming a thing of the past in modern computers. Bringing all communication under the umbrella of IPC has advantages and simplifies the system.

[8] Again, the term *driver* originates with this very asymmetrical view of peripherals where all the managing of the peripheral was done by the processing system. This configuration is changing.

characteristics, not by assumptions about the applications for which they will be used. The role of device drivers is assumed by applications, in most cases what have been called kernel processes or threads, that use IPC to communicate with a peer.

A computing system is defined to correspond to our traditional view of "my computer" (i.e., the collection of processing systems taken together for a particular purpose). In many cases, these are one physical hop away, but there is no requirement that this be the case. Basically, a computing system is the collection of processing systems under a common management regime.

Basic Structures and Their Principles

A layer is a distributed IPC facility, DIF. A distributed IPC facility is a distributed application consisting of at least one IPC process in each processing system participating in the DIF. (Although rare, more than one IPC process in the same processing system may be a member of the same DIF. It is more likely that multiple IPC processes on the same processing system will be members of different DIFs. This would occur with VPNs or DIFs [lower layers] handling specific media.)

Traditionally, the scope of an (N)-layer has been defined as the set of protocol machines that communicate without relaying at the (N+1)-layer. This is still the case. But a more correct characterization would be that the scope of an (N)-layer is the set of cooperating IPC processes that comprise an (N)-DIF. Generally, the scope of layers increases with greater N. However, there exist configurations where an (N+1)-DIF may have less scope, such as VPNs or other distributed applications, mail, transaction processing, and so on. Throughout we will speak of DIFs rather than layers.

An (N+1)-DIF with less scope should involve a proper subset of the (N)-DIF processing systems. If an (N+1)-DIF with less scope involves processing systems of more than one (N)-DIF, there is a potential for security compromises potentially allowing corrupting data (viruses and so on) from a less-secure DIF to be introduced to a more-secure DIF.

There can be more than one DIF of the same rank. More frequently, the sets of processing systems participating in different DIFs are mutually exclusive. When this is the case, systems in different (N)-DIF cannot communicate without relaying at the (N+1)-DIF. Communication between peer DIFs within the same processing system must use either an AP with only local knowledge (e.g., a protocol converter or NAT) or with knowledge of a wider scope (for instance, relaying by an (N+1)-DIF).

Applications in the same processing systems may use different DIFs. Note that the (N)- notation does not apply to APs. APs operate over any (N)-DIF that they have access to and has sufficient scope to communicate with any destination AP required. Hence, an application may communicate with more than one DIF at the same time. However, this does create the potential for security compromises. Where security is a concern, the only APs capable of communicating with two or more DIFs should be an (N+1)-IPC process (i.e., a member of an (N+1)-DIF). The operating system would have to enforce this constraint.

The Structure of Applications and Protocols

For two processes to communicate, they must have some shared "understanding." There must be a set of objects they have in common and an agreement on a "language" for talking about these objects and for performing operations on them. This common understanding is the protocol specification, and the language is the set of formats of the messages they exchange and the rules governing their generation and action taken when they are received.

A protocol, as indicated by the earlier definition, creates a shared domain of discourse (a fancy term for the set of things they know how to talk about) about a set of objects. A protocol establishes the rules and formats for exchanging PDUs to create and maintain this shared state and is implemented by a finite state machine. (This is a constraint. All protocols are no more computationally complex than an FSM.) A PDU consists of PCI and optionally user-data. PCI is *information* on the state of those shared objects, and the user-data consists of uninterpretable *data*. In other words, PCI is what the protocol understands, and user-data is what it doesn't.

There are two kinds of protocols: application protocols and data transfer protocols. Application protocols to perform operations "on shared state external to." For example, FTP performs operations on a computing system's file system, a management protocol performs operations on a Management Information Base (MIB), and so on. Data transfer protocols, on the other hand, perform operations on shared state internal to the protocol. The only "external affect" of a data transfer protocol is delivering SDUs transparently. As discussed in Chapter 6, "Divining Layers," the relaying and multiplexing protocols described in Chapter 3, "Patterns in Protocols," degenerate into a common PCI fragment. Strictly speaking of course, this is a protocol. Any written procedure is a protocol.

This description of protocols is taking a necessarily purist stance so that we can clearly see the forms. I fully recognize that real protocols may not (and today do not) follow these definitions. However, there are good arguments that following these definitions would greatly streamline protocol processing and open the door to simpler much more effective implementations

Protocols progress through two phases: a *synchronization phase* in which the shared state necessary to support this communication is created, and the *data transfer phase* in which the communication takes place. For application protocols, the synchronization phase is primarily concerned with establishing that correspondents are who they say they are. A discussion of these methods can be found in Aura and Nikander (1997). The synchronization phase of data transfer protocols is concerned only with creating the initial shared state necessary to support the mechanisms of the protocol. This was discussed in some detail in Chapter 2, "Protocol Elements," and Chapter 3, "Patterns in Protocols." We have tended to consider establishment as a single concept. But we see here that there are two very different forms: IPC synchronization and application initialization.

The data transfer phase of an application protocol is concerned with performing operations on external structures and ensuring the proper sequencing of those operations. The data transfer phase of a data transfer protocol is concerned with ensuring that the properties requested for the communication (e.g., bit-error rate, loss rate, jitter, and so on) are provided. This shared state allows the application to act on information at a distance. However, it should always be kept in mind that the representation of state maintained by any PM about its peer is only an approximation. There is always a time delay in the exchange of state information such that events may occur such that the information no longer represents the state of the peer.

Conjecture: Any state associated with the correspondent in an application protocol is part of the application and not associated with the application protocol. Any shared state that must be maintained during a communication is associated with IPC. For example, checkpointing is an IPC function corresponding to acknowledgments in traditional data transfer protocols. Similarly, "recovering a connection" reduces to recovering the state of the application, not the connection. An application may record information about a correspondent and about actions taken for the correspondent, but this is independent of what the correspondent does. This is not shared state in the sense we have used it. This would imply that all application protocols are stateless, whereas data transfer protocols may or may not be stateless.

It appears that all application protocols can be modeled as a small set of remote operations (e.g., read, write, create, delete, start, and stop) on objects. Differences in the "protocols" primarily involve the structures to control the sequencing and parallelism of these operations, or common sequences of operations. This is more the domain of programming languages than communicating remote operations.[9] The other "difference" is whether operations are requested (client/server) or notified (publish/subscribe). But Telnet showed us that this

---

[9] If we include these "control structures" and sequences of operations in the protocol, we are basically sending small programs, which is simply a write one level down. One must draw the line somewhere, and doing so at this elemental level seems to create the fewest problems. Also it seems reasonable that IPC gives way to "programming."

kind of request/response or publish/subscribe of an information base can be seen as symmetrical and does not warrant a distinct protocol. Therefore, we can conclude that architecturally there is only one application protocol and it is stateless.

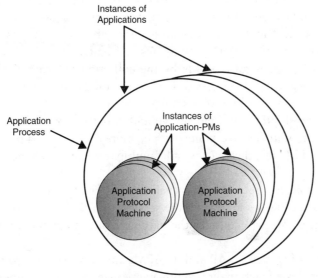

Figure 7-2 An AP contains one or more application protocol machines. A system may have multiple instances of the same application. And an application may have multiple instances of application PMs.

Application Protocol Machines

An AP is the instantiation of a program in a processing system to accomplish some purpose (see Figure 7-2). The component of the AP that implements an application protocol is called an APM. This construction of the APM is done for two reasons: First, it must be a component or else there is an infinite regress. Second, the APM is a module that may appear in more than one AP. This is the structure discussed in Chapter 4, "Stalking the Upper-Layer Architecture," and applied in Chapter 6, "Divining Layers."

An AP may contain any number of different APMs and may also have multiple instances of the same APM. An AP must have at least one APM. Otherwise, it would have no input or output and hence serve no purpose. APs (and consequently their PMs) are constructed by combining *application protocol modules* (AP-Mods), some of which may implement common functions (see Figure 7-3). A coordinating FSM governs the interaction of these modules. (It is not a PM because it does not generate PDUs.) Some modules may have fairly complex state machines themselves. (Although this construct is not strictly required, it is intended to indicate that commonality and reuse of components is possible.) The concept of an application protocol (and protocol machine) is inherently recursive.

But we just indicated that there is only one application protocol. If that's the case, aren't all APMs just instances of this one protocol? The reader has caught my "oversimplification." Strictly speaking, yes. But in practice, one will want to combine these elemental operations on external objects operations on the IPC channel, such as synchronization, two-phase commit, and so on. Also, it will be useful to further distinguish APMs by the collection of external objects they manipulate for purposes of access control and so on. So, there really are "different protocols"; they just look very similar.[10]

Conjecture: All protocols involve two and only two correspondents. Shared state involving multiple correspondents (i.e., more than two) is a property of the AP, not an APM. In other words, all "multiparty" protocols are distributed applications.[11]

To communicate, the APM must exchange information with its peer. To do this, it generates PDUs and invokes the services of a DIF via an API to pass the PDU to its peer. We will consider the nature of this interaction in more detail later.

The relation between an AP and its APMs varies widely. For some APs, the APM has very little functionality; in others it is essentially synonymous with the AP itself. The APM APIs are internal to the AP and may be ad hoc or published (i.e., the subject of standardization). They may be general or quite specific to the AP and may run the gamut of rich APIs that correspond almost 1:1 with the objects of the application protocol;[12] to APIs that resemble the IPC API; or to an API that simply populates an Information Base that is then accessed by the AP or other APMs and so on.

---

[10] OSI called this the application entity not the application protocol, for several good reasons: consistency with the use of *entity* in the other layers and to emphasize that the AE was part of the communications environment, whereas the AP was not wholly contained in it; because they realized that it wasn't *just* the protocol, and it created abbreviation problems (two APs). I used APM here to give the reader a familiar concept.

[11] This might appear to be a pedantic nit. However, this appears to follow from our previous conjecture and is the case for traditional routing protocols, multicast, P2P, and transaction-processing protocols. As we apply this model both here and beyond this book, this distinction will prove useful.

[12] These may be rich APIs but they are poor black boxes.

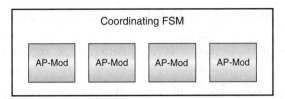

Figure 7-3 An application protocol consists of one or more ASMs. Some perhaps are common building blocks.

The components for application protocols would be defined as common modules that could be reused in different protocols. Given the complexities of providing security, one can expect that common modules would be made available for authentication and similar security functions and so on.

Naming Concepts for (N)-DIFs and Applications

Definitions

- **Application process name space.** The set of strings that may be assigned to the APs and used to reference them by other applications in the same naming domain.

- **Application process name, AP name.** A string assigned to an AP from an AP name space and assigned to no other AP while bound to the one it is assigned.

- **Application process instance.** The instantiation of an AP on an operating system.

  These definitions provide for multiple instances of the same application and allows them to be separately accessed.

- **Application process instance-id.** This is an identifier bound to AP instance that when combined with the AP name is unambiguous AP name space.

- **Application PM name space.** The set of strings that may be assigned to application PMs and used to reference them by other applications in the same naming domain.

- **Application PM-id.** This is an identifier that is unambiguous within the scope of the AP. An application PM-id when concatenated with an AP name is also unambiguous AP name space.

These definitions allow an AP to have multiple application protocols.

- **Application PM instance.** The instantiation of an application PM within an AP.

- **Application PM instance-id.** This is an identifier that is unambiguous in the AP name space when qualified by the AP name, AP instance-id, and the application PM-id.

These definitions allow naming multiple instances of application protocols within an instance of an AP.

- **IPC process name.** An AP name that is assigned to an IPC process. This is the external name of an IPC process.

There is nothing special about IPC processes or their names. A different term is used purely to make it clear when we are talking about the elements of IPC.

- **Distributed application name, DAN.** A name generally taken from the same name space as APs to identify a distributed application. An important type of distributed application is a DIF (i.e., the set of cooperating IPC processes). A DAN acts as an anycast or multicast name for the set of APs comprising this distributed application depending on the operation.

- **(N)-port-id.** An identifier unambiguous within the scope of the processing system used to distinguish a particular (N)-IPC allocation.

Application Naming

The scope of an AP name space is arbitrary and subject to the discretion of network design. At a minimum, the scope of an AP name space must be at least as great as the scope of an (N)-DIF. However, there is no logical constraint on its maximum size, given that there can be multiple DIFs of the same rank in the same system.

The scope of AP names can be as great as the union of the scope of all DIFs with processing systems in common. This requires essentially following a chain of commonality as follows:

Pick a DIF, A. Consider the processing systems of all IPC processes comprising A. The AP name space must cover all the applications reachable by this DIF. In addition, if any of these processing systems have distinct DIFs other than A, the scope of the application name space must also include all applications reachable by these DIFs (i.e., by their IPC processes and so on). (This is true because applications in processing systems with more than one DIF may relay between them.) The set thus formed represents the scope of the AP name space.

Scope defined in this way allows any two APs with names within the scope of the name space to communicate, although an AP acting as either a protocol converter or an (N+1)-DIF may be required. (A relay would be required when two APs wanted to communicate that did not have a DIF in common. If the relay uses local knowledge to relay PDUs to a destination, it is called a *protocol converter*. If the relay is the member of a DIF, it is an IPC process.)

The structure of these name spaces will depend on their scope. In domains of small scope, they may be simple and flat. For domains with large scope, they may be hierarchical (or some other organization). These name spaces may exhibit structure that can be exploited in their use. As noted earlier, how the name structure is reflected to humans is a matter of user-interface design. Here we are only concerned with the kinds of names required, their properties, and the relations among them.

The name space for the APM is a component of the AP and generally would be coordinated with it. A name space is required for the APs and APMs for all the APs that need to communicate. This name space should be location independent or more precisely have the capability of being location independent. For most applications, it does not matter where they are, but there are a few for which it does matter. For example, the name of a printer application that indicates where the printer is, as in PrintStation3rdFloorSWCorner, could be useful. There is no need to artificially disguise this fact; but on the other hand, there is no reason to impose it on all applications.

The DIF is composed of a number of IPC processes. For external purposes, each IPC process is assigned an AP name.[13] The DIF is a distributed application that is identified externally by a distributed application name. The distributed application name is used to distinguish it from other distributed applications in the same name space, whether a DIF or not. Note that a distributed application name is a multicast-application-name, see Chapter 9, "Multihoming, Multicast, and Mobility."

---

[13] We stress that these names have external visibility, because we will also want to discuss important classes of identifiers that are internal to (N)-DIFs.

In most cases, requests for IPC will not require communication with specific instances of APs, but only with the AP and perhaps the APM[14] resulting in the instantiation of a new instance of the AP or APM. There are situations, such as recovery or certain long-lived processes, where the initial request will require communication with a particular instance on an AP/APM. Similarly, there are situations where it is known at the outset that there will be no communications initiated to an instance (e.g., dedicated IPC).

The use of APs, APMs, and their instances is not rigid or unique. For example, a teleconferencing service might be implemented such that the application name designates the service and each teleconference is a distinct application protocol instance. It might just as well be implemented such that each teleconference is an AP instance. Either is possible, and there are good arguments for both. The model should not force the designer to one or the other, nor should the designer not have the choice.

When an APM requests service from the IPC facility, it is given an (N)-port-id. The port-id is used by the APM instance and the DIF to refer to all interactions regarding this flow. In general, the scope of the port-id should be the processing system. We explore why this is the case in more detail latter.

As mentioned earlier, these represent the complete set of names required for applications. Some combinations will see much less use than others. It is highly doubtful that all of them would be presented to the human user, although they would probably be available to the developer. The kind of naming syntax and the conventions necessary for human use will and should be quite different. This is just the bare bones of the structure required.

The (N)-Distributed IPC Facility

Definitions

- (N)-error-and-flow-control-protocol (EFCP). The data transfer protocol required to maintain an instance of IPC within a DIF between corresponding port-ids. The functions of this protocol ensure reliability, order, and flow control as required.

---

[14]   An application that uses only a single protocol would not necessarily have to specify the application PM.

This is equivalent to UDP, TP2, TP4, HDLC, delta-t, and TCP.

- **(N)-relaying/multiplexing-task (RMT).** The task within IPC process that performs multiplexing/relaying of (N)-PDUs and prepends the Relaying PCI to all PDUs primarily for purposes of addressing.

- **(N)-connection-identifier.**[15] An identifier internal to the DIF and unambiguous within the scope of two communicating EFCPMs of that DIF that identifies this connection. The connection-id is commonly formed by the concatenation of the port-ids associated with this flow by the source and destination EFCPMs.

- **(N)-address.** A location-dependent identifier *internal* to the DIF and unambiguous within DIF. This identifier is used in the coordination and maintenance of the DIF's state.

- **(N)-EFCPM.** A task within the IPC process that is an instance of the EFCP that creates a single instance of shared state representing a full-duplex channel, connection, association, flow, and so on.

- **(N)-delimiting.** The first operation performed by the DIF, usually by the API primitives, to delimit an SDU so that the DIF can ensure being able to deliver the SDU to its recipient.

- **(N)-Relaying-PCI.** The designation of the Relaying PCI used by the RMT of a IPC process. This is the PCI of the data transfer phase of the distributed IPC application.

This corresponds to IP, CLNP, or MAC protocols.

- **(N)-SDU-protection.** The (optional) last operation performed by RMT to ensure the SDU is not corrupted while in transit.

- **Resource Information Exchange Protocol (RIEP).** An application protocol internal to a DIF used to exchange resource information among the IPC processes of a DIF. Logically, RIEP is updating the distributed Resource Information Base (RIB).

---

[15] I have debated about the name of this term. Early drafts used *flow*. *Connection* is a heavily laden word, and many will want to associate much more with it than is intended. But just as I dislike having a half-dozen terms for PDU, I don't want to do it here. The reader is reminded that here the term identifies the entire range of possibilities from minimal shared state of a flow (e.g., UDP-like) to considerably more shared state (e.g., TCP-like).

This is a generalization of routing update protocols.

- **IPC access protocol (IAP).** An application of RIEP that finds the address of an application process and determines whether the requesting application has access to it, and communicates the policies to be used.

The (N)-IPC-Process

What we need to do now is to describe in the abstract the elements that make up an IPC process. We will not be concerned with specific protocols or algorithms, but with the class of functionality represented by each element. It is in the next level of abstraction down where specific sets of protocols and algorithms would be specified.

The IPC process is an AP, a component of a distributed IPC facility, consisting of two major components: the IPC task and the IPC management task. The IPC task consists of a RMT and one EFCPM for each connection/flow that originates in this IPC process. There is one IPC management task in an IPC process. (All instances within an IPC process have the same concrete syntax and policy range.)

The IPC task itself naturally divides into four functions:

1. Delimiting and PDU protection, which consists of fairly straightforward functions amenable to pipelining

2. Relaying and multiplexing, which is concerned with managing the utilization of the layer below

3. Data transfer, which distinguishes flows and sequencing if necessary

4. Data transfer control functions responsible for feedback mechanisms and their synchronization, which control data transfer queues and retransmission, requiring high performance but having a longer cycle time than data transfer and more complex policies

This is not the first recognition of this pattern, although I have yet to see a textbook that points it out to students. Complicating the matter is that protocols with a single PDU syntax make it difficult to take advantage of it. As noted in Chapter 3, this structure allows a single protocol to address the entire range of protocols from connectionless to fully reliable connections.

The IPC management task uses RIEP. RIEP is used to exchange information among the IPC processes necessary for the management of the DIF. Events, including timeouts, can cause RIEP to issue updates (in a publish/subscribe mode), or an IPC process or network management system may request information from an IPC process (client/server mode). The IPC management task corresponds to what some investigators have referred to as the *control plane*. However, this term is strongly associated with the beads-on-a-string model. As discussed in Chapter 6, IAP performs the function of search rules and access control for distributed IPC. One major use of RIEP can be seen as a generalization of routing update protocols.

Notice that this yields a fundamental structure for the IPC process consisting of three relatively independent loci of processing with decreasing "duty cycles" loosely coupled by some form of Information Base.

The (N)-IPC-APM

The IPC APM consists of six distinct subtasks:

1. IPC API

2. SDU delimiting

   The EFCP, which provides the error and flow control on a per-connection basis. This protocol decomposes into two parts:

3. EFCP data transfer PM, which handles tightly coupled mechanisms and carries user data

4. EFCP control PM, which provides the support for loosely coupled mechanisms

5. The relaying and multiplexing task, which appends the Common Data Transfer PCI, also known as the relaying and multiplexing protocol

6. PDU protection, consisting of CRC and encryption functions

The IPC API

The IPC service primitives[16] are used by an AP to request IPC facilities. The primitives are as follows:

What Is Wrong with "Control Plane"?

"Are your prejudices showing?" Perhaps. The concept of control plane implies that this management functionality is a distinct process from the data transfer process, that IPC consists of two processes. This implies further complication and overhead in management doing its task of monitoring and manipulating data transfer. Modeling them as tasks (threads) of an IPC process is in more alignment with what the relation needs to be. This does not mean it can't be implemented as two processes, but "buyer beware." So is it just my anti-beads-on-a-string prejudice? I don't think so, he rationalizes!

---

16 As noted in Chapter 1, service primitives are a language- and system-independent abstraction of an API. It is assumed that a real API would look different and include parameters of local necessity. Other service disciplines are possible. This one is provided just so there is one we can talk to.

- **Reason <- Allocate_Request (Destination, Source, QoS Parameters, Port-id)**   An asymmetrical request/response issued by an application to the IPC facility to create an instance of a connection with an application,[17] or by an IPC process to an AP to notify it of a request for communication.

- **Reason <- Allocate_Response (Destination, QoS Parameters, Port-id)**   An asymmetrical request/response issued by an application to the IPC facility to respond to a request to create an instance of a connection with an application, or by an IPC process to notify the requesting AP of the result of its request.

- **Reason <- Send (Port-id, buffer)**   Issued by either AP to send an SDU to the destination application on this port.

- **Reason <- Receive (Port-id, buffer)**   Issued by either AP to receive an SDU from the destination application on this port.

- **Reason <- De-allocate (Port-id)**   Issued by either AP or DIF to request or notify of the de-allocation of the resources held for this allocation and destroys all shared state associated with it and notifies the communicating applications.

The IPC API communicates requests from the APM to the DIF. Contrary to current designs that see the API as a direct input to the EFCPM, the Allocate_Request goes to the IPC management task (described later), which determines what action is to be taken. The APM communicates the characteristics of the IPC it wants, but it is the IPC management task that determines what policies will be utilized to provide those characteristics. It is important that how these characteristics are communicated by the application is decoupled from the selection of policies. This gives the DIF important flexibility in using different policies but also allows new policies to be incorporated. But first it must find the destination application and determine whether the requestor has access to it.

Previously, we said that all communication goes through three phases: enrollment, allocation, and data transfer. Earlier in this chapter, we noted that the EFCP has a synchronization phase. This is not a contradiction. Allocation is the function that occurs at the API (layer) boundary with the DIF. Applications request the *allocation* of communication resources. The DIF then determines how to provide those resources, which will require assigning port-ids, allocating resources, and instantiating an instance of the EFCP, which depending on the mechanisms required to support the request may require *synchronization*.

---

[17] Note that whereas the interface must be asymmetrical to ensure the requested AP can respond to a specific request, the underlying protocol can and should be symmetrical.

Chapter 6 showed how the IAP decouples the EFCP from requests by the APM. This decoupling is important and has been missing in our previous thinking. Allocation is an asymmetric operation. Synchronization is (generally) a symmetric operation. The decoupling of allocation and EFCP instantiation is key. It allows the IPC process greater flexibility in managing the allocation and binding of EFCP connections to the APMs.

The EFCP Protocol

This protocol provides the IPC connection/flow associated with each allocation request. It provides for the transfer of data between APs. The discussion in Chapter 3 made it clear that the protocol cleaves naturally into tightly bound mechanisms and loosely bound mechanisms. Chapter 6 showed how the distinction between the IPC function and a common header for relaying and multiplexing arises.

The binding of an APM connection to an IPC connection is made after a successful response by the IAP, not by the EFCP as is common today. The decoupling of allocation requests and EFCP synchronization would also allow a pool of EFCP connections to be maintained between frequently used destinations and simply bound to an APM request once it was determined the requested AP existed and access was permitted. Of course, an IPC with weak access control requirements could further optimize this procedure.

The IPC function requires a protocol to maintain synchronization and provide error and flow control. The EFCP is divided into two cooperating protocols. These are described as two separate protocols and are implemented by two distinct protocol machines, sharing a state vector. The EFCP supports both stream and idempotent operations. Different PDU types facilitate flexibility simplifying execution when mechanisms are not used.[18]

In the late 1970s and early 1980s, one of the differences in transport protocol proposals was whether two establishment requests to the same ports created two, one, or no (an error) connections. The Americans said one, preferring the elegance of the symmetric establishment. The European proposals preferred either two or none, being inclined to explicit control and special cases. Here we can work out the answer. The *protocol* should be symmetrical, but the *service* is necessarily asymmetric because one side or the other initiates the allocation. Of course, if the protocol is timer based, the point is moot.

Delimiting

An application protocol will deliver an amount of data to a DIF, called a SDU or *service data unit*. An SDU is a contiguous piece of data that has meaning to the

---

[18] It differs from TCP by having different PDU types for loosely coupled mechanisms. However, traffic analysis of TCP indicates that it is used as if it had different PDU types, so in fact it isn't that different.

application's correspondent. Unless otherwise directed, the DIF will deliver the same SDU to the other side. To do this, the layer may find it necessary to either fragment the SDU or concatenate it with other SDUs. Hence, the first operation on an SDU will be to delimit it.

The IPC Data Transfer PM

This is the Data Transfer PDU used for the IPC tightly coupled mechanisms. It is a very simple header requiring minimal processing. The PDU contains only source and destination port-ids as a connection- or flow-id, a length field, a PDU-id (message-id), and an optional checksum. For some IPC connections/flows, this is the only PDU required (i.e., traditionally referred to as unit data). There is a distinct instantiation (flow) of this protocol for each Allocation request. Interactions between flows are performed by the RMT and IPC management task. The only change to this protocol to support more robust connections is that the PDU-id is interpreted as a sequence number. Actually, it is always a sequence number; it is just that sometimes it isn't used for ordering.

The IPC Control Protocol

The IPC control protocol provides the loosely coupled mechanisms as required. There is a distinct instantiation (flow) of this protocol for each Allocation request that requires initial state synchronization. Coordination of the data transfer PM and the control PM is done through a shared state vector. Interactions between flows are performed by the RMT and IPC management task. The IPC control protocol has three modes of operation that are present, depending on the mechanisms and policies, depending on the QoS the application has requested and the QoS provided by the underlying (N–1)-DIF:

- **No synchronization.** Null, corresponding to the functionality of UDP. The binding of an instance of the IPC data transfer is made by the IPC Management Task upon receipt of a successful IAP request. In this mode, there is no instantiation of the control protocol in this case.

- **Weak synchronization.** The synchronization mechanism establishes shared state between the endpoints. This weak synchronization may use a two-way handshake. The PDU-id field of the PCI is interpreted as a sequence number. Only tightly bound mechanisms are available (i.e., PDUs may be ordered) but no feedback mechanisms.

- **Strong synchronization.** Synchronization may require a three-way handshake. Loosely bound mechanisms are available, such as retransmission control (i.e., acknowledgment and flow control mechanisms). The IPC control protocol operates independently (in parallel) of the data transfer protocol but shares the same state vector.

Although this description might seem a radical departure from the traditional EFCP designs, it is actually quite close to protocols such as UDP, OSI Transport Unit-Data, delta-t, CYCLADES TS, and TP2/4. However, using a timer-based approach found in delta-t (Watson, 1981) would avoid the need for distinct two-way and three-way handshakes. The necessary levels of synchronization could be achieved by just modifying the policies associated with the timers. This would clearly be the simplest solution.

Relaying and Multiplexing Task (RMT)

As discussed in Chapter 6, the primary purpose of this task is to moderate the multiplexing and relaying of all PDUs passing through this IPC process. The RMT is responsible for the real-time delivery of PDUs to the lower layer. RMTs come in three forms depending on where they occur in the architecture[19]:

1. A multiplexing application primarily found in hosts and the lower layers of routers

2. A relaying application primarily found in the "top" layer of interior routers

3. An aggregation relaying application primarily found in the "top" layer of border routers

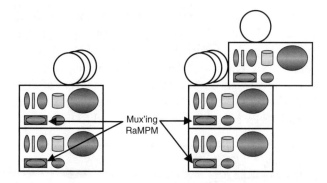

Figure 7-4 A typical host supporting applications (left) and a host supporting a mail relay and mail application (right).

All PDUs for all EFCP connections have Relaying PCI prepended to the PDUs. This Relaying PCI is associated with the relaying and multiplexing function. When a DIF has more than two IPC processes (i.e., most of the time), this task must also add addressing information to the PCI. The PCI contains the source and destination addresses. This corresponds to IP or CLNP in traditional

---

[19] As you will see, the three forms differ little in functionality.

models. Note that with a recursive architecture, the requirements for other
capabilities, such flow-ids, and various options are avoided. Flow-ids are provided by the EFCP of the layer and different policies can be the policies associated with different flow-ids. In other words, the only PDUs that would invoke a
"slow path" would be IPC Control Protocol PDUs, which weren't going any
further any way.

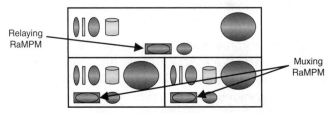

Figure 7-5 A typical interior router with relaying and multiplexing RMTs. IPC protocol
in the top DIF may also be present for network management. Depending on the media,
the RMT and IPC protocol may or may not be present in the two lower DIFs.

A Host RMT is primarily responsible for managing the use of local resources
and multiplexing traffic onto local interfaces (see Figure 7-4). Typically, it does
not have much to work with (unless it is a system with a large number of APs
[for example, a server]).

The Interior Router RMT (see Figure 7-5) handles transit flows. It must have
high performance and minimal processing overhead. This process most closely
resembles traditional packet forwarding. It receives PDUs from an input queue,
inspects the destination RMT-id, refers to a forwarding table, and sends PDUs
as quickly as possible to an output queue. (Lower layers of an interior router
will have RMTs similar to a host.) Aggregation is degenerate in interior routers.
PDUs have already been concatenated and assigned to flows.

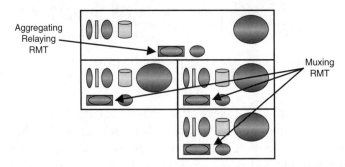

Figure 7-6 A typical border router where interior flows are created and PDUs are
aggregated over a subnet.

The Border Router RMT (see Figure 7-6) does relaying but also manages high-traffic intermediate flows. Traffic with similar QoS requirements and common intermediate paths are aggregated onto these flows, and the (N+1)-PDUs may be aggregated to increase efficiency and lower switching overhead.

Actual systems may well be various combinations of these.

PDU Protection

The last function performed on PDUs before they are delivered to the layer below is taking necessary precautions to safeguard their integrity. Any data-corruption protection over the data and PCI, including lifetime guards (hop count) and/or encryption, are performed here. Not only is the last function performed on outgoing PDUs, but it also must be the first function performed on incoming PDUs, and as such is a component of the DIF, not the protocol.

Note that delimiting and PDU protection are components of the DIF, not the protocols used by the DIF. This is contrary to the common view. It is not possible to have more than one delimiting or PDU protection function operating in a DIF because the DIF would have no way to determine which one to apply (because it cannot inspect the PDU until it has performed the function).

The IPC Management Task

(N)-IPC-Access-Protocol (IAP)

As shown in Chapter 6, a protocol is required to carry the source and destination application names to the remote IPC process along with the necessary access control and authentication information, but first it must find the IPC process of this DIF that resides on the processing system that has access to the requested application. Note that the destination application is not necessarily resident on this processing system. It may be acting as a relay.

This protocol accomplishes three functions:

1) Finding the address of the destination IPC process with access to the requested AP

2) Determining whether the requested AP is actually at that destination and the requesting AP has permission to access the requested AP

3) Carrying information to the destination IPC process on the policies to be used for the requested communication and returning the destination's response to the source

The IAP response will return a PDU indicating success or failure. If successful, destination address and connection-id information will also be returned along with suggested policy choices. This gives the IPC processes sufficient information to then bind the port-ids to an EFCPM instance (i.e., a connection)[20] so that data transfer may proceed (as described below).

This protocol may use the (N–1)-DIF. As shown in Chapter 6, the requirement for this protocol corresponds to the search rules and access control functions of an operating system. There are a variety of ways in which it may work, none of which require changes to the protocol. It is easy to see how this could start out as a local cache of recent activity, which broadcasts queries when there are cache misses, and evolve into any number of dedicated caches, a hierarchical directory, and so on, with search rules on where to go next. A failure at a cache could be noted with updates to these caches when the request is satisfied. As with an operating system, the search rules should be configurable.

If the necessary address information is not in a local cache, it must be found in distributed caches. Then, any cache where the information is found is "on the way" to the destination. The likelihood is fairly strong that it will be found closer to the destination than to the source. Regardless, it would be inefficient to pass a request most of the way (or even part way) from the source to the destination, just to go back to the source, and then immediately back to the destination to determine access control and to complete the request. It is simpler, more efficient, and more useful to continue to the destination and complete the operation.

The cache where the information was found may be incorrect. We will only know for sure that the application is accessible at the address in the cache when we get to the IPC process indicated by the address and determine whether the requested AP can be accessed. At that point, it may be useful to send the response directly back to the source IPC process and a separate update back along the cache trail to update the caches. If the application is no longer at the address found, but has been and left a forwarding address (or more likely, the new information is propagating out from this host and had not reached the database where the out-of-date information was found), the request merely continues looking for the destination.

As we see, the DNS or X.500 approach inherently assumes that any information found is correct, and if not, puts the onus of finding the correct information on the application, which has no means to redirect its search, except blindly trying again. This approach believes that such assumptions cannot be made. Instead, this approach withholds a response until the location of the application has actually been confirmed and the requestor has access. By taking this approach, we also provide for important aspects of mobility as a natural consequence. Furthermore, it is the IAP that can cause the databases to be updated and thus fix the out-of-date information problem.

---

[20] In some cases, this will be redundant.

Similarly, APs can be made available to the DIF in a variety of ways. Application processes might be registered with the DIF, or all APs made available. A more interesting possibility is because IAP carries access control information, systems using the DIF could create access control domains associated with distributed services, making only those applications that are members of the domain visible.

Resource Information Exchange Protocol (RIEP)

A DIF is a distributed application and as such it must exchange information on its state to effectively allocate resources. Traditionally, this has been referred to as the routing update protocol and was associated only with routing. Given our more general context, we generalize the concept and decouple it from routing. We will view it as a general tool for sharing information among the members of the DIF. Routing-related information is only one kind of information exchanged within the DIF, whether related to connectivity, queue length, processing load, resource allocation, and so on. RIEP can be used in both a request/response mode and a notify/confirm mode using the same managed objects. This allows IPC processes to notify the other members of the DIF when there is a significant change or to request information. It also allows the RIEP to act as the management protocol. In general, the (N)-RIEP of an (N)-DIF uses the IPC facility of the (N–1)-DIF, but there is no prohibition on using the (N)-IPC task, too.

The RIEP is responsible for disseminating from other subsystems in this DIF the information necessary to coordinate the distributed IPC. This includes information on the mappings of AP names to the IPC process names (and addresses) of nearest neighbors, the connectivity provided by the DIF, and resource usage and allocation information. There is no requirement that the same update strategy be used for all information in the DIF. It will be advantageous to use different strategies for different kinds of information. The RIEP collects information from other RIEPs in the DIF. Several events can cause a RIEP to query or update peers: events (e.g., failures) in the network, new subsystems, periodically, or as a matter of policy imposed by its users. Some of these events may involve some or all members.

This protocol could be confused with a *Network Management Protocol* (NMP) and should be. The difference being that the NMP uses the request/response mode. The NMP is used by a network management system to monitor and manage the systems comprising the network. The object models used by the two are the same. The NMS will generally retrieve aggregated data from the systems under its management, but it will also access the same kind of detailed information when diagnosing and repairing a problem.

At the higher layers, this information may be characterized by a large number of destinations and a small number of relays. However, this does not change the basics. In these cases, a RIB is a cache of the mappings required by this IPC process. If a mapping is requested that is not in the cache, this RIEP-PM communicates with its peers to obtain the necessary information. At lower layers, the RIB tends to have complete information on all members of the DIFs; at higher layers, this is less often the case.

Resource Information Base

The Resource Information Base is the logical store of local information on the state of the DIF. Each IPC process maintains a RIB. The RIB is a replicated Information Base. The assumption is made that if all data transfer activity ceased, the collection of RIBs in the DIF would reach a consistent state. However, tasks using this information can never assume that is the case. This is very similar to what is traditionally called the MIB or Management Information Base. A different term was used here to indicate that this may include information for other than network management (recognizing, however, that any information that is kept may prove useful for management).

The IPC Management Task

The information distributed and collected by REIP is then used by various IPC management functions. We briefly survey these to give some flavor of what they are

- **Enrollment.** Enrollment was defined as those procedures required to create sufficient shared state that allocation could occur. Traditionally, enrollment has been ignored, swept under the rug, or done by ad hoc or even manual procedures. DHCP has been our only slight foray into enrollment. In multicast, there has been a tendency to confuse enrollment and allocation operations (Chapter 9).

  In this model, enrollment falls out as an integral part of the model. Enrollment occurs when an IPC process establishes an application connection (using an (N–1)-DIF) with another IPC process, which is already a member of an existing DIF, to join the DIF. Once this occurs, the IPC process may authenticate the newcomer, using RIEP initialize various managed objects and their attributes, including assigning an address. These parameters characterize the operation of this DIF and might include parameters such as max PDU size, various timeout ranges, ranges of policies, and so on, as well as a full update of routing and resource allocation information. Similarly, the new IPC process will have new information to share with the DIF. The robustness of the authentication is a policy of the DIF. It may range from null or a simple password to a more robust cryptographic-based authentication procedure.

- **Routing.** This task performs the analysis of the RIB to provide connectivity input to the creation of a forwarding table. To support flows with different QoS will in current terminology require using different metrics to optimize the routing. However, this must be done while balancing the conflicting requirements for resources. Current approaches can be used, but new approaches to routing will be required to take full advantage of this environment. The choice of routing algorithms in a particular DIF is a matter of policy.

- **Directory.** As shown in Chapter 5, "Naming and Addressing," each DIF must maintain the mapping (N)- to (N–1)-names and addresses of nearest neighbors for both its upper and lower boundary; that is, name to address at the upper boundary (usually referred to as a directory function) and address to point of attachment at the lower boundary (to select the path to the next hop). The primary user of this information is IAP and routing. Because scope tends to increase with higher layers, we should expect the number of elements for which this mapping must be maintained to increase dramatically with higher DIFs. Hence the caching strategies and search rules will vary radically across DIFs. Updates to these caches are made using RIEP and are triggered by local events. IAP requests forwarding requests to other caches.

- **Resource allocation.** If a DIF is to support different qualities of service, different flows will have to be allocated, and traffic for them treated differently. To meet the QoS requirements, different resources will have to be allocated to different flows, and information about the allocations distributed to the members of the DIF. There are three classes of such flows:

    1. Flows requested by an AP, usually in a host

    2. Flows created by IPC management for distinct classes of QoS to aggregate traffic and enhance efficiency, generally in border routers and among them

    3. Flows that transit a system (i.e., traditional routing)

When an IAP request returns successfully, IPC management must determine whether and how to allocate the flow/connection to a new or existing flow (a matter of policy). This process uses input from routing, current allocations, and current conditions within the DIF. This may include creating flows of similar or aggregated QoS, creating high-density flows between intermediate points in the network, and so on, depending on the context in which the DIF operates. It should be remembered that *flows* in this context does not necessarily imply that traffic is following a single fixed route through the DIF, and it is unlikely there would be much, if any, error control, and flow control would probably be done by pacing. One would expect that the management of such flows would be more useful nearer the backbone. Flows between intermediate points in DIFs nearer the backbone will tend to have very long lifetimes of hours, days, or even months.

Some IPC processes may only be transit subsystems and thus have relatively simple resource-allocation functionality, whereas those on the borders of subnets may be more complex. The degree to which this is automatic or under direct control of a central network management system is a matter of policy. There is considerable opportunity for policy differentiation. DiffServ and IntServ could be considered opposite extremes of this task. With this model, it is straightforward to support much more diverse approaches to resource-allocation strategies.

- **Security management.** A DIF requires three security functions:

    1. Authentication to ensure that an IPC process wanting to join the DIF is who it says it is and is an allowable member of the DIF. This is similar to the application authentication requirements that any AP should have when establishing communication with another AP.

    2. Protection against the tampering or eavesdropping by an (N–1)-DIF.

    3. Access control to determine whether APs requesting an IPC flow with a remote application has the necessary permissions to establish communication. The particular security procedures used for these security functions are a matter of policy.

A DIF need place very little trust in (N–1)-DIFs: only that an (N–1)-DIF will attempt to deliver PDUs to something.

The most that a DIF can guarantee is that the IPC process with the destination address believes that it has created an IPC channel with the requested application. There can be no guarantee that it is. Therefore, it is the responsibility of every AP, including the IPC processes of a DIF, to ensure that the application it is exchanging PDUs with is the intended application (authentication) and to protect its PDUs from eavesdropping and tampering (confidentiality and integrity). The only information that an application has about the communication is the local port-id for this IPC and the application name of the destination.

An *authentication* mechanism is used to ensure that an IPC process is a valid member of the DIF. This part of enrollment is able to use existing techniques. If a DIF distrusts (N–1)-DIFs, authentication is used to ensure that PDUs are being delivered to the appropriate IPC process, and PDU protection is used to protect against tampering and eavesdropping.

IAP provides access control generally implemented as capabilities, which are used to determine whether the requesting application has access to the requested application.

Network Management Protocol and Management Architecture

While the IPC processes that comprise the DIF are exchanging information on their operation and the conditions they observe, it is generally necessary to also have an outside window into the operation of DIFs comprising the network. Normally, this will require monitoring of the multiple DIFs that constitute a network (i.e., a management domain). The purpose of network management is *monitor and repair, not control*. Each processing system in the network (which may include hosts) contains a management agent responsible for collecting information from IPC processes in all DIFs in the system and communicating it to a *network management system* (NMS).

The NMS exerts a strong influence on enrollment. The enrollment tasks acts for the NMS. The NMS may determine when a layer is to be created and initiate the action, but it is the enrollment tasks that carry it out. This includes creating the ability for the enrollment agents to sense the correct conditions and to make the decision automatically. The NMS management strategy may run the gamut from hands-on to quite light.

This is one of the few places in this architecture where it is necessary to recognize the systems that are hosting the IPC process. We assume that there is a *management agent* (MA) that is an AP (see Figure 7-7). An MA has access to all DIFs in a system. It communicates with an NMS, just as any other application, using a DIF. Although Figure 7-7 shows the MA as above all other DIFs, this should not be taken too literally. The MA only has to use an (N)-DIF with sufficient scope to be able to communicate with the NMS. An MA can communicate over a lower DIF and still collect information from higher DIFs.[21]

---

[21] I realize that this sounds contradictory. Management always has a role, a bit like the sphere visiting Flatland (Abbott, 1884). An MA is an application in a processing system and, hence, can access anything it is given permission to access by the operating system.

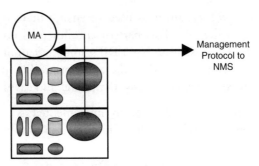

Figure 7-7 Schematic of a management agent (MA) that collects information on each DIF for a network management system (NMS).

It is easy to imagine situations where it would be convenient to allow multiple MAs responsible for different DIFs in the same processing system. For example, one might create DIFs as VPNs and allow them to be managed by their "owners"; or one could imagine different DIFs belonging to different providers at the border between two providers and so on. Although there are good reasons to do this, and one can fully expect it to be done, the network designer must be careful. There is only one processing system to meet the requirements of these MAs. One MA (and management system) must be empowered to resolve conflicts or to bound the capabilities of other MAs.

In general, a processing system in a network can be managed by one and only one manager at any particular time. Other managers may be given permission to read (i.e., observe) the system but not write to it (i.e., change configuration). Management systems will have mechanisms for defining management domains and changing their composition.

The Nature of Layers

It is time to step back and take a look at what we can now say about the nature of layers. In Chapter 6, we noted that there has been considerable dissatisfaction with layers as an organizing principle, but on the other hand, the inherent nature of distributed shared state of different scopes implied that there was something like a layer inherent in the problem. A repeating structure of common elements makes it much easier to characterize the nature of a "layer." You might have already gotten an inkling of the model we are moving to with the description in this chapter. To some degree, we have been too stringent in our characterization of layers and have also not fully taken into account the environment in which it exists. We were looking for easy answers and not listening to what the problem was telling us.

A distributed IPC facility or DIF is a layer. The ranking (stacking) of DIFs is purely a relation among DIFs and hence apply only to DIFs. Applications belong to no layer, unless they are IPC processes and a member of a DIF. This is why in the definitions in this chapter, the (N)- notation does not appear in front of any application related concepts. Applications execute on a processing system. Layering based on concepts of kernel or user applications is a property of the operating system and not of the communications. If any rank is applied to an application it is only that implied by its use of a DIF of a given rank. Potentially any application can use any DIF of any rank as long as the DIF has sufficient scope to access the necessary remote applications and appropriate access controls. An application may have IPC connections with other applications using DIFs of different ranks at the same time as long as the access control policies permit it. The same is true of applications, which are IPC processes. In this case, there are constraints that must be recognized to ensure that shared state for data transfer is maintained and PCI is properly removed.

Working out the repeating structure of a DIF has also cleaned up the interactions at the layer boundary. In other architectures, layers caused problems where conflicts were constantly appearing about what goes in what layer. This is now rendered moot by the realization that all layers/DIFs do one thing and only one thing: IPC. The primary purpose of layers is organizing the scope of shared state, on the one hand, and organizing information (PCI) for processing in layer order on the other. This is very much the case for the primary purpose of IPC: the data transfer aspect.

This shifts the data transfer model from moving PDUs between layers to process, moving along the PDU processing PCI as required. The feared data copy is only an artifact of the hardware, not of the architecture. And context switches across DIFs are only necessary if desired; they're not implied by the architecture. This, along with the natural partitioning of information flow into three largely independent functions of differing duty cycles, opens the door for much more effective processing models for routers and hosts.

As we have seen, management is "extra-dimensional." As shown in the preceding section, not only is network management the sphere that can see inside all the data transfer inhabitants of Flatland but, IPC management has this property, too. IPC management must maintain mappings of (N+1)- to (N)- (nominally application names to node addresses) and (N)- to (N−1)- (nominally node addresses to point of attachment addresses). Data transfer is Flatland, and management is the sphere visiting it. IPC management must have the ability to share information among adjacent layers.

Notice I said *adjacent* layers, not all layers. A consequence of the recursion that we touched on earlier in this chapter is that most processing systems have a rank of DIFs no more than three deep. Hosts might have more, but not many more, and these would be specialized DIFs for other IPC-related distributed applications (e.g., mail or transaction processing). For the hosts and routers, this creates something of a hook-and-eye structure across layers. Only the NMS potentially has the ability to see information about DIF operation across all DIFs in a network. If the access control is appropriate between adjacent layers, so that addresses are available, effective mappings between (N)-addresses and (N–1)-addresses can make routing much more effective.

This gives us a structure that is layered as the loci of shared state requires, but is at one and the same time more structured and more flexible than our previous attempts and also translates into a simple implementation.

Operation of the DIF

In this section, we briefly consider the operation of a DIF. In particular, we look at three fundamental operations: how an IPC process joins a DIF, how a new DIF is created, and how an application requests IPC services. The operation of a DIF is driven by the action of the APs (i.e., its users and by its internal coordination). The IPC processes must coordinate their actions with the other members of the DIF.

Traditionally, the enrollment phase has been ignored as a collection of ad hoc procedures that must be done at startup that are very implementation specific. In this model, the enrollment phase is an integral part of the model and essential to its operation. There are two aspects of enrollment: new systems joining an existing DIF, and creating a new DIF.

Adding a New Member to an (N)-DIF

Let's consider how a processing system joins a DIF. One variation of this process is a new system attaching to a network. Suppose that DIF A consists of a number of IPC processes on a set of systems, a_i. Suppose that the DIF B wants to join the DIF A. The DIF B represents a single IPC process. The IPC process, **b**, in B has the AP name of an IPC process, **a**, in A (or it might have the name of the DIF A), not its address. B has no way to know the addresses of any elements of A. A and B are connected by the (N–1)-DIF, which ultimately will be the physical media (see Figure 7-8).

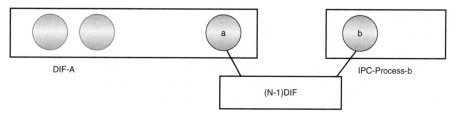

Figure 7-8 A new system B wants to join the DIF A. B is connected to A by an (N–1)-DIF.

Using the (N–1)-DIF, **b** requests that the (N–1)-DIF establish an IPC channel with **a** in the same manner it would with any other application using the AP name of **a**. The (N–1)-DIF determines whether **a** exists and whether **b** has access to **a**.

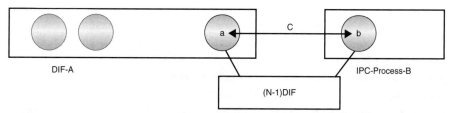

Figure 7-9 b sets up an application connection with a using the DIF. The DIF returns separate port-ids to a and b (no different from any other IPC request).

After the application connection has been established (see Figure 7-9), **a** authenticates **b** and determines whether it can be a member of A. If the result is positive, **a** assigns an (N)-address to **b**.[22] **b** uses the (N)-address to identify itself to other members of the DIF A. This (N)-address is used in the Data Transfer PCI of the enrollment application protocol, also called the Relaying PCI. Other initialization parameters associated with DIF A are exchanged with **b** (see Figure 7-10).

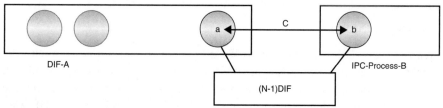

Figure 7-10 b is authenticated and an address is assigned to it along with other initialization parameters.

---

[22] Or based on where the IPC process, **b**, is in the topology of the DIF A and the address space (see Chapter 8). For (N)-addresses in the model, we will retain the (N)- notation to minimize confusion with other uses of the term *address*.

The IPC process, **b**, is now a member of the DIF A (see Figure 7-11). Soon after this, **b** also establishes similar communication with all members of A that are nearest neighbors. (Because the (N–1)-DIF may have less scope than A, there may be members of A that **b** cannot communicate with directly.) These flows are used to exchange RIEP information to maintain the shared state of the (N)-DIF. The **b** is now ready to participate in the (N)-DIF and can now accept requests from its applications for IPC.

Figure 7-11 A new system has just joined the network, been authenticated, and assigned an (N)-address and is now ready to participate as a member of the DIF.

Some readers will jump to the conclusion from what I have just described that this is a connection-oriented architecture. Nothing could be further from the case. *Enrollment* is simply creating the necessary shared state among the IPC management tasks, so that there is sufficient shared state for IPC. Whether IPC within the DIF is connectionless or connection-like is an entirely separate matter. That will depend on how the routing and forwarding are done. In a sense what we have done is to establish the logical "wires" over which this DIF will operate. Of course, these "wires" are a little "cloudier" than normal wires. To the DIF, they range in quality and type: Some are point to point and fairly reliable (real wires); some are multipoint and unreliable (wireless); some are multipoint with a few stations on them and fairly reliable (LANs); some are multipoint with large numbers of stations on them and somewhat reliable (subnets with multiple routes); and so on.

Although this is described in terms of a single DIF, the protocols could be designed to allow several DIFs (layers) to be joined at the same time within the constraints of the security policies for the DIFs.

Creating a New DIF

Creating a new DIF is a simple matter. An NMS or similar application with the appropriate permissions causes an IPC process to be created and initialized, including pointing it at one or more (N–1)-DIFs. As part of its initialization, the IPC process is given the means to recognize allowable members of the DIF (e.g., a list of application process names, a digital signature, and so on). Or it might be directed to initiate enrollment with them or to simply wait for them to find this initial IPC process. When this has been achieved, the creation of the DIF proceeds as described earlier.

Data Transfer

When enrollment initialization is complete, the DIF is available to provide IPC to APs residing on its processing system or to act as a relay. APs will request the allocation of IPC resources via library calls.

Let's assume (see Figure 7-12) that the AP, **A**, wants to establish an IPC connection with the AP **B**. **A** resides on a processing system using a DIF that is represented by the IPC process, **a**.

Figure 7-12 Application A wants to establish communication with application B, using its supporting DIF.

A generates an Allocate request that will cause the IPC management of **a** to evaluate the request according to its allocation policies. The IAP request will contain the application process name of **A**; **a**'s address, **a-addr**; the local port-id, **a$_i$-port**; **B**'s application process name; access control and capability information for **A**; and the proposed policies for the connection. If the request is acceptable and the (N)-address of the IPC process **B** is not in the local RIB, **a**'s local IPC management task will use IAP to find **B**. **a** uses its search rules to forward the IAP request to another IPC process in the DIF (see Figure 7-13). For this information, the search rules may organize the elements of the DIF into a logical hierarchy.

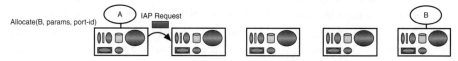

Figure 7-13 An Allocate request from A for IPC with B generates an IAP request with A's and B's names, resource and access control parameters, and the local port-id to be assigned A's request. The IAP request follows search rules to find the address of the IPC process with access to B.

The IAP request may be forwarded within this hierarchy until the location of **B** is found. When the address of the destination IPC process is found, the information may be forwarded back through the intermediate IPC processes to update their caches. The IAP request is forwarded to the destination IPC process, **b** (see Figure 7-14). When the presence of **B** can be confirmed, **b** determines whether it can honor the request and **A** has access to **B**. (The degree of access control is policy. It could be quite elaborate or like the current Internet, none.)

Figure 7-14 When a cache entry is found, the IAP request is forward to b to confirm it has access to B and to determine whether A has access to it.

If it does, **B** may be instantiated if it was not active and notified of the request from **A** using the IPC API primitives. **b** will allocate a local port-id, **b_i-port**, and make a suggestion for policies on the IPC connection to be created and send an IAP response back to **a**. Now is a much better time to forward the result of the IAP request back through the intermediate IPC processes because we know the information is correct (see Figure 7-15).

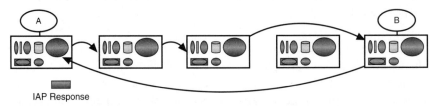

IAP Response

Figure 7-15 The IAP response returns indicating success and the port-id assigned to the communication with b. The IPC processes a and b have the necessary information to create an appropriate EFCP flow between a and b for this communication.

When the IAP response arrives at **a** and with a positive result, the Allocate_Request is returned[23] to **A** with the destination, source, a port-id to be used with all subsequent interactions on this allocation, and a positive reason code.[24] At the same time, **a** allocates an EFCPM instance (i.e., a connection); binds the port-id assigned to **A** to it, with the appropriate policies; and initiates any synchronization exchanges, if they are required (see Figure 7-16). **A** may now start sending Application PDUs to its peer by invoking the transfer API primitive. The transfer primitive is used to pass APM PDUs to the IPC facility as an SDU. The SDU is delimited and transformed into user-data for a PDU.

---

[23] Whether the Allocate request is returned immediately or only after the requested APM accepts is a matter that can be left for later. With this approach, the requested APM may refuse the request, in which case a De-allocate will have to be delivered to the requesting APM to notify it.

[24] This might seem like a radical departure from the current behavior of the Internet, which never refuses any new traffic. It isn't. If one desires all new allocations to be accepted, that is a matter of policy. This approach allows both without additional overhead or the inflexible constraints of circuits.

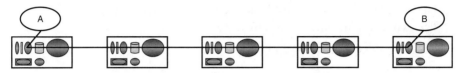

Figure 7-16 The EFCP flow/connection is created and bound to the port-ids returned to A and B. The applications are now free to exchange SDUs.

The SDU is delivered to the EFCPM specified by the port-id and is processed. The resulting PDU(s) are delivered to the RMT for transmission. The RMT may have created a number of (N–1)-flows of various QoS characteristics to various destinations. Based on the allocations determined by the IPC manager, the PDU is queued on an outgoing (N–1)-flow to be sent by the (N)-RMT, which may also combine it with other PDUs into a single (N–1)-SDU.

Figure 7-17 When the applications are finished, the bindings are terminated. Whether the EFCP flow is terminated is a matter of policy. With a timer-based EFCP protocol, the question is irrelevant.

When **A** has finished its communication and terminated its communication with **B**, **A**, **B**, or both invoke the close API primitive to inform the DIF that it may release the resources (see Figure 7-17). **a** and **b** will de-allocate their respective local port-ids. Whether the EFCP instance is de-allocated is a matter of policy. Of course, if a timer-based protocol is used this consideration is moot.

Identifiers in an (N)-DIF

We have found that six kinds of identifiers are needed (three externally visible, one internal to the processing system, and two internal to the DIF). The three external identifiers are as follows:

1. The distributed application names that designate a set of APs cooperating to perform a particular task

2. AP names to identify APs

3. The APM names that identify application PMs, which are unambiguous within the AP

The one identifier internal to the processing system is the port-id. The two identifiers internal to DIF are as follows:

1. The (N)-addresses assigned to the IPC processes

2. The connection-id used in the EFCP to distinguish connections

The (N)-Port-ID

The DIF requires identifiers to distinguish multiple IPC flows. APs need them for the same purpose. When the connection is established, the APM and the DIF use the port-id when referring to the communication. The port-ids are unambiguous within the processing system. When the IPC protocol creates shared state with its correspondent, the connection is distinguished by a connection-id. The connection-id is generally formed by concatenating the port-ids of the source and destination, thus unambiguously identifying it within the scope of the communicating IPC processes.

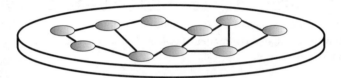

Figure 7-18 By exchanging information on connectivity and resource usage and allocation, the IPC processes that constitute the layer create a distributed application, essentially a distributed operating system. The (N)-addresses need only be known among the IPC processes (i.e., internal to the distributed operating system). Application names are externally visible in the layer; (N)-addresses are not.

The port-ids play a crucial role in linking the (N)-addresses to the (N–1)-addresses in adjacent layers while at the same time insulating (N)-addresses from both AP names and (N+1)-addresses, if they exist. The only identifier an AP has associated with a flow is the port-id and the destination application name. It has no knowledge of the destination port-id or the (N)-addresses.

All IPC requests are assigned a local port-id to distinguish multiple instances of IPC within a processing system. Port-ids are defined to be unambiguous within a processing system. This choice is not made arbitrarily. This choice implies that PDUs need only carry addresses and connection-ids (created from port-ids). If the scope of port-ids is defined to be unambiguous only within the DIF *and* the system was allowed to be a member of more than one DIF at the same rank, the PDUs must include the DIF name, too. By defining the port-id as we have, the DIF name is only needed when an IPC process is joining a DIF.

Application Process Names

Application process names are used by a new system to establish initial communications when it joins a DIF. Traditionally, it has been assumed that a processing system participated in one and only one DIF per rank, except at the bottom, where there was one per interface. In some cases, there are good reasons for this to be the case. But this does not have to be the case. However, this does have some implications for naming that must be understood. It is possible (and actually useful) to have more than one DIF in the same systems or set of systems. This implies that when there is more than one DIF in a system and a new system wants to join a layer, it must know which DIF it is joining (i.e., it must have its distributed application name or DAN). The DAN is used to establish communication with the DIF using the (N–1)-DIF.

(N)-Addresses

The names used for routing PDUs are not just the names of the IPC process but are identifiers *internal* to the DIF formed by the collection of IPC processes. In other words, they are not visible outside the DIF. Addresses are used by the IPC processes of the DIF for their *internal* coordination. This may not have been apparent looking at traditional network layer routing but is more obvious if one considers relaying applications, such as mail. E-mail addresses are used for routing mail and strictly speaking are internal to the mail application. E-mail addresses and IP-addresses are two examples of the same concept.

The routing function of IPC requires two kinds of information:

1. Information on the graph of RMTs (node addresses in Saltzer's terms) formed by being directly connected by the (N–1)-DIFs

2. The mapping of (N)-addresses to (N–1)-IPC process names[25] (Saltzer's point of attachments) for all nearest neighbors (i.e., capable of direct connection) at the (N–1)-DIF

A traditional routing application uses the connectivity information to calculate routes from a source to a destination. This is, in turn, used to construct a forwarding table to the "next hop" or next RMT to which PDUs are sent for relaying or delivery. The mapping of the neighboring (N)- to (N–1)-addresses is used to choose the specific path to the next hop.

---

[25] Or (N–1)-addresses, depending on the level of trust between the (N)-DIF and (N–1)-DIF.

(N)-DIFs, in general, have greater scope than (N–1)-DIFs. However, this is not the case with configurations such as virtual private networks or specialized applications, where a closed subnet is created on top of DIFs. The RIEP protocol collects information to create a local database of the mapping of (N)-addresses to (N–1)-addresses and the logical connectivity of the IPC processes constituting this DIF (i.e., routes). As the scope of layers increases, the number of "nearest neighbors" will tend to increase combinatorially. This will require more complex distribution and caching strategies (e.g., imposing a hierarchical structure on the RIBs). These applications exchange information on the contents of their caches and to respond to queries that cannot be answered with the information in their local cache.

The primary function of (N)-addresses in a DIF is to establish and maintain the mappings among (N)-addresses, the (N+1)-addressing above, and the (N–1)-addresses below, and as a consequence facilitate routing. Enrollment is used to assign addresses and to manage changes of addresses. These mappings of the current connectivity are maintained by the tasks associated with resource allocation and routing protocols. These protocols maintain databases of routes to different parts of the network topology and "forwarding tables" indicating the (N–1)-addresses PDUs are to be sent on. These databases are also interrogated to get information necessary to initiate communication. This is generally referred to as a directory function.

Saltzer and everyone else agree that an address is a location-dependent name. From the beginning of networking, the analogy to operating systems was utilized to recognize that names specified the *what;* addresses, the *where;* and routes, the *how* to get there. For most networks to date, addresses were not location dependent. They were flat identifiers. None of the routing protocols in use today utilize the location-dependent property. The names used by these algorithms are used purely as labels, not as indications of *where*. For small networks, this is adequate. But in large networks or networks where less-complex operations are desired, true addresses can be used to great advantage.[26] The key aspect of this problem, which has always been recognized, was how to make addresses location dependent and route independent. In other words, how to achieve the properties that addressing serves on a Midwest grid on a much less-regular network graph. In the next chapter, we consider how to develop the concept of addresses, which are location dependent without being route dependent.

---

[26] Recently, location dependence has been used to aggregate addresses for purposes of route calculation, but this preprocessing simply moderates the scaling issues associated with the fact that the route calculation itself uses addresses as labels.

The scope of the address space is the DIF within which it is used. This is the set of (N)-IPC processes that can communicate either directly or by relaying and without relaying at a higher layer. Although this is still true, it is less important. An (N)-address is an internal location-dependent identifier assigned to each (N)-IPC process.

The scope of the (N)-address is the DIF to which it belongs. Route dependence is at least relative to the layer in which the relaying occurs. A (N)-address is route independent, but the (N–1)-address (or point of attachment) is necessarily route dependent relative to relaying in layer (N). From the point of view of an IPC process, choosing an (N–1)-address is the act of choosing a path. Thus, all (N–1)-addresses available at the lower boundary of an IPC process are route dependent with respect to that IPC process. Each one represents the first hop on all routes going in that direction. The same (N–1)-addresses may be (and should be) route independent relative to relaying in (N–1)-DIF and so on to the physical layer where addresses must be, by their nature, route dependent. Route dependence is an inherent property of addresses only at the physical layer.

Postponing the introduction of explicit route-dependent addresses into a network architecture (i.e., not adopting a naming convention that is inherently route dependent) will greatly improve the flexibility of the configurations that the network can have. However, it is always possible to create an address space that is inherently route dependent. For example, traditionally, the most common means to make an address route dependent is to include an (N–1)-address as part of the (N)-address (e.g., a MAC address or EUI-64 address) as part of the network address. It is these architectures that are unnecessarily plagued with problems.

As a consequence of layer independence, a good architecture makes this transition at each layer. A viable addressing scheme must make a transition from physical (route dependent) to logical (route independent) at least once. In a very real sense for the recursive structure we have developed here, the (N)-layer provides the "logical" addressing for the "physical" addressing of the (N–1)-layer. In this approach, we have simply made this relation relative. In other words, Saltzer's concepts of node address and point of attachment address are relative. An (N)-address is a node address; and an (N–1)-address is a point of attachment address. In a complete architecture, addresses at the layer below are points of attachments for the layer above.

However, one can make address spaces in adjacent layers too independent and make routing inefficient. A judicious choice of a relation can be very advantageous. In particular, a topological relation between adjacent spaces can be quite useful. This is discussed in the next chapter.

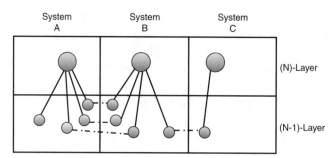

Figure 7-19 Routes are sequences of (N)-addresses. A next hop is an (N)-address. But each IPC process must also know mappings of (N)-addresses to (N–1)-address of the (N)-layer nearest neighbors to determine the path to the next hop.

Taking Stock

This is a good point to contrast this with Internet. In the current Internet architecture, the closest thing to an application process name is the URL. The syntax of the URL allows specifying an application protocol and the host on which it resides. The host part has essentially become the application name. It is not at all clear how one would build an application with multiple application protocols and whether it would work in all cases. Would ftp://ftp.myappl.com and http://www.myappl.com actually create connections to the same AP? Doubtful. If I want my corporate websites on a hosting service and my internal company websites, I must have multiple domain names or other such subterfuge. Rather than simply having a branch for my corporate application names that I can assign and locate the applications wherever I please. If there were a special protocol for my project, say mynewprot, it would have to be registered with IANA. There is no support for connecting to specific multiple instances of either APs or application protocols associated with specific APs. This makes constructing anything but the most rudimentary distributed applications difficult if not prohibitive.

There is only a partial equivalent of the IPC access protocol. DNS allows the *application* to determine the address of the destination application. This puts more burden on the application and also represents a security problem. There is no access control and the application has knowledge of the address.

The Internet is based on a "one size fits all" model or maybe two sizes: UDP, and TCP. However, this now seems to be breaking down with the addition of RTP, SCTP, DCCP, and others. This contributes considerable complexity to the architecture. The inability to couple these EFCPs with resource allocation associated with IP further adds to the problems.

In the current Internet architecture, there are only point-of-attachment addresses. Hence, routes are calculated as a sequence of (N–1)-addresses.

Consequently, it is difficult to accommodate multiple paths[27] between adjacent nodes. It is done, but it is a kludge. Each path is a separate segment of a route. Consequently, the existence of multiple paths increases the number of routes combinatorially. In a very real sense, today multihoming is not even supported in the routers let alone the hosts. In these architectures, multihoming and mobility cannot be supported without expensive and cumbersome mechanisms. As we saw in Chapter 5, although the CLNP approach had both node addresses and points of attachment, it didn't solve all the problems. Scope is either very local or the whole world. Nothing in between. Changes in points of attachment can be handled effectively, changes in node address take too long to update because the scope of the network layer is too great. In this model, with topological addresses and repeating layers, both capabilities work easily and scale. (We look at this more closely in Chapter 9.)

The problem here is not that there are not workarounds to solve all of these problems. There are. Lots of them. Therein lies the problem. They all increase the "parts" count and hence the complexity, which reduces the reliability and increases the effort required to field new capabilities and manage the ones already there. Just finding something that works isn't good enough. It has to simplify as well.

All applications using a DIF are "one hop" away. The traditional concept of a directory or DNS is an inherent part of the information associated with the mapping of (N)- to (N−1)-address information collected for routing, in essence a degenerate case of the layer structure. But some applications, such as mail, do relay. Mail relaying[28] is simply this same structure (i.e., another layer) that uses a particular set of addresses. E-mail addresses are another form of address. Strictly speaking, a mail protocol should only be concerned with the composition and sending of the "letter." The delivery of the letter is merely the routing of an often, large PDU.

IPC Facilities

IPC Structures

A DIF always interfaces to an (N−1)-DIF or the physical media. In general, each DIF interfaces to **m** (N−1)-DIFs, because the scope of IPC tends to increase with higher rank.

---

[27] The reason being that the routing now interferes with load balancing.

[28] As is peer to peer, OLTP, or another distributed application that involves relaying.

To the DIF, a request may contain either an AP name or (N+1)-address. The DIF maintains a mapping between its addresses and these AP names and (N+1)-addresses. In other words, it is responsible for knowing what applications are available to whom on its system.[29] The mapping of AP names to (N)-addresses is arbitrary (by definition). However, the mapping of (N+1)-addresses to (N)-addresses may be a topological mapping.

However, a DIF must be able to confirm that an AP is an (N+1)-IPC process and can be guaranteed to obey certain rules (i.e., that addresses are valid and have not been tampered with). (Because the (N)-DIF carries the (N+1)-IPC facility PDUs transparently, the possibilities for compromise are limited to the parameters passed as part of the API and relate mostly to addressing.)

At enrollment, a DIF may be authenticated with the (N–1)-DIF. This is how the (N–1)-DIF knows that the AP requesting services is itself part of an IPC facility. If this is done, the (N–1)-DIF knows it can trust the (N)-address information it is given from the DIF. The (N)- and (N–1)-DIFs exchange information on their capabilities and policies. Each determines the degree it can trust the other. The (N–1)-DIF is in a better position to protect itself because it can always refuse requests by the DIF. The two biggest threats are that regardless, the (N)- and (N–1)-DIFs share the same processing systems and the possibility of a rogue IPC process successfully negotiating the enrolment authentication policy. If no authentication agreement can be reached, all communication is done with application names. It still works, but is less efficient.

Multiple (N)-DIFs of the Same Rank

We have already seen that a single IPC process is necessary to manage multiple users of a single physical interface. We have also seen that having a single IPC process to manage multiple users of multiple interfaces is also advisable. But this raises the question of whether this is always the case.

Multiple IPC processes can occur at any rank. Let's consider briefly the conditions where this makes sense. Layers are created for essentially two purposes: for organizational reasons and for managing specific ranges of bandwidth and QoS.

Starting at the bottom, it would seem at first blush this is the one place where there would be one IPC process per physical interface. However, this is not the case. Consider, for example, a TDM physical medium, which creates some number of independent channels. Theoretically, each one could have a separate IPC process to manage its use. The number of IPC processes that are possible in this case is between one and the number of channels.

---

[29] As part of access control policy, a processing system may not make all (N)-application names available to a particular (N)-DIF.

There are two forms that a lowest DIF may take:

1. A point-to-point media, which will have an EFCP, but no RMT

2. A multiaccess media, which will require both an RMT and EFCP policies determined by the error

Our early, constrained view of layers prohibited (at least discouraged) routing in the data link or media layer. Bridges began the slippery slope, which was promoted by the use of spanning trees by LANs and so on. With this model, we step back and do what should have been done sooner, recognize routing is a natural capability in all layers. In this case, LAN spanning trees become a minimal form of routing. Similarly, many of us (me included) looked at LLC in LANs as acquiescence to the beads-on-a-string proponents and not appropriate for LANs at all. LANs are sufficiently reliable that an EFCP with robust policies is not required. But with the popularity of wireless media, we see cases where a more robust EFCP might be required. (In other words, not all layers need all the capabilities but be careful about claiming that they are never needed.)

Error control in the data link layer should be sufficient to make error control at the transport layer cost-effective. In other words, if the purpose transport layer error control is to handle losses due to routing, data link error control should ensure that losses are at a lower rate than the rate of loss due to routing. Recognize that propagating errors to the wider scope of a higher layer will incur greater cost to recover, while keeping in mind the impact on delay incurred by retransmissions. We will want to generalize this relation with this model.

Above this level, the same principle applies. Depending on the desired configurations, one or more DIFs may exist. Above the first layer, creating DIFs will essentially create distinct and separate networks.

In the some common configurations, there would be one (N–1)-DIF per interface and one (N)-DIF for the system. Above this, (N+1)-DIFs might be created as closed networks (e.g., VPNs, transaction processing, peer-to-peer application, and so on). In these upper layers, we are likely to have multiple DIFs within a system that are not dedicated to a specific media. Note that (N–1) here is with respect to the architecture but may not be the (1)-layer within a particular subnet (i.e., immediately above the physical medium). In Chapter 8, "Making Addresses Topological," we explore the relation between public, private, organizational, and provider networks.

Implications for Security

We will not attempt a thorough security analysis at this point, but a few remarks are worthwhile. We assume that all the current security mechanisms can and would be applied to the protocols and procedures developed to fit an architecture based on this model.

As a first step, let's assume that only applications are threats, not other IPC processes; then we will relax this assumption to consider that case. First, we note that the only IPC-related information that an application has access to is the destination application name and its local port-id. The application has no access to addresses or destination port-ids. The access control mechanisms of the IAP have limitations. The most that can be guaranteed is that the DIF is providing access to an application that to the best ability of the DIF is the application being requested. It is then the responsibility of the requesting application to determine that this is the application it requested.

Because IPC processes are applications, this also applies to IPC processes. As we saw with the sequence for joining a DIF, the DIF determines whether the requesting IPC process can join according to the authentication policies of the DIF. This is part of the initial enrollment phase. This leads to the conclusion that the degree of trust that an (N)-DIF can put in an (N−1)-DIF can be characterized as follows:

> A (N)-DIF can only assume that the (N−1)-DIF will try to deliver PDUs to something and may copy or modify them in the process. If the (N)-DIF does not trust the (N−1)-DIF, it should invoke the appropriate PDU protection and authentication mechanisms. If the applications using the (N)-DIF trust the (N−1)-DIF less than the (N)-DIF does, that is their responsibility.

Let's consider a compromised IPC process joining a DIF. We will assume that compromise is such that the new member can pass the authentication and become a member of the DIF. What damage can it do? The answer is some. However, unless the policies of the DIF are incredibly loose, it will always be possible to find the offender and terminate its membership. If a timer-based EFCP is used, SYN attacks are not possible. The offender could try to flood IAP requests, but these will be fairly diffuse and mostly negative responses. There are no well-known sockets to attack. Depending on how access control and application naming is handled, many application names may not actually be recorded in any RIB. In general, the potential threats are at best fewer than with current architectures and at worse no more than current architectures.

As we can see, the nature of the recursion of DIFs is such that any system will only have access to management information in the (N+1)-, (N)-, and (N−1)-DIFs that it implements. Further, the (N−1)-DIF will have less scope, and thus information available to the system will have much less utility. The only (N+1)-information available will be about the application names available to the (N)-DIF. This too has limited ability. The greatest threat that a compromised system can have is to distribute bad resource allocation and routing information with its peers.

One aspect that this model has no affect on is virus attacks perpetrated on communicating applications. Compromises based on weaknesses in the application software or the local operating system cannot be addressed by this model. Although stronger authentication by IPC can help, it cannot prevent such compromises.

Conclusions

This chapter has defined the elements of an abstract model for a IPC model of networking. By taking our cues from key elements of our past experience, and carefully listening to the problem, we have been able to assemble a simple model that is much less complex than previous architectures and far more capable. But at the same time, it has greater capability and solves problems with little or no additional mechanism that cannot be solved in previous architectures. The recursive structure implies that the architecture will scale indefinitely. There will still be bounds, but they won't be because the architecture has "run out of gas." In the process, we have found that the internal structure naturally cleaves into three functional areas of increasing complexity and longer "duty cycle" times. This points the way to significant simplifications in implementations.

It is curious that from the earliest days of the ARPANET we saw operating systems as our guide, but now we find that we just didn't follow it closely enough. Looking back from this vantage point, our current architecture looks more like DOS than UNIX—more like a collection of partial solutions strapped together with Moore's law, baling wire and binder twine—but mainly Moore's law.

Some will say that this is a general theory of networking. It isn't. It may be a model on which we can construct such a theory, but this is not the general theory. Some will be disappointed that I have not addressed important issues such as performance, congestion control, quality of service, routing, and so on. This was quite deliberate. This book has been purposely restricted to only the architectural problems. The first task must be to get the fundamental structure right. Now that the structure is in place, we can consider these other issues.

This model now forms a foundation for tackling these problems. It provides the needed orthogonality and regularity at different scales that help to shed light on the solution of these problems. Of course, these issues had to be a consideration while working this model out. But truthfully, the structure of the problem was a greater factor in determining the direction than these issues. In a very real sense, the problem provided the answer, once it was well stated.

Now we have one more problem to look at—not so much how to solve, but how to think about it: how to think about location dependence in a network that is not route dependent.

Then we look at the implications that this structure has for multihoming, mobility, and multicast.

Chapter 8

Making Addresses Topological

A 64-byte address is too long, it won't fit on my business card.

—Any of several CCITT delegates (didn't get or want their names)

Q: So, how long should an address be?

A: Processing the address should halt.

Introduction

Previously in Chapter 5, "Naming and Addressing," we reviewed the current state of naming and addressing. We saw how the early development of networking often looked to operating systems for guidance and have seen that perspective pay off with addressing, too (even though many OS designs, including UNIX, failed to understand the importance of IPC). From operating systems, Shoch noted that networks needed the same separation between logical names and physical addresses that is useful in operating systems. And Saltzer extended that analogy to include the distinction between virtual and physical addresses, yielding location-independent applications names, location-dependent node addresses, *point-of-attachment* (PoA) addresses, and routes, arguing that these were the necessary components of a network architecture. We also saw that Saltzer missed (understandably) that, in general, routing was a two-step process of choosing the next hop (from sequences of node addresses) and then choosing the specific path to that next hop.[1] We also found that the information necessary to determine the path (i.e., the mapping of node address to PoA address of nearest neighbors) was the same mapping as the application name to node address or directory at the layer above. This presaged our "discovery" in Chapter 6, "Divining Layers," that network architecture consists of a single recursive

---

[1] Remember, this is the architectural view and does not change the nature of the forwarding table in real implementations.

283

layer, further implying that the addresses of an (N–1)-layer were the points of attachment of the (N)-layer and some applications using the (N)-layer might be members of an (N+1)-layer for which the (N)-layer are points of attachment. The relation between node and point of attachment is relative: a not uncommon recurring theme in science that things that at first appear static often turn out to be relative and, in fact, practice has been doing this for some time, although as special cases rather than as a general method.

In Chapter 5, we talked often about addresses being location dependent without being route dependent. We found that it was easy to say but far less easy to translate into action. At the time when Saltzer wrote, it seemed best to wait until there was a better understanding of addressing. It is now 20 years later. The Net is no longer a research project, and addressing problems are legion. Moore's law has saved the Internet from needing to act on Saltzer's results. However, there are indications that Moore's law is no longer going to save us, and we must save ourselves. We have incorporated Saltzer's observations and generalized them to a recursive structure that not only solves a number of addressing issues, but also solves issues of resource management, security, and scaling.

However, there is still one problem (at least) that remains a major stumbling block: What does location dependent mean in a network? How in a graph does one indicate *where* something is without indicating *how* to get there? Especially in a graph that is changing! Location dependence is a straightforward concept in operating systems, where the relation between application names and logical and physical address spaces is well understood: Memory address space has a highly regular structure. But that is a much easier problem. Clearly, to follow the analogy, node addresses and PoA addresses are supposed to correspond to logical and physical address spaces. But how do we make addresses location dependent? Location dependence is well understood in the other favorite analogy: street addressing, especially in cities that were founded after Descartes. The street-addressing analog is closer to what we are looking for: Given an address, it is easy to derive many routes to a destination. But networks seldom have the regular structure exhibited by a city street grid. Intuitively, we know what it should mean. Putting that into something we can implement has proven to be a wholly different matter. The often knee-jerk response when location dependence is mentioned is to suggest latitude/longitude or some similar scheme (once again jumping to the arithmetic, before doing the algebra). But it fundamentally misses the point: We are trying to find something in a network, not on the surface of a sphere.

Terminology Inflation

Our field is notorious for abusing terminology, and *topology* is another example of that abuse. (We seem to like words that sound more important than what we need.) In the overwhelming majority of cases in networking, the word *topology* is used to mean "graph." Unfortunately, most practitioners could not define a topology. Some try the cultural relativism argument of, "Networking has a different definition." Hogwash. The origins of our use came from mathematics, and we should have the intelligence and honesty to use it correctly.

It is clear that the graph of the network is not suitable. Links in a network come and go with some frequency. It would not be effective to tie addressing to anything quite so volatile. In addition, the graph is too tightly bound to the *how*, not the *where*. We need an abstraction of the graph, an abstraction that would remain relatively invariant to changes in the graph.

The area of mathematics that concerns abstractions of spatial relations and graphs and properties of invariance is topology. If we consider addresses to have topological properties, we may be able to create addresses that are location dependent but not route dependent.

A word of warning that I will repeat often: Topological addresses are not magic, not a panacea. They are a technique for leveraging an abstraction of the network graph. They can only be effective to the degree that the abstraction effectively reflects the network graph. If the network graph bears little resemblance to the abstraction, topological addresses will not be effective.[2] There is a little mutual coercion here. The structure of the topological address space is determined by an abstraction of the network graph. And as the network grows, "things" are easier if it grows in such away that it reflects the abstraction of the topology. The structure of the address space influences how the network changes, and the nature of the network affects the topology of the address space, not unlike the fact that country roads in the U.S. Midwest follow section lines,[3] not because it is legislated they should (and they don't always), but just because "things" are easier if they do.

In what follows, we build on the definitions for naming and addressing in Chapter 7, "The Network IPC Model." We consider how a topological structure may be used to this end. Given that the definition of *topology* will be unfamiliar to most readers, we spend some time on the basics, laying some groundwork for further investigation of various topologies for addressing. We then discuss how this could apply to addressing and develop one example of a topological address space, using at once the simplest and perhaps the most useful example in real networks: the hierarchy.

---

[2] In such a case, it makes one wonder why a particular topology was chosen as the abstraction, if it isn't one. Or as a great computer scientist once said, "If you don't do it right, it won't work."

[3] The Northwest Ordinance of 1787 caused all the U.S. Midwest (Ohio and east of the Mississippi was the Northwest United States then) to be surveyed into 1-mile squares called sections. An area of 6 by 6 sections is a township. As luck would have it, the land was fairly flat, it was a reasonable scheme to carry out.

Is It Worth It?

Does it really matter if we have topological addresses? Remember the "Or is it?" sidebar in Chapter 5 where noted how finding a route in the U.S. Midwest differed from much of the rest of the world? Using topologically dependent addresses makes the shift to a Midwest view. We don't do routing because we want to know the route. We do routing because we need a forwarding table to generate the "next hop." In the Midwest view, the forwarding decision is derived from the address in the PDU and the address of the router we are passing through. For a network which reasonably coincides with the topology of its address space, the forwarding decision is made directly from the address in the PDU. Routing information would need to be exchanged when there were distortions in the topology. The equivalent of "the road doesn't go through," or of a "short-cut." But this information only needs to be known in the vicinity of the distortion, not everywhere. If a PDU is not going near the deviation, it does not need to know about it. Routing exchanges are only needed in the neighborhood of a distortion. Some routers would store no routes at all, and those that did would store 10s, not 100s of thousands! This inherently scales. The benefits are huge. We still need to accommodate the effect of load on forwarding, but that is a resource allocation problem and better handled as resource allocation.

General Properties of Addressing

Names and Addresses

In logic, there are basically two approaches to names: denotation and connotation. In natural language (much to the chagrin of the various academies), the assignment of names is connotative. Words or names get their meaning from their usage. However, computer and communication systems are not that smart, so for the most part the assignment is denotative. Names are essentially labels on objects. Following directly from Wittgenstein's *Tractatus*, this implies that any arbitrary label can be applied to any object. If one wants the string of glyphs *B* followed by *E* followed by *D* to stand for a four-legged mammal that barks and is often referred to as "man's best friend," that is their prerogative. In some sense, this is what the *Académie Française* does, but not what the "harmless drudges"[4] who compile the *Oxford English Dictionary* do. To get started:

> **Definition 1.** A *name space, NS,* is a set {N} of names from which all names for a given collection of objects are taken. A name may be bound to one and only one object at a time.

> **Definition 2.** A *name* is a unique string, N, in some alphabet, A, that unambiguously denotes some object or denotes a statement in some language, L. The statements in L are constructed using the alphabet, A.

Any name, $n \in N$, may be either *bound* to an object or *unbound* (and thus available for binding). An unbound name is called a *free name.* Names from a given name space may be bound to so-called atomic objects, to other names from this name space, or to sets of objects or names within this scope. One or more names may be bound to the same object. Such names are called *aliases* or *synonyms.* Names are objects, too. Some systems will define aliases or synonyms to apply to other names, rather than to the entity named. This can be an important distinction.

There are fundamentally two operations (and their inverses) associated with managing names: assignment/de-assignment and binding/unbinding.

Assignment allocates a name in a name space, essentially marks it in use. *De-assignment* removes it from use. Assignment makes names available to be bound. This allows a name space to defined and certain portions of it to be "reserved" and not available for binding.

---

4   Samuel Johnson's definition of *lexicographer* in the first English dictionary, 1755.

Binding binds a name to an object. Once bound, any reference to the name accesses the object. *Unbinding* breaks the binding name bound to an object. Once unbound, any reference will not access any object. Because names can be reassigned to different objects, it is often advisable that once a binding is broken that the name not be de-assigned (and thus available for reassignment) for some period of time to avoid errors.[5] The length of time will depend on the use of the name space, and in some cases, it may be advantageous for some names that the length of time be zero or nearly so. In general, more than one name may be bound to an object. This is often referred to as an *alias*. There are two forms of aliases: direct, where the alias refers to the object itself; and indirect, where the alias refers to a unique name for the object.

The words *unique* and *unambiguous* are significant here. *Unique* is used to note that there is one and only one. *Unambiguous* is used to indicate that referencing a given name will yield the same result without implying that it is the only name that when referenced will yield this result; that is, there may be more than one name for an object. Direct aliases are allowed. Thus, a name is a unique if there is one and only one string unambiguously denotes an object. Only indirect aliases may occur.

The *scope* of a name or name space is the set of all objects to which it may be applied. This will most often be used in reference to the scope within which a name is unambiguous. Let $A \supseteq B$, if the name, a is unambiguous in the scope of A, then the there is no other bound or unbound occurrence of the name a in A. Any reference to a in the context of A will yield the same object. However, there may be an occurrence of a in B where $B \cap \neg A = \varnothing$, such that a reference to a will not yield the same object as a reference to a in the context of A. For example, we may say that an (N)-address is unambiguous within the scope of the (N)-layer. This means within the (N)-layer, no specific (N)-address will be bound to two objects at the same time. However, the same address may occur in two layers of the same rank. The same address can be assigned to different objects as long as they are in different scopes and different address spaces. When we speak of the scope of one address space being larger or smaller than another, we are comparing the number of bound and unbound elements in each set.

As noted previously, it was well understood that addresses should be location dependent. Here we solve this problem by defining a topological relation between an address space and the elements it names (and later, topological relations between address spaces in adjacent layers).

---

5   In networks, there are practicalities that must be considered. Because there is always some time delay in propagating any changes in state, we will want to delay de-assignment so that references made during the change can be referred to a possible new assignment, followed by a period after de-assignment and before reassignment when a reference results in an error to minimize the chances of a wrong reference after reassignment.

Definition 3. An *address space*, AS, is a name space defined over a set {A} of strings, **a,** in the language, L, which is a topological space. Associated with {A} is a function, **F:O -> A,** that maps objects, **o** ∈ **O,** to be assigned addresses to addresses, **a** ∈ **A.** Taking our cue from Frege, F is a function of one or more properties of the object that exhibits the appropriate attribute of "nearness." The set {A} has a topologically structure to some level of granularity, **g.**

Definition 4. An *address* is a topologically significant name, which unambiguously identifies an object or a set of objects.

If we are going to define an address as a topologically dependent name, we should also have a term for the nontopological names, just to keep the pedants off our backs. Laziness suggests that we create the definition:

Definition 5. A *title space* is a topologically independent name space.

Definition 6. A *title* is a topologically independent name that unambiguously identifies an object or a set of objects.

A title is a specialization of a name. A title is a label for an object and can be chosen entirely arbitrarily. The only constraint is that the chosen string in the name space is not bound to another object. Therefore, there is no structure imposed on the elements of the name space. Such a name space is often referred to as flat. In other words, we use *title* to refer to names that aren't *addresses*.

An address space is a name space with a topology imposed on it. An address is a specialization of a name. Although an address is a label for an object just as a name is, the label cannot be chosen entirely arbitrarily. An address space has a structure. There is the additional constraint that the name must be chosen to be topologically significant (within some degree of granularity). Therefore, there is a structure imposed on the elements of the address space to reflect this topology and assigned according to an algorithm that maps elements of the address space to the objects being named. Now let's consider the definitions of a topology.[6]

---

6   The definitions found here can be found in any basic text on topology. Here we have relied on (Newman, 1964), (Mendleson, 1971), and most especially, as always, on (Bourbaki, 1990).

Introducing Topology to Addressing

Definitions

Definition 7. A *topological structure* (or more briefly, a topology) on a set **X** is a structure given by a set **A** of subsets of **X,** having the following properties (called axioms of topological structures):

(O1) Every union of sets of **A** is a set of **A.**

(O2) Every finite intersection of sets of **A** is a set of **A.**

The sets of **A** are called *open sets* of the topological structure defined by **A** on **X.**
Another way of considering a topology that is more helpful for these problems is that it is the study of those properties of an object that are invariant under deformation. To be more precise, consider Definition 8.

Definition 8. A *topology* is defined as follows: Let **X** be a nonempty set and **T** a collection of subsets of **X** such that

A1. $X \in T$

A2. $\emptyset \in T$

A3. If $O_1, O_2, ..., O_n \in T$, then

$$O_1 \cap O_2 \cap ... \cap O_n \in T$$

A4. If for each $a \in I$, $O_a \in T$, then $\cup_{\alpha \in I} O_a \in T$.

The pair of objects (**X, T**) is called a topological space. The set **X** is called the *underlying set,* the collection **T** is called the *topology on the set,* **X,** and the members of **T** are called *open sets.*

Definition 9. A *topological space* is a set endowed with a topological structure.

Definition 10. *Topology* is the study of properties that remain invariant under a homeomorphism.

Definition 11. A *homeomorphism* is a continuous function, **F: X →Y,** which is one-to-one and onto, and maps each point $x \in X$ to a point $y \in Y$, and F^{-1} exists and is continuous. This mapping ensures that points "near" **x** are mapped to points "near" **y.**

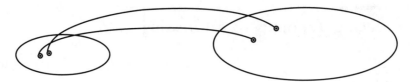

Figure 8-1 A homeomorphism is a continuous function *F:D->R* that is one-to-one and onto and has a continuous inverse and hence preserves "nearness."

Definition 12. A *homeomorphism of a topological space* X onto a topological space X' is an isomorphism of the topological structure of X onto that of X'; that is, in accordance with the general definitions of a bijection of X onto X' which transforms the set of open sets of X into the set of open subsets of X'.

The definition says that two points may be near each other in one set and far apart in another, but the distortions (mapping) maintain the relation of the points to each other (Figure 8-1). It also means that all surfaces with one hole are equivalent (doughnuts and coffee cups) or with two holes are equivalent, and so on. All of this derives from the definition of *homeomorphism*. The definition states that there is an *onto* mapping from one surface to another without any rips or holes; that is, it is continuous and there is an inverse. It is this concept of nearness that we are most interested in. And in particular for network addresses, we are interested in metrizable topologies.

When one says a network has a certain topology, one means that there is a function, which is a homeomorphism between the graphs of two or more networks. So in fact, when one says that a network has a certain topology, one is saying that there is a set of graphs that maintain certain structural properties in common. One may talk about star topologies, hierarchical topologies, mesh topologies, and so on. These all refer to sets of graphs with certain *invariant* interconnection properties. One may say that two networks have the same topology even if the lengths of the arcs are different but the number of nodes is maintained, and so on. However, one must be careful. Often in the networking literature, *topology* is used when *graph* would be more correct; that is, the use refers to a single network in isolation, not to a class of networks or graphs.

Addresses are used as an indication of *where* without indicating *how* to get there. An address space is a name space with a topological structure (Figure 8-2). A one-to-one and onto function **F:A –> A** on a set creates a topology. In other words, one wants addresses to be location dependent without being route dependent. This is desirable because there may be more than one route to a given location and most of the time the choice of how to get there may change much more frequently than where the destination is. So it is desirable to postpone choosing a route as long as possible. It is advantageous to be able to change the path while en route to the destination.

The mapping of addresses to the network reflects where things are for some notion of *where*. To make it easy for the routing algorithms, it is necessary to encode this sense of *where* in the address without constraining *how*, so that objects near each other have similar addresses. One would like an address to be useful in the sense that if I know where I am and where I want to go, the address provides some indication of which possible paths or directions will get me closer to the goal. This implies that the mapping of identifiers in the address space to the network elements is not arbitrary. In fact, the mapping defines a topology. Think of the address space as having a topological structure such that when the graph of a network is laid over this space the nodes in the network are assigned addresses according to which points are near the nodes. Purely as an analogy, consider a city laid out on a grid. Part of the plan for the city is the "address space." Before a street is constructed and buildings are built on it, one knows what addresses they will have. The addressing is imposed on the streets and buildings by the plan. Essentially, we want to construct an abstract version of this for network graphs.

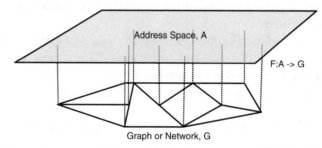

Figure 8-2 The address space, A, has a topological structure defined by the function **F:A -> G**. Points near each other in G will be near each other in A.

From a practical point of view, it is useful to distinguish nearness only to a certain resolution. Note that *resolution* for purposes of addressing is not the same as *resolution* for purposes of finding a physical object. Hence, we will define *granularity* to capture this concept.

Definition 13. The *granularity*, **g**, of the address space, **AS**, is defined as follows:

Consider two addresses, **a** and **b** in **A**

if **d(a,b) < g**, then **d(a,b)** = ε

as **lim** ε→ 0

In other words, while **a** and **b** are distinguishable (i.e., $\mathbf{a} \neq \mathbf{b}$), referencing **a** will yield a different object than referencing **b**. But as far as the topology of the address space is concerned, they are in "the same place," even though physically they may be a great distance apart (different topology with a different granularity). This property is common in address spaces. For example, in the telephone system, numbers within the same exchange exhibit this property. Two numbers in the same exchange are "in the same place" even though they may be tens of kilometers apart. The *topological* distance between any two telephone numbers in the same exchange is less than **g** for that topology.

The "granularity" of the address space is essentially a subset of the address space in which the "distance" between two addresses is considered to be zero; that is, they are topologically in the "same place." This implies that for any topology, addresses within the same domain of granularity $\mathbf{g_i}$ (i.e., $\mathbf{d(a, b)} < \mathbf{g}$), all routes to these addresses must be the same; that is, any path into this granularity domain, $\mathbf{g_i}$, has the ability to reach any address in the granularity domain (within given some number of concurrent failures within the domain). In other words, the connectivity within the domain of granularity is such that any address within $\mathbf{g_i}$ can be reached by paths leading into $\mathbf{g_i}$ assuming some number of links within $\mathbf{g_i}$ are not down at the same time. This is consistent with our intuitive notion of granularity and at the same time puts bounds on its size that are not entirely arbitrary.

Two other mathematical properties will prove useful in applying topological addresses to networks: distance and orientation. When these properties are used, they represent special types of topologies.

Definition 14. A *metrizable topological space* is a topology for which there is distance function.

Definition 15. A *distance function is* defined as a function, $\mathbf{d:x} \longrightarrow y$

Where $\mathbf{x,y} \in \mathbf{X}$ such that

1. $d(x,y) \geq 0$

2. $d(x,y) = 0$ if $x = y$

3. $d(x,y) = d(y,x)$

4. $d(x,z) \leq d(x,y) + d(y,z)$

We will define an address space, **A**, to have an *orientation* if and only if there exists a relation **R** on **A** that is a partial ordering, which is defined to be reflexive, antisymmetric, and transitive. This construction is adapted from and uses the definitions found in (Bourbaki, 1968).

Definition 16. There exists a *relation* **R** on a set A such that for all x, y, and z in **A**

1. x **R** x,

2. if x **R** y and y **R** x, then x = y

3. if x **R** y and y **R** z then, x **R** z.

Further, we know that an *ordering* on a set **A** is a *correspondence*

$$\Gamma = (G, A, A)$$

where **A** is the domain and range of **G** and $\ni \forall (x,y) \in G$ is an order relation on **A**.

Definition 17. If **R** is an *order relation* on **A**, it has a graph that is an ordering on **A**. Where the graph, G, is defined as follows (Bourbaki, 1968):

G is said to be a graph if every element of **G** is an ordered pair (i.e., if the relation

$$(\forall z) (z \in G \Rightarrow (z \text{ is an ordered pair}) \text{ is true.}$$

An address space is a set with a topological structure and in some cases a distance function and/or an orientation. One must be aware that while the definitions here appear to be the familiar ones from analytical geometry, there is no requirement that the distance function be, in fact, Cartesian. Other distance functions may be more useful with address spaces. A topology with orientation relation imposed on it gives us an abstract notion of "direction." Both of these can be used to advantage in translating a designation of *where* to a definition of *how* to get there. The topology of an oriented address space maps the elements of the address space to the elements of the network, which form the graph of this layer. In essence, we create a homeomorphism between the address space and the elements of the graph of the layer (i.e., the connectivity of elements with respect to their layer). The effectiveness of the routing and resource management for the layer can be greatly enhanced if the topology is metrizable and has an orientation.

Topologies for Addressing

As anyone who has tried to use a Chinese dictionary can verify, naming does not scale.[7] One of the advantages of the relatively short Western European alphabet is that it allows an effective topology to be imposed on the name space with the

---

[7] In the official Chinese/English dictionary, the PRC made the dictionary easier to use with a step that while infinitely pragmatic was nonetheless completely unparalleled for a lack of nationalistic chauvinism quite uncharacteristic of any country. The dictionary is organized by the Pinyin spelling of the characters, rather than the traditional count of strokes and radicals. The traditional collation could yield as many as 85 different characters under the same entry. Using Western collating sequence will still yield many characters under the same entry, but the granularity of the resulting topology is much smaller.

benefit of a more manageable dictionary. The collating sequence of the language is the property used to determine where the word goes in the topology of the address space (i.e., the dictionary). The nature of current routing algorithms has caused us to combine route determination and cost optimization. Because we want to consider multiple metrics, we will try to separate determining connectivity and cost optimization/route selection.

Actually, a better analogy for our purposes might be a thesaurus. A thesaurus maintains a mapping between two name spaces each with a different topology. There is one table that is arranged in the collating sequence of the language (i.e., alphabetical) and another table arranged in some semantic topology that attempts to place words with similar meaning "near" each other for some concept of "near." The first table has pointers into the second.

The primary difference between application naming and IPC addressing is the nature of the topology. IPC addressing topologies are used to locate IPC processes relative to each other within the DIF and are, therefore, location dependent. This is why they often seem to be based on spatial topologies and why the naïve approach assumes location dependent means geography. Application naming topologies are used to locate applications within a semantic space (or a set of semantic attributes). For example, we structure file directories in a way that is meaningful to us and helps *locate* files within the organization of files, not physical devices, and may, therefore, be location independent.[8] It is possible to create location-dependent application naming, just as it is possible to create route-dependent network addresses.[9] As indicated earlier, in some situations this is even desirable.

Thus, applications will have addresses drawn from topological spaces, although in some cases, not metrizable spaces, although the semantic Web may be trying to rectify this. However, address spaces for IPC will most likely be metrizable and, if not, at least have an orientation. Because the nature of the address spaces is so radically different (and is supposed to be), mappings from an application address space to a distributed IPC address space are unlikely to be homeomorphic. A router wants to determine two things: given PDUs with different addresses, which addresses are "near" each other so that it can send the PDUs in the same direction; and given the address, which "direction" to

---

[8] Well at least not for any post-1960 operating system technology have we had to know what physical drive files were on. Although such operating systems continued to be written after 1960, generally as class projects, this does not change their vintage.

[9] Traditionally, application names have been assumed to be human readable. However, a current trend might seem to indicate that search engines, such as Google and Yahoo!, are displacing this view. This tends to confuse names and attributes and relies on the same attribute list and yielding the same results over time, an iffy proposition at best.

send it. Thus, the relation between address spaces of layered (N)-DIFs should have similar concepts of nearness to facilitate routing within their layers or subnets. We can expect that mappings between layers will in most cases be homeomorphic.

Network address architectures without this topological dependence do not define addresses, only names. MAC and pre-CIDR IP "addresses," for example, are names, not addresses. This is not a problem for MAC addresses[10] because of the limited scope of LANs and the broadcast nature of the media, although more and more we are seeing demand for routing in LANs. However, it is often called something else, partly for marketing reasons and partly to avoid turf conflicts. Ethernet has been backing into routing since spanning trees were proposed. With Ethernet coming full circle to wireless, there is no doubt that routing occurs in the media layer. And in fact, the theory developed in this book endorses that move.

Their scope is essentially less than the granularity of the address space to which routing is applied. The scope of these subnetworks is sufficiently small that scaling is seldom an issue. Unfortunately, this is not generally the case for IP; and where it is the case, it seldom matters.Consequently, IP addressing fails to scale on two counts: It is (pre-CIDR) a name space, not an address space and is route dependent.

So, is an addressing scheme based on country codes, such as the NSAP scheme, better? Sort of. The existence of the syntax identification of the address, the AFI, is clearly not topological. It might be interpreted as either the name for the syntax of the address space but probably would be interpreted as, "Route this to that kind of network in as few hops as possible." The country codes make the space topological, but do network boundaries coincide nicely with political boundaries? Sometimes, but by no means always. This will work well for large countries or densely populated ones, but even here it might be better to have more than one domain per country at the same level of the hierarchy for some countries (and in regions with a number of small countries or not so small, but less densely populated countries where there would be advantages to a higher-level domain serving several countries). So the domains implied by the country codes may not correspond well to the logical topology best suited for routing purposes. But this could be accommodated by a judicious choice of country codes, as is done now with two-digit numbers for large European countries and three-digit numbers for smaller ones (e.g., France, 33; Germany, 49; but Lichtenstein 352; Gibraltar, 350; and so on).

---

10   MAC addresses are a case of overloading the semantics of the address as both an address and a serial number.

Telephone networks grew generally under government sponsorship, and so nonoverlapping national boundaries tended to occur naturally. Multinational corporations, on the other hand, have built data networks, in a period of deregulation. Consequently, national boundaries may not coincide with the structure of the network as naturally. It may well be the case that the convenient routing domains would not correspond well with any national boundaries. Some of these cases would have been helped perhaps if the NSAP scheme had allowed for a "regional domain" above the countries. It will seldom be the case that the domain boundaries of the addressing topology and political boundaries will coincide.[11] However, many individuals and thus institutions place considerable weight in "having *their* block of addresses,"[12] or perhaps more to the point where countries are concerned, that their domain is at the same level as other countries. Clearly, such chauvinism can play havoc with an effective addressing architecture. And all the more reason that we should remove considerations of addressing from the visibility of the end users. This is somewhat understandable in traditional networks such as the telephone network or an IP network, where the address was all there was to hang on to. Removing the prominence of the address by recognizing it as an identifier internal to a distributed IPC facility and focusing on application naming should go a long way to defusing some of these issues.

The primary question is what topologies for address spaces make sense, are easily maintained, scale, have nice properties for routing, and so on. The problem then is to find useful and effective algorithms for creating and configuring topologies of address spaces based on the abstractions and aggregation and the topologies of subnets without tying it to the physical topology of the network but at the same time providing a convergence to that physical graph. The physical graph should be guided as much by the topology of the address space as by other considerations. Or with an allusion to Einstein, it is the theory that determines the data, or it's the topology that determines the network! If the graph of the network differs significantly from the topology chosen for the address space, the wrong topology has been chosen. Consequently, there is no single answer.

---

[11] There was a country that once had an RFP for a network that required that each of its 20 or so provinces have its own network management system, but the national network only required 6 or 8 switches! A phrase about "Too many cooks ..." comes to mind.

[12] Not unlike our friend who wanted his network address on his business card. A prominent corporation believed they should have a block of Class A IP addresses because they were prestigious. Because they were prestigious and only dealt with the most important customers, they had many fewer offices than companies that dealt with the multitudes and had offices everywhere. The fact that numbers of systems was what counted and they didn't have the numbers simply didn't register. Clearly, a Class A network was "better" than having Class B subnetworks, and *they* were definitely Class A.

The topology of the address space and the graph of the network need to be worked out together. The best we can do is to explore common network graphs for useful topologies.

The Role of Hierarchy in Addressing

To date, all address architectures for large domains (networks as well as others, such as the postal system, the telephone system, and so on) have utilized hierarchical topologies for everything except the terminal sets of the address space. There has been considerable use of other topologies in these local environments, spatial, Cartesian, flat (enumeration), time, random (another form of enumeration), and so on. The small scale allows almost any assignment procedure to be used.

Of course, hierarchical routing schemes have been proposed, notably Kleinrock (1977) and, more important, O'Dell (1997). In these cases, these routing schemes are used in a single layer reflecting a graph that is primarily hierarchical. Here we will do something a bit different that has greater effectiveness and flexibility.

As yet, there are no logical arguments (i.e., proofs) that a hierarchy is the only topology that can be used for large domains. On the other hand, we have no examples or proposals of any other topology actually being feasible on a large scale. This makes it difficult to make many general statements about addressing without assuming a hierarchical topology. Therefore, we will develop the concepts for a hierarchical topology while issuing a challenge to others to develop nonhierarchical topologies.

There are three distinct hierarchies in network architectures that are all useful but are often confused and sometimes combined:

- The hierarchy of layers

- The hierarchical address space

- The hierarchical arrangement of subnetworks

All three are important to an addressing architecture. There is a tendency to confuse them or to assume one implies the other. We saw in Chapter 5 the inclination to confuse the hierarchy of layer and the hierarchy of addressing by putting the MAC address in the IP address and thereby defeating the purpose of their being distinct. However, there are three distinct independent hierarchies. The distinctions among them must be kept clear. If assumptions are made that meld them, they must be clearly made and understood. I will attempt to keep them as distinct as possible to clarify the role each has in developing an effective addressing architecture.

The Hierarchy of Layers

Network architectures are organized into a hierarchical stack of layers. In traditional network architectures, these have been layers dedicated to different functions. Consequently, pictures of such stacks of layers seldom illustrate the salient properties we are concerned with. The common "tower" figure implies that there is a set of layers stacked one on top of another, all with the same scope in all systems in the network, often leading some to conclude that the same protocol is under all higher layers at all places, which is seldom the case. The "hourglass" figure of layers is used to represent the diversity of protocols at the top (applications), narrower in the middle with many fewer protocols usually only one or two, and widening again at the bottom reflecting the diversity of media. This diagram illustrates the taxonomy associated with the layers but does not illustrate the layers in an operating network. These diagrams were tightly bound to our ideas that layers had different functions. Now that we consider layers to all have the same functions, our interest is in the scope of layers, in their ability to partition and organize the problem. In this case, we arrive at the "hill and valley" model of the last chapter.

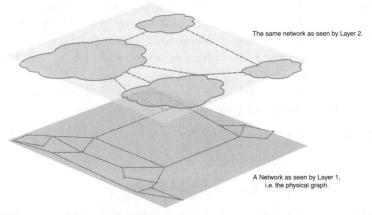

The same network as seen by Layer 2.

A Network as seen by Layer 1,
i.e. the physical graph.

Figure 8-3 The use of layering to abstract the graph of a network.

Layers have two major properties that are of interest to us: abstraction and scaling (i.e., divide and conquer). Layers hide the operation of the internal mechanisms from the users of the mechanisms and segregate and aggregate traffic. But most important, they provide an abstraction of the layers below. To create a topological address space, we need an abstraction of the physical graph of the network. Layering will prove to be an effective tool for creating that abstraction.

Lower layers in this hierarchy have smaller scope. In general, scope increases as one moves up through the layers. This forms the equivalent of a tree with many more leaves (bottom layers) than branches. This provides the mechanism by which we can "divide and conquer" the problems tackled by the layer. At lower layers, we deal with issues at a finer granularity over few objects; whereas at higher layers we deal with less granularity but over more elements, such that the amount of work to accomplish these functions remains relatively constant from layer to layer.

These layers allow efficiencies in routing and resource allocation to be achieved. When there are multiple flows between the same intermediate points, these flows can be combined into a single lower-layer flow, encapsulated at a lower layer, where "same place" may be a host or some intermediate router (i.e., part of a path). The latter is more likely. This will be effected by a lower layer with a smaller scope and address space than the layer above. The smaller scope of lower layers means that PCI overhead will decrease with the lower layers, which will also reduce the complexity of the routing tasks (i.e., fewer routing decisions on fewer flows requiring less routing computation and routing traffic). We can use how the scope of layers is chosen to impose a particular topology on the network. Figure 8-3 illustrates how layering might be used to abstract the graph of a network. At the upper layers, we get a more mixed bag, layers of both greater and lesser scope.

Layering is our primary tool for abstraction and scaling.

The Hierarchical Topology of Address Spaces

Layers with a relatively large scope will have a large number of elements to be assigned names from its address space (Figure 8-4). The management of the address space is much easier if a hierarchy is imposed. The address will consist of a sequence that corresponds to the branches of the hierarchy. This sequence does not specify a route but only a location within the granularity of the address space. A nonterminal domain identifier identifies a set of domains (i.e., a set of sets of addresses). The nonterminal domain-ids can be used to encode finer and finer granularity location information and may also indicate distance and direction. The terminal domains reflect the granularity of the topology. Within the terminal domains, addresses are assigned in some arbitrary fashion. This does not imply random or simple enumeration for assignment, although it may be either. Put simply, this implies that the assignment of values in the terminal domain is not necessarily topological. We have previously defined this point at which the structure of the topology disappears as the granularity of the topology: The points are distinguishable, but their "distance" is indistinguishable within the topology.

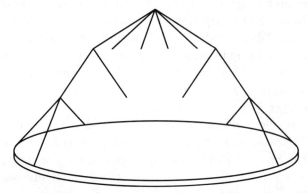

Figure 8-4 Hierarchical addressing of a single layer is used to manage the size of the address space.

This is similar to the addressing scheme found in Japanese cities, where a series of proper subsets (prefect, neighborhood, block) finally gives way to simply numbering houses in the order they were built. The use of hierarchical address space is very common and very old and seems quite natural. However, this can hardly be considered an endorsement. Where addressing is concerned, intuition and "naturalness" have too often proved not just fallible but a trap. The postal system is probably the most ubiquitous form of hierarchical addressing. As networks began to get larger, hierarchy is imposed on the addressing. And as with the postal system, it has often been along geographical lines at least down to countries and distribution points within those countries then shifting to a different topology for delivery. We have already pointed out some of the problems with these approaches, but hierarchy remains the only useful and scalable approach, we have found.

We have already defined earlier the basic properties of an address space. We now need to consider how those properties are manifested in a hierarchical topology. In this topology, the points are represented by a string of domain identifiers:

$$(d_n, \ldots, d_1, d_0)$$

The primary property that we must develop is the concept of distance. Above, we defined the granularity of the topology to be the minimum distance between two points that can be distinguished by the distance function. In this topology, we define that granularity, **g,** as follows:

$$d(a, b) < g \Leftrightarrow$$

$$\forall a = (a_n, \dots , a_1, a_0) \text{ and } b = (b_n, \dots , b_1, b_0)$$

$$\ni a_i = b_i \; \forall i \ni 1 \leq i \leq n$$

In other words, the distance between two addresses in the same leaf domain is indistinguishable in the topology. Let's define the distance between two addresses, **a** and **b,** to be:

$$d(a, b) = 2 * \Sigma (a_I \neq b_i) \; 1 \leq i \leq n$$

The summation measures the depth of the subtree to be traversed from **a** to **b,** and then to get there it is necessary to go up to the first domain in common and then back down, hence *2. This of course is for the easy case where the tree has equal depth on all branches. A somewhat more complicated equation will be necessary for trees with unequal depth.

Hierarchical addressing is our primary tool for organizing and locating addresses within a single layer. A hierarchical address space applies to one layer and only to one layer. Figure 8.4 illustrates how a hierarchical address space might be used to organize and locate elements of a layer.

The Hierarchy of Networks

In the early days of data comm, hierarchical networks were common. This generally consisted of terminals at the leaves with various forms of concentrators and stat muxes as intermediate nodes and a mainframe at the root. These tree networks had limited routing capabilities. These have not entirely disappeared but are not what we are concerned with. Hierarchies of networks are represented by subnets, which are arranged hierarchically with more connectivity within the subnets than between subnets, but seldom a single connection. Real networks are generally organized into a *rough hierarchy;* of subnets with smaller corporate or organization subnets connected to metro subnets, connected to regional subnets connected a backbone subnet. "Rough" in this sense implies that the hierarchy is not strictly followed. There might be shortcuts between nodes of the tree (which are subnets) that create loops.

The levels of subnets attempt to minimize the number of hops required to deliver a PDU between any source and destination. Also, by working with subnets, redundant connections between subnets can be provided while maintaining the hierarchy. The desire to keep network diameter small also moderates the depth of the hierarchy. This sort of tree will on average lessen the number of hops between any two points. Figure 8.5 illustrates a hierarchy of subnets.

The potential inefficiency of strictly following a hierarchical topology for routing is well known, especially for "local traffic" or traffic between "popular" sites within a network. Hence, networks in the wild are seldom strict hierarchies. Additional arcs will often be added to "short-circuit" the path between branches of the tree with a considerable traffic. Exchange points are used to short-circuit the hierarchy and to further optimize the route between points with lots of traffic. We would see that these are easily recognized, and it is easy to take full advantage of them.

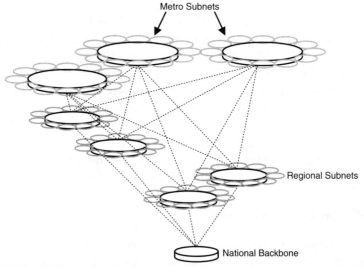

Figure 8-5 Typical hierarchy of subnets. Backbone connects only to regionals. Regionals connect only to backbone and metro subnets. Hosts connect only to metro subnets.

The number of levels in a hierarchy (Figure 8-5) will vary depending on the number of elements in the network as well as organizational considerations. For example, one feeder subnet might be a small corporation with several subnets, or a local ISP with residential or corporate customers with their own subnets, and so on. Some networks such as the public Internet are not rooted in a single subnet, nor are the connections between subnets strictly hierarchical, nor should they be. The hierarchy is imposed as the minimal (or default) connectivity of the subnets, although not necessarily the primary or optimal connectivity. The tree is the minimal connectivity that a router needs to know. The links that make the connectivity a lattice can be considered elements of alternative subnet hierarchies (i.e., "shortcuts"). Also, user systems will not be attached only to "leaf" subnets but to whatever subnet is closest to the user's system physically. However, this latter practice is fast disappearing as networks become very large and the realities of "impedance matching" the relative low load of host access with a much higher load backbone become more pronounced.

Early in the history of networking, there was considerable work to optimize network design. The early work was based on optimizing flows in graphs using the mathematics developed for optimizing pipelines and other such systems. The primary concern was ensuring that there was a minimal number of sufficiently large "pipes" to support the expected traffic to achieve a reasonable level of redundancy. As networks grew, the number of nodes in a typical path through the graph also became an issue. The more nodes, the greater the switching delay. This naturally leads to a hierarchy to reduce the diameter of the network.

By the same token, the network design should be guided by the topology imposed by the address space. The more the graph follows the topology, the easier routing will be. On the other hand, a network design must accommodate less-ideal constraints, such as high-volume traffic between particular nodes or completely irrational considerations such as tariffs.

Entire books have been written on the design of such networks to optimize throughput and delay. However, here we are interested only in the relation of this hierarchy of subnets to addressing. Although the address architecture is ultimately concerned with finding a route from the source to the destination, the address itself must limit its role to "locating" the addressable element. This will be made much easier if we are able to recognize and use the hierarchy of subnets in the assignment of addresses. Clearly, a near optimal path would be to route toward the backbone (unless a shortcut is encountered) and then back down the tree. The obvious approach would be for the hierarchy of the address space to correspond in some way to the hierarchy of subnets. However, we can't make the correspondence too close because physical network topology tends to change. The address space is supposed to be dependent on location but independent of route. Thus, while an address space should recognize the hierarchy of subnets, it should not be too tightly bound to its connectivity. As discussed later, the Internet is actually many hierarchies superimposed.

The first two hierarchies described here are tools to facilitate creating an effective topological address space. The hierarchy of subnets is a structure that many real networks follow to a greater or lesser degree. Some readers will no doubt be thinking this: The Internet topology is not hierarchical. Many papers have said so. There are two responses to this: 1) The public Internet is not the only network or even the only Internet in the world. As scientists and engineers, it is good to have an understanding of more than one corner of the problem space. 2) No, the Internet is not *a* hierarchy. It is a collection of hierarchies with shortcuts, which are, in turn, hierarchies with shortcuts. It would seem that some observers have difficulty seeing the *trees* for the forest. In what follows, we consider how keeping theory close to practice can leverage each other. We first look at the implications for a single layer and then look at how this applies to multiple layers. Finally, we consider how this can be applied to networks consisting of several overlapping and nonoverlapping hierarchies of layers.

Melding Address Spaces and the Hierarchy of Layers

Before beginning our example, let's consider how we can use our tools to create an effective naming scheme for a hierarchy of subnets.

Address spaces are finite point set topologies. Networks are finite graphs. The graph of an (N)-layer as seen from above the (N)-layer boundary (i.e., by its user) is a fully connected graph; that is, everything is directly connected. Each node (i.e., application) is one arc from every other node. The applications appear one hop from each other at this layer.

The graph of the (N)-layer as seen just *below* the (N)-layer boundary is an (N)-network consisting of the collection of (N–1)-layers, which form a covering of the (N)-layer and the (N)-relays providing the connectivity among the (N–1)-layers (or subnets). Thus, the (N)-network consists of all nodes in the (N)-layer (i.e., (N)-IPC-processes) either multiplexing at the edge or relaying in the interior, and arcs connecting those nodes (i.e., (N–1)-layers). A topology is imposed by a mapping between the elements of an address space and the graph of the (N)-layer.

The composition of subnets chosen to constitute the (N–1)-layers creates the topological structure of the (N)-network (i.e., the abstraction of the graph). The end nodes of the network are directly connected to one or more (N)-relays (i.e., they are one hop across an (N–1)-subnet from one or more (N)-relays). k(N–1)-layers are required to cover the (N)-network (i.e., support the scope of the (N)-layer). To be less abstract for a moment, an (N)-network looks like a WAN connecting a set of LANs. As one goes up through the layers, the "WAN" gets larger and the "LANs" get smaller.

There is a "covering" of layer (N) if and only if every (N)-layer relay has a binding with an element of some (N–1)-layer (i.e., a binding between an (N)-IPC-process and an (N–1)-IPC-process in the same system). A covering does not require every (N)-IPC-process to have an (N–1)-IPC-process. In particular, an (N)-IPC-process that is not an (N)-relay may not have such a binding.

Each of (N–1)-layers as seen by the (N)-layer is fully connected. The resulting graph formed by the (N)-relays spans the (N)-layer. This is an abstraction of the underlying physical network.

This abstraction is refined (made less and less abstract) down through the layers until the topology of the (N)-network is isomorphic to the physical graph of the network.

Moving from top to bottom, the layering decomposes the connectivity and resource-allocation problems into manageable pieces by creating a covering of (N–1)-layers of fewer elements and greater bandwidth. The layers between the "top" and "bottom" are created as a combination of abstracting the physical network graph and aggregating the flows of the layer(s) above. The higher the layer, the more aggregation dominates; the lower, the more the physical network dominates. At some layer, the connectivity of the layer (i.e., its graph) becomes isomorphic with the graph of the network, ultimately at the physical layer. The graph created at layer (N) represents the connectivity at this level of abstraction. (Other characteristics are changing, too, but here we are only concerned with those that relate to addressing.)

The binding between the elements of the point set topology formed by the (N)-layer address space and the graph of the (N)-network is the basis for routing. Maintaining this mapping is the directory/routing function.

In general, the address space at layer (N) is larger than the address space at (N–1)-layer owing to the smaller scope of the underlying layers. Each successively lower layer contains fewer elements than the layer above. (Lesser scope implies fewer elements reachable within a layer and therefore shorter addresses.)

Mappings from (N)-application-names to (N)-addresses will not be homeomorphic because they are very different kinds of names. Application naming is intended for an external location-independent purpose rather than the internal location-dependent purpose. But the mapping between DIFs of internal (N)-addresses to the (N+1)- or (N–1)-layers may be homeomorphic. There are basically three exceptions:

1. For (N)-layers with a scope that is sufficiently small (i.e., smaller than the granularity of typical address spaces that the address space need not be topologically dependent; in other words, flat). The bottom layer will seldom have a topological structure because it has such small scope and is so close to the physical graph for "topology" to be effective (although there are exceptions).

2. There may be a discontinuity in the mapping between layers belonging to different domains, such as a layer between a private and a public addressing domain or from one provider to another. This mapping may or may not be a homeomorphism. (If there is no homeomorphism, clearly there has been a major discontinuity in the abstractions in adjacent layers.)

3. The (N+1)-layer does not meet the interfacing security requirements of the (N)-layer. The (N)-layer does not trust the (N+1)-layer and only creates flows/connections between applications (i.e., it does not recognize the applications as (N+1)-IPC-processes).

For media with physical layer addresses that may be assigned at installation, it might be possible to make even this last mapping homeomorphic. Our challenge is to find a topology that leverages the mappings between layers and to leverage the network graph.

As we have seen, a hierarchical address space is commonly used as much to facilitate the management of address assignment as it is to be a useful addressing topology. Each layer has a distinct and independent address space.[13] If the scope of the layer is large enough, it will have a hierarchical address space imposed on it. The hierarchy breaks up the address space into manageable pieces with various levels having their own subauthorities for allocating subtrees. Each nonterminal level of the tree defines a set or domain that may be administered independently and can also correspond to regions of the subnet.

The choice of domains is not entirely arbitrary, although there is considerable flexibility in choosing them (and choosing well is highly desirable). In general, these domains will correspond to geographical regions, spatial loci of organizational facilities, subnetworks, and so on, taking into account likely exchange point arrangements and granularity. However, they should not be along organizational lines that do not correspond with some form of spatial locality; that is, members of a department spread through multiple buildings would probably not be a good domain choice. (Remember that here we are concerned with creating topologies to facilitate routing. Defining VPNs to create subnets that cut across the routing topology is a very different problem and best accommodated with a layer on top of the "routing layers.") Although the choice does not directly reflect the connectivity of the network, it is important to recognize that things near each other may be connected by a single subnet. As discussed later, it is possible to define an addressing architecture for an organization of layers that is simple to maintain. As we will see, choosing domains can be used effectively when mapping one layer to another.

The sign "=" should be read as "is easily confused with."

—attributed to G. Frege

---

[13] This does not imply that there can't be relations or conventions in how address spaces for layers are designed but only that there is no requirement for such relations to exist. However, such conventions may be highly desirable.

Hierarchical Addressing Architecture

The challenge then is to effectively use the hierarchical tools on the naturally occurring hierarchical network to create an addressing architecture. The address space is our primary concern. We want the assignment of addresses to facilitate finding the location of the IPC-processes to the greatest degree possible.[14] The address is our primary "key" or "index." We have already observed that the only topology that has been found to scale for a wide range of size, granularity, and other properties is a hierarchy. It would seem fortuitous then that the seemingly preferred organization of physical networks is roughly a hierarchy with "shortcuts" between subtrees; and that all we would want to do is design the address space to loosely coincide with the hierarchy of subnets. The "shortcuts" are optimizations for "routing" and not concerned with "locating" (and "loosely" here is the key). Locating must remain independent of routing. However, we know that the physical connectivity represented by the subnet structure is subject to change. And although we recognize that this change will affect addressing, experience has shown that it is not wise to tie the addressing structure too tightly to the physical structure. We need to decouple the two; we need a separation of logical and physical, but not complete independence. This is a role that layering has traditionally performed, although less so in traditional network architectures. Layers close to the physical media closely reflect the characteristics of the media. Although successively higher layers provide greater and greater abstraction (i.e., are more logical than physical).

Thus, it would seem that our goal in constructing an addressing architecture should be a hierarchical address space that reflects the "ideal" subnet hierarchy. Addresses then would be assigned to reflect that ideal structure even if the physical reality diverges somewhat. This may lead to occasional reassignment of addresses, but even then it would be rare if such a change would alter an addressable element's position in the hierarchy by more than a single level. Furthermore, the choice of subnets (i.e., the set of elements in different (N+1)-layers) defines the topology.

So far, we have discussed the basic concepts of topology and have seen how they might be used. We have reviewed three distinct kinds of hierarchy in networks and that two of these occur naturally, in the physical organization and logically to manage complexity. We can leverage both topology and hierarchy to develop a more effective approach to the problem of assigning addresses so that

---

[14] It is probably worthwhile to remind the reader of two things: 1) The observation by some that "the Internet graph is not a hierarchy, but heavy tailed" is an artifact of the Internet graph being a large number of networks with a generally hierarchical structure being superimposed; and 2) that the Internet is seldom the only internet of concern to most providers.

they fulfill our requirement of indicating "where" such that it aids *forwarding*. Working with a single recursive or repeating layer rather than individually crafted specialized layers further leverages our ability to find useful solutions. Our goal is not to provide *the* answer, because there is no single answer, nor is one required. Nor are we concerned with the problems of competing groups. Our goal is to show how it might work, indicate the possibilities, and expect ourselves and others to continue to explore its possibilities.

In this section, we explore several idealized cases on the assumption that if we work out these cases, the real-world problems will most likely be combinations of them or variations on them. We first consider a single layer and the use of hierarchy, then a hierarchy of layers, and finally overlapping and nonoverlapping of multiple hierarchies of layers. The section finishes with some speculation about how this might be used in a multiprovider, multiuser network, such as those found in the wild.

Single-Layer Address Topology

As shown in Figure 8-2, the address space has a topological structure that is mapped to the graph of the network. When nodes are added to the graph, addresses are assigned according to "where" they are relative to other nodes and hence to the topology of the address space.

The problem now is to determine what sort of topology would be a useful "aid" to routing. The answer, of course, depends on the network. To create a not-so-extreme example and to illustrate that our analog to Midwestern grids might not be too far-fetched, one might want to have a network that was highly reliable and resilient to physical failures in a chemical plant or refinery. The network for such a plant might actually be a two- or three-dimensional grid with routers at all intersections such that even in the case of a catastrophic failure (i.e., an explosion) it would still have a high likelihood of maintaining contact with operational parts of the plant.[15] This could be a useful topology for a "campus" network, but only on a local scale. It should not be hard to find other environments where other topologies are useful.

Single-Layer Hierarchical Address Topology

As we have seen, most networks are organized as hierarchies. Let's see what we can do with them. If a network is large enough to be organized as a hierarchy, it

---

[15] Yes, wireless might be used, but it is unlikely. Given the nature of the equipment in such plants, there would be sufficient EMI and shielding created by the equipment to make wireless problematic.

is large enough to organize its addresses hierarchically, too. Such a network, as pictured in Figure 8-6, would have three or four levels of hierarchy (let's say campus, metro, regional, and backbone for the sake of argument). Each level constitutes a subnetwork of its own with multiple paths among its members and multiple paths to its parent and child subnets. In addition, we will assume that because the owner of the network is responsive to its users' needs, there are various paths (shortcuts) installed that cut across the hierarchy either within the same level or across levels.

We can construct our address topology to reflect this structure. The hierarchy of addresses would reflect the hierarchy of the subnets. Note that because we are considering a single layer, we must allocate terminal levels of the hierarchy to routers in nonterminal subnets. From inspecting at an address, one can tell in what campus, metro, and region the host or router is located.

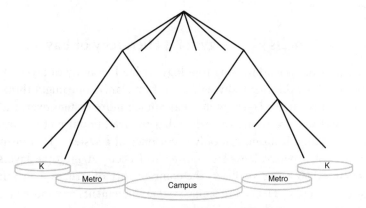

Figure 8-6 A single-layer hierarchical address space, with k regions, m metro areas, and m campuses with a maximum p elements in each requires $\log 2 \ (1 + k(1 + m(1 + n)))p$ bits in the address.

As we know from the O'Dell GSE proposal, such a hierarchical address topology has many advantages.[16] First of all, because the addresses indicate where the node is, the address represents an abstract route, a sort of "anycast" route. We say "anycast" because the address does not indicate a specific path but any of several paths through the subnet hierarchy. The routers know that at least as a default they can route along paths that move up or down the tree of subnets.

The network may have added shortcuts not only because of heavy traffic between parts of the network but also to improve the resiliency of the network

---

[16] The O'Dell proposal considers hierarchical addressing more in the context of a hierarchy of subnets, whereas the Kleinrock paper considers it more a hierarchy of switches.

Note on Nomenclature

People seem to put a lot of weight in these words *router* and *switch*. It is sometimes hard to tell a difference. Whether the operation is done in hardware or software is not a significant difference. We will use the following definitions:

- A *router* uses information in the PDU to make the relaying decision.

- A *switch* uses information outside the PDU to make the relaying decision.

- A *hub* uses no information about the PDU to make the relaying decision.

to failure. It might even be the case that all adjacent regions are connected as well as being connected to the backbone. Taking advantage of these shortcuts is equally easy. As routers learn the addresses of their neighbors, they can easily recognize by the address which neighbors represent paths to a parent or child subnet. It is equally easy to recognize which routers are "across" the tree because their address indicates they are neither a parent nor a child. Furthermore, the address indicates which part of the tree they provide access to (i.e., what they are a wormhole to). In addition, such a topology reduces the number of routes to be calculated or stored. Basically, routes only need to be calculated for paths within a level. The addressing structure allows considerable route aggregation to be done, thereby reducing the computation load.

Address Topology for a Hierarchy of Layers

Let's now consider the addressing topology with a hierarchy of layers. First, we must consider how this hierarchy works. At first glance, one might think that an architecture of recursive layers would have much more system overhead. However, it doesn't take one long to realize that the traditional picture of layers is not quite the same. Routing can only occur once in a system. There is no point in the graph of a network where routing will occur at multiple layers in the same system. (And as we shall see, the commonality of structure also improves processing efficiency.) Hence, no single system implements any more layers than it does in a conventional system. In this configuration, border routers mark the boundary of routing layers. It is at the boundaries that layers are used to both contain and bound the routing problem (and, limiting the routing computation within a layer).

The bottom layer is always a media access layer. Its policies will be determined primarily by the constraints of the physical media. In many cases, it will be a degenerate layer for either a point-to-point (which require no addresses) or multiaccess media (which require addresses). It is not uncommon for multiaccess to be routed. In general, the physics of the physical media limits the scope of a single media access layer to well within the bounds of flat addressing. (Again, the introduction of switching and routing in the media access layers may also remove these physical limitations. Then, the major limitations are those of management and scaling.) Because this condition is so common, we will make that assumption. However, removing the assumption does not affect our conclusions.

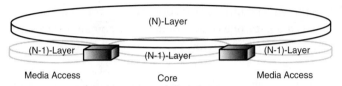

Figure 8-7 The (N)-layer has addresses only for elements of the (N)-subnets. Border routers are one hop across the (N–1)-layer of the core network. The (N)-layer address space requires log2 mp bits, where m is the number of subnets of p elements.

As noted in Chapter 7, it is at border routers where recursion occurs. The configuration of border routers differs from traditional routers in that their "interior" side goes down a layer. Returning to our analogy of the valley, where we noted the deeper the valley, the greater the effective bandwidth; and the greater the determinism of the traffic, the greater the aggregation and where we will implement internal congestion control. At a border router, we move down a terrace in the valley (Figure 8-7), multiplexing edge hosts or subnets toward the core of the network. This construction yields an (N)-layer with greater scope than the (N–1)-layers as we would expect. There are two kinds of (N–1)-layers: Some (N–1)-layers are the media access layers of the edge subnets, and there is (in the ideal case) one large (N–1)-layer in the middle (see Figure 8-6). But remember, this is not a spatial diagram but a logical one. There is no "hole" where there is an area uncovered. All border routers appear to be directly connected at the (N)-layer: They are one hop from each other at the (N)-layer. We will be most interested in the relation of the addressing of the "core" (N–1)-layer to the (N)-layer.

For large networks (Figure 8-8), we can assume that a hierarchical address will be used for most of the nonmedia access layers, if for no other reason than to manage the large numbers of addresses. We want to choose the composition of the subnets to reflect the topology (and granularity constraints) or to choose the topology to reflect the structure of the subnets. If we assume that the (N)-layer address space is hierarchical, it will be advantageous (not necessary) if the upper *domains* of the address reflect the subnet structure of the core, while the lower domains of the address reflect the topology of the edge subnets. Because each subdomain of the address can be assigned independently of the others, not all edge subnets need to have the same topological structure but can be allowed to match the local topology. (N)-addresses are only used by the (N)-layer elements. The (N)-address space will only name elements of the (N)-subnets (whereas in the previous case, the address space had to name all elements of all subnets). The top layer of a border router has an (N)-layer address, but the middle layer and the top layer of all routers of the core subnet have (N–1)-addresses only. There is no special domain of (N)-addresses for core network routers. There is no requirement that there is a one-to-one correspondence of domain-ids to subnets. A subnet might have a "locally" hierarchical address space of its own.

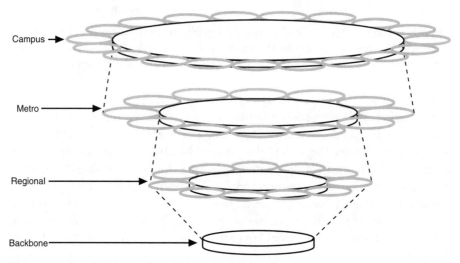

Figure 8-8 A typical hierarchy of layers for a network.

We gain several advantages here: The (N)-address space can be smaller because it is not used for the core of the network. As we will see, we can construct a network such that users (whether hosts or subnets) are assigned addresses from a distinct address space from providers. Also, the (N–1)-address space can be much smaller. Because these core layers are essentially stable transit subnets, their elements will not vary over nearly as a great a range as subnets nearer the edge. This means that shorter addresses are possible. We aren't forced into the tyranny of requiring a single address space. Although each edge subnet is part of the same layer, its routing policies can be independent of all other edge subnets in this layer. (There are constraints that all routing policies must obey to keep them from working at cross-purposes, but within those constraints routing policy within different subnets can be independent.) The routing it must perform is only within its subnet to the border routers. The border router then picks the destination subnet, which is, by definition, one hop away. The PDU is then handed down to the (N–1)-layer for routing across the core subnet. Because every border router at this level is directly connected to every other one, the number of potential next hops could be quite large. This is where a topological mapping between the address spaces of the (N)- and (N–1)-layers can be very advantageous. This corresponds to "choosing the path to the next hop" step. Essentially, we use the topological structure between the (N)- and (N–1)-address spaces to simplify the mapping.

The routing policies of the core (as well as its topology) may be completely different from the edge subnets and done by an entirely separate layer with its own address space. The only routes a router must store are those local to its subnet and any wormholes that terminate in its subnet. (If its underlying connectivity closely reflects the topology, this could be very small.) One needs to calculate routes and determine the next path when traversing a subnet and to know which exit from the level the packet should take; otherwise, the address is sufficient. This, of course, means that failures of links in the default tree (i.e., connecting parents and children) will result in more routes being stored. In any case, the amount of routing information to be exchanged has been drastically reduced. It may even be bounded.

Addressing Topologies for Multiple Hierarchies of Layers

The preceding section described what is basically a single-provider network. Although some networks today might fall into that category, not many do. Some might draw the conclusion that the structure just described could only be applied to such simple networks. This is not the case. Let's see how more complex networks could be accommodated.

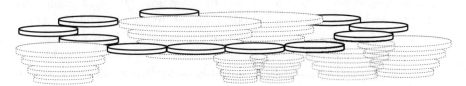

Figure 8-9 Corporate subnets are supported by overlapping and nonoverlapping providers.

Let's take a simple example to illustrate how it might work. Consider a corporation with a number of installations spread around the world. In some cases, there are multiple installations in the same area. The company finds that in some places it must use one provider (and perhaps multiple providers to support certain critical facilities). The key to the solution is that layers are independent. As noted in the preceding section, although there are advantages to aligning the topology of one layer with the address topology of the underlying layers, it is not a requirement. The company's chief network architect has designed a "top" layer to span all the installations with a subnet for each installation or region of installations. As we see in Figure 8-8, within an installation the company is the provider, and if the installation is large enough has its own set of layers. Border routers at the edge of these subnets might connect to other subnets or to one or more supporting providers. Corporate data is encapsulated by the border routers and sent over one of the providers. Only corporate border routers recognize the corporate addressing structure. The providers' addresses appear as points of attachment to the corporate border routers. In areas with several installations, a provider network might provide the subnet underlying the corporate local subnet. (Yes, this does closely resemble a VPN. However, it is much simpler to create and manage.) The corporate network is "floated" over the providers' networks. It is essentially a VPN. Hosts have no access to the address space of the providers. Providers (and corporate users) are the sole owners and are in complete control of their address space.

Modeling the Public Internet

But what about the Internet? How does the public Internet fit into this structure? And most important of all, that all-important question intended to stymie change: What is the transition? Basically, the Internet is just another "organizational" network, a very large one, but nothing special. It is a layer that would lie alongside (at the same rank) as the corporate networks just described. Applications in the corporate network would request application names that were not on the corporate network but on a more "public" network. (The local IPC API would determine which DIF to invoke, the corporate DIF or a public DIF, implicitly also determining what DIFs the requestor has access to.) Provider networks would support this public layer from underneath. Although it would not be necessary, it could be the case that only hosts that want to join a public network would need public addresses. Regardless, hosts have complete control over what applications are accessible by whom and over which DIFs. The provider would immediately map this to an address private to the provider encapsulating the traffic from the hosts. This eliminates the tyranny of the single address space, which requires hosts to be visible to the world whether they want to be or not. In fact, there is no reason why a host or subnet needs to have any "public" addresses at all. Furthermore, depending on one's point of view, NATs are either a seamless degenerate case and occur at nearly every subnet boundary or don't exist at all.

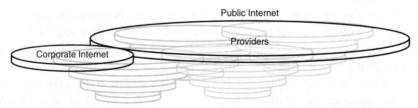

Figure 8-10 The public Internet is just another "top" layer that applications may access. It is supported by multiple providers, as is a corporate network.

Because not all hosts would be serviced by all providers, this brings up how exchange between providers would work. Would packets have to be routed back to the top layer to move between providers? Only in rare cases, where exchange relations did not exist between providers. Otherwise, an exchange address space at a lower layer subscribed to only by providers would provide a common topologically dependent address space for providers. Two points of practicality: 1) It is very likely that a "topologically dependent" multiprovider address space is better described as a geographical topology where the tree would reflect the finest granularity of exchange. And 2), neither the public layer or exchange layers would have to be distinct layers. They could be simply a distinct address space with enrollment, where these addresses were treated as aliases within an existing layer. (Although there might be security advantages to having a distinct layer.) Although common exchange address spaces for different levels of exchange seems to have some advantages, one could easily imagine pairs or groups of providers creating their own exchange address spaces or layers to facilitate their interworking, reflecting corporate alliances.

The other topic that must be considered is transition. There does not need to be a transition at all, only adoption. It is more prudent to simply allow the current Internet to remain in place supported by NIPCA. New applications and services could be developed either for use in the traditional public e-mall like today's Internet or on a modern secure public e-mall, or other networks using NIPCA as appropriate. These new capabilities would take advantage of the greater support for distributed applications, security, and QoS. The public Internet offers the equivalent of POINS (*Plain Old InterNet Service*) and becomes the equivalent of a vast e-mall that one may choose to visit. Other e-malls with other services could develop, as well. For a NIPCA subnet to support a legacy IP network (or any network for that matter) is straightforward. The public Internet is simply a layer above that floats on one or more layers below. The first router of a NIPCA provider subnet would interpret the IP address as a foreign IPC-process name and determine the appropriate exit point from the subnet. Then, it would encapsulate the IP traffic and forward it to an adjoining IP provider. Only the TCP and IP protocols within the legacy architecture would operate. Much of the overhead of the current TCP/IP machinery would only be needed when traversing legacy subnets. The NIPCA subnet would only participate in IP routing at its boundaries with other IP subnets.

The recursive architecture also has the advantage of returning control of networks to the owners who are now able to do more than order more bandwidth and are able to offer new services. Also, as pointed out earlier, network providers and equipment vendors are no longer in the data communications or telecom business, but the distributed IPC business. This opens up new opportunities that the traditional static layering had precluded. At the same time, this model also opens up competition for traditional providers by facilitating the confederations of wireless viral networks being proposed—creating a much more interesting level playing field than the current Internet with its traditional boundaries between providers and users.

Conclusions

We should pause here and step back; we don't want to trip up at this point. We need to be aware that although our recursive architecture didn't seem to change much superficially, it has in fact changed things significantly. Among the things that have changed is that what had been a static absolute structure has shifted to being relative. In the past, our focus has been on "*the* network" or "*the* Internet."

As we explore the implications of the recursive model, we see (as we just have) this emphasis on *the* changes to an emphasis on "*a.*" The preoccupation found in the telephone network and the public Internet with a central addressing scheme and standard resource management strategies is much less important. This common structure will still exist but merely as one among many, rather than in the central role it has played historically. What we saw start here and what we will continue as we explore the properties of this architecture either in this book or elsewhere is that resource management is still key, but we do not have to inflict the "one size fits all" tyranny of the past on the future. In the past, the management of the media (i.e., the "lower layers"), although owned by private entities, was a public affair. Everyone had to do it the same way. As we are seeing emerge here, managing the media is a private affair, and one user may be public. Is this complete independence, total freedom? No, as in the political sphere, with freedom comes responsibility. There will be a need for boundary conditions on how DIFs should behave. Of course, as in the political sphere, we should strive for the minimal set of constraints that yields responsible behavior. And what about those that choose not to play by the rules? Don't join their DIFs. Providers have the option to not carry their traffic. The rules should be self-correcting.

Chapter 9

Multihoming, Multicast, and Mobility

It moves.

—Galileo Galilei

Introduction

In Chapter 5, "Naming and Addressing," we looked at our understanding of naming and addressing. The main insights we took from that were Saltzer's results and our insights about Saltzer as well as naming for applications and application protocols that followed from our understanding of the upper layers in Chapter 4, "Stalking the Upper-Layer Architecture." In Chapter 6, "Divining Layers," we realized that addresses were not quite what we thought they were: not just the names of protocol machines, but identifiers *internal* to a distributed IPC facility. In Chapter 7, "The Network IPC Model," we assembled an architecture model based on what we had learned in the previous chapters, assembling the elements for a complete naming and addressing architecture. Then in Chapter 8, "Making Addresses Topological," we considered what location dependent means in a network and showed how concepts of topology apply to addressing and, when used with a recursive architecture, can create a scalable and effective routing scheme.

Now we must consider a few other addressing-related topics: multihoming, multicast, and mobility. In the process, we will also consider so-called anycast addresses as the contrapositive of multicast. This will also provides the opportunity to apply this model to see what it predicts.

317

Multihoming

As related in the Preface and Chapter 5, the problem of multihoming raised its head very early in the history of networking and the ARPANET. As we saw by naming the point of attachment, the network could not tell that redundant connections went to the same place. To the network, two connections looked like two different hosts (see Figure 9-1). The host could make a choice of which interface to use when it opened a connection, thus providing some degree of load leveling. However, if one link to the router failed, so did all connections over it. Any traffic in transit to that host would be lost. This was a problem that the telephone system had not faced. The solution was clear: A logical address space was required over the physical address space.

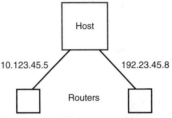

Figure 9-1 The multihoming is when a host has more than one attachment to the network. By having different addresses for the interfaces, the routers can't tell that both interfaces go to the same place.

For some reason, solving this problem never seemed a pressing matter to the Internet or its sponsors, which seems peculiar given that survivability was always given as a major rationale behind the design of the Net and seemingly what the DoD thought it was getting.[1] To recap our earlier brief discussion, many argued against implementing a solution if it imposed a cost on the entire network and because so few systems required multihoming that it was unfair to impose the cost on everyone. Of course, that small number of multihomed hosts were the ones that vast number of PCs needed to access! This lead to a deft piece of political engineering ensuring conditions in which no solution would be acceptable. As we have seen from Saltzer, there is no additional cost to supporting multihoming. Why wasn't Saltzer's paper applied? Who knows? It was certainly cited often enough. One gets the impression that there was more concern with protecting the status quo than making progress.

---

[1] To reiterate, the original justification to *build* the ARPANET was resource-sharing to reduce the cost of research. However, Baran's original report and many subsequent arguments to continue the Net appealed to reliability and survivability.

Others have argued that any multihoming would have to be with different providers on the assumption that one could not get multiple physical paths from the same provider. This, of course, is not true. Companies quite commonly buy redundant paths from the same provider. However, it is wise to physically check and recheck that the distinct paths being paid for actually are distinct, even if they are from different providers. The argument continues that it would be near impossible for the routing algorithms to recover and reroute a PDU destined for an interface on one provider's network to another provider's network. Although it is true that it is likely that either the hop count or the TCP retransmission timer would make delivery moot for PDUs nearing the failed interface, rerouting is not impossible. This argument assumes either that any interruption will be short-lived i.e., similar to the time to reroute or that the rather coarse-grained exchange[2] among providers that has existed in the past will continue to be the case. As local traffic increases,[3] so will the desire of providers to get traffic to other providers off their network at the earliest opportunity.

There was an opportunity during the IPng process to fix this problem. And frankly, many expected it to be fixed then. The developers of CLNP (ISO, 1993) and the OSI reference model had understood the necessity of naming the node rather than the interface. Because the problem had first surfaced in the ARPANET, it was always assumed it would be fixed in IP. So, it was quite surprising when in the IPng discussions it became apparent that so few IETF "experts" understood the fundamentals of network addressing that it would not be fixed. Naming the node was seen as something OSI did, so the Internet should not do it. And the opportunity was lost.

The multihoming problem has been ameliorated by the continuing progress of Moore's law. Faster, cheaper processors and memory have kept the price of routers low enough that the increasing routing load was not painful. The argument was often made against developing a new solution, when the hardware was still quite capable of accommodating the problem. Of course, the problem with this argument is that the longer one waits to fix it, the more painful the day of reckoning. As computers tended more toward workstations and servers, the

---

2 For example, until recently peering for traffic between two Boston area users on different providers took place 500 miles away in Virginia.

3 There seems to be a penchant among humans to believe that things as they are will remain as they are forever. Even though there is overwhelming evidence that this seldom the case, we still insist on it. Therefore, many argue that the granularity of exchange will remain as it is and not become any finer. An increase in local traffic does not necessarily imply new behavior in the network but can result simply from growth. The decision for more exchanges is driven by absolute cost, not relative numbers. Unless the the growth of the network begins to slow which seems unlikely, if anything there will be orders of magnitude more growth.

problem became less critical as the problem evolved from a host being multiply connected to a subnet being multiply connected. The existing methods were better at masking that problem. However, as we have seen, not having a solution for multihoming also applies to routers and increases the number of route calculations combinatorially. Later in this chapter, we will see how solving multihoming simplifies mobility, too.

As one would expect, the Internet has attempted to develop a number of workarounds (a politically correct word for *kludge*) for the lack of a multihoming solution. They run the gamut from being mostly spin to a genuine attempt to address the issue. All have their drawbacks. We consider a couple here before looking at how multihoming is supported by NIPCA. The least satisfying claim of multihoming support has been made by SCTP (RFC 3286, 2002; RFC 2960, 2000). The designers of SCTP use the well-known approach to solving a problem by simply changing the definition to something they can solve. It should be clear from the description of the earlier problem that there is nothing that a transport protocol can do about multihoming. The support SCTP provides is the ability to change the IP address (that is, the *point of attachment* [PoA]) without disrupting the transport connection. This is not possible in TCP because of the pseudo-header. TCP includes the source and destination IP addresses (as well as other fields from the IP header) in the TCP checksum.[4] Hence, should the IP address change, the checksum will fail, and the PDU will be discarded.

If the IP address named the node rather than the PoA, this would not be a problem. Changing the PoA would not affect the pseudo-header. The SCTP solution has no effect on responding to the failure of a PoA. If a PoA should fail, any traffic in transit will be discarded as undeliverable. The sending transport protocol machine would have to be cognizant of the routing change. In the current architectural approach, this would be difficult to do. Unfortunately, we must classify SCTP's claims of supporting multihoming to be more in the nature of marketing than solving the problem.

The situation is quite different with *Border Gateway Protocol* (BGP) (RFC 1654, 1994; Perlman, 1992). BGP is an interdomain routing protocol. Because the multihoming problem is both an addressing issue and a routing problem, BGP at least stands a chance of being able to do something about it. For this discussion, I assume the reader has a basic knowledge of how interdomain routing works. To assume otherwise would require another chapter on that alone. Suffice it to say that BGP adopts a hierarchical approach to routing and groups collections of border routers into what are called *autonomous systems* (ASs). Routing information is exchanged about ASs. The solution to multihoming then is essentially to treat the AS as a node

---

[4]   This is called the pseudo-header. The necessity of this has been questioned for many years. The rationale given was as protection against misdelivered PDUs.

address. The host or site that wants to be multihomed acquires an AS number from its ISP and advertises routes to it via BGP. There are some drawbacks to this. The scope of BGP is the entire Internet. The intent of ASs was to serve as a means for aggregating routes among the thousands of ISPs that make up the public Internet. To also assign an AS to every host or site that wants to be multihomed significantly increases the routing burden on the entire Internet infrastructure. Consequently, some ISPs ignore the smaller ASs (that is, those that correspond to small sites or multihomed hosts), making it the same as if the AS were not multihomed. Clearly, although this approach solves the problem, it has scaling problems and is a band-aid to another problem. ASs are band-aids on top of the path-vector algorithm to allow it to scale to a large flat network like the current public Internet.[5] But the BGP solution does solve the problem by trying to emulate the right answer within the political constraints of current Internet.

Several other band-aids are used to provide solutions for multihoming. All are somewhere between these two. All increase the "parts-count" (that is, the complexity) to solve the problem or a part of it and complicate the solutions of other problems none of them scale, and none are really suitable for production networks, although they are used in them every day. Further, they only solve one particular part of the problem. They don't make anything else easier. There is really no solution other than the one Saltzer proposed a quarter century ago.

Then in late 2006, a new crisis arose (Fuller, 2006; Huston, 2006). Router table size was on the rise again. The cause of the rise was laid at increased multihoming. Now that businesses rely heavily on the Internet, many more find it necessary to be multihomed. Based on estimates of the number of businesses large enough to potentially want multihoming, the conclusion was that we could not expect Moore's law to solve the problem this time. This has led to much discussion and a spate of meetings to find another patch that will keep the problem at bay. The discussion has revolved around the so-called location/identifier split issue mentioned in Chapter 5. This only addresses part of the problem and does not *solve* it. As this book goes to press, a consensus has not been reached on the solution but probably will be by the time the book appears. Although for about ten days there was talk of *solving* the problem, but then more "pragmatic" heads prevailed. It appears that the consensus will be yet another band-aid. (Not to be cynical, but stopgap measures do sell more equipment than solving the problem.)

This is a problem that has been known for more than 35 years and ignored. It would have been much easier to fix 30 years ago or even 15 years ago. Not only fix but solve. What was it that Mrs. McCave said? Ensuring the stability of

---

[5] Some contend that because ASs were originally designed into BGP, it is not a band-aid. ASs are a band-aid on the architecture. Routing is based on addresses carried by PDUs, not by out-of-band control traffic. This has more in common with circuit switching.

the global network infrastructure requires more vision and more proactive deployment than we are seeing. (It is curious that the major trade journals were silent on this topic for a year even though it was the hot topic at every IETF meeting that they covered.) This episode, along with a string of others, calls into question whether the IETF can be considered a responsible caretaker of the infrastructure that the world economy has come to rely on.

The model we have constructed here adopts Saltzer's approach and generalizes it in the context of the recursive model. In keeping with our shift from a static architecture to a relative one, an (N)-address is a node address at the (N)-layer and a PoA address for the (N+1)-layer. In this architecture, the relation is relative (see Figure 9-2). Clearly, multihoming is supported as a consequence of the structure. If we had the right structure to begin with, we would probably never noticed there was a problem.[6] Routing is in terms of node addresses, with path selection (that is, the choice of the path to the next hop) done as a separate step.[7] Unlike the current Internet, NIPCA supports multihoming for both hosts and routers. This in itself significantly reduces the number of routes that must be calculated.[8] Furthermore, the recursive structure ensures that the mechanisms will scale.

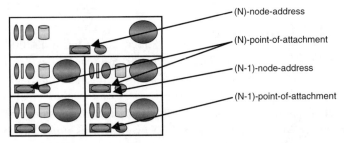

Figure 9-2 A rare layer configuration to illustrate that the relation between node and PoA is relative.

---

[6] This is reminiscent of Needham's short discussion of irrational numbers in Volume III of *Science and Civilization in China*. After recounting the problems irrational numbers caused in Western mathematics, Needham turns to China and says, that because China adopted the decimal system so early, it is not clear they ever noticed there was a problem! They simply carried calculations out far enough for what they were doing and lopped off the rest! Ah! Ever practical!

[7] These separate steps are in terms of route calculation to generate the forwarding table, not in forwarding itself. However, this does imply that path calculation (that is, changing the path to the next hop) could be done to update the forwarding table without incurring a route calculation.

[8] Strictly speaking, current algorithms must calculate all the possible routes and then aggregate the common ones. Various workarounds have been introduced to avoid this at the cost of additional complexity. By calculating on node addresses rather than points of attachments, the bulk of the duplication is never generated in the first place.

The problems described earlier need not exist. The problem of coarse exchange between providers that we referred to earlier is driven primarily by "cost" (where *cost* is not just capital cost, but also the cost associated with meeting customer expectations of performance). As long as the amount of traffic for other providers is sufficiently low within an area that the cost of not exchanging within the area is cost-effective, providers won't bother. If the amount of traffic increases, especially intraregion traffic for the other providers, the advantage of finer-grained exchange would gain advantage. Finer-grained exchanges might not be driven by the volume of traffic but by the need to ensure less jitter for voice and video traffic. Even so, a move to finer granularity of exchange is not helped by the fact that in general an inspection of the IP address will only indicate to a router what provider the address belongs to, not where it is. The application of topological addresses, as described at the end of Chapter 8, would further facilitate a move to finer granularity of exchange and would also facilitate rerouting to multihomed sites. Accommodating more fine-grained exchange in the address topology costs very little, and it doesn't have to be used, but it does plan for the future in a manner unlike any from the past.

Multicast Architecture

Introduction to the Multicast Problem

Multicast transmission has captured the imagination of networking researchers almost from the start of networking. Multicast is the ability to send a single PDU to a selected set of destinations, a generalization of broadcast (where *broadcast* is the ability for a sender to send a PDU that is received by *all* destinations on the network). Clearly, this derives from the wireless or multiaccess broadcast model. For the multiaccess media, the PDU generally has a special address value that indicates that the PDU is for all destinations. Because the media is multiaccess, all stations on the media see the broadcast or multicast address and determine whether to receive the PDU. This ancestry has led some researchers to assume multicast to be defined as purely one-to-many communication, and to coin the term *multipeer* to represent the more general many-to-many group communication one might require for various sorts of collaborative systems. We will use *multicast* for both unless there is a need to emphasize the difference.

Clearly, for inherently broadcast media, multicast is straightforward. But, multicast becomes a much more interesting problem in traditional wired network. Here it is generally implemented by computing a minimal spanning tree over the graph of the network generally rooted at the sender (see Figure 9-3). A PDU sent by the sender traverses the spanning tree being replicated only at the branching nodes of the tree. This saves considerable bandwidth. To send the same PDU to M destinations would normally require M PDUs to be sent. With multicast, M PDUs are delivered to M destinations, but the entire network does not have to carry the load of all M PDUs. Distributed spanning-tree algorithms were developed quite early. However, multipeer changes the problem: Rather than a different spanning tree rooted at each sender, one must find a single spanning tree that is optimal for the group of senders.

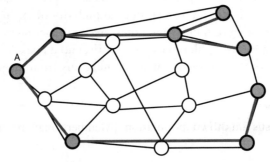

Figure 9-3 A multicast spanning tree rooted at A to the set of all members of the multicast group.

Although many proponents wax eloquent about multicast as a new and different distributed computing model, in the end it is ultimately a means for conserving bandwidth. Its primary importance is to the network provider in allowing it to carry more traffic using fewer resources and manage it better. The advantage to the user is minimal.

This is where the simplicity of the problem ends. There are a myriad of complications, whose intellectual challenge has generated extensive literature on the subject. However, multicast has not found much adoption outside the research community. The complexity and overhead of setting up multicast groups combined with the precipitous drop in bandwidth costs have continued to make the brute-force approach of sending M copies over M connections acceptable. As applications that could use multicast continue to grow, however, especially in the area of multimedia, we can expect that even with the advances in fiber, the need to make more effective use of bandwidth will reassert itself, and the complexity and cost of managing M pairwise connections will exceed the cost of managing multicast groups; so, multicast may find greater use. Of course, anything that can be done to simplify multicast deployment can only help.

Most of the research has concentrated on particular applications and provided solutions for each particular problem, with little or no consideration of how that solution would work along with other multicast applications with different requirements. However, because multicast is primarily a benefit to the provider rather than the user, a provider is going to want a solution that covers many multicast applications. If every class of application that could use multicast requires a different solution, this would be a nonstarter. We will not even try to survey the literature[9] but will refer to key developments as we proceed. We want to use this experience in traditional networks as data and hold it up to the structures we have developed here to see how it either improves or simplifies or complicates the problem.

The first problem with multicast (one ignored by most researchers) is that there are so many forms of it. It is fairly easy to construct a list of characteristics, such as the following:

Centralized versus decentralized (Multicast or multipeer?)

Static versus dynamic population (Can the membership change with time?)

Known versus unknown population (Members may be unknown with wireless?)

Isotropic versus anisotropic (Do all members behave the same?)

Quorum (Is a minimum membership required?)

Reliable versus unreliable

Simplex versus duplex

And so on

Within these characteristics are multiple policies that might be used, making the range of potential protocols quite large. One would not expect a single solution to effectively accommodate the entire range. But to create specific solutions for specific applications would lead to proliferation and complexity within the network. Providers are not enthusiastic about introducing another parallel routing system, let alone many. But perhaps not all combinations would find applications. Perhaps a small number would cover the major applications.

The latter assumption turns out to be wrong. One of the myriad standards organizations to look at multicast actually took the time to explore the matrix

---

[9] Unfortunately, most of the literature must be classed as more thesis material than truly concerned with advancing understanding of multicast.

of multicast characteristics. It expected to find clusters of applications for some parameters and others that clearly would not occur. It fully expected to find that a small set of characteristics covered the great majority of cases (a common result in engineering, allowing the designer to concentrate on the important combinations rather than a fully general solution). Although there were a very few combinations for which it was unlikely to find an application, quite likely scenarios could be found for the vast majority of combinations. Not a welcome result.

The Multicast Model

Just with the connection/connectionless problem, we need to consider the service of of multicast and the function of multicast separately. Multicast is viewed as communication with a group (a set of users). Some models assume that all participants are members of the group (that is, multipeer). Others assume that the group is an entity that others outside the group communicate with (that is, multicast)—in a sense, unicast[10] communication with a group. This difference will be most pronounced in the consideration of multicast naming (see the following section). In the literature on multicast, one will generally find a service model that differs from the model for unicast communication. The sequence of API calls required is different. The application must be aware of whether it is doing multicast.

In the traditional unicast model, communication is provided by primitives to connect, send, receive, and disconnect, executed in that order. (Here we have replaced *connect* with *allocate* to include initiation of connectionless communication.) In multicast, the service primitives are generally connect, join, leave, send, receive, and disconnect.

The connect primitive creates the group and makes the initiator a member. Join and leave are used by members of the group to dynamically join and leave the group. Disconnect is used to terminate participation in the group. There is some variation in how the initiator may leave the group without terminating it. This, of course, creates a different sequence of interactions than unicast. The application must be cognizant of whether the communication is unicast or multicast, just as we saw earlier that the user had to be cognizant of whether the communication was connection or connectionless. In this model, a multicast group of two members is different from a unicast communication. We would clearly prefer a model in which one collapses cleanly into the other. Or more strongly, why should the application have to be aware of multicast at all?

---

10 *Unicast* being the term coined to denote traditional pairwise communications to contrast it with multicast.

But notice that the primary purpose of the "connect" primitive is creating the group, essentially creating sufficient shared state within the network to allow an instance of communication to be created. This is what we have called the enrollment phase. In fact, if the service model is recast so that creating the group is an enrollment function, join and leave become synonymous with connect and disconnect. The initiator would issue a primitive (enroll) to create the multicast group and in a separate operation initiate communication with the group with a join/connect/allocate/attach. Hence, the interaction sequence (that is, the partial state machine associated with the service interaction) is the same for multicast as for the unicast and connectionless cases. In fact, the only difference would be that the destination naming parameter would name a set of names rather than a single name (or is that a set of one element?). Furthermore, it is consistent with our model and eliminates another special case. We have found an effective single model for all three "modes" of communication: connectionless, connection, multicast.

Multicast "Addressing"

As always, the problems surrounding naming and addressing are subtle and often less than obvious. There have been two models for multicast addressing. What has become the generally accepted definition is that a multicast "address" is the name of a set of addresses, such that referencing the set is equivalent to referencing all members of the set.

Initially, the Internet adopted a different definition. The early Internet multicast protocols viewed a multicast address as essentially an ambiguous or nonunique address. Simply viewed, several entities in the network had the same address so that a PDU with a multicast address was delivered to all interfaces with that address. This is an attempt to mimic the semantics of broadcast or multicast addresses on a LAN: Multiple interfaces on a LAN have the same (multicast) address assigned to them. As a PDU propagates on the LAN with an address (of whatever kind), the interfaces detect the PDU and read its address. If the address belongs to this interface, the PDU is read. In effect, if more than one station on the Ethernet has the same address, it is multicast.

This is straightforward with LANs, but for other technologies it means we have to ensure that every node sees every PDU. This means that flooding is about the only strategy that can be used. Flooding is generally considered pathological behavior. Instead of reducing the load on the network, it increases it. This is not good. Essentially, multicast in this model is broadcast, which is then pruned. This defeats the advantage of multicast of saving bandwidth in the network. It does retain the advantage that the sender only sends the PDU once rather than M times. Not much of a savings. Why can't we use a spanning tree as with other schemes? A spanning tree would require a correspondence between a normal address and the multicast group name. For all intents and purposes, this would bring us back to the set model of the address stated earlier. Flooding as a distribution mechanism does not scale and is not greeted by providers with enthusiasm.

The other peculiarity of this early Internet model was that it was built around what we referred to earlier as "unicast communication to a group." The sender is generally not part of the group but is sending PDUs to a group. This would seem to presume a simplex communication model—best suited for a "limited broadcast" model rather than the kind of more general distributed computing models required by multipeer applications. Also, the inability to resolve the multicast address to a unicast address has negative security implications. Given its problems, it is odd that this definition ever arose considering the earliest work (Dalal, 1977) on multicast used the set definition of a multicast address.

We must consider one other somewhat pedantic issue related to multicast addresses: They aren't addresses. As we have defined them, addresses are location dependent. Multicast "addresses" are names of a set. The elements of the set are addresses, but the name of the set cannot be.

The concept of location dependent that we wanted was to know whether two addresses were "near" each other—so that we knew which direction to send them and whether we could aggregate routes. Although one could attribute the smallest scope of the elements of the set with the concept of a "location," this seems to be not only stretching the spirit of the concept, but also not really helpful either. At first blush, one thinks of nicely behaved sets and how the concept of location would apply to them. But it doesn't take long to come up with quite reasonable "monsters" for which it is much less clear how the concept would apply. It is far from clear what utility this would have. The most location dependence a multicast address could have would have to be common to the entire set. But this property will arise naturally from the analysis of the members of the set and in the computation of the spanning tree. It might be of some utility to nonmembers attempting to communicate with the group, but here again this would have only limited utility to route PDUs to some idea of the general area of the group (if there is one). Multicast distribution relies on one of two techniques, either some form of spanning tree or the underlying physical layer is inherently multiaccess, a degenerate spanning tree. In either case, what a sender external to the group needs to know is where the root of the tree is, or where it can gain access to the group (not some vague idea of the area the group is spread over). There is not much point in having a multicast address (that is, location dependent). They are simply names of sets of addresses.

The conclusion we are drawn to is that multicast addresses, although they may be represented by elements from an address space, are semantically names. We will use the term *multicast name* throughout to remind ourselves that these are not location-dependent names (that is, not addresses). To be very precise and in keeping with the model we have developed here, the application would have a multicast application name defined as a set of application names. We have already defined this: a distributed-application-name. Interesting, isn't it? This would be passed in an open request to the DIF, which would allocate a multicast name from the DIFs address space. This multicast name would name the set of addresses to which the applications were bound. (Rules for adding or deleting addresses from the set would be associated with the set.)

Multicast Distribution

The primary focus of multicast research has been on solving the multicast distribution problem at the network layer for networks without multiaccess physical media. Many approaches have been tried, including brute-force flooding. But most of the emphasis has been on distributed algorithms for generating spanning trees. Not only is this much more efficient, it is also an intellectually challenging problem. The first attempt to solve this was Yogen Dalal's Ph.D. thesis (1977). Since then there are have been many theses and papers. Although there has been some emphasis on pure multicast (that is, a single sender to a group), much of the interest has been on "multipeer," where each member of the group would be communicating with the group. This has led to several problems:

1. Scaling the techniques to support large groups

2. Maintaining an optimal or near-optimal spanning tree when the members of the group change

3. Reducing the complexity of multipeer by not requiring the computation of a separate spanning tree for every member of the group

This has led to a number of standard multicast protocols being proposed: DVMRP (RFC 1075, 1988), PIM (RFC 2362, 1998; Estrin et al., 1996) and CBT (RFC 2189, 1998). The focus of these algorithms is to find optimal spanning trees given multiple senders in the group. Hence, the root of the spanning tree is not at one of the senders, but at some "center of gravity" for the group. The problem then becomes finding that center of gravity. We will not review these techniques here. They are more than adequately covered in numerous textbooks. The major problem confronted by most of these is the complexity of the computation in current networks with large groups.

Sentential Naming Operations and Their Resolution

This would be a good place to consider how these names work. The heading of this section uses the term *Sentential* because we will be concerned with the two forms of sentential naming that we find: universal and existential.[11] We have just covered the "universal" naming operator (that is, multicast). We will also consider the "existential" naming operator, known colloquially in the field as an "anycast" name.[12] We can define an anycast name as the name of a set such that when the name is referenced one element of the set is returned according to some rule associated with the set.

In both cases, the use of the sentential name resolves sooner or later to an address. This then raises the question of when does this name resolution take place. With the anycast name, it may be immediate or at various points along the path, whereas with a multicast name it will be done at several points along the way. We would like an answer that minimizes special cases. This leads to the following:

The rule associated with the set is applied when the forwarding table is created to yield a list of addresses that satisfy the rule. When a PDU with a sentential destination address is evaluated at each relay, it is then sent to the elements of the list. (Of course, a list can have one element.)

The sentential names are placeholders for the set and its associated rule. At each relay (hop), the set is evaluated according to the rule. For anycast, this means selecting an address from the set and forwarding toward that address. For multicast, it means selecting the addresses downstream on this spanning tree and forwarding a copy of the PDU toward all of them. Given topological addresses, the addresses in the multicast set can be ordered into a virtual spanning tree based on the topology of the address space. (The structure of the addresses would imply a spanning tree or, more precisely, which addresses were near or beyond others.) This then simplifies the task of each node, which given its own address knows where it fits in the spanning tree of that multicast set and which branches it must forward copies of the PDU on. In fact, with a reasonable topological address space, the addresses of the nodes of the spanning tree can be approximated. This implies that specialized multicast protocols are unnecessary. We still need the distributed spanning-tree algorithms. The definition of the sets will have to be distributed to each member of the DIF along with the policies

---

[11]   The term used in symbolic logic to refer to these two operators. See, for example, Carnap (1958).

[12]   They are called anycast "addresses" in the literature, but they are names of sets; and the same arguments we just used to argue that multicast "addresses" are not addresses apply to anycast, too.

associated with it and the spanning-tree algorithm applied. This information is then used to generate entries in the forwarding table. The only difference being that a forwarding table's lookup results comprise a list, admittedly a list with one element most of the time, but a list just the same.

Sentential addresses are used in building the forwarding table. The rule is only evaluated when the forwarding table is generated. Any changes in network conditions that would change the outcome of the rule are equivalent to the same conditions that would cause a recalculation of the forwarding table. In the multicast case, this means determining to which branches of the spanning tree the PDU is to be forwarded. For an anycast address, this means the PDU is forwarded toward the address returned by the rule associated with the set. (This of course implies that the rule could yield different results at different nodes along the route. This envisions a concept of anycast that is both simpler and more powerful than allowed by IPv6.)

Unicast is a subset of multicast, but multicast devolves to unicast.

Multicast Distribution in a Recursive Architecture

A multicast group at layer N, (N)-G, is defined as a set of addresses, $\{(N)$-$A_i\}$, such that a reference to (N)-G by a member of the group yields all elements of $\{(N)$-$A_i\}$. It is sometimes useful to consider traditional "unicast" data transfer as a multicast group of two. (N)-G is identified by an (N)-group-address, (N)-GA.

$$(N)\text{-group-name } \forall \ (N)\text{-}A_i \ni (N)\text{-}A_i \in G = \{(N)\text{-}A_i\}$$

The order of an (N)-G (that is, the number of elements in the set) is $|\{(N)$-$A_i\}|$ or $|(N)$-$G|$.

Although there is no logical reason that the set cannot contain a group name, there are practical reasons to be cautious about doing so (for example, duplicates).

The primary purpose of multicast is to reduce load on the network for those applications that require the same data be delivered to a number of addresses. Several mechanisms are used to accomplish this ranging from brute-force flooding to the more subtle forms of spanning trees. These spanning trees may be rooted at the sender(s) or at some intermediate point, sometimes referred to as the "center of gravity" or "core" of the group.

A minimal spanning tree is an acyclic graph $T(n,a)$ consisting of n nodes and a arcs imposed on a more general graph of the network. This tree represents the minimal number of arcs required to connect (or span) all members of (N)-G. The leaf or terminal nodes of the tree are the elements of the set $\{(N)$-$A_i\}$. The nonterminal nodes are intermediate relays in the (N)-layer. Let's designate such a spanning tree for the group, G as $T_G(n,a)$. Then the bounds on the number of nodes in the spanning tree are given by the following:

$$\min |T_G(n,a)| = |\{(N)\text{-}A_i\}|$$

$$\max |T_G(n,a)| = |\{(N)\text{-}A_i\}| + (d\text{-}1)\, |\{(N)\text{-}A_i\}|$$

where d = diameter of the network

Let (N)-B be a group name and (N)-A_i be the addresses in the group, then ∃ a spanning tree, (N)-$T_B(A_i, c_i)$ which covers (N)-B.

$$\forall\, (N)\text{-}A_i \in (N)\text{-}B, \exists\, (N-1)\text{-}A_i \ni F{:}(N)\text{-}A_i \Rightarrow (N-1)\,A_i \text{ and } (N-1)\text{-}A_i \in$$
$$(N-1)\text{-}G_i$$

Or some elements of (N)-B such that (N)-A_i is bound to $(N-1)$-A_i. This binding creates a group at layer $(N-1)$ in each of these subnets. In current networks, F is 1:1, ∀ A_i. This may or may not be the case in general.

$$\forall\, (N-1)\text{-}A_i \exists\, m \text{ subnets, } S_i \ni (N-1)\text{-}A_i \supseteq S_i$$

If $|\,(N-1)\text{-}G\,| = k$, then ∃ m $S_i \ni \forall (N-1)\text{-}A_i \in (N-1)\text{-}G$, m ≤ k

As we saw previously, to the user of layer N there is one "subnet," a user of layer (N), that appears directly connected to all other users of that layer. From within the (N)-layer, there are m subnets connected by the (N)-relays. A subset of these (N)-relays form the nonterminal nodes of the spanning tree, (N)-$T(A_i,c_i)$. Thus, there are k addresses that belong to m subnets with m ≤ k. This decomposes the (N)-$T_B(A_i,c_i)$ into m(N-1)-$T_B(A_i,c_i)$.

Let $\{(N\text{-}1)\text{-}A_i\}_j$ be the (N-1)-G_j of addresses in subnet S_j

At the m(N-1)-layers, ∃(N-1)-$G_j \ni \{(N-1)\text{-}A_i\}_j$

(N)-GA is supported by the services of the $(N-1)$-layers (subnets) that form a covering of the (N)-layer. A subset of this covering provides services in two distinct ways (see Figure 9-4):

1. The p end subnets, G^e_j, $\{(N-1)\text{-}A_i\}_j$

2. The m − p transit subnets, G^t_j, that connect the p end subnets

The spanning tree of the end subnets would be rooted at a border relay at which it enters the subnet. The (N)-GA is supported by p $(N-1)$-Ge and (m–p)G.

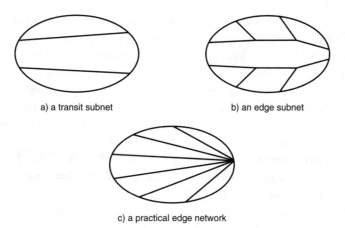

a) a transit subnet   b) an edge subnet

c) a practical edge network

Figure 9-4 In a recursive architecture, multicast groups decompose into two cases: a) transit subnets that are unicast, and b) edge subnets, which use spanning trees. Practically, however, the latter case is simpler **if c)** unicast flows from the border router are used with no internal branching (making multicast distribution a subset of unicast routing.)

Note there may be more than one such entry point and thus more than one independent spanning tree for the same group in the same subnet.

As one moves down through the layers, the number of end subnets decreases, the degree of branching decreases, and the number of transit subnets increases.

Multiplexing Multicast Groups

Multicast has always been considered such a hard problem that multiplexing multicast groups for greater efficiency was just too much to consider. But given an approach that allows us to decompose the problem, multiplexing becomes fairly straightforward. There are two cases that must be considered: transit groups and end groups.

Assume layer N has m subnets. Any group from layer $(N+1)$ will be decomposed into n segments $n \leq m$ consisting of p end groups and q transit groups, $n = p + q$. Suppose there are k such groups at the $(N+1)$-layer, each with its own value of n, p, and q.

The number of subnets is much smaller than the number of hosts participating in the group, as is the number of (N)-relays. Therefore, it is likely that there will be a number of transit groups that have flows between the same (N)-relays. These are candidates for multiplexing.

A transit group is distinguished by connecting only (N)-relays. A transit subnet group consists of q pairwise connections, where $1 \leq q \leq m$. The decision to multiplex them will be no different than for any other unicast flow.

An end group is rooted at (N)-relay, and leaf nodes are either end systems or other (N)-relays. Multiplexing the spanning trees of the end groups is more difficult. One could require that the trees be the same, but this would not lead to many opportunities to multiplex. It would be better to allow similar trees to be multiplexed, the only question is what does "similar" mean.

Here we have a number of spanning trees rooted at the same (N)-relay. To multiplex; we will want (N)-G^e with similar if not the same tree. Let's define λ-similarity, as λ is the number of leaf nodes of the $G_1 \ldots G_k$ have in common. Suppose $G_1 \ldots G_k$ are the end groups of an (N)-subnet of distinct (N+1)-groups, then

$$\forall \ G_i \in G_1 \ldots G_k < \lambda \text{ then } G_i \text{ may be multiplexed.}$$

Then construct a spanning tree for $>> G_1 \ldots G_k$. This will cause some PDUs to be delivered to addresses that are not members of the group and so be discarded. (Other QoS parameters may cause G_i to be multiplexed with a different (N)-G_j.)

Reliable Multicast

One of the first problems researchers took up along with multicast distribution was multicast transport. If the multicast distribution algorithms were the network layer, then what did the mechanisms look like for a multicast transport protocol to provide end-to-end reliability? It was a natural topic to pursue. Can we adapt protocols like TCP to provide reliable multipeer? This has been a favorite topic with tens of proposals, a great thesis generator. However, this proves to be a less-than-straightforward problem.

Just defining what service multicast transport provides is problematic before one even gets to considering the mechanisms for providing it. Consider the following issues:

- What is done if one member falls behind and can't accept data fast enough? Is everyone slowed down to the same rate? Is data to the slow ones dropped? Is the slow member dropped? Is data for the slow one buffered? For how long?

- Is retransmission to all members of the group or just the ones that either nack'ed or timed out? If the latter, doesn't this defeat the advantage of multicast? By making it into (m-1) unicast connections?

- What happens if one member doesn't receive something after several retries? Drop the member? Terminate the whole group?

- Can multiple senders send at the same time? If so, what order is maintained if there are multiple senders in the group? Relative? Partial ordering? Total ordering? No order?

- If the group has dynamic membership and a new member joins, at what point does it start receiving data? If it leaves and rejoins, is the answer different?

The list can go on and on. It doesn't take long to realize that most, if not all, of these may be desirable by some application. The design of a single protocol or even a small number of related protocols satisfying the range indicated by these questions is a daunting problem. Of course, the strategy of separating mechanism and policy developed here can be used to address this at least partially.

The problems don't stop there. A prime characteristic of error- and flow-control protocols is that they have feedback mechanisms. Feedback is inherently pairwise. This brings us to the other problem with multicast transport: ack implosion. What is the point of multipeer distribution if the error- and flow-control protocol is going to impose a service of (m–1) pairwise connections? The senders must keep separate state information for each receiver in the group so that it knows who has received what and how fast it can send. But weren't we trying to avoid the burden of keeping track of each member of the group? If each sender must maintain state for each receiver, multicast will reduce load on the network but not for the sending systems.

Acknowledgment and flow control are feedback mechanisms and thus return information to the sender. For a multicast group, this means that for a group of *m* members (m – 1) acks or credits will need to be sent back for the sending protocol machine to process. Do these pairwise acks destroy the group nature of the communication? One can easily imagine that for large values of *m* the sender could become overwhelmed by feedback PDUs. (*Ack implosion* has become the shorthand term for this problem, even though it involves both ack and flow-control information.) Does this mean there needs to be flow control on the flow-control PDUs? Many proposals have considered techniques that aggregate the control messages as they return up the spanning tree (thus reducing the number of control PDUs the sender must see). In traditional architectures, this was problematic. The aggregation function of the transport protocol required knowledge of the spanning tree in the layer below. Furthermore, the transport protocol is relaying and processing PDUs at intermediate points. Doesn't aggregating break the "end-to-end"-ness of the transport protocol? What happens if an aggregating mode fails? Also, does the process of aggregating impose a policy with respect to systems that fall behind, and so on? It also raises the question of whether it really saves anything. Is this a step back to

X.25-like hop-by-hop error and flow control? It reduces the number of PDUs received, but the amount of information must be close to the same. Consider the following:

What the sender needs to know is what sequence number is being ack'ed and by whom. The aggregated ack might contain the sequence number and the list of addresses and port-ids corresponding to all of the receivers who have ack'ed this. The list can't be assured to be a contiguous range, so the aggregated Ack PDU must be able to carry the list of port-ids, perhaps representing ranges as well as individual ports. This reduces the number of control messages being delivered (probably fixed format), but it is doubtful it reduces the processing burden or reduces the memory requirements. Nor have we considered the delay and processing overhead incurred by aggregating. Are acks held at interim spanning tree nodes to await PDUs that it can be aggregated with? Does this mean that these nodes must keep track of which acks have been forwarded? Or one could assume that each node collects all downstream acks, and so only a single ack for all the members is finally delivered to the sender. Now we are up against the slow responder. This implies a fixed timeout interval for all members so that any member that didn't respond within the time interval was assumed to have not gotten the PDU and is a candidate for retransmission or being dropped from the group. As one moved in the reverse direction up the spanning tree, the timeout for each node would have to be progressively longer to allow for the delay by nodes lower in the tree. This could lead to much longer retransmission timeouts than seen for pairwise connections, but that might be acceptable. Do retransmissions go to everyone or just the ones that didn't report? This strategy is possible for acknowledgment, but flow control is a bit different. What does one do about members who are slow? A member may be delayed a considerable amount of time. Is traffic stopped by one member of the group? Etc. etc.

As you can see, the questions surrounding a reliable multicast protocol are legion. Those proposed in the literature have generally been designed for a specific environment where specific choices can be made. Separating mechanism and policy can cover some of this variability. It remains to be seen whether it can or should cover it all. In the structure developed here, the error- and flow-control protocol and the relaying and multiplexing process are in the same DIF and can share information. Because the EFCP is structurally two protocols, the Control PDUs could be routed separately from the Transfer PDUs. One spanning tree could be used to support data transfer, while a separate parallel spanning tree supports the control flow with protocol machines at each node aggregating them as they percolate back up the tree.

In the NIPCA structure, this is not a layer violation because the EFCP and relaying process are in the same DIF/layer. In fact, it actually fits rather nicely. However, a major design consideration of EFCPs to ensure end-to-end integrity is that its PDUs are interpreted only at the "ends," not by intermediate points. Aggregating acks (and credits) is not a "layer violation," but simply combining PDUs, a well-accepted mechanism of the relaying and multiplexing function of a layer. However, to do more (that is, combining the semantics of the acks and credits to reduce the number of actual PDUs) does raise questions about the end-to-end integrity of the protocol. Most multicast applications can tolerate some loss (that is, streaming video or voice). One might consider a stock ticker, but given the timeliness of the data it could not tolerate the retransmission delays either. Assuming that there are applications that will arise for reliable, it seems that we need to review and possibly refine the theory of EFCPs with respect to the degrees of integrity and the role of intermediate processing.

Interpreting multicast and anycast in terms of a distributed IPC architecture makes many things more clear. We have been able to integrate multicast into the operation of the layer such that the application sees the same interface at the layer boundary. The only difference is that when the application requests communication, it passes the name of a set rather than the name of an application. Of course, we could interpret it as always being a set—just that often the set has one element. We have also found that it is fairly easy to architecturally integrate multicast and anycast operation into routing. Given that the set of potential routes from any given router is a spanning tree, future research will undoubtedly increase the degree of integration. We also found that in a recursive architecture, multicast can be limited to border routers and hosts, further simplifying the problem and opening the door to multiplexing multicast trees, which not only allows greater transmission efficiency but also reduces the complexity of its support.

NIPCA also sheds light on the nature of reliable multicast. We won't be so bold as to say that NIPCA solves all the problems. It is fairly clear that as long as tightly coupled feedback mechanisms are used to create reliable protocols, the problems of reliable multicast are inherent. The separation of mechanism and policy does make it possible to accommodate much if not all of the range of reliable multicast. The structure of the DIF (three loci of processing with different duty cycles) would appear to neatly accommodate ack aggregation at the border routers. (Similarly, I will use *ack aggregation* as a shorthand for aggregating ack or flow-control feedback information being returned to the sender.) As we saw, we could map multicast data transfer and multicast "control" to separate spanning trees. In this case, normal operation would allow for aggregating acks and credits at they flow back up the tree to the sender.

What is questionable is doing any more "compaction" (that is, having a single ack reflect the ack of several ends). This would seem to drag the model to a hop-by-hop paradigm, rather than our preferred end-to-end paradigm for error control. Why is this bad? Partly because this is error control in adjacent layers with nominally the same scope. Why do the same thing twice? What did the layer below miss that the layer above is detecting? This is imposing a policy about the nature of ack and credit across multiple endpoints. This may be the desired policy. And we can create a very reasonable rationale, such as "any policy that can be performed by the source that can be distributed transparently among the IPC processes in the DIF." In other words, any operation can be performed on EFCP Control PDUs that does not modify the state vector. Unicast is then a degenerate case where the function is null.

This would seem to avoid the concerns that ack aggregation impairs the "end-to-end" nature of an EFCP. Any "impairment" of end-to-end-ness (determining what to do with delayed acks, and so on) is a matter of policy, and policy is a parameter selected based on what the application has requested, and any action that changes the state vector is only being done at the "ends." In terms of assembling a theory, we would like a better rationale. Was our traditional view of the end-to-end-ness of an EFCP—that acks are simply relayed to the source and not interpreted along the way—focused on a special case? Is multicast the general case that we must consider. Being able to relate such rationale to a consequence of the fundamental structure would be more assuring that there was truly some basis for such rationale and it wasn't just an expedient. Is this it?

But at the same time, the wide range of special cases generated by reliable multicast seems to indicate that they are all kludges and multicast is purely a routing and distribution phenomena. Recognizing that this is computer science, so that most anything can be *made* to work, one still is unsure whether feedback mechanisms should not be part of multicast.

Mobility

Mobility has become a hot topic in networking. Although mobility does present some new issues, they turn out to be either more of the same or requirements to be more explicit and formal about things we were already doing or should have been. There are basically three common forms of mobility:

1. Hosts or edge subnets mobile relative to a fixed network for example, traditional cellular networks

2. Hosts or subnets mobile with respect to each other for example, ad hoc networks

3. Applications that move from host to host regardless of whether the hosts are fixed or mobile

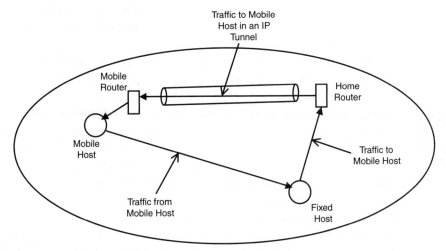

Figure 9-5 Mobile IP requires an IP tunnel to be configured.

Mobile network systems appear more difficult than they are because we didn't finish building the basic architecture before moving on to consider mobility. Mobile applications by their nature are confined to the periphery of a network or to relatively small standalone networks or subnets. But as always, many view mobility as an opportunity for new special cases, rather than as an application of a general model. This is not helped by the way that mobility must be supported in the Internet owing to its incomplete addressing architecture.

Mobility in IP and Cellular Networks

To support mobility in IP (see Figure 9-5; Perkins, 1998), a router in the "home subnet" of a mobile host is assigned the role of a "home router." The mobile host's IP address, S, in that subnet continues to identify the mobile host; but when it moves into the new subnet, it is assigned a local IP address, M, in that subnet. An IP tunnel is created between the home router and a router in the new subnet with a direct connection to the mobile host. When PDUs are sent to the mobile host with the IP address S, they are routed to the "home router"; the home router knows the mobile host is not where it is supposed to be; so the PDU is encapsulated and sent down the IP tunnel to the foreign subnet. There the PDUs are forwarded on the interface that connects the mobile host to the foreign router. The foreign router knows that traffic from the tunnel is to be forwarded to the IP address of the mobile host that is on a known local interface of the foreign router. Traffic from the mobile host to the sender can take a more direct route or can be funneled back through the tunnel. The mobile host's IP address is only used by the home router and by the mobile router. These two know the mobile host was or is directly connected to them. They must know that this address requires special handling.

Mobile routers and home routers are special cases and would have to be identified in advance. Furthermore, there are two single points of failure: the home router and the foreign router. If either fails, communication is lost. This approach is more suitable for "static" mobility, where a mobile host is removed from the network at one point and reattached at another temporarily. It is less suitable for roaming, where the mobile host is moving and the IP tunnel from the home router has to follow it. (It is done, but relies on the fact that MAC addresses have greater scope than IP addresses and don't change.)

Why is IP mobility so complicated? As we have seen, in the Internet architecture the IP address is the only means for identifying anything. Well-known sockets are extensions of IP addresses and not independent of them (although there is a global location-independent host name that is mapped to the IP address by DNS). For purposes of mobility, domain names are synonyms for the IP address; they do not name a distinct object. The update time for DNS, averaging 8 to 12 hours globally, is far too long for updating IP as a point-of-attachment address.

The telephone system initially had a similar problem when they began to consider mobile phone service. As noted earlier, in the telephone system the phone number was the name of the wire coming from the central office to the phone. This would clearly not work for a mobile system. The handset would need to establish communication with a cell tower. As the handset moved, the cellular system would have to follow the handset and hand it off from tower to tower. The phone number would have to name the handset because that was what one would call. (Already we are in better shape.) The cell phone system would need a distinct address space for the cell tower antennas. The telephone number identified the handset (a node address) that was communicating at a lower layer with a cell tower (PoA). As the cell phone moved around its area, it communicates with one cell tower after another, often to more than one at a time (multihoming). It is doubtful the cell phone developers realized that in networking terms they were being forced to make a distinction between node address and PoA address, but they were.[13]

Cell phone use was initially restricted to a local area, just as the phone system was in its early days. If a cell phone user left his "home" area, special arrangements had to be made for "roaming" (for an additional charge). Entries were

---

[13] Odd that the staid, conservative, old-model telephone carriers could part with tradition, but the innovative, visionary Internet has not been able to.

made in a special roaming database called the *Visitor Locator Register* (VLR). As cell phone use increased, so did the number of people needing to roam. Travelers making special arrangements every time they were about to jump on a plane quickly became unworkable. Cellular systems needed to allow any phone to roam outside its home area without human intervention.

Clearly people's phone numbers couldn't change, but cell phone providers needed a more effective way of finding the handset when it wasn't where it was suppose to be. This meant that the phone number in the handset would not indicate where the phone was. The phone numbers would become location independent. (We have seen this before.) Without disrupting their customers, the cell phone operators jacked up their architecture (again), making node addresses of phone numbers, application names, and other newly assigned numbers. Contrary to how this might have looked at the time, this wasn't that big of a change. The phone system had already been purposely confusing phone numbers as both node addresses and location-independent names (that is, application names) with 800 numbers and 411 and 911 numbers. In one's home area, it was likely that one's application name and node address were the same string of bits; as the phone moved beyond its home area, however, the node address was changed to one local to the new area, but the phone number seen by the user (and those calling her) remained the same. The cell phone system merely changed the mapping in its directory databases so that connect requests to the application name are routed to the subnet indicated by the node address, which in turn is mapped to a point-of-attachment address so that the call is routed to the correct cell tower.

In effect, the cell phone system first "jacked up" the PoA address space of the traditional phone system to make them node addresses and then did it again to make them application names (with the result that cell phone numbers were "portable"). Although the cell phone system started out with a concept of "home" much like that found in mobile IP, it evolved to the point that its primary utility is for management and billing. Because the form of the numbers never changed, most users never knew that there was a difference or that one was necessary.[14] One should not conclude that the current cell phone system is as clean as described here. Cell phone providers backed into the solution, and so there are a number of warts on the implementation that give away its history. But the basic idea was correct. Armed with a full addressing architecture, one finds that

Mobility is simply dynamic multihoming.

---

[14] And because no networking text teaches the principles of network naming and addressing, we are constantly inundated with demands to make IP addresses portable. After all, if the telephone company can, why can't the Internet. Of course, the answer is that the phone company doesn't make point-of-attachment addresses or node addresses portable and neither can the Internet. But every few months, some Internet "expert" calls for it.

Mobility in NIPCA

So, networking should just replicate the cellular approach? Not quite. As shown earlier, mobile communications is just a matter of the mobile host moving along acquiring new points of attachments as they come into range and discarding old ones as it moves out of range, being multihomed at times. A mobile system is a bit like a monkey brachiating from vine to vine through the jungle; the mobile system swings from tower to tower. The primary difference between networking systems and cellular systems is that in a cellular system it is the *vine* that decides when to let go! Clearly, we would much prefer to let the monkey decide when to let go, especially if *we* are the monkey!

But joking aside, letting the mobile system determine which points of attachments it has good communication with and which ones it wants to drop or which new ones it wants to acquire makes sense. At the very least, it knows whether it has the necessary signal strength with a new signal, *and* it knows where it is going. The cell phone approach came about when cellular was analog and the phones had little or no computing capacity. Cell phones today are orders of magnitude more powerful than the largest ARPANET hosts. This approach also fits nicely into our model of layer or DIF operation developed in Chapter 7.

Basically, a mobile system is acquiring new physical PoAs as it moves. Strictly speaking, each of these new physical PoAs is joining a new DIF or layer.[15] Although an address indicates where a system is in that DIF, the lowest layer (traditionally called the data link layer) has such small scope that the address space is generally flat. As we saw, addresses have a certain granularity or resolution in the degree to which the address indicates *where*. PoAs to the physical media are generally within this granularity. So even though the physical PoA will change most frequently, it isn't necessary that the lowest-level address change as frequently. (Remember that PoA and node addresses are relative in our recursive model.) As the system joins each new lowest layer, it will only be necessary to ensure that the address is unambiguous within the layer. As the system moves, the signal strength of some physical layer POAs will drop below a usable threshold and membership in the layer will be terminated.

---

[15] In the same way that an Ethernet segment constitutes a data link layer, each cell phone tower or wireless base station should be modeled as a single layer. Note how this is reflected in an 802.11 header by having four addresses, two for each layer (one for the base station, and one for the "Ethernet segment" operating over it).

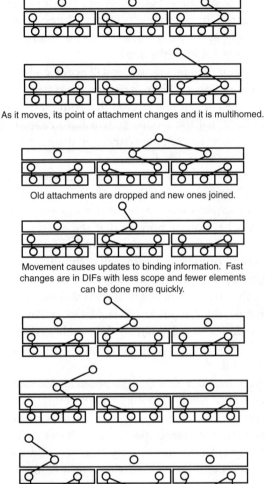

As it moves, its point of attachment changes and it is multihomed.

Old attachments are dropped and new ones joined.

Movement causes updates to binding information. Fast changes are in DIFs with less scope and fewer elements can be done more quickly.

Figure 9-6 As a mobile host or application moves, it joins new DIFs and drops its participation in old ones, at times being multihomed to more than one. The rate of change is commensurate with the scope of the layer. The smaller scope, the faster it may traverse it, and the fewer elements of the layer that need to be notified.

It is a design trade-off whether the addresses do not need to change or don't need to change often. Ethernet made the choice in favor of easy deployment in a trusting environment, so that addresses don't need to change and that new nodes don't need to be authenticated. The cost of this is, of course, larger addresses. If there is significant verification of the identity of the system when it joins a lowest layer (that is, is this serial number allowed to join this network?), the advantage of the global media access addresses is lost. The cost of assigning an address when a new system joins the network is lost in the cost of authentication. This could argue for using much shorter addresses and lower overhead for data transfer. Although strictly speaking more efficient, unless PDUs are fairly small, this savings is lost in the noise.

When a mobile host moves far enough, it will acquire a lowest-layer PoA that is bound to a different upper layer. The mobile system will then join this (2)-layer and be assigned an address in it. At this point, it may be multihomed at both layers 1 and 2. When the mobile system has dropped all layer 1 POAs associated with its original layer 2, the system will drop the PoA and exclusively use the new layer 2 (and so on; see Figure 9-6).

So, while we might like to speak of the addresses associated with mobile systems changing to reflect its new location in the layer, it is more correct to say that a mobile system acquires new addresses and ceases to use old ones. Above the first layer, it will be more important that the addresses assigned indicate *where* the system is attached to the network. It will also become more important to track the changes in routing and ensure that routing updates are made in a timely manner. Although the number of IPC processes in an (N)-DIF increases with higher layers, the rate of change will decrease. However, it will be advantageous to ensure that nearby systems are updated sooner. And this is precisely the environment we noted for IAP in Chapter 7. In addition, it will also be useful for PDUs in transit to be redirected to different IPC processes. Techniques for this are well understood.

How many layers would a mobile system have? As many as needed. The answer to this question is fundamentally an engineering problem that depends on the size of the network and the rate of new address acquisition. We have seen that the cell phone system performs quite well with two layers and three levels of addressing. But this is based on relatively long new address acquisition rates on the order of minutes and hours. And although it could without doubt perform at a rate of seconds and minutes, a system with a faster address acquisition rate might require more layers to ensure that routing updates could be made in a timely manner.

Will there be a problem with propagating these changes in address throughout the network?

This is the first question that comes to mind. The reason is that there is a tendency to see this as a directory update and to compare it with update times for DNS. This is a not the right view. This is a routing update. The changes only need to be propagated to other IPC processes within the (N)-DIF. The change does not need to be reflected in the (N+1)-DIF (yet) because the (N+1)-DIF is still topologically significant. The lower the layer, the greater the rate at which the binding will change. The higher the layer, the slower the rate of change. This is a direct consequence of the larger scope of higher layers. Changes will be the greatest in those layers with the smallest scope and where the time for the propagation of updates will be the shortest.

Actually, DNS updates are routing updates, too, but that was not understood when DNS was proposed. For mobility, where routing changes occur more frequently, it is important to maintain a balance between the scope of a layer (subnet) (that is, the number of elements that must be updated) and the rate of routing changes. We have seen that a traditional cellular system works reasonably well with three levels of addressing. But if the density of base stations were increased to accommodate more users, or more rapid movement between subnets were required, additional layers might be used so that updates would affect fewer nodes. In fact, given the recursive nature of the architecture, this could lead to a network with a different number of layers in different parts of the network (more in densely used areas, and fewer in less densely used areas).

Isn't this at odds with the hill and valley model described in Chapter 8? Not at all. Mobile networks by their nature are subnets that are either independent of or at the periphery of a fixed network. In a sense, mobile networks surround the hill and valley model of the fixed network (see Figure 9-7). The common layer that user applications communicate over runs "over the top." The border between a fixed network and mobile network would meet at the "top of a hill," just below this common layer. No one incurs any more overhead than required to meet the requirements of the network and the applications.

Remember, too, that these changes are entirely internal to the operation of the distributed IPC facility at that rank. The application names of the user applications and of the IPC processes in all DIFs/layers do not change. However, new instances may be created. This makes it clear why mobility in IP networks is so complicated: With no built-in support for multihoming and not enough names, there is no way to make mobility straightforward. The lack of a complete addressing architecture again takes its toll.

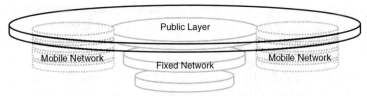

Stacked Layers of a Mobile Network and the Hill and Valley
Layers of a Fixed Network supporting a common public Network

Figure 9-7 Stacked layers of a mobile network and the hill and valley layers of a fixed network supporting a common public network.

For wireless mobility, we can surmise that each (N)-IPC process will monitor the QoS (signal strength) of its PoAs dropping those that fall below certain parameters and acquiring new ones whose QoS has exceeded some threshold. At the bottom, this will entail frequent enrollments in new lower layers and less frequent enrollments in new higher DIFS. One could view this constant monitoring of the lower-layer QoS with the result that PoAs are dropped as unique to mobility. But this is not the case. It is more common with mobility but not unique. Wireline systems should be (and are) in effect doing the same thing as they monitor the QoS of various PoAs to make decisions about routing. The only difference is that the "failure" rate for wireline systems is generally much lower.

Ad Hoc Mobile Networking

Another major form of mobility that we need to look at is what has come to be called ad hoc networking, where mobile end systems or subnets communicate with other mobile end systems or subnets. Let's see what the architecture has to say about this and what new problems it might pose.

The operation of a layer in an ad hoc network works in the same way. Each system in the ad hoc network has one or more (1)-layers, one for each wireless channel it can send and receive on. Each (1)-layer is essentially a star topology. Because the physical medium is multiple access, there will be multiple systems participating in this (1)-layer. The constraints on the single wireless channel are such that the (1)-layer will have sufficiently small scope that we can assume a flat address space. As noted earlier, it is an engineering design choice whether the addresses are unambiguous across many instances of a (1)-layer (as with MAC addresses) or only unambiguous within a single (1)-layer, or somewhere in between.

The boundaries of the (1)-layer are determined by the physical medium. The boundaries of higher layers are less constrained and determined by considerations of locality, management, traffic patterns, and so on. Generally, subnets are made up of elements in the same area. Determining such proximity in a truly ad hoc network can be difficult. Reference to an external frame of reference (for example, GPS or the organization of the user) would make it easier. But even with that there is the problem of characterizing and recognizing viable clusters as subnets with truly fluid movement of ad hoc systems. How this could be accommodated would depend on the specific ad hoc network. These are really issues of policy and do not impact the architectural framework. It is sufficient to see that the architecture as developed supports a consistent set of policies. One might, for example, have an ad hoc network with a flat layer address space for all (2)-layers. In this case, systems could join a (2)-DIF as described previously and essentially self-organize into a (2)-DIF. There might be an upper bound on the number of participants and further rules for creating a second one and creating a (3)-DIF for relaying between them and so on.

The further question is this: Can topological addresses be assigned in an ad hoc network? Again, this will to a large degree depend on the specific ad hoc network. Is it large enough that there is an advantage to using topological addresses? Is address acquisition sufficiently constrained or the rate of change sufficiently slow to warrant their use? The Internet makes a good case for large networks without location-dependent addresses, but the constraints of ad hoc networks may argue for smaller subnets. In our development of topological addresses, we found that the topology adopted should be an abstraction of the underlying graph of the network or the desired graph (that is, according to a plan). The same applies to an ad hoc network. The expected deployment may imply a topology. The collected (1)-layers are a set of overlapping star networks, with each system being a center. Clustering algorithms might be used to self-organize higher layers. Again, the rate of change would be a major factor in the practicality of applying such techniques.

Any topology is going to be an abstraction of the relation among the (1)-DIF stars. But the very nature of ad hoc networks is that this relation is fluid. This would seem to imply that these topological addresses are not applicable to purely ad hoc networks (that is, those that have no reference to an external frame of reference). Ad hoc networks with an external frame of reference may be able to use this frame of reference as a basis for a topological structure.

Mobile Application Processes

The last case we need to consider is application processes moving from host to host. This problem was actually investigated before the other forms of mobility on the UC Irvine ring network in 1972 (Farber, 1972). Since then, many distributed systems projects have contributed to the problem. Here we are primarily interested in what this model tells us about this form of mobility.

Clearly, the only case that is interesting is applications moving while they are executing. We saw that with recovery that all the state that must be "recovered" is in the application process, not in the IPC or the application protocol, which are stateless. For IPC, there is no difference between a recovered flow and a new flow. The dialog must resume from the last information the application received.

The solution to mobile applications is similar in that we are not so much concerned with moving executing processes as we are with initiating a new instance on another system and then synchronizing state with the existing copy, and then the existing copy can disappear. How might we accomplish this? Consider the following example:

You are in a voice conversation on your computer at your desk. However, you need to leave for another meeting but want to continue the phone call. For the sake of argument, let's assume that the AP name is a multicast name. Your APM and the APM on the other end are the only members of the multicast group.

To move your phone call, you direct your "cell phone" to join the conversation. The phone creates an instance of the phone conversation APM on your cell phone. The APM joins the AP using the AP name as a multicast name. The phone conversation is now a multicast group consisting of three participants: the person you are talking to, you on your computer, and you on your cell phone. When you are satisfied that the cell phone application is in the call, the APM on your computer can drop out of the call and you can continue to use your cell phone. Or maybe it doesn't. Perhaps your computer continues to record the conversation for you.

Put simply, mobile applications are just a form of multicast. Very straightforward and, with our simpler approach to multicast, much more easily implemented. One could easily imagine using this with other, more complex applications that were not streaming. In this case, the new APM would join the multicast group, open a separate connection with the primary synchronize state, and then assume the role of the primary or of a hot spare. A nice little trick for applying the model.

But upon reflection, one realizes that this little trick has deeper implications. There is an invariance in the addressing architecture that we had not previously called out: system dependence/independence. Application process names/multicast names are location dependent and system independent; but application PM-ids are location independent and system dependent. This yields a very nice progression:

(N-1)-addresses (PoAs) are location dependent and interface or route dependent.

(N)-addresses (node addresses) are location dependent and interface or route independent.

APM-ids are location independent and system dependent.

AP names are location independent and system independent.

Conclusions

In this chapter, we have looked at the problems of multihoming, mobility, anycast, and multicast; and we have found that all four fit nicely within the NIPCA structure. No new protocols are required. Multihoming and mobility are an inherent part of the structure and can be provided at no additional cost. Multicast and anycast require only the ability within layer management to distribute set definitions and the algorithms for evaluating the set at the time the forwarding table is updated. But more important, we have found that in a recursive structure multicast comes down to what is essentially two cases of unicast. We have also explored the properties of multiplexing multicast groups. This would increase the efficiency of multicast and make its management easier.

All of these are accommodated without special cases, and none of these capabilities was a consideration when we derived the IPC model back in Chapter 6, one more indication that we may be on the right track.

Chapter 10

Backing Out of a Blind Alley

Its not as if there is some killer technology at the protocol or network level that we somehow failed to include. We need to take all the technologies we already know and fit them together differently. This is not about building a technology innovation that changes the world but about architecture....

—Dave Clark, MIT, 2005

Introduction

The Preface noted seven fundamental questions uncovered in the early forays into networking. Interestingly, these questions were lost in the ensuing conflict over protocols and remain unanswered 30 years later. What happened? As the 20th century drew to a close, the excitement over the Internet had begun to wane, with prominent Internet researchers finally beginning to realize that research was stagnating. In 2001, a study into the state of network research by the National Research Council (2001) made a jarring and embarrassing observation:

A reviewer of an early draft of this report observed that this proposed framework—measure, develop theory, prototype new ideas—looks a lot like Research 101.... From the perspective of the outsiders, the insiders had not shown that they had managed to exercise the usual elements of a successful research program, so a back-to-basics message was fitting.

An entire field's research program being so strongly criticized for losing sight of the fundamentals? Outrageous! But worse, it was becoming more and more apparent that the current Internet architecture was running out of steam. There were severe problems with scaling, security, addressing, routing, and so on; and although there were endless proposals for fixes to specific problems, the fixes were just that: more band-aids, not fundamental new insights. They tended to further complicate the structure. There was a crisis in fundamentals. DARPA funded MIT and ISI to convene the NEWARCH project, consisting of prominent researchers from those two centers and elsewhere. After two years, their final report (Clark et al., 2003) essentially came up dry.[1] Sessions on new architecture have been held at various conferences, but the results were always the same. It became so bad that proposing new architectures became the subject of satire. Then with great fanfare, NSF discovered the issue. A grand effort to build an infrastructure (how does this differ from the rationale for Internet2?) to investigate the major questions plaguing the Internet today (a variation on trying all kinds of cannons?) was initiated, along with a new initiative to *find* a new Internet design. "Clean-slate" has become the new hot topic. But if their announcements are any indication, the slates haven't been erased well, let alone washed. Few of the problems it sees as important seem to be any of our seven fundamental questions. In the one or two cases, where they have come close to a key issue, they have failed to recognize it as having fundamental implications. There seems to be an inherent assumption that the foundations are firm (leaving the slate less than clean). It is not clear whether this is a blind spot or the old guard protecting its legacy. But so far, the grand effort seems to be recycling old wine in new bottles. Perhaps, it has become just another source of funding. A new take on Alyosha's dream: We can't actually solve the problem or the funding will dry up. But there is more going on here. We must look at the socioeconomic forces that got us here. So, where do we stand with our fundamental questions?

Consolidation and the Next Generation

Going back to the chronology in the Preface, the first thing that hits one is that none of the outstanding issues have been resolved, with the exception of replacing NCP with TCP, and that is now clearly showing its age. We can see now that TCP was designed to address the immediate problems of the day and had little ability to adapt to the future,[2] as indicated by the proliferation of transport protocols within the IETF. The Internet is at its core an unfinished demo.

---

[1] For those who may dispute that characterization, I can only offer that if NEWARCH did not come up dry, why is FIND necessary?

[2] But, it has worked well for 30 years! Yes, but there were no new applications for 20 of those years.

Then why is the Internet seen as such a success? Basically five reasons: abstraction, insensitivity, Moore's law, military spending, and hard work.

- The layer abstraction hides most of the problems from those who use the Net. This was true of the ARPANET, too, and contributed strongly to its success. Only a relatively few people have to deal with the underlying issues; the vast majority are given the illusion that it simply works.

- For better or worse, one property of computer systems is that they are relatively insensitive. As some software manufacturers have demonstrated very successfully, you can make almost any piece of sh*@ er, sorry, software work, no matter how bad. And a prime contributor to this insensitivity is....

- Moore's law. Moore's law has provided the cheap computing power to keep the problems at bay. This is especially true for the routing and addressing problems we faced.

- ARPA willingly spent money overprovisioning the early Net. In the early 1970s, 56K lines were enormously fast and expensive. No other experimental network built at the time used such high-speed, long-distance lines (most were 9.6K). Although tests could stress the network, normal usage never came close to a significant load. One cannot overstress the role that this overprovisioning played in the perception of that early success and in masking unsolved problems.

- And, the intense nonstop efforts of thousands of engineers to keep it going.

Many people point to this success as proof that the Internet suite of protocols is a paragon of technical achievement and that there is little fundamentally wrong with the Internet. This is the same argument that apologists for DOS used to justify its technical excellence. To quote Stan Lee, "'nuff said."

If one looks carefully over this chronology, one is inexorably drawn to the conclusion that the Internet did not begin to stagnate at the turn of the century, but in the late 1970s. It is here that conservative behavior begins to take hold. It is here that each juncture is not seen as an opportunity to fulfill the earlier vision or to synthesize new insights with previous achievements to create a new innovative direction, but more the minimal change is made to solve the immediate problem and go no further. It begins to seem that people are the keepers of some flame and dare not tamper with what has been entrusted to them, the classic behavior of a "second generation" i.e., not the founding generation. Some will argue that this was the policy of small incremental change that has been a stalwart of Internet development. And they are right; caution in maintaining a production system is a necessity but a slow death for research and the research was far from done. But isn't that just what one would expect from the inheritors of the flame? Is that just a rationalization of a much deeper malaise?

We can now see that after 1975 we were entering a period of consolidation. We were implementing TCP,[3] the network was expanding, but no efforts were creating new requirements on the Net, efforts that would have forced us to look deeper at some of the things we hadn't done in that first push.[4] All the while, Moore's law was at work pushing the edges further and further out, making problems less and less pressing. In addition, there was never a clean split between operations and research. In some sense, the researchers never let go of *their* network, but at the same time it *was* operational supporting more and more people who were not network researchers who could live with the Net being a little flaky on a Tuesday morning. So researchers had to make incremental changes. There was no place to try out major new ideas. Although a period of consolidation was probably necessary and unavoidable, without new developments in other areas the Internet was essentially marking time. Each change becomes permanent. Any attempt to addresses shortcomings of a previous change must be built on top of it. There is no replacement of modules by new solutions as with most products. This has more in common with biological evolution than incremental engineering. We know that with biological evolution, the vast majority of trials (species) reach a dead-end and become extinct. For nature, this is not a problem; it does millions if not billions of trials. We don't have that luxury.

This mode of operation was reinforced by newcomers to the Net who were mostly nonresearchers and lacked the broad background of the initial developers and who finding a working system (and few alternatives to look at) saw the existing structure as the only way to build a network (early imprinting works again). Myths grew up as to how various stopgaps, kludges, and shortcuts were wonderful pieces of forethought and design.[5] These myths became "design principles," making them virtually impossible to overcome and return to the original vision. More than once, the decisions of the early Net have been described as

---

[3]   Which was no small task. A TCP implementation from scratch took 18 man-months and was pretty much a one-person effort. And as one would expect, the first one was a throwaway, as we learned that the specification was not a good guide for implementation.

[4]   As noted previously, there were some large networking projects done by various ARPA contractors, but they only involved those groups and did not really affect the general use of the Net.

[5]   The human species' ability to ascribe meaning to things that was never intended is truly amazing.

if "handed down on stone tablets." This was further reinforced by textbooks, which described what existed as the best or nearly best solution instead of doing the extra work of describing the principles along with particular implementations.

Reflecting on the events of the past 35 years, I have come to suspect that not pursuing the upper layers, the squelching of USING (the Users Interest Group, see Chapter 4, "Stalking the Upper-Layer Architecture") may have been a crucial juncture. I had always thought the upper layers should have been explored in the mid-1970s, mostly because there were all of these "neat" things we should use the network for! (The engineer in me.) It was the next obvious thing to look at. But more recently, I have begun to suspect that it was more than just doing the next neat thing. That not pursuing the upper layers removed the driver that would have forced us to complete the architecture; forced a complete addressing architecture; forced greater attention to security, more requirements on the lower layers, and probably many other things. Growth alone was not enough with the effects of Moore's Law. With no impetus, there was no reason to change, especially given the "second-generation" effects.

In addition to the internal social forces, there were external forces the intensity of which no other effort in computer science (or perhaps any science) had ever been subjected to. Starting in 1974 and 1975, we became aware of the PTTs' effort to standardize packet-switched networking with X.25. This was our first foray into the world of electro-political engineering and power politics. We were rank novices compared with European researchers, but we were learned quickly. Unlike today, CCITT meetings were open only to telephone companies and countries.[6] For any U.S. manufacturer (other than Western Electric) to attend, they had to be accredited by the Department of State. This began the ongoing war between the "beads-on-a-string" and layered approaches to networking and the incredibly intense connection/connectionless debate.[7] There was much more at stake for the Europeans. With no Carterphone decision in

Where Are the Ivory Tower Academics?

I am afraid that much of the fault here lies with academia for not distilling principles and insisting on intellectual discipline. Engineers building product and keeping a network running can't be expected to be working out fundamental principles. But those teaching should be. They are really the only ones in a position to do it. They should ensure that students have a deeper understanding of what is going on, of the principles that can be derived from our successes and our *failures!* (The failures are more important than the successes.) It wasn't something that everyone had to do, but it also couldn't be no one. For example, the fact that not a single networking textbook discusses what must be named, only the format of names, is unconscionable and is a major contributor to our current crisis. I have met many professors, "experts" in networking, who were unaware that an IP address named the interface, not the computer.

---

6 Which in most cases were one and the same, except in the United States.

7 It is interesting at this time to consider how symbiotic the PTT architecture and the IBM SNA architecture were. Each very carefully avoided the other's turf.

Europe, the European PTTs could claim that the only equipment that could be attached to their data networks would be theirs. In other words, you had to lease their computers, just as you did their telephones. Research was being pushed into a world of power politics at a very early stage. And not just the power politics of standards; there was also immense pressure to commercialize packet switching and, very soon after, LANs.

Packet-switching networks had always been the underdog, both scorned and feared by the phone companies, beginning with the ARPANET demo at the ICCC conference in 1972. Scorned because the bellheads had been building networks for a 100 years, and the Net flew in the face of everything they knew. Feared by the engineers because computers were at the heart of it, and they didn't really understand this new world. Feared by management because the layered architecture, and the transport layer in particular, relegated the phone companies to what was clearly a commodity business (unless, of course, they wanted to leave their cushy monopoly for the rough-and-tumble world of competition). In 1975, they saw no reason to. It would be easier to squash the upstarts, or just let it die out when it was realized that it didn't work very well.

The tensions between the connection and connectionless camps began to heat up. From the beginning, these were some of the most emotional arguments I have ever witnessed or participated in. The first attempt to affect the outcome of X.25 had only modest results.[8] The connection model held out a possible escape from the commodity trap with so-called value-added networks. The PTTs believed that connectionless was an academic infatuation that would fade away (or at least they hoped). Several PTTs were already well on their way to building networks and were not going to change very much. Because the PTTs were monopolies in most countries, the attitude that customers had to buy what they decided to offer was common.

If communications were going to use computers, it was a new market for the computer industry, and they weren't going to miss it. The computer industry recognized that they would never have a voice in the CCITT. So, they attempted an end run by creating a network standards effort in ISO, a nongovernmental voluntary standards body. OSI was formed in 1978 over the objections of the traditional ISO data-comm committee.[9] While OSI was initiated by the

---

8 LAPB was aligned with HDLC, and a datagram packet type was added, but no PTT had any intention of implementing it.

9 This committee, essentially controlled by IBM, represented the current status quo with the phone company. It didn't want to see its lucrative boat rocked.

proponents of connectionless, the European computer companies wanted and needed rapprochement with the PTTs. Very quickly, with the aid of AT&T, the CCITT effort in this area was made a joint effort between ISO and CCITT. This was unavoidable and at the same time sealed the doom of OSI. On the one hand, a competitive effort in CCITT would have severely weakened any computer industry effort, especially with no inkling of deregulation on the horizon. At the same time, the difference in paradigms was irreconcilable, at least given our knowledge at the time. No one could see a synthesis of the two, and "professional" standards committees did not do the kind of elegant synthesis seen in the early APRANET, but just jammed two (or more) contending approaches together and called them options.

Beginning in 1974 as the International Network Working Group (INWG) and later becoming IFIP WG6.1, INWG broadened the scope of similar groups within the ARPANET, NPLet, and CYCLADES, along with other researchers. 6.1 had been working on an international transport protocol also doing work on a VTP that was a very elegant example of extensibility and the beginnings of the application of FDTs to protocols. Just before OSI started (March 1978), INWG chose a revised CYCLADES TS as the international transport protocol over the NPLnet protocol and TCP (Cerf, et al. 1978). This output was carried onto the OSI process as an IFIP liaison contribution and became the basis for the OSI Transport Protocol Class 4 (TP4). Soon after this DARPA researchers ceased participating in OSI. Over time, this separation led to the Internet preception of the OSI connetionless work as a rival rather than an ally against the phone companies.

Those Crazy Americans!

A story has circulated in the past few years that the DoD offered TCP to OSI in the 1980s and they turned them down. This is offered in the vein of a "missed opportunity." The story is true, but not complete. From the OSI point of view, they had already accepted Vint Cerf's and the DoD's recommendation years before as the output of the open IFIP WG6.1 process. (Cerf and McKenzie were the first two of the four authors of the report.) Years later, when the DoD brought TCP to OSI, the Europeans chalked it up to yet another case of the American's right hand not knowing what the left hand was doing.

The resulting separation of the Internet participants from OSI led to essentially a three-way competition between the connection-oriented PTT proponents, the Internet, and the OSI connectionless proponents who saw their effort as essentially the next step in developing connectionless networking. It was clear by the late 1970s that DARPA no longer had an interest in continuing the revolution it had begun. If any of the open issues were going to be resolved, it would have to be elsewhere. OSI offered the only forum where there was a chance to resolve some of the issues the

ARPANET/Internet had not had a chance to do.[10] However, with the confusion created by the warring connection/connectionless factions, it didn't matter what OSI was trying to do; whatever advances it made were completely obscured by the internal conflicts. The strife within OSI was not limited to connection versus connectionless, but also Japan versus Europe versus the United States, and the computer industry versus the phone companies and everyone against IBM.[11] The push for OSI was signaled in early 1982 when IBM changed the diagrams in its advertising of SNA from five layers to seven.

After IBM's endorsement,[12] the desire to lead the commercialization of OSI yielded many interests who all had their own agendas, fighting over who would get a piece of the pie, who would essentially control its implementation: NBS/NIST, MAP/TOP, EMCA, COS, DEC, IBM, and others. IBM played them like a violin. It was truly magical to watch.[13] IBM played them not by direct action or pushing specific proposals but by creating an environment that would maximize confusion and complicate whatever the result. IBM played on the egos of a few key people to create new initiatives, separating the designers from the implementers (a standard organizational tactic to kill a project) by encouraging the formation of implementer's workshops distinct from the standards organizations.[14] As it usually turns out, the designers had a much better idea of how to implement than the implementers did. The implementation profiles were supposed to be a means around the connection/connectionless dichotomy.

Different environments would use different profiles. It merely served as predicted as a forum to rehash the same arguments in different groups, adding to

---

10 Things such as a full addressing architecture, à la Saltzer, and developing the upper layers. (As we saw in Chapter 4, OSI still got it wrong, partly because there was more to understand and partly because of action of the PTT faction. But it was a step along the way.)

11 Which held the head of delegation position for most European countries and the United States.

12 Well, not entirely. IBM endorsed the seven-layer model but contended that OSI didn't do management. (Sound familiar?) IBM already knew that the symmetrical layered model was completely incompatible with its flagship SNA, a hierarchical architecture. You can always subset a symmetrical model to be hierarchical, but you can't go the other way. IBM didn't want this to happen in a major way.

13 It truly was. I think I could write a "Discourses on Livy" for standards committees.

14 IBM was in a multifront war during this period. IBM always sold to the person who signed the check. In the 1960s and 1970s, the person who could sign a check for millions of dollars of computer equipment had little or no computer expertise. As we moved into the 1980s, that was changing and check signers were more willing to consider minicomputers and PCs. IBM was probably more successful delaying the assault on networking than they were at delaying the assault on the mainframe.

the confusion. The dichotomy in OSI immensely complicated its output. Because vendors were unwilling to bet on the outcome, they felt they had to implement the whole thing. As with all organizations, it is the internal problems that are the most deadly. There were just too many disparate camps under one umbrella, too many wanting to "lead" OSI, and no common direction for OSI to have ever succeeded.[15] And while there were elements buried in OSI that would have advanced the state of the Internet, it would have been impossible to extract them in the political climate, and there were still many things that were not "right." The lesson to take away from the OSI experience is plain: No matter how reasonable it may appear, collaborating with the legacy will lead to failure. If the new model does not have enough advantage to stand on its own, it does not have enough to stand with the old guard either.

Probably the greatest beneficiary of all this turmoil was the Internet, which for the most part was left out of this multisided conflict. The Internet had been left to its own devices and was in the best position to push the technology ahead while everyone else was distracted. But, this did not happen. At the same time, the isolation had its own effects when the IPng effort brought them together again. By this time the Internet had rewritten its history to reflect its crowning achievement, having lost sight of the list of open issues and that the Net was really an unfinished demo that had never been "productized."

What was required was a true synthesis of connections and connectionless, like the syntheses that the early ARPANET had been so good at pulling off. However, the political situation was so intense and the problem so much more difficult that it was hard to find the middle ground.[16] Instead, a bunker mentality set in, each group unwilling to bend for fear of losing the whole thing. One cannot stress too much the intensity or affects of this bunker mentality on all three camps. A less-intense environment might have been able to find the synthesis, but it was impossible in the environment that existed.

It is also worthwhile to bring up another factor that is sensitive and embarrassing for many of us: immaturity. Although there were many "standards professionals" who knew the ropes and understood how to get things done, the vast majority of participants in all three camps were young, bright, hotshots

---

[15] This has necessarily been a very high-level account of these events touching on the first-order effectors. There is fertile ground here for those interested in the process of and sociology of science and technology.

[16] At the time, they were characterized as extremes of shared state, which it is. But this characterization does not lead to a useful middle ground.

New Architecture and the IETF

Clearly, one contributor to these problems has been a misconception about what the IETF can accomplish. It is fundamental that all committees behave conservatively. (James Madison was one of the earliest to realize this property.) This is not where new understanding will come from, nor should it. The job of the IETF is to ensure the stability of the operational public Internet.

But for the problem we are concerned with, the situation is worse. It is very hard for organizations to change culture. The history of business has shown that the few companies that do succeed do so by doing what they were founded to do, but very few are able to adapt to do the "next thing." The drag by the original proponents is generally sufficient to deflect or diffuse the new effort. It has always seemed that making such changes should be easier for companies being driven "top down," but we know they aren't. It is orders of magnitude more difficult, if not impossible, in standards organizations, that are directed bottom up. This alone makes it virtually impossible for a committee to radically change its culture or pursue a radically new direction. Too many participants have too much invested personally and commercially to want to see it displaced. This implies that should a new direction be found, it must be done by a different organization. There are too many interests in the status quo for such a change to succeed in the IETF. Trying to do a new architecture within the IETF would be worse than OSI bringing in the PTTs. It would make that look like a tea party. Anyone who demurs is either hopelessly naïve or represents such an interest.

So, is there a way forward for the IETF and for the Internet? There might be. However, most participants see the Internet as a string of crowning achievements, not as a list of missed opportunities. This has to change. Until a new crop of young Turks comes along who are willing to look at the efforts of their seniors and find them lacking, I am afraid we are stuck. Where is Oedipus when you need him?

new to the game. We had been weaned on the kind of raucous design sessions that were prevalent in the 1970s and 1980s, and I am afraid that our behavior often contributed poorly to the process. Often ridicule and loud abusive language was substituted for logic and reason and trying to understand the opposing view. The idea of winning the position at whatever cost overrode any need to "get it right." Although it has moderated considerably, a strong current of intolerance and lack of listening still characterizes these discussions on all sides (often compared to religious fervor).

If OSI buffered the Internet from the bulk of the turmoil with the PTTs and the connection/connectionless debate, how does any of this affect the Internet? This is one of the oddest effects in this whole story, and one I still don't understand. The Internet participants developed a deep visceral aversion for anything associated with OSI, which exists to this day. Much of what is believed about OSI is not based on firsthand knowledge and is often simply wrong. It is an odd reaction for something that was doomed to fail on its own.

But as I noted in Chapter 5, "Naming and Addressing," the oddest reaction is that if OSI did something, then the Internet wouldn't. The reaction wasn't, "They didn't understand it; let us show you how to do it right." The reaction was to do anything else but (hardly the behavior of professional scientists or engineers and often resulted in "cutting off their nose to spite their face"). We saw this with the decision to continue to name the interface in IPng. Something we had known was wrong since 1972 in the ARPANET. And something like this may have been at work in the rejection of an object-oriented approach for network management that chose SNMP over

HEMS.[17] As discussed in Chapter 4, SNMP was a step backward from even the rudimentary IEEE 802.1 protocol that preceded it.

We also see it with respect to the concept of layers. Internet proponents try very hard to avoid layers, primarily because it is strongly associated with OSI, although it is doubtful any would admit it. However, they can't completely forsake them. To do so would put them squarely in the beads-on-a-string camp. Recently, however, it does seem that some prominent Internet researchers have lost faith with the connectionless model, just when a renaissance is in the offing. Many papers have been written trying to get rid of layers. Most still assume that a layered architecture implies a particular implementation strategy. And they assume that the only possible layers are the ones arrived at in the early 1970s. Both of which we have seen in this book are not the case. They have de-emphasized interfaces to the point that the lack of clean interfaces was a major source of the work in doing IPv6, and the interfaces provide little or no abstraction. They have tried to concentrate everything in the network and transport layers to the point that the Internet architecture is more beads with stripes than layered, with TCP/IP rather than X.25/LAPB.

It is easy to see how in all the turmoil, research has suffered.

From reading the popular press, one has the impression that the Internet is an amazing intellectual achievement, a triumph of American innovation. But a close look reveals a quite different picture. There are only two major innovations: the central one, Pouzin's connectionless insight for a French network;[18] and Saltzer's application of operating system naming to networks. Technologically, the Internet has been languishing since the mid-1970s, creating one band-aid after another as it rode Moore's law around the hard problems facing them. When OSI self-destructed from its internal contradictions and the corporate squabbling over whom would set its agenda, the Internet much to its own surprise was the only thing left. And the Internet was only standing because of the effort of Al Gore and others to make it freely available in the United States. So in the end, it was more politics and economics that determined the success, not the technological innovations.

Maybe Al Gore did invent the Internet![19]

---

[17] Although that may have had more Luddite, anti-intellectual overtones, as in "real programmers don't use high-level languages."

[18] There is a lesson here for both the Americans and the French. The Americans have not been the innovator they thought they were but were able to capitalize on the ideas. The French, although creative, were not able to capitalize on the new idea because it threatened entrenched institutions. One must admit that this is typical of both.

[19] And now he champions action on the global warming crisis and goes down in history as the most influential U.S. politician to never be president? How strange that would be.

Maybe it is time we quit loafing and get back to doing some serious intellectual work, if we still know how.

How Did This Happen?

The short answer is a combination of effects. The push to commercialize networking came on very fast, before the science was really understood. The business world and the research community to a large extent assumed that the "productization" of networking would occur in commercial products. And academia was intimidated from exercising its responsibility to distill fundamentals by the intense flame wars that erupted when pointed questions were asked. "Facts" were often articles of faith, and desires were couched as principles, and wonderful technical doubletalk was created to obscure the lack of hard evidence. By the time it became clear that the Internet was to be the focus of those products, no one in the Internet remembered (or ever knew) that it had not been finished.

The effect of business cannot be underestimated. The press to commercialize networking had a tendency to freeze solutions much too early. But by the same token, the public success of this commercialization led to research taking up the pattern of venture capitalists looking for a quick ROI. Each agency or program director measured by how much they are on the "bleeding edge." This has led to research programs that are not so much concerned with solving problems as funding for two or three years, declaring victory and moving on to the next big problem. (Clearly, the "bleeding edge" can't be the same as three years ago.[20]) Meanwhile, researchers must adjust their research program to the new fads to keep the dollars on which they are measured rolling in. No one is measured on *solving* problems and producing science. This leads to a proliferation of technique, with no theory to distill them and to hold them together. And with no theory, there is no way to determine how good the results are.[21] Note that in other sciences, the fact that they are trying to understand an external object (e.g., nature) to a large extent keeps this from happening. It is only in computer science, where we don't have nature, that this seems to occur. We have nothing to keep us close to Clauswitz's "proper soil." It seems that it is as important to keep practice close to theory as it is to keep theory close to practice! As in any science, it is the boundary conditions that are the most enlightening. Computer science provides an interesting boundary condition to the "philosophy" of science.

---

[20] It isn't the same attitude that all problems can be solved in a one-hour TV show, but it is close.

[21] However, there is some question whether anyone wants to make or can afford to make such a determination. To do so would jeopardize their funding.

Much more damaging was the political milieu that networking found itself thrust into. Almost immediately (within just a few years of its first proposal), the concept of the connectionless network was under relentless attack by the PTTs. This led not only to a bunker mentality, but also to a feeling of being a "chosen" elite initially, because the Net was so much more advanced than anything the PTTs could do, and later with the exponential success of the Web. In the 1970s, this was the camaraderie of excitement about new ideas. In less than two decades, this perception had become institutionalized, so that today the mindset of the Internet bears a stronger resemblance to the mindset of the PTTs of the early 1970s than to the ARPANET of the early 1970s. Our textbooks present the Internet as the only network. (Just as 40 years earlier, the study of telecommunications was the study of how the telephone system worked.) Rationales are invented to portray what was done 30 years ago as near perfect, rather than our partial understanding at the time. Even when it is recognized that a "Copernican revolution" in networking is required, it is with the caveat not to change what we have. What sort of revolution is that?

There are uncanny parallels elsewhere in science. In Lee Smolin's recent book, *The Trouble with Physics* (2006), he describes the "seven unusual aspects of the string theory community:"[22]

1. *Tremendous self-confidence,* leading to a sense of entitlement and of belonging to an elite community of experts.

2. *An unusually monolithic community,* with a strong sense of consensus, whether driven by the evidence or not, and an unusual uniformity of views of open questions. These views seem related to the existence of a hierarchical structure in which the ideas of a few leaders dictate the viewpoint, strategy, and direction of the field.

3. In some cases, *a sense of identification with the group,* akin to identification with a religious faith or political platform.

4. A strong sense of *the boundary between the group and other experts.*

5. A *disregard for and disinterest* in the ideas, opinions, and work of experts who are not part of the group, and a preference for talking only with other members of the community.

---

[22] Quoted in their entirety both to emphasize the similarity and to assure the reader I have not been selective in quoting them.

6. A tendency to *interpret evidence optimistically*, to believe exaggerated or incorrect statements of results, and to disregard the possibility that the theory might be wrong. This is coupled with the tendency to *believe results are true because they are "widely believed,"* even if one has not checked (or even seen) the proof oneself.

7. *A lack of appreciation for the extent to which a research program ought to involve risk.*

This is a striking list. Smolin could be describing networking rather than theoretical physics. He notes that sociologists recognize these characteristics as *groupthink* and quotes Irving Janis of Yale as defining *groupthink* as "a mode of thinking that people engage in when they are deeply involved in a cohesive in-group, when the members' strivings for unanimity override their motivation to realistically appraise alternative courses of action." He goes on to quote a description of groupthink excerpted from an Oregon State University Web site dealing with communication:

Groupthink members are themselves as part of an in-group working against an outgroup opposed to their goals. You can tell if a group suffers from group-think if it

1. Overestimates its invulnerability or high moral stance

2. Collectively rationalizes the decisions it makes

3. Demonizes or stereotypes outgroups and their leaders

4. Has a culture of uniformity where individuals censor themselves and others so that the façade of group unanimity is maintained

5. Contains members who take it upon themselves to protect the group leader by keeping information, theirs or other group members' from the leader

As Smolin says about theoretical physics, this doesn't match up one for one with what we see in networking, but it is close enough to be worrying! And as Smolin points out, the in-crowd of networking will have no problem countering these critiques. But all one has to do is look at the contributions surrounding the current NSF initiative to see this groupthink at work. They are all remarkably similar, and yet none get at the core of the problem or strike out in a new direction. It would appear that the groupthink arose as part of the bunker mentality created during the "protocol wars" of the late 1970s and 1980s, when the connection versus connectionless battles were most intense. The attitude has persisted. Note how some commentators still drag out the OSI bogeyman even though it is long dead. This is reminiscent of a tactic used by countries who create an incident with a traditional rival to direct attention away from their own internal problems. Part of the problem in networking is that we now have generations of engineers and professors who have never seen anything else and don't seem to be able to imagine another way to do things; reinforced by luminaries saying there is no point in changing the underpinnings, even though the underpinnings are deeply flawed (our seven unanswered questions). To not question the under-pinnings is not only intellectually dishonest, contrary to the scientific tradition, but is building on sand!

Smolin goes on to attribute this to the increased professionalism of the field, and the same thing seems to apply to networking. He distinguishes between master craftsmen and seers. Smolin characterizes them as follows:

Master craftsmen go into science because, they are good at it. They are usually the best students in their math and physics classes from junior high school all the way up to graduate school, where they finally meet their peers. They have always been able to solve math problems faster and more accurately than their classmates, so problem solving is what they tend to value in other scientists.

Seers are different. They are dreamers. They go into science because they have questions about the nature of existence that schoolbooks don't answer.

I would refer to Smolin's seers as "theoreticians." These are people who need to get to the bottom of things to understand the deep structure and assure them-selves that everything is based on something firm, to find the similarities, the invariances. A recent article (Kramer, 2007) in CACM touched on this in lamenting the decline of abstraction in computers science. We can see how net-working (and to some degree computer science) has been selecting for the excel-lent programmer (master craftsman). But reading between the lines of Kramer's paper, one realizes that the characteristics of the super-coder are essentially anti-thetical to the characteristics of someone good at abstraction and theory.[23]

Looking back over the events chronicled in the Preface, we see the work of master craftsmen. At each juncture, a stopgap patch is found. There is no con-sideration of how it fits into a theory or whether it does. No consideration is given to how this sets things up for the next step because there is no vision of the goal. Only once does a theoretician insert an idea (Saltzer), and it is lauded but studiously ignored.[24] Smolin traces this distinction back to Kuhn's *Structure of*

---

[23] There are intersections, but they are exceedingly rare.

[24] Today you are told "we have moved beyond that" when it is not at all clear that it was ever really understood.

Scientific Revolutions (1968) and points out that master craftsmen are precisely what is required during periods of "normal" science: the period in which a new paradigm is established and is being explored and exploited. But when the new paradigm becomes the old paradigm and is showing its age, it becomes clear that a new paradigm is necessary; a different perspective is necessary.

It is when a new paradigm is needed that a period of revolutionary science has been entered, when Smolin's seers are needed. To find a new paradigm requires seeing new distinctions, questioning everything, looking carefully at what is *really* going on. Master craftsmen are not suited to finding the new paradigm. Their characterization of the problems tends to look at the edges, at the surface. Their reaction tends to be to start building things, anything, in the hope that it will be better. It is disconcerting to realize that a paradigm one learned as a student and that has always appeared hugely successful and that the world has heralded as a wonderful achievement (perhaps that one has built a career on knowing its ins and outs) will not meet fundamental needs and must be replaced. After all, the paradigms' success was based not on its own merits but elsewhere (Moore's law and politics). But this is where we find ourselves.

That Blinding Flash

Many times over the past 35 years, I have seen a new insight put forward only to watch it be greeted with "Oh, yeah, now I get it!" but of course they didn't get it, and then watch them run off to do what they thought they heard, only to get it wrong. Then, of course, it is the idea that is bad, not that they lacked the subtlety to get it right. There are a million ways to get a concept wrong but only a few ways to get it right. There are hints that possibly this was at work with connectionless, too. We saw its immediate elegance, but we failed to dig further to gain a better understanding of it, inhibited in part by the attacks of the beads-on-a-string forces and the need made unnecessary by Moore's law.

In our case, however, it appears the craftsman took over before the new paradigm shift was complete. In 1974, we were just beginning to get an understanding. Saltzer tried to jump-start a look at theory, but we lacked a driver. It would seem that we have a case of arrested development. It is interesting to note how various stalwarts of the Internet—small incremental change, the emphasis on running code, the rejection of technical sophistication—are all characteristics of an artisan tradition rather than a scientific one. There is science, actually more engineering, in specific topics, but overall the tradition has become artisan, dedicated to the development of technique, not to comprehensive theory.

We have an added problem. Hundreds of millions of people rely on our unfinished demo. But they are just a drop in the bucket of what is to come. There is no way that the current model will provide what is needed for the next 50 years or more.[25] The change has to come, and the sooner the better.

---

[25] And don't even mention IPv6. It is less than too little too late. A waste of time.

In most fields, the fundamental science comes first, at least a basic under-standing. First, we understand how nature works and predict what it will do, and then we figure out how to build things that exploit that knowledge, i.e., engineering. It seemed that in networking we were doing the engineering but not the science. But before condemning too quickly, it is good to remember that in computer science, *we build what we measure*. Not only does this make it dif-ficult to separate artifact from principle, but it also means we must build some-thing (engineer) before we can measure (science).[26]

Networks present a much different problem than our experience with, for example, operating systems. With operating systems, it is relatively easy for many different approaches to be tried. All one needs is a machine. For a net-work, one needs considerably more. By the time Multics and VMS were designed (usually considered the canonical bases for most modern operating systems), there had been at least 20 or 30 different operating system designs tried and explored. We might say that Multics and VMS are roughly v30 of operating system designs. With networks, it is much more difficult to try differ-ent approaches. At most, we had XNS, CYCLADES, NPL, ARPANET, and the few X.25 networks to draw on, and they were all small networks. This is not to say that we still would not have done something fairly close to what we have, but we had much less experience with the problem space when we settled on what we do have. And it was much more difficult to try other forms. Even doing just one new protocol was (and is) a major effort, let alone a new architecture.

When we step back and look at what we have, given what we have seen here, it is apparent that what we have is closer to DOS, what we *need* is Multics, but we would probably settle for UNIX.

Very quickly, research on networks became more "engineering the Internet." How many good ideas have been squashed by "But how would it work in the Internet" or "You could never do *that* in the Internet." When did good research start to be predicated on whether it could be deployed in a single product? The telephone network prior to the 1970s? With that attitude there would never have been an Internet. Little work has been done to understand general proper-ties of networks, to understand the deep structure and how architectures other

---

26 One might argue that this is true of any experimental apparatus in any science, but I contend there is a big difference between building an inclined plane to study the motion of balls in a constant gravitational field and building gravity to measure its properties!

than the one we have may work. Basically, we have been engineering and not doing much, if any, science. There has been too much emphasis on the next neat whiz-bang thing, too much emphasis on the latest hot topic, too much emphasis on academic research as angel funding, and not enough emphasis on *science* on what these new hot topics tell us about general principles.

The difference between science and engineering is crucial. When most people think of "doing science," their first thought of experimental method, as we saw in the NRC report cited at the beginning of this chapter. But experimental method is a key element of both good science and good engineering. This is not what distinguishes science and engineering. The crux of the difference between science and engineering is that science is concerned with understanding, whereas engineering is concerned with applying that understanding to real-world situations. One might say that engineers are fascinated by exploiting the differences, whereas scientists are fascinated by the similarities, with finding the invariances. The Holy Grail of every scientist is to do for his field what Euclid did for geometry. What Newton did for mechanics. What Maxwell did for classical electricity and magnetism. What Mendeleev did for chemistry. Accomplishing the goal matters less than striving for it. We have lost sight of that in our corner of computer science.

Previously in computer science, this kind of abstraction and theory was common. Everyone knew the basic results of automata theory, for example. Today one would be hard pressed to find a computer science graduate who had ever heard of the halting problem, let alone knew what it means. Perhaps this is because everyone has been trained in a field where theory and abstraction is part of the tradition. But some bad experiences with theory run rampant, and a continuing push for applicability, not to mention visions of dollar signs, has seen a waning of theory (as well as appeals to futility, as in "X is 80% of the market. Why worry about knowing what is the right way?"). It has been decades since theory has been seen in networking. Maybe I don't read the right journals. But if it exists, it isn't in the mainstream, and it needs to be. Everyone needs to be aware of how what he is doing fits into the bigger picture (or doesn't).

The Importance of Theory

We have seen another example in the history of science where a rich and successful scientific tradition stagnated and lost information. For millennia, China had such a successful scientific tradition that China was ahead of Europe, some-times by centuries. The Chinese developed Pascal's triangle 300 years before Pascal, and Western medicine did not surpass the cure rate of Chinese medicine until the beginning of the 20th century. These are just two examples of the sophistication of the tradition. But ultimately, Chinese science stagnated. In his multivolume magnum opus, *Science and Civilization in China* (1965), Joseph Needham concludes that the reason for stagnation was that the merchant class was low in the social hierarchy. Without merchants to create demand for new innovations, the need for progress declined when the power structure lived as well as it thought it could. Half-jokingly, one could turn Needham's argument around to say that it was a strong reliance on government funding that caused science to stagnate in early China. China was a hegemony, a very strong one. If you were in favor with the emperor, everything was golden, if not.... This was in contrast to Europe, where there was no hegemony. When Galileo first got into trouble with the Pope, he went to teach at Padua, then under the control of Venice, a major power and could afford to be independent. There was little the Pope could do. In Europe, if new ideas caused political problems and made things a bit untenable, there was always someplace to go.[27] My enemy's enemy is my friend.

But there is more to the stagnation of science in China. It is sometimes difficult to compare Western science with what one finds in China. Much of what is in Needham's comprehensive survey (seven volumes, some volumes consisting of multiple books, all quite copious) is more technology than science. Many of the advances came out of an artisan tradition, as they did in the West during this period. But unlike Western science, they stayed there. This belies what is perhaps the greatest difference between Western and Chinese science. Although Needham recognized the lack of theory, neither he nor other historians have assigned much importance to it as a factor in maintaining a vibrant scientific tradition. The most significant difference is that more than a lack of theory it is that

China had no Euclid.[28]

There was essentially no tradition of *theory* in Chinese science, and certainly not axiomatic theory, of systematizing the results. Needham points out that the body of knowledge represented by Chinese science was more a set of individual techniques than an organized corpus of knowledge.[29] There was no attempt to develop the kind of overarching theory to integrate a set of results into a com-prehensive whole that has characterized Western science. It is hard to find much

---

[27] Galileo's problems started when he got homesick and returned to Florence to teach at Pisa.

[28] Ricci translated Euclid for the Chinese in the early 17th century (Spence, 1984).

[29] This is consistent with the strong artisan aspect of the tradition.

evidence of attempts (outside of astronomy) to develop predictive theories, or anything analogous to the discipline of proof found in Western science. [30] The pressure of commerce alone would generate new results but not the impetus for consolidation that comes from theory. As we have said, the Holy Grail of every scientist is to do for his field what Euclid did for geometry: reduce it to a small number of concepts from which every thing can be derived.[31] Early China is not the only example. There is definite evidence that artisan or craft traditions have a tendency to become insular and protective—more concerned with perpetuating the guild than invalidating its *raison d'être*. In other words, they stagnate.

Working toward a comprehensive theory, even if one is not found, is beneficial. We seem to have fallen into a bad habit that our only criteria for a solution to a problem is whether the code can be made to work in a reasonable amount of space.[32] Every time we solve a problem, we should consider how it fits the current theory. If it doesn't, we need to ask which is wrong: the solution or the theory. What is it we don't understand? As different models are proposed and tested, a deeper understanding of the problem domain is achieved, even if the proposed model is wrong. It will get better. A good theory is, at the very least, a good mnemonic. There is less to remember. One only need remember the central concepts, a few intermediate principles, and roughly how things relate, and everything else can be derived. Many major results of Chinese science were forgotten, some because they weren't needed very often. For example, when Matteo Ricci first entered China at the end of the 16th century, he was convinced that he had brought the knowledge that the Earth was round (Day, 1995). As it turns out, the Chinese had determined this 300 years earlier, but the knowledge had been lost.[33] We are seeing similar loss of knowledge today in computer science as the same solutions are published as new, as the technological pendulum swings back and forth.

Without a unifying theory to simplify knowledge, the amount of information was eventually overwhelming. But theory is much more than just a mnemonic.

---

[30]   Expecting something like scientific method or predictive theory may be expecting too much. Scientific method, even in a rudimentary form, did not arise in the West until science had already begun to stagnate in China. It is possible that a critical mass of results was necessary for "science" to arise. One could argue, however, that China should have achieved that critical mass earlier. Another factor is that while China changed dynasties several times between the Han and Ming (~ 2,000 years), they didn't change bureaucracies. Just as, according to de Tocqueville, the French didn't change bureaucracies between the *ancien regime* and the Republic.

[31]   Well, okay, nearly everything, thanks to Gödel.

[32]   Not unusual for craftsmen.

[33]   Probably lost due to lack of use. The fact that the earth is round is a prominent issue for a culture focused on maritime ventures as Europe was, but since most Chinese trade was overland, the knowledge was seldom needed.

A theory, even a partial one, leads to deeper understanding of the phenomena being studied and to further insights. Proposals of a unifying theory (even if unsuccessful) raise questions relating disparate phenomena that would not otherwise arise. When there is a theoretical framework, results can be derived that were far from obvious before. Theory not only provides a simpler, more logical explanation, but it also has a tendency to simplify individual techniques (making them easier to understand and apply). Many techniques coalesce to become degenerate cases of a more general method. To see this, one only need read accounts of electricity and magnetism before Maxwell, chemistry before the periodic chart, or geology before plate tectonics.

It is the individual discoveries combined with the search for an encompassing or simpler theory that is the essential tension that gives science direction and allays stagnation. Theory questions the meaning of the observations and techniques that make it up. Theory points at experiments that test its veracity and attempt to invalidate it. Theory points at its own limits. Theory becomes a map of our knowledge and thus pushes us toward better theories.

The processes that have been operating on our science are creating a situation similar to the one found in China of the late Ming Dynasty. Network research has come to this juncture by a different route. Hopefully, it will not have the same end. While we have innovation being driven by the merchant class, they are looking for a quick ROI, i.e., technique, not great leaps forward. To compound the problem, research funding is flitting from fad to fad every few years, generating techniques but giving theory little time to gestate. This, in turn, has a strong effect on researchers. Ross Ashby (1956) noted that the longer a state machine operated, the output became independent of the input and began to reflect the structure of the machine itself.[34] We are conditioning researchers to produce techniques, not science. There is no theory.[35] It isn't that the basics of Research 101 are unfamiliar in our field. What is unfamiliar is that our research must contribute to building a theory. The problem is that the bulk of our researchers have not had training in doing good theory. In mathematics, yes, but not in science.

As anyone who has taken a science course knows, the first step in science is not to measure as the NAS study says. The first step is to state a *hypothesis*. To state a hypothesis, one must *start* with a theory to be invalidated.[36] As Einstein

---

[34]   His favorite example of this principle was that when you met someone in the UK, you could immediately tell what public school they had gone to.

[35]   It must be admitted that theory as sometimes practiced by academia and even corporate research labs has sometimes given theory a bad name. Big investments made in too many big claims have failed to live up their promise leading to more demand for early practical results.

[36]   As Popper showed, you can never prove a theory correct; you can only invalidate it.

is often quoted, "It is the theory that determines the data." Without theory, you don't know what questions to ask, and you don't know what data is relevant or how to measure it.

I once asked a good friend and a Nobel laureate[37] in physics about Galileo as a theorist and got a strong reaction, "*No!* Galileo was the great experimentalist!" True, Galileo's experimental method was exemplary and important to the development of science. But his method would have meant nothing had he not had the insight to see the model that was at the core of the problem. Galileo had thought long and hard before those famous experiments were done. Galileo's brilliance was in picking the right model on which to base his experiments: falling bodies in relatively controlled conditions. If Galileo had attacked a problem of practical value such as predicting where cannonballs would land (and I am sure that APRAF[38] would have funded him), he would have found his equations useless. In fact, people did try to apply his results to cannonballs and found his equations were off by as much as 50%.[39] But Galileo did not start by trying to find equations that would take into account wind drift, air resistance, or that cannonballs were not perfect spheres. The solution to where a cannonball lands requires far more complex equations, at least a system of three-dimensional second-order partial differential equations.[40] Whereas Galileo's model could be described with a simple polynomial and confirmed by relatively simple, well-controlled experiments. After the basics of the theory had been worked out, the results for cannonballs could be reasonably achieved by enhancements to Galileo's equations; but almost impossible if you were to try to start it from the start with a clean sheet of paper. *Galileo had the insight to pick an initial model that had a small number of independent variables, could be tested experimentally, and could form the basis to solve more complex problems.* But then (and I hesitate to say this), Galileo and his colleagues had the faith to believe in the elegance of the solution even when it contradicted experience, the great Aristotle, and important real-world data. (This is not uncommon in the annals of science [Fleck, 1981].)

Needham recognized that a strong central government as the only patron of science could lead to stagnation. Not surprisingly, he did not foresee that the short ROI demanded by a successful merchant class could have the same effect.

---

[37] Who was more an experimenter than a theorist.

[38] *"Agenzia di Progetti di Ricerche Avanzate di Firenze."*

[39] Today you could not get funding for the equivalent of rolling balls down an inclined plane or dropping them off a tower; it has to have practical application. Is it any wonder our field is in stagnation?

[40] Not to mention that calculus had not yet been invented and to some extent required these results to create the impetus for its invention.

It would seem that we have created the conditions for stagnation. Depending on your degree of pessimism, it is now up to us to avoid it or get ourselves out of it.

Finding a New Path

Avoiding the proliferation of technique or, more positively, encouraging the consolidation of technique by theory is difficult. Although, the private sector is more interested in technique, or as they call it product differentiation, theory is not just the responsibility of the research community. Such consolidation is just as important to the private sector for decreasing cost, improving performance, and creating new opportunities. Furthermore it occurs at many levels, some only the purview of those building product. At the same time, we must keep theory from its flights of fancy and close to "its proper soil," the practical.

There are many platitudes for encouraging theory and good research. As previously mentioned, it is exceedingly hard to rush theory but it is easy to discourage it. It often seems that all one can do is to create a fertile environment and hope for the best. But there are some things that will help create fertile ground. One can argue that research programs and funding should do more to stress theory. But how many researchers have a sufficiently broad exposure to multiple paradigms, the history of science, and to some extent philosophy to be able to think about it from the outside? And how quickly will it be viewed as just another means to exploit the funding process? This could harbor a lot of less than serious work, and it would be very hard to distinguish between that with real potential and that that had done. Clearly, keeping an eye on the fundamentals is important, always holding proposals up to those fundamentals. A better understanding of the fundamentals is never a waste of time or money. On the other hand, this book demonstrates that new insights are more a product of hard thought than hard cash.

But what are the fundamental principles that can be taken from theory in computer science? Fundamental principles are relations that are invariant across important problem domains. The more fundamental, the greater the scope of their use. To have principles, we need good theory. But developing theory in computer *science* is much more difficult than in any other field because as I have said many times before,

we build what we measure.[41]

Because there are few principles to rely on, we often see new efforts going all the way back to the beginning. Hence, many different decisions are made in each

---

[41] I know I keep repeating this, but it is *that* important.

new effort, which in turn makes it more difficult to compare different approaches to the same problem, which further complicates our ability to discern principle and artifact.

But we can leverage this unique nature of computer science to get our arms around the problem of separating theory from artifact. There are essentially two parts to computer science: a part that is mathematical, and a part that is scientific. Mathematics is not a science. In mathematics, the only requirement is that a theory be logically consistent. In science, a theory must be logically consistent *and* fit the data. Many aspects of computer science are purely mathematical: automata theory, complexity theory, algorithms, even to a large extent programming languages, and so forth. Although they are rooted in mathematics, it is the "systems" disciplines of computer science that are the more scientific: computer system design, operating systems, networks, database systems, and so on.[42] For theory to consolidate knowledge, it must find models that emphasize the invariants in the logical structure. This is much of what we have tried to do in this book.

Because mathematics is independent of the data, this can provide us with a means to develop theory in the systems disciplines of computer science. In a real sense, there are principles in these fields that are independent of technology and independent of the data. Principles follow from the logical constraints (axioms) that form the basis of the class of systems.[43] This is the *architecture*.[44] Within this structure, there are additional principles, which are dependent on the data and independent of the technology or implementation. Specific choices in this space yield specific designs. These two should form the content of university-level texts in a field. And finally, there are the "principles" or relations that are dependent on the technology. These form the basis of product manuals and technical books.

The first two are pure theory. Here is where the pressure to emulate Euclid is most felt. One wants to find the minimal set of principles needed for a model that yields the greatest results with the simplest concepts. The general principles derived from the empirical will often take the form of a trade-off or principles that operate within certain bounds or relations between certain measures. Goodput in networking is a good example of this. We have seldom distin-

---

[42] I do not propose that to draw this distinction too finely, but see it as a useful way to think about our discipline. And in fact, some curricula make this distinction.

[43] One should not assume that there is a single set of "axioms" for operating systems or networks any more than there is a single set of axioms for geometry. The set of axioms merely serves to create a footing on which to build a theory to test.

[44] Our field also has a tendency toward "term inflation." Architecture is used to be synonymous with hardware; architect with chief engineer, topology when we mean graph, and so on. We need to be more careful.

guished these three forms of knowledge. We have not subjected ourselves to the same discipline that other sciences follow. This tendency contributes to the proliferation of techniques and ultimately to the stagnation of our field. This is hard work. It requires disciplined experiments. But it is possible. And it beats working in a stagnant field.

As a start in extracting us from this malaise, this book has attempted to show how we have come across more of the principles than we may have thought. To lay the groundwork for a general theory of networking. To tease out the fundamental structure of a complete network architecture, not just an unfinished demo. So, let's review the high points of what has been covered here and consider their implications.

The High Points

In the first five chapters of this book, we looked at major aspects of networking and what we had learned along the way. We considered the patterns that fell out when we extracted the invariances from protocols, and how we might create a synthesis for the connectionless/connection dichotomy. And while we found that there was no upper-layer architecture, we did find concepts that would prove crucial to understanding the structure. We dug into naming and addressing and found much good work had been done that was still waiting to be applied, which when extended to accommodate new conditions presaged the structure we found when we came to sorting out layers. Sorting out layers proved to be a little embarrassing; the answer had been staring us in the face all along, being precisely what we had always said it was: IPC! We had been skipping steps and getting sloppy! But after we assembled it, there was a lot to reflect on:

- First and foremost, there is one layer that provides interprocess communication and it repeats. All layers have the same complement of functions (in particular instances, some functions may be null) but are configured (with policies) for different ranges of the problem.

- The IPC model makes it clear that the network or Internet layer was the last vestige of the "beads-on-a-string" model. It disappears. The data link layer developers got it right, but only because we only gave them one layer to work with! Networking is very much a discipline of computing systems. Telecommunications is dead or applies only to the physical media. There are implications for operating systems here that are yet to be fully explored.

- This model confirms our understanding that security functions belong in the application. Even IPC security is just a specific form of application security, because IPC processes are applications.

- The distributed IPC model is inherently more secure in that it minimizes information available to attackers, requires minimal information from applications, makes it possible to put requirements on its members, and requires minimal trust in supporting services. When combined with current security techniques, it can create a network secured to the degree required by its developers. The enrollment phase establishes the level of trust in the DIF.

- Layers (also called distributed IPC facilities) have different scope (or if the same scope, are of different ranks) and serve significantly different ranges of effective bandwidth.

What About the End-to-End Principle?

Nearly every architecture paper in the field cites it, but I have a simple question: Why not? The astute reader will have already realized the answer: It simply never came up. And, in a recursive architecture, the concept of "end" is a non sequitor.

- The decomposition of the structure into three loci of processing with different cycle times—ranging from the very simple and fast for data transfer; to somewhat slower, somewhat more complex control; to slower, yet more complex management—all decoupled from each other through a RIB/state vector is quite elegant and satisfying.

- Our thinking about EFCP-like protocols and the fact that we weren't clear about the bounds on what went into them had to some degree obscured this structure. When we understand that this is the per-instance IPC channel, limit what should be in them, and remove the invariances (that is, separate mechanism and policy), we see that UDP and TCP are actually part of the same protocol. This then leads to a somewhat unexpected result: There are only two protocols in networking.

1. An error- and flow-control protocol to create the equivalent of an IPC channel. It consists of a single Transfer PDU and optional Control PDUs to support loosely coupled mechanisms. Common PCI is added under two conditions:

To carry internal addressing information, if the IPC facility has more than two members

For PDU protection (that is, CRC, time to live, encryption)

2. An application protocol that provides information exchange for the distributed IPC, including the following:

An IPC access for implementing search rules and access control.

A Resource Information Exchange for distributing near-real-time resource information necessary for managing the IPC facility. Connection setup for this protocol provides the means to authenticate new members and assign addresses.

A DIF management that performs the role of a traditional network management.

- delta-t turns out not just to be a good example of an EFCP but fits into the structure as if it were made for it. I had always known that it was probably the intellectual paragon in protocol design but had not realized how much better it fit the context. Early on, I realized that for an EFCP to support a wide range of services, as it must in the higher layers (transport), separate PDUs for loosely coupled mechanisms would make degenerate cases fall out more simply and make it easier for the implementation to exploit the natural separation of control and data. That implied that protocols such as SeqPkt or TP4 might be a better choice than TCP.[45] But after the rest of the IPC structure was in place, it was clear that delta-t fit like a hand in a glove. This was a surprise. It allowed for an elegance in the structure that had not been foreseen. It also emphasized the importance of the decoupling.

- Decoupling application requests from the protocol action as a key element of the structure. Determining what to do with a user request for communication resources isn't just invoking the EFCP protocol machine, as we have all seen it for the past 35 years, but involves invoking the DIF's management. This clarifies all sorts of aspects of resource management.

- The application protocol is probably best served by a generalized and updated version of HEMS, as discussed in Chapter 4.

---

[45] I had always been uncomfortable with the fact that TCP didn't separate control and data (something that seemed fairly iron-clad in protocol design, but it had seemed like a good idea at the time).

• As noted in Chapter 4, OSI figured out that there were no general-purpose upper layers. There might be common functions that some applications used, and specific application domains might have additional layers (that is, relaying and error control with greater scope). OSI might have made more progress on the implications of that had the PTTs not stolen the session layer. The design sensibilities of the telecom tradition were misguided and continue to be as we have seen with WAP, Bluetooth, and now IMS. OSI's other contribution was working out the relation between the application process and application protocol. This not only makes logical sense, but it has also proved to have wider implications, clearly explaining constructs that were unforeseen to be related. What was surprising was that this relation became key to understanding the structure of the "lower layers" (IPC).

• The "session layer," whatever it was to be, turns out to be part of IPC management. A case where two kludges (the theft of the session layer in OSI and DNS as not quite a directory in the Internet) made it hard to see the answer. But the natural way that it fits—corresponding to operating system search rules and access control and how the case of "out of date" DNS/directory information (also known as a mobile application) is a degenerate case of normal operation—indicates that this is clearly "right."

• We also found that protocol-ids are unnecessary. At first it looked like protocol-ids identified syntax, and they did. But after the IPC model was understood, it was clear that they were completely unnecessary. If there is a protocol-id in a protocol design, the layer design is faulty; either the layer boundary is in the wrong place or there is no EFCP or no enrollment or both.

• By the same token, the flow-id in IPv6 would be unnecessary if the existing flow-id hadn't been used for something else. One kludge leads to another. Not having the equivalent of the IPC access protocol leads to well-known ports and leaves no flow-id available.

• Connectionless turns out to be maximal state, not minimal state. This was a rude turn of events and completely upset everything I had thought (and claimed loudly) for 35 years! As it turns out, we had been drawing the boundaries too tightly and comparing apples and oranges. Like trying to do a conservation of energy problem with the wrong bounds on the system! Connection-oriented concentrated on congestion control and put routing at the edge, while connectionless concentrated on routing and did nothing about congestion until it hit us over the head. When it is put this way, it makes a lot of sense and points the way to some interesting, new directions to providing connections with connectionless properties and to providing QoS without having to resort to strong connections as in MPLS. It appears that the dumb network wasn't so dumb after all! When we compare apples and apples, the amount of state appears to be about the same. The difference is in where it is. This therefore argues that connectionless is characterized by maximal distributed state, whereas connection-oriented is characterized by concentrating state, primarily at the ends.

- Layers recurse. We should have seen this coming. Dijkstra and the 1960s were so resource constrained that it focused our attention on differences rather than similarities. And although there are allusions to recursion in the original catenet paper (Cerf, 1978), it seems to have been forgotten. The lesson of large bridged LANs should have told us to expect the same for large routed networks.

- When the layers have a common structure, the implementation is streamlined and does not incur the overhead of traditional layers. In effect, it organizes the processing and doesn't get in the way, which makes implementation more compact and effective. This undoubtedly has significant implications for moving functionality into silicon.

- We had always assumed that addresses were names of protocol machines as application names were the names of applications. So, it was quite surprising to realize that in the context of the distributed IPC model, addresses are identifiers *internal* to the DIF to coordinate its operation. The IPC process is an application process and as such has an application name. This is what is used to initially establish communication with it.

- Saltzer's addressing model from the 1980s requires only slight generalization to include a case that didn't exist when Saltzer wrote and provides an elegant example of "throwing away the ladder." It presages the recursive model, and then Saltzer's distinction of node and point of attachment turn out to be relative and, when combined with the last bullet, a natural consequence of the IPC structure. We needed Saltzer's result to see the answer, but after we had the answer we no longer needed the result!

- But we also found a nice parallel progression in the roles that names and addresses have in a network. The architecture of external application names is essentially a projection onto internal DIF addresses:

Application names:		location-independent	system-independent
Application instance-names:		location-independent	system-dependent
Sentential names:		location-independent	system-independent
Sentential identifiers:	route-independent	location-independent	system-independent
Node addresses:	route-independent	location-dependent	system-dependent
Point-of-attachment addresses:	route-dependent	location-dependent	system-dependent

- "Private" addresses turn out to be the general case, and "public" addresses are a specific kind of private address. This was totally unexpected, and I am sure is not going to be popular among those whose utopian desires outstrip their scientific discipline. But this is consistent with the world we now find ourselves, where potentially everyone owns their own network, not just large corporations or governments. It appears now that the idea of the global public address that everyone has to have was an artifact of artificial constraints of early technology that are no longer necessary. One can break out of the tyranny of being accessible within a single global address space: one more blow for freedom, privacy, and security, another blow against the Orwellian tyranny of having to be always connected to *the* public network.

- The layer as distributed IPC reveals minimal information and allows strict control over the information made available to the application. This provides a much more robust structure within which to provide security services.

- And last but not least, this model seems to do an admirable job of meeting Newton's guidelines. We will be hard pressed to find a simpler model that solves as many problems that isn't isomorphic to this one. In other words, this isn't just a nice model, it is *the* basis for a general theory of networking.

Reflecting on this model and looking at what we have been working with, it is clear that what we have today is more analogous to a rudimentary operating system like DOS than to a full-fledged operating system like Multics or VMS. Like DOS, all the pieces are there to call it an operating system, but there are a few things missing that give it everything we think of when we think of an operating system. There are many reasons why this was the case and we have discussed many of them. But still, it should serve as a lesson for the future. We should have seen this sooner (me included).

I must admit this model was constructed not so much looking to solve specific problems, but carefully analyzing interprocess communication between distinct systems with an eye to extracting invariances and minimizing discontinuities. Trying to see what was really going on. It would not be going too far astray to say that finding an elegant, simple structure was the primary overriding concern.[46] But, of course, this pursuit of elegance was not without a clear knowledge of the problems it needs to solve. Even so, on numerous occasions it

---

[46] I must admit that I did not follow the steps that any system design book tells you to follow: requirements analysis and all that. And I believe that if I had, this structure would not have resulted.

became clear only long after arriving at the structure that the structure solved a particular problem, not something I had consciously set out to solve. With this structure, we find that it has a number of interesting properties:

- Most important, the model scales over any range of bandwidth, number of elements, distance, and so on.

- This allows a complexity implosion that eliminates the need for hundreds of specialized standards, makes networks much easier to manage, and allows more effort to be brought to bear on doing more sophisticated services with the network rather wasting it on twisting an incomplete structure to new ends.

- Initializing a DIF is just a case of setting up an application connection. The application authenticates its peer. In this case, that authentication corresponds to ensuring that the process is an acceptable member of the DIF. All that the DIF can guarantee is that as far as it can tell this is what the source asked for. IPC can't not guarantee it.

- This model provides a strong foundation for doing science and for teaching university-level networking, not vo-tec. This model allows us to eliminate variables so that we may better compare results of experiments.

- Multihoming is inherent in the structure.

- Mobility is dynamic multihoming, a consequence of simply configuring the structure appropriately. All forms of mobility (mobile subnets, systems, or applications) are easily accommodated without special cases.

- The model simplifies multicast by more closely integrating it into routing and similarly makes anycast generally useful.

- Then multicast turns out to facilitate aspects of mobility.

- The structure can be secured to whatever degree necessary. The repeating structure also means that it is less work and that if bugs are found they only have to be fixed once.

- Among the things that scale is router table size. With topological addresses and recursion, the number of routes that any one router has to store can be bounded. In the worst case, the total number of routes in a network might be the same, but no router would have to store anything close to all of them.

- Congestion control can be utilized in many places either with or without the cooperation of applications. (Far beyond the scope of this book, there are early indications that this structure makes much better congestion control and QoS possible, which then provides much finer control over a network.)

- With a full naming and addressing complement, sophisticated distributed applications are possible without additional protocols. (Voice call management is a fairly simple use of these capabilities.)

- Other application structures turn out to be cases of IPC—mail relaying (or any application relaying), aspects of transaction processing, and so-called peer-to-peer protocols. This also has the odd implication of removing the "transport layer" barrier from the network providers that started the protocol wars in the first place. Network equipment vendors and network providers, it could easily be argued, are in the IPC business. IPC doesn't stop at the network but continues up into what has traditionally been seen as applications.

- But probably most important, a common repeating structure will have a profound affect on network management. Rather than layers crafted with all sorts of bells and whistles, all with delusions of being the answer to everything, layers (DIFs) are configured to address well-defined ranges of bandwidth and QoS with protocols that are configured to behave in similar and complementary ways. This will promote scalability, repeatability, orthogonality, and commonality, greatly simplifying and improving the effectiveness of network management.

Does this throw out much of the work of the past 20 years? Not really. As with any shift in thinking, there will be a few topics that were once popular that will be mentioned much less frequently. However, because much of the research of the past 20 years has been on technique, much of it can be translated into what we would call policy; this work can be carried over. In fact, more research may find application since there is less requirement that all equipment do the same thing and hence greater diversity in the networks and layers that may occur. This model will make it easier to evaluate when which policies should be used and the boundary conditions within which well-behaved policies should be constructed.

Where do we go from here? This book is an attempt to bridge the gulf between what we have seen in our experience with networks over the past nearly 40 years and to get us out of the blind alley we seem to have marched into. With any luck, this book will help to restart the revolution begun by the

ARPANET, CYCLADES, NPLnet, and all of those other "old guys" but was derailed by two decades of conflict. With even more luck, this book will serve as an inspiration for a new generation of young Turks[47] to have the excitement that we had and to make the kind of mark we made. I hope this book helps rally the seers still left in computer science to throw off the corruption of Moore's law and return to distilling principles and abstractions and maybe even theory, making the advances that have been lying in wait all these years. Rescue us from the stagnation of mounting technique.

By the time this book publishes, there should be specifications available for a DIF that can be debated and implemented and for which policies can be written. Discussion, experimentation, and exploration can begin—working out the policies for different forms of DIFs from what used to be called the data link layer through the resource-allocation layers and into what we called applications. I hope this book opens up new ideas about providing QoS and routing using addresses. I intend to also begin assembling a textbook that uses this model and its results as its organizing principle (a book based on invariances and principles, a true university-level textbook).

What do I expect the reaction to this book to be? Some are going to be intrigued and probably enjoy the read (I hope). I would hope that people will read this, consider its foundation in IPC, and realize that although it doesn't agree with much accepted wisdom, it is well founded and might just represent the basis for a new generation to have their day in the sun. Clearly an approach to networking like this benefits the owners of networks more than the vendors. Major vendors will hate it because it represents further commodization and simplification. Engineers will hate it, because it requires many fewer engineers to develop and configure policies than developing whole new protocols and will come up with all sorts of excuses to continue their expensive proliferation of special cases and unnecessary optimizations. The greatest expense in networking today is staff, both operations and engineering. This direction requires much less of both.

But the bulk of the reaction? That is easy. In Hafner's *Where Wizard's Stay Up Late*, Bob Metcalfe describes the reaction of the AT&T engineers to the ARPANET demo at ICCC in 1972. Pretty much the same response is likely here. I hope not, but I won't be surprised. Do we care? They are the new bellheads and already well past their prime. The future belongs to IPC!

No, technology does not change the world. Imagination does.

---

[47]   That's what they called us.

Appendix A

Outline for Gedanken Experiment on Separating Mechanism and Policy

January 1993

Part I
Service Definitions

  0 Introduction

  1 Scope

  2 References

  3 Definitions

  4 Compliance with other Specifications

  5 Overview of the Service

      5.1   Narrative Description of the Service

      5.2   Basic Service and Options

  6 Detailed Specification of the Service

      6.x   Name of the Service Primitive

            6.x.1   Description of the Function

            6.x.2   Conditions for Generating (This Primitive)

<This section should contain both the prose description and the formal description.>

6.x.3   Action on Receipt (of This Primitive)

\<This section should contain both the prose description and the formal description.\>

6.x.4   Semantics of the Parameters (of the Primitive)

\<This section should contain a complete specification (or a pointer to complete specification) of the parameters in the primitive.\>

Part II
Protocol Specifications

0   Introduction

1   Scope

2   References

3   Definitions

4   Compliance with Other Standards

5   Overview of the Protocol

    5.1   Narrative Description of the Protocol

    5.2   Reference to the Service Definition

    5.3   Services Required by This Protocol

    5.4   Basic Protocol and Extensions

6   Detailed Specification of the Protocol

    6.1   Detailed Specification of Common Functions

    (Subsections giving a detailed specification of common functions following the style used for the PDUs in 6.2)

    6.2   Detailed Specification of PDU Behavior

        6.2.i.1   Name of PDU

        6.2.i.2   Function

        6.2.i.3   Conditions for Generating (This PDU)

            6.2.i.3.1   Prose Description

            6.2.i.3.2   Formal Description

Part III
Mechanism Specifications

5.6 Additional Actions Associated with the Generic Protocol

 5.6.1 Data.submit

  5.6.1.1. Informal Specification

  5.6.1.2. Formal Specification

 5.6.2 Data PDU

  5.6.2.1. Informal Specification

  5.6.2.2. Formal Specification

5.7 Actions Associated with Imported PDUs

5.8 New PDUs or Timers Associated with This Mechanism

 5.8.1 New PDU Name

  5.8.1.1 Description

  5.8.1.2 When Generated

   5.8.1.2.1 Informal Specification

  5.8.1.3 Action

   5.8.1.3.1 Informal Specification

  5.8.1.4 Syntax

  5.8.1.5 Semantics of the Fields

 5.8.2 New Timer Name

  5.8.2.1 Description

  5.8.2.2 When Activated

  5.8.2.3 Action upon Expiration

Bibliography

Abbot, E. *Flatland, 2nd Edition.* 1884 (republished Dover, 1953).

Ashby, R. *An Introduction to Cybernetics.* New York: John Wiley & Sons, 1963 (first published Chapman & Hall, 1956).

Aura, T and Nikander, P. "Stateless connections." Technical Report A46, Helsinki University of Technology, Digital Systems Laboratory, May 1997.

Baran, P. "On Distributed Communications: I. Introduction to a Distributed Communications Network." *Rand Report* RM-3420-PR, August 1964.

Belnes, D. "Single Message Communication." *IEEE Transactions on Communications* COM-24:2, February 1976: 190–194.

Birrell, A.; Levin, R.; Needham, R.; and Shroeder, M. "Grapevine: An Exercise in Distributed Computing." *CACM* 25:4, April 1982.

Bourbaki, N. *Elements of Mathematics: General Topology.* Berlin: Springer-Verlag, 1990 (originally published as *Éléments de Mathématique, Topologie Générale,* 1971).

Bourbaki, N. *Elements of Mathematics: Theory of Sets.* Paris: Hermann; Addison-Wesley, 1968 (originally published as *Éléments de Mathématique, Théorie des Ensembles*).

Carnap, R. *Introduction to Symbolic Logic and Its Applications.* Dover, 1958.

CCITT/SGXI Recommendation Z.101–Z.104. "Functional Specification and Description Language." 1988.

Cerf, V.; McKenzie, A.; Scantlebury, R.; and Zimmermann, H. "Proposal for an Internetwork End-to-End Transport Protocol" Rev. 1 (revision edited by M. Gien, G. Grossman, C. Sunshine). IFIP WG 6.1 INWG General Note 96, January 1978.

Cerf, V. "The Catenet Model for Internetworking." IEN #48, July 1978.

Chesson, G.; Eich, B.; Schryver, V.; Cherenson, A.; and Whaley, A. "XTP Protocol Definition" Ver. 3. Silicon Graphics, 1988.

Chiappa, N. "Endpoints and Endpoint Names: A Proposed Enhancement to the Internet Architecture." internet-draft, March 1995.

Clark, D; Jacobson, V.; Romkey, J.; and Salwen, H. "An Analysis of TCP Processing Overhead." *IEEE Communications Magazine* 27:6, June 1989: 23–29.

Clark, D. and Tennenhouse, D. "Architectural Considerations for a New Generation of Protocols." ACM Proceedings of ACM SIGCOMM, 1990.

Clark, D.; Sollins, K; Wroclawski, J.; Katabi, D.; Kulik, J.; Yang X.; Braden, R.; Faber, T.; Falk, A.; Pingali, V.; Handley, M.; and Chiappa, N. "New Arch: Future Generation Internet Architecture." DARPA/ITO (issued by Air Force Research Laboratory, Rome), New York, 2003.

Curran, J. "TCP & UDP with Network-independent Endpoints (TUNE)." internet-draft, October 1992.

Dabek, F.; Burnskill, E.; Kaashoek, M. F.; Karger, D.; Morris, R.; Stoica, R.; and Balakrishnan, H. "Building Peer-to-Peer Systems with Chord, a Distributed Lookup System." Procedings of the 8th Workshop on Hot Topics in Operating Systems, IEEE, 2001: 71–76.

Dalal, Y. "Broadcast Protocols in Packet Switched Computer Networks." Digital Systems Laboratory, Department of Electrical Engineering, Stanford University, 1977.

Danthine, A. "Modeling and Verification of End-to-End Transport Protocols." Proceedings of National Telecommunications Conference, Los Angeles, December 1977.

Day, J. "The Search for the Manuscript Maps of Matteo Ricci." *Imago Mundi* Volume 47, 1995.

Day, J. and Sunshine, C. " A Bibliography of Formal Description Verification of Computer Network Protocols," Proceedings of Computer Network Protocols Symposium (Leige, Belgium), February 12–15, 1978.

Day, J. The (Un)Revised OSI Reference Model, ACM SIGCOMM *Computer Communications Review,* October 1995.

Day, J. "The Reference Model for Open Systems Interconnection," *Computer Network Protocols and Architectures, 2nd Edition* (edited by C. Sunshine). Plenum, 1990.

Dijkstra, E. "The Structure of THE Operating System Multiprogramming System." *CACM* 11:5, 1968: 341–346.

Estrin, D.; Fariaacci, D.; Helmy, A.; Jacobson, V.; and Wei, L. "Protocol Independent Multicast (PIM): Dense Mode Protocol Specification." draft-ietf-idmr-PIM-DM-spec.01.ps, 1996.

Farber, D. Larson, K. "The System Architecture of the Distributed Computer System—The Communications Service," *Computer Communications Networks and Teletraffic* (edited by J. Fox). Brooklyn: Polytechnic Press, 1972.

Fermi, L. and Bernardini, G. *Galileo and the Scientific Revolution.* Dover, 2003 (originally published by Basic Books, 1961.

Fiorini, D.; Chiani, M; Tralli, C.; and Salati, C. "Can We Trust HDLC?" ACM SIGCOMM *Computer Communications Review* 24:5, October 1995.

Fleck, L. *The Genesis and Development of a Scientific Fact.* University of Chicago Press, 1981.

Frege, G. *On Sense and Meaning* (first published in *Zeitschrift für Philosophie und Philosophische Kritik* Volume 100, 1892): 25–30. Reprinted in *Translations from the Philosophical Writings of Gottlob Frege* (edited by P. Geach and M. Black) Oxford: Basil Blackwell, Oxford, 1952 (3rd Edition 1980).

Frege, G. *The Basic Laws of Arithmetic.* Translated by M. Firth. Berkeley: University of California Press, 1967 (first published as *Grundlagen der Arithmetik,* 1884).

Hadzic, I.; Marcus, W.; and Smith, J. "Policy and Mechanism in Adaptive Protocols." Technical Report, University of Pennsylvania, 1999.

Hafner, K. and Lyon, M. *Where Wizards Stay Up Late.* New York: Simon & Schuster, 1996.

Holton, G. *Thematic Origins of Scientific Thought.* Cambridge, MA: Harvard University Press, 1988.

Huston, G. "IPv4: How long do we have?" *Internet Protocol Journal* 6:4, 2003.

IEEE Standard 802.1B-1992. "Standards for Local and Metropolitan Area Networks: LAN/MAN Management." 1992.

ISO/IEC 7498. 1994. "Information Processing Systems—Open System Interconnection—Basic Reference Model" (also published as ITU X.200).

ISO/IEC 7498-3. 1997. "Information Processing Systems-Open Systems Interconnection-Basic Reference Model, Part 3: Naming and Addressing."

ISO/IEC 8073. 1992. "Information Technology—Telecommunications and Information Exchange between Systems—Protocol for Providing the Connection-mode Transport Service."

ISO/IEC 8208. 1993. "International Standards Organization—Data Communications—X.25 Packet Layer Protocol for Data Terminal Equipment, 3rd Edition."

ISO/IEC 8327. 1987. "Information Processing Systems—Open Systems Interconnection—Basic Connection Oriented Session Protocol" (also CCITT X.215).

ISO/IEC 8348. 1993. "Information Processing Systems-Data Communications-Network Service Definition.

ISO/IEC 8473. 1993. Information Technology—Protocol for Providing the Connectionless-mode Network Service. Part 1: Protocol Specification."

ISO/IEC 8473-1. 1993. "Information Technology—Protocol for Providing the Connectionless Network Service, Part 1 Protocol Specification" (also CCITT X.233).

ISO/IEC 8648. 1987. "Information Processing Systems—Data Communications—Internal Organization of the Network Layer."

ISO/IEC 8650. 1987. "Information Processing Systems—Open Systems Interconnection—Protocol Specification for the Association Control Service Element" (also CCITT X.227).

ISO 8807. 1994. "Information Technology—Open Systems Interconnection—LOTOS—A Formal Description Technique based on the Temporal Ordering of Observational Behavior."

ISO/IEC 8823. 1987. "Information Processing Systems—Open Systems Interconnection—Basic Connection Oriented Presentation Protocol" (also CCITT X.226).

ISO/IEC 8824. 1990. "Information Processing Systems—Open Systems Interconnection—Specification of Abstract Syntax Notation 1 (ASN.1)" (also CCITT X.208).

ISO/IEC 8825-1. 1990. "Information Processing Systems—Open Systems Interconnection—Specification of Basic Encoding Rules for Abstract Syntax Notation 1 (ASN.1)" (also CCITT X.209).

ISO/IEC 8825-2. 2002. "Information Processing Systems—Open Systems Interconnection—Specification of Packed Encoding Rules for Abstract Syntax Notation 1 (ASN.1)" (also CCITT X.691).

ISO 9074. 1994. "Information Processing Systems—Open Systems Interconnection—Estelle: A Formal Description Technique based on an extended state transition model."

ISO/IEC 9545. 1989. "Information Processing Systems—Open Systems Interconnection—Basic Application Layer Structure" (also CCITT X.207).

ISO/IEC 9594. 1990. "Information Processing Systems—Open Systems Interconnection—The Directory" (also CCITT X.500).

ISO/IEC 9595. 1991. "Information Processing Systems—Open Systems Interconnection—Common Management Information Service Definition" (also CCITT X.710).

ISO/IEC 9596-1. 1991. "Information Processing Systems—Open Systems Inter-connection—Common Management Information Protocol" (also CCITT X.711).

ISO/IEC 9805. 1990. "Information Processing Systems—Open Systems Inter-connection—Protocol Specification for Commitment, Concurrency and Recov-ery" (also CCITT X.852).

ISO/IEC 10026. 1992. "Information Processing Systems—Open Systems Inter-connection—Distributed Transaction Processing" (also CCITT X.861).

ISO/IEC 10021. 1990. "Information Processing Systems—Open Systems Inter-connection—Message-Oriented Text Interchange System (MOTIS)" (also CCITT X.400).

ISO/IEC 13392. 1999. "Information technology—Telecommunications and information exchange between systems—High-level data link control (HDLC) procedures."

Ji, P.; Ge, Z.; Kurose, J.; and Towsley, D. "A Comparison of Hard-state and Soft-state Signaling Protocols." Proceedings of ACM SIGCOMM, 2003.

Kurose, J. and Ross, K. *Computer Networking: A Top Down Approach Featur-ing the Internet*. Addison-Wesley, 2005.

Lamport, L.; Shostak, R.; and Pease, M. "The Byzantine Generals Problem." ACM Transactions on Programming Languages, 4:3, July 1982.

Levin, R.; Cohen, E.; Corwin, W.; Pollack, F.; and Wulf, W. "Policy/mechanism separation in HYDRA." Proceedings of the 5th Symposium on Operating Sys-tem Principles, November 1975: 132–140.

Kleinrock, L. and Kamoun, F. "Hierarchical Routing for Large Networks, Per-formance evaluation and optimization." *Computer Networks*, 1977: 155–174.

Kuhn, T. *The Structure of Scientific Revolutions*. University of Chicago Press, 1968.

MacArthur, R. *Geographical Ecology*. New York: Harper & Row, 1972.

McKenzie, A. "The ARPANET Control Center." Proceedings of the 4th Data Communications Symposium, Quebec, 1975.

Madison, J. *The Federalist Papers* Number 35, 1778.

Mendelson, B. *Introduction to Topology, 2nd Edition*. Boston: Allyn and Bacon, 1971.

Millstein, R. "The National Software Works: A distributed processing system." Proceedings of the ACM, 1977.

National Research Council, "Looking over the Fence at Networking." Committee on Research Horizons in Networking, National Research Council, 2001.

Needham, J. *Science and Civilization in China* Volume 1. Cambridge University Press, 1965.

Newman, M. *Elements of the Topology of Plane Sets of Points.* Cambridge University Press, 1964.

Nordmark, E. and Bagnulo, M. "Level 3 Multihoming Shim protocol." draft-ietf-shim6-proto-07.txt, 2006.

O'Dell, M. "GSE: an alternative addressing architecture for IPv6." draft-ietf-ipngwg-gseaddr-00.txt, 1997.

Oppen, D. and Dalal, J. "The Clearinghouse: A Decentralized Agent for Locating Named Objects in a Distributed Environment." ACM Transactions on Office Information Systems 1:3, 1983: 230–253.

Organick, E. *The Multics System: An Examination of Its Structure.* Cambridge, MA: MIT Press, 1972.

Pelkey, J. *Computer Communications: 1968—1988 A History of Technological Innovation and Economic Growth* (in preparation). Unpublished manuscript, 2000.

Perkins, C. *Mobile IP Design Principles and Practices.* Prentice Hall, 1998.

Perlman, R. *Interconnections.* Addison-Wesley, 1992.

Perlman, R. *Interconnections, 2nd Edition: Bridges, Routers, Switches, and Internetworking Protocols.* Reading MA: Addison-Wesley, 1999.

Peterson, L. and Davie, B. *Computer Networks: A Systems Approach, 3rd Edition.* Morgan Kaufman, 2003.

RFC 407. Bressler, R. "Remote Job Entry Protocol." October 1972.

RFC 493. MacKenzie, A. "TELNET Protocol Specification." 1973.

RFC 542. Neigus, N. "File Transfer Protocol for the ARPANet, Aug 1973.

RFC 740. Braden, Robert. NETRJS Protocol." November 1977. (Obsoletes RFCs 189, 599)

RFC 791. Postel, J. (ed). "Internet Protocol Specification." 1981.

RFC 793. Postel, J. (ed). "Transmission Control Protocol Specification Postel." 1981.

RFC 0882. Mockapetris, P. "Domain names: Concepts and facilities." November 1983. (Replaced by RFCs 1034, 1035, and numerous updates in 1987)

RFC 0883. Mockapetris, P. "Domain names: Implementation specification." November 1983. (Replaced by RFCs 1034, 1035, and numerous updates in 1987)

RFC 1021. Partridge, C. and Trewitt, G. "High-level Entity Management System (HEMS)." October 1987.

RFC 1022. Partridge, C. and Trewitt, G. "High-level Entity Management Protocol (HEMP)." October 1987.

RFC 1023. Partridge, C. and Trewitt, G. "HEMS monitoring and control language." October 1987.

RFC 1024. Partridge, C. and Trewitt, G. "HEMS variable definitions." October 1987.

RFC 1075. Waitzman, D.; Partridge, C.; and Deering, S. "Distance Vector Multicast Routing Protocol." November 1988.

RFC 1157. Case, J.; Fedor, M; Schoffstall, M.; and Davin, C. "Simple Network Management Protocol." May 1990.

RFC 1518. Rekhter, Y. and Li, T. "An Architecture for IP Address Allocation with CIDR." September 1993.

RFC 1519. Fuller, V.; Li, T.; Yu, J.; and Varadhan, K. "Classless Inter-Domain Routing (CIDR): An Address Assignment and Aggregation Strategy." September 1993.

RFC 1541. Droms, R. "Dynamic Host Configuration Protocol." 1993.

RFC 1633. Braden, R.; Clark, D.; and Shenker, S. "Integrated Services in the Internet Architecture: An Overview." June 1994.

RFC 1654. Rekhter, Y.; Li, T. (eds.). "A Border Gateway Protocol 4 (BGP-4)." July 1994.

RFC 1887. Rekhter, Y.; Li, T. (eds.). "An Architecture for IPv6 Unicast Address Allocation." December 1995.

RFC 1945. Berners-Lee, T.; Fielding, T.; Frystyk, H. "Hypertext Transfer Protocol—HTTP/1.0." May 1996.

RFC 2189. Ballardie, A. "Core Based Trees (CBT version 2) Multicast Routing—Protocol Specification." September 1997.

RFC 2205. Braden, R. (ed.); Zhang, L.; Berson, S.; Herzog, S.; and Jamin, S. "Resource ReSerVation Protocol (RSVP)—Version 1 Functional Specification." September 1997.

RFC 2362. Estrin, D.; Farinacci, D.; Helmy, A.; Thaler, D.; Deering, S.; Handley, M.; Jacobson, V.; Liu, C.; Sharma, P.; and Wei, L. "Protocol Independent Multicast-Sparse Mode (PIM-SM): Protocol Specification." June 1998.

RFC 2373. Deering, S. "IP Version 6 Addressing Architecture." July 1998.

RFC 2430. Rekhter, Y.; Li, T. (eds). "A Provider Architecture for Differentiated Services and Traffic Engineering (PASTE)." October 1998.

RFC 2460. Deering, S. and Hinden, R. "Internet Protocol, Version 6 (IPv6) Specification." December 1998.

RFC 2616. Fielding, R; Gettys, J.; Mogul, J; Masinter, L.; Leach, P.; and Berners-Lee, T. "Hypertext Transfer Protocol—HTTP/1.1." June 1999.

RFC 2766. Tsirtsis, G. and Srisuresh, P. "Network Address Translation—Protocol Translation (NAT-PT)." February 2000.

RFC 2960. Stewart, R.; Xie, Q.; Morneault, K.; Sharp, C.; Schwarzbauer, H.; Taylor, T.; Rytina, I.; Kalla, M.; Zhang, L.; and Paxson, V. "Stream Control Transmission Protocol." October 2000.

RFC 2993. Hain, T. "Architectural Implications of NAT." November 2000.

RFC 3178. Hagino, J. and Snyder, H. "IPv6 Multihoming Support at Site Exit Routers." October 2001.

RFC 3286. Ong, L. and Yockum, J. "An Introduction to the Stream Control Transmission Protocol (SCTP)." May 2002.

RFC 3510. Herriot, R. and McDonald, I. "Internet Printing Protocol/1.1: IPP URL Scheme." April 2003.

RFC 3587. Hinden, R.; Deering, S.; and Nordmark, E. "IPv6 Global Unicast Address Format." August 2003.

RFC 4340. Kohler, E.; Handley, M.; Floyd, S. "Datagram Congestion Control Protocol (DCCP)." 2006.

RFC 4423. Moskowitz, R. and Nikander, P. "Host Identity Protocol (HIP) Architecture." May 2006.

Raman S. and McCanne, S. "A model, analysis, and protocol framework for soft state-based communication." Proceedings ACM SIGCOMM 1999. (Skip Section 3).

Saltzer, Jerry. Name Binding in Computer Systems.1977.

Saltzer, Jerry. "On the Naming and Binding of Network Destinations." *Local Computer Networks* (edited by P. Ravasio et al.). North Holland, 1982: 311–317 (republished as RFC 1498).

Shoch, J. "Internetwork Naming, Addressing, and Routing," IEEE Proceedings COMPCON, Fall 1978: 72–79.

Sotica, L.; Morris, R.; Karger, D.; Kaashoek, M.; and Balakrishnan, H. "Chord: A Scalable Peer-to-Peer Lookup Service for Internet Applications." Proceedings of SIGCOMM '01 Conference ACM, 2001: 149–160.

Selga, J. and Rivera, J. "HDLC Reliability and the FBRS Method to Improve It," Proceedings of the 7th Data Communications Symposium, ACM SIG-COMM, 1981: 260–267.

Snoeren, A. and Raghaven, B. "Decoupling Policy from Mechanism in Internet Routing." SIGCOMM 34:1, January 2004.

Spector, A. "Performing Remote Operations Efficiently on a Local Computer Network," CACM 25:4, April 1982: 246–260.

Spence, J. The Memory Palaces of Matteo Ricci. Penguin Books, 1984.

Tanenbaum, A. Computer Networks, 4th Edition. Upper Saddle River, NJ: Prentice Hall, 2003.

Touch, J.; Wang Y.; and Pingali, V. "A Recursive Network Architecture." www.isi.edu/touch/pubs/ isi-tr-2006-626, October 2006.

Watson, R. and Fletcher, J. "An Architecture for Support of Network Operating System Services." Computer Networks 4, 1980: 33–49.

Watson, R. "Timer-Based Mechanisms in Reliable Transport Protocol Connection Management." Computer Networks 5, 1981: 47–56.

Watson, R. "Delta-t Protocol Specification." Lawrence Livermore Laboratory, UCID-19293, December 1981.

Wittgenstein, L. Tractatus Logico-Philosophicus. London: Routledge & Kegan Paul, 1922.

Xerox Corp. Xerox Network Systems Architecture. General Information Manual, 1985.

Zimmermann, H. "A Contribution on the Internetwork End-to-End Protocol." INWG General Note, May 1975.

Index

F

Farber, David, 144
Fast Select, 68
fate-sharing, 87
FDTs (Formal Description
  Techniques), 16-19
    development of, 16
    finite state machine methods, 18
    guidelines, 17
    lack of support by IETF (Internet
      Engineering Task Force), 18
    mathematical or language-based
      techniques, 17
    temporal logic approaches, 18
feedback mechanisms, 79
File Transfer Access Method
  (FTAM), 115
File Transfer Protocol. *See* FTP
finite state machines. *See* FSMs
first-order effectors, 7
flag sequences, 45
flow, 37
    definition, 28
    flow-control protocols. *See*
      error-control protocols
    flow-id, 47
Forester, Heinz von, 87
Formal Description Techniques.
  See FDTs
fragmentation, 48
France Telecom, 111
free names, 286
Frege, Gottlieb, 147, 306
frictionless motion, 57
FSMs (finite state machines)
    compared to threads, 28
    definition, 24
    diagrams, 24
    methods, 18
    modified state machine
      approach, 25-26

protocol machines (PMs). *See also*
  data transfer mechanisms
    associations, 28
    bindings, 28
    data transfer PMs, 82-85
    definition, 26
    flow, 28
    interactions, 30, 37
    interfaces, 29-31
    model of, 37
    *(N)-PM relation to other
      PMs, 30*
    as procedure calls, 36
    *protocol machine types
      (PMTs), 27*
    QoS (Quality of service), 43-44
    rankings, 27
    state maintenance, 37-38
    state explosion problem, 25
FTAM (File Transfer Access
  Method), 115
FTP (File Transfer Protocol), 102-105
    ARPANET FTP model, 103
    network virtual file system
      (NVFS), 103
    Return Job Entry (RJE), 104-105
full addressing architecture, 358*n*
Fuller, Buckminster, 170
functions, 147
    distance functions, 292

G

Galilei, Galileo, 57-58, 317, 369, 372
gedanken experiment on separating
  mechanism and policy (outline)
    mechanism specifications, 387-388
    protocol specifications, 386-387
    results, 75
    service definitions, 385-386
General Motors, 2*n*
Geographical Ecology, 1*n*
Gore, Al, 361

overview, xxvi*n*
relaying protocols, 79
   adjoining protocols, arguments against, 80
   architecture, 82-85
   compared to error-control protocols, 82
   embedded into applications, 81-82
   tasks, 209

N

(N)-addresses, 164, 249, 273-275
(N)-API-primitive, 238, 251-253
(N)-associations, 163
(N)-connections, 163
(N)-data-transfer-protocol. *See* data transfer protocols
(N)-DIF. *See* DIF (distributed IPC facility)
(N)-entities, 162-164
(N)-entity-titles, 164
(N)-IPC-process, 204, 238, 250-251
(N)-layers, 162, 219, 237, 240
(N)-PCI. *See* PCI (protocol control information)
(N)-PDUs. *See* PDUs (protocol data units)
(N)-PM. *See* PMs (protocol machines)
(N)-port-id, 246, 248, 272-273
(N)-protocols. *See* protocols
(N)-SDUs. *See* SDUs (service data units)
(N)-subsystems, 162, 219
(N)-user-data, 31, 238
N systems, communications with
   cheap communication, enabling, 214-219
   DIF (distributed IPC facility), 212-213
   directories, 213
   initial conclusions, 219-223

operation of communication, 210-213
   RIEP (Resource Information Exchange Protocol), 211-213
n2 problem, 107
nack (negative acknowledgment), 50
Name Binding in Computer Systems, 153
name spaces, 245-247, 286
name-resolution systems. *See* NRSs
naming. *See also* addressing
   aliases, 287
   anycast names, 330
   application instance names, 379
   application names, 196, 379, 246-248
   application process names, 245-246, 273
   ARPANET, 143-145
   assignment/de-assignment, 286
   bound/unbound names, 286-287
   complex names, 147
   connotative names, 286
   DANs (distributed application names), 246
   definition of names, 286
   denotative names, 286
   DIF (distributed IPC facility) naming concepts, 245-248
   early IP (Internet Protocol), 154-161
   foundations of mathematics and symbolic logic, 146-151
   free names, 286
   importance of, 142
   incomplete names, 147
   IPC process names, 246-247
   multicast names, 329
   name spaces, 245-247, 286
   in operating systems, 153
   origin of naming problem, 143-145
   OSI application addressing, 178-182

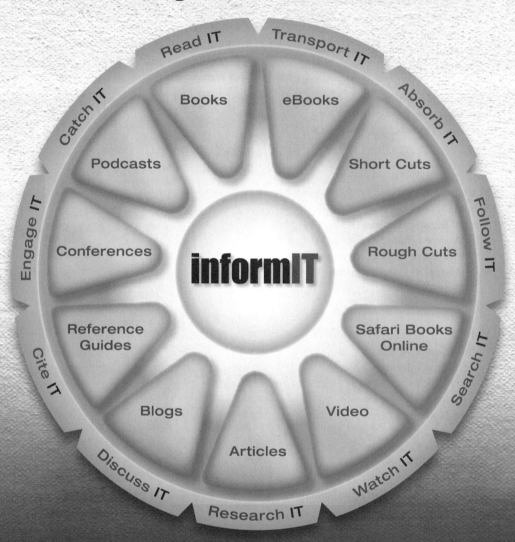